Understanding Governance

Series Editor
R. A. W. Rhodes
Professor of Government
University of Southampton
Southampton, UK

Understanding Governance encompasses all theoretical approaches to the study of government and governance in advanced industrial democracies and the Commonwealth. It has three long-standing objectives:

1. To develop new theoretical approaches to explain changes in the role of the state;
2. To explain how and why that role has changed; and
3. To set the changes and their causes in comparative perspective.

The origins of the series lie in the renowned Whitehall Research Programme funded by the Economic and Social Research Council. Since 1997, it has published some 26 books by the best known names in the field including Colin Hay, David Marsh, Edward Page, Guy Peters, R. A. W. Rhodes, David Richards, Martin Smith and Patrick Weller.

Over the past twenty years the 'Understanding Governance' book series has constantly defined the state-of-the-art when it comes to the analysis of the modern state. From accountability to agencies, party politics to parliamentary power and from crisis-management to the core executive this book series continues to set the agenda in terms of world-class scholarship.

—**Matthew Flinders**, Professor of Politics and Director of the Sir Bernard Crick Centre at the University of Sheffield

More information about this series at
https://link.springer.com/bookseries/14394

Kristoffer Kolltveit • Richard Shaw
Editors

Core Executives in a Comparative Perspective

Governing in Complex Times

palgrave
macmillan

Editors
Kristoffer Kolltveit
Department of Political Science
University of Oslo
Oslo, Norway

Richard Shaw
School of People, Environment and Planning
Massey University
Palmerston North, New Zealand

Understanding Governance
ISBN 978-3-030-94502-2   ISBN 978-3-030-94503-9   (eBook)
https://doi.org/10.1007/978-3-030-94503-9

© The Editor(s) (if applicable) and The Author(s), under exclusive licence to Springer Nature Switzerland AG 2022
This work is subject to copyright. All rights are solely and exclusively licensed by the Publisher, whether the whole or part of the material is concerned, specifically the rights of translation, reprinting, reuse of illustrations, recitation, broadcasting, reproduction on microfilms or in any other physical way, and transmission or information storage and retrieval, electronic adaptation, computer software, or by similar or dissimilar methodology now known or hereafter developed.
The use of general descriptive names, registered names, trademarks, service marks, etc. in this publication does not imply, even in the absence of a specific statement, that such names are exempt from the relevant protective laws and regulations and therefore free for general use.
The publisher, the authors and the editors are safe to assume that the advice and information in this book are believed to be true and accurate at the date of publication. Neither the publisher nor the authors or the editors give a warranty, expressed or implied, with respect to the material contained herein or for any errors or omissions that may have been made. The publisher remains neutral with regard to jurisdictional claims in published maps and institutional affiliations.

Cover illustration: © Getty Images / hamzaturkkol

This Palgrave Macmillan imprint is published by the registered company Springer Nature Switzerland AG.
The registered company address is: Gewerbestrasse 11, 6330 Cham, Switzerland

Contents

Part I   Setting the Scene   1

1 In the Beginning: The Story of a Concept   3
   Kristoffer Kolltveit and Richard Shaw

2 Core Executive Studies in the Wild   27
   Richard Shaw and Kristoffer Kolltveit

3 Court Politics: From Metaphor to Theory   53
   R. A. W. Rhodes

Part II   Core Executives in Westminster Contexts   77

4 Court Politics in an Age of Austerity: David Cameron's Court, 2010–2016   79
   R. A. W. Rhodes

5 Ireland's Core Executive at One Hundred Years of Self-government: Navigating Coalition, Crisis and Complexity   123
   Bernadette Connaughton

6 New Zealand: The Core Within the Core   143
    Richard Shaw and Rose Cole

Part III Core Executives in Continental Countries   163

7 On a Wild Goose Chase? The (Core) Executive
    in Germany   165
    Anna Hundehege and Thurid Hustedt

8 The Netherlands: How Weak Prime Ministers Gain
    Influence   189
    Erik-Jan van Dorp and R. A. W. Rhodes

Part IV Core Executives in Scandinavia   209

9 The Swedish Executive: Centralising from Afar   211
    Erik Brinde, Thurid Hustedt, and Heidi Houlberg
    Salomonsen

10 The Danish Core Executive: From 'Duopoly' to
    'Monopoly'?   235
    Heidi Houlberg Salomonsen and Amalie Trangbæk

11 The Norwegian Core Executive: Baronial Courts and
    Inner Circles?   255
    Kristoffer Kolltveit and Jostein Askim

Part V Conclusion   277

12 Continuity and Change: Explaining Developments and
    Looking to the Future   279
    Kristoffer Kolltveit and Richard Shaw

Index   303

Notes on Contributors

Jostein Askim is a professor at the Department of Political Science, University of Oslo, and adjunct professor at the Department of Administration and Organization Theory, University of Bergen. His research and teaching concern administrative reform, performance management, political-administrative relationships and cabinet government in parliamentary systems. His research has appeared in *Public Administration*, the *Journal of Public Administration Research and Theory*, *International Public Management Journal*, *Political Studies Review* and *Government and Opposition*.

Erik Brinde is a Master's student in International Administration and Global Governance at Gothenburg University, Sweden, and also holds a Master's degree in Global Political Economy from Stockholm University. His present research focuses on the politics of Industry 4.0 technology, and he is particularly interested in questions of power and democracy.

Rose Cole is a postgraduate researcher affiliated to Victoria University of Wellington in New Zealand. She has held a variety of leadership roles in New Zealand's public service and community sector. Her PhD thesis researches the role of non-partisan advisers—departmental private secretaries—in New Zealand's core executive, and has been published in leading journals such as *Parliamentary Affairs*, the *International Review of Administrative Sciences* and the *Australian Journal of Public Administration*.

Bernadette Connaughton is Senior Lecturer in Public Administration at the Department of Politics and Public Administration, University of Limerick, Ireland. Her main research interests include politico-administrative relations, Ireland's relationship with the EU and environmental governance. She has published on those areas and specifically in relation to Irish governance in authored, co-authored and edited books and journals such as *Public Administration*, *Irish Political Studies*, the *Journal of Environmental Policy and Planning*, *Regional and Federal Studies* and *Administration*.

Anna Hundehege is a doctoral researcher at the Hertie School in Berlin. Her research focuses on bureaucratic policy-making and EU multi-level administration.

Thurid Hustedt is Professor of Public Administration and Management at the Hertie School in Berlin. Her research focuses on relations between politics and administration, policy advisory systems and government coordination.

Kristoffer Kolltveit is a professor at the Department of Political Science, University of Oslo. Kolltveit's research interests include political and administrative élites, media impact in the central administration, cabinet decision-making and bureaucracy. His research, which is largely based on interview and survey data, has been published in several international journals such as *Public Administration*, the *International Journal of Press/Politics*, *European Journal of Communication*, *International Review of Administrative Sciences*, *Policy and Politics* and *Scandinavian Political Studies*.

R. A. W. Rhodes is Professor of Government (Research) at the University of Southampton (UK) and Director of the Centre for Political Ethnography. He is the author or editor of 40 books, including, most recently: *Comparing Cabinets* (with D. Grube and P. Weller, 2021); *The Art and Craft of Comparison* (with J. Boswell and J. Corbett, 2019); *Networks, Governance and the Differentiated Polity. Selected Essays. Volume I* (2017), *Interpretive Political Science. Selected Essays. Volume II* (2017), *Narrative Policy Analysis* (editor, Palgrave Macmillan 2018) and the *Routledge Handbook of Interpretive Political Science* (edited with M. Bevir, 2015). He has also published some 200 articles and chapters in books. He is a fellow of the Academy of the Social Sciences in Australia and a fellow of the Academy of Social Sciences (UK). In 2015, the European Consortium for Political Research (ECPR) awarded him their biennial Lifetime

Achievement Award for his 'outstanding contribution to all areas of political science, and the exceptional impact of his work'.

Heidi Houlberg Salomonsen is Professor of Public Management at the Department of Management, Aarhus University, Denmark. Her research focuses on public management and leadership, core executives, relationships between top civil servants, ministers and political advisers as well as reputation and trust in the public sector.

Richard Shaw is Professor of Politics at Massey University, New Zealand. He has authored or edited several books on public policy and executive government, most recently, *The Edward Elgar Handbook on Ministerial Advisers* (with C. Eichbaum, 2022). His research interests lie in core executive studies, political-administrative relationships and the roles and responsibilities of political advisers, and his work has been published in leading international journals, including *Governance*, *Public Administration*, *Public Management Review* and *Parliamentary Affairs*, as well as in various handbooks on political leadership, governance, the policy process and the public service.

Amalie Trangbæk is a PhD fellow at the Department of Political Science, Aarhus University, Denmark. Her research focuses on top civil servants' roles and careers as well as their relationships with ministers, political advisers and other civil servants.

Erik-Jan van Dorp is a PhD candidate at the Utrecht University School of Governance in the Netherlands. He studies senior civil servants up-close and personal. His work has been published in various peer-reviewed journals.

List of Figures

Fig. 8.1   The cabinet process in Dutch executive government   194
Fig. 8.2   The prime minister's court (2012–2017)   197

List of Tables

Table 4.1	The forums of the UK core executive	97
Table 5.1	Numbers of government meetings and memoranda (information and decision)	130
Table 11.1	Cabinets, parties and parliamentary support in Norway 2001–2021	257
Table 11.2	The importance of decision arenas to reaching an agreement in the cabinet; percentages and means per cabinet	267

PART I

Setting the Scene

CHAPTER 1

In the Beginning: The Story of a Concept

Kristoffer Kolltveit and Richard Shaw

INTRODUCTION

In 1990 Patrick Dunleavy and R. A. W. Rhodes unveiled a concept that has changed the shape, language and contours of the scholarship on executive government. These days, the rhetoric of the 'core executive' is more or less ubiquitous, its authors having largely succeeded in displacing old debates about the relative powers of the prime minister and cabinet with a focus on the functions of governing, the trading of executive resources and the politics and positioning of the executive court(s). But the world has since changed, and 30 years on it is time to take stock of progress and to chart a way ahead. To those ends, the primary purposes of this book are to evaluate the use and utility of Dunleavy and Rhodes' concept, to

---

K. Kolltveit (✉)
Department of Political Science, University of Oslo, Oslo, Norway
e-mail: kristoffer.kolltveit@stv.uio.no

R. Shaw (✉)
School of People, Environment and Planning, Massey University, Palmerston North, New Zealand
e-mail: R.H.Shaw@massey.ac.nz

© The Author(s), under exclusive license to Springer Nature Switzerland AG 2022
K. Kolltveit, R. Shaw (eds.), *Core Executives in a Comparative Perspective*, Understanding Governance,
https://doi.org/10.1007/978-3-030-94503-9_1

provide a framework for the study of contemporary executives and to offer a comparative study of core executives across different systems and traditions.

The first of those aims is the focus of Chap. 2, in which we set out a systematic review of the scholarship, distinguishing studies that use the construct of the core executive analytically to direct attention to certain developments, actors and arenas from those in which it is simply deployed as a noun for the central administration apparatus. Before that, however, and by way of establishing a broader context for the book, in this chapter we discuss a series of societal developments that (might) have changed the composition or functioning of core executives—or which at the very least have had an impact on the environments in which executive actors and institutions operate. There are numerous candidates, but at least in part because each has global application we have opted to emphasise developments in the media and in post-New Public Management (NPM) thinking, and on coalition dynamics, the rise of populism and the impacts of the COVID-19 pandemic. Taken jointly, the foci of Chaps. 1 and 2 contribute to a framework for the study of contemporary core executives which informs the country chapters in the book (Chaps. 4, 5, 6, 7, 8, 9, 10 and 11).

The balance of this chapter is as follows. In the following section we tease out the signal characteristics of and motivations informing the two seminal definitions of the core executive. We then connect the core executive approach with the literature on coordination, and examine several contemporary societal and technological developments which shape the material circumstances core executive scholars seek to understand. Finally, we set out the structure of and the logic informing the rest of the book.

Marking Out the Terrain: A Brief History of the Core Executive

Defining the Core Concept

The concept of the core executive was first defined by Dunleavy and Rhodes (1990) and subsequently revised by Rhodes (1995). There are subtle distinctions between the two conceptions. Dunleavy and Rhodes (1990, p. 4) take the core executive 'functionally to include all those organizations and structures which primarily serve to pull together and integrate central government policies, or act as final arbiters within the executive of conflicts between different elements of the government machine'. Rhodes' later definition is a little tighter. For Rhodes the core executive 'refers to *all those organizations and procedures which coordinate central government policies, and act as final arbiters of conflict between different parts of the government machine*' (1995, p. 12; original emphasis). Place those two definitions alongside each other and several small but significant differences are apparent: by 1995 (1) the earlier and institutionally fixed 'structures' has been replaced by the more fluid and relational 'processes'; (2) there is a sharper, less qualified emphasis on coordination; and (3) the discretionary 'or' has become the obligatory 'and', such that the empirical focus is firmly locked on both coordination *and* conflict.

In this volume we lean towards Rhodes' revised definition, which has three significant elements. The first is the reference to 'all those organizations and processes' which collectively transact the business of executive government. The signal contribution of core executive studies stems from those five words. Rhodes was not the first to posit a differentiated model of the executive: earlier contributions of similar ilk include Richardson and Jordan's (1979) analysis of the extent to which exogenous forces can splinter the exercise of executive authority, and Armstrong's (1971) distinction between 'spine' and 'ring' administrative functions. Rhodes was also indebted to organisational theory and the sociology of organisations, drawing on their insights into organisations' interests and the ways in which they command their own resources (see Hanf & Scharpf, 1978). For instance, in an early piece on intergovernmental relations Rhodes cites Hanf and Scharpf's discussions about the exchange and substitutability of participants' resources (1980, p. 306).

However, it is Rhodes' model that led to the setting aside of the then-orthodox concern with the institutions of the prime minister and cabinet in favour of a more capacious view of who and what counts as 'government', one which extends beyond the political executive to encompass the civil service and, depending on circumstances, various other administrative bodies. At a stroke, boundaries were loosened and institutional margins became mutable.

Second, Rhodes' conception draws attention to coordination as the central function of government. The insertion of the verb transformed a field of study that had hitherto focused on sketching the institutional contours of the political executive and mapping interactions between prime ministers and their cabinet colleagues into something much more active. Rhodes' is a functional definition: the central questions are 'Who does what?' and 'With what resources?' (Rhodes, 2007, p. 1247). It is the *doing* of government rather than its formal *description* that really matters.

And mostly what is done is coordination, whether by interlocking networks of courtiers or via institutional mechanisms such as cabinet or officials' committees. Some of this activity, of course (and certainly many of the really important bits), occurs within the inner sanctum, but the central insight of core executive studies is that the management and coordination of government—whether horizontally (across the machinery of government; see Craft, 2015) or vertically (within departments; see Robson, 2015)—also involves people who will rarely if ever sit in a cabinet or cabinet committee meeting. Ministers and prime ministers are central actors, but the actions of myriad others are also important, such that what is critical is making sense of the rituals, practices and agency of the institutional actors who carry out these functions.

Thirdly, and relatedly, the core executive encompasses those who 'act as final arbiters of conflict between different parts of the government machine'. This aspect of the definition has, as we shall see in Chap. 2, received rather less explicit empirical attention than has the coordination imperative, but it is important not to lose sight of the extent to which Rhodes positioned conflict resolution as a core function of government. Intuitively it makes sense, of course: after all, beyond a certain point it is difficult to envisage successful coordination co-existing with systemic conflict. However, it also means that there is a touch of the conservative to the concept of the core executive, not in the partisan political sense but insofar as the functions of government are essentially to maintain continuity and stability (which is about as close as core executive studies gets to a normative position, albeit one that is not often mentioned).

One further observation at this point. Implicit in the seminal definition is the matter of the nature and exchange of governing resources. How—and with what—is all this coordinating and resolving of difficulties to be done? The distribution and trading of intellectual, fiscal, relational and other resources in the context of the executive court has emerged as a central focus of core executive studies, not least in Rhodes' own work on the beliefs and practices of the actors who inhabit political and bureaucratic courts (Rhodes & Salomonsen, 2020; Rhodes & Tiernan, 2016). Whether or not the terms 'executive court' and 'core executive' are synonyms remains a matter for consideration (the inference in Rhodes and

Tiernan (2016, p. 351) is that they are): the point here is that the issue of resources—what they are, where they are to be found and who has and does not have them—has become a major cleavage in the literature on the core executive.

Why Bother?

All of this thinking was driven by two major considerations. The first was the need for a new conceptual, rhetorical and methodological approach to the study of executive government. In the British context, in particular, traditional debates regarding the relative powers and influence of the prime minister and cabinet had become increasingly arid. The orthodox treatment of these 'chestnuts of the [British] constitution' (Dunleavy & Rhodes, 1990, p. 4) was problematic both descriptively and normatively: not only was (and is) it wrong to assume that cabinet is the primary institutional locus of the coordination of government business, whether or not things should work according to the strictures of standard thinking was also up for debate.[1]

At heart this is a tussle over the importance of hierarchy. Rhodes' definition of the core executive—which reached back both to his earlier work on policy networks and communities and forwards to later theorising on governance and the hollow state (Elgie, 2011)—directly confronts the assumption that influence and power are ineluctably woven into formal hierarchy. Rather, institutional location (e.g., occupancy of the premiership or membership of the cabinet or its committees) is eschewed—entirely so for late period Rhodes (especially with Mark Bevir; see Bevir & Rhodes, 2008) but only in part for others who also embraced the new orthodoxy—in favour of a focus on function. It is what people do and the relationships through which that agency is transacted that matters to coordinating policy-making and resolving conflict, not where they are located on an organisational chart.[2]

Having decoupled function from location Dunleavy and Rhodes turned to the second imperative, which had to do with articulating the conceptual preconditions for a more expansive research agenda than they felt was possible under the extant terms of debate. Epistemologically, Rhodes' seminal definition of the core executive is a heuristic; an 'analytical tool' (Craft, 2015, p. 63); a means of framing a site of empirical analysis and theorisation. Crucially, unlike the lens it sought to supplant (the language of which is particular to parliamentary democracies), the construct of the core executive is methodologically agnostic: it contains no description of a specific set of institutional arrangements or constitutional conditions, and therefore lends itself to the study of executive government in a range of disparate contexts.

Specifically, Dunleavy and Rhodes pointed out that a 'focus on the core executive has the considerable advantage of being applicable to other countries with radically different systems of government' (1990, p. 4). The invitation, clearly, was for scholars to engage in comparative research across diverging national, cultural and institutional contexts—and in particular for theoretical and empirical hands to be stretched across the boundaries delimiting parliamentary, presidential and (by logical extension) semi-presidential contexts. We address this in greater detail in Chap. 2, assessing the distance the concept has travelled by systematically reviewing the scholarly use of the concept. While many studies use it as an analytical tool, others merely use it as rhetoric gloss, as a label for the institutions or actors under study. Notwithstanding some notable exceptions, relatively few efforts have been made to compare core executives across systems. Clearly there is work to be done: despite the value of a flexible concept with few specifics and conditions, in our view certain dimensions of the core concept should be elaborated and/or common questions formulated to enable comparative research.

COORDINATION, COORDINATION, COORDINATION

Dunleavy and Rhodes' main intention was to get people to focus on what core executive actors actually do. There is a form of materialism at work here; an encouragement to ground analyses in observable conduct rather than to impute intent or influence on the basis of organograms and formal titles. Activity and action count in core executive studies.

And what matters in particular is coordination. To reiterate: the core executive perspective draws attention to all those organisations and procedures which 'coordinate central government policies' and act as 'final arbiters' (Rhodes, 1995, p. 12) of or 'tiebreakers in deadlocked conflicts' (Dunleavy & Rhodes, 1990, p. 16). For our purposes, then, coordination is the centre piece of core executive studies, providing the point of departure for operationalising the core concept and developing an analytical lens that facilitates comparisons across countries and systems (Elgie, 2011, p. 72). However, it seems to us that much (although certainly not all) of the core executive scholarship tends to skip quickly over the meaning of 'coordination': our preference is to address this propensity and sharpen up our own analysis by explicitly locating our approach to the core executive in the coordination literature.

We begin with Peters, who defines coordination as an 'end-state in which the policies and programmes of government are characterized by minimal redundancy, incoherence and lacunae' (1998, p. 296). Coordination can also be conceived as a process (which may or may not produce a desired end-state). In this vein, Bouckaert et al. (2010, p. 16) characterise coordination processes as 'the instruments and mechanisms that aim to enhance the voluntary or forced alignment of tasks and efforts'. Coordination instruments and mechanisms are utilised by actors to create coherence, and to reduce redundancy, lacunae and contradictions within and between policies, implementation or management (Bouckaert et al., 2010).

Within the traditional coordination literature, it is common to distinguish between different *degrees of coordination*. Fritz Scharpf (1994) separates negative from positive coordination: the former occurs when decisions in an organisation are made to avoid conflict, while the latter requires organisations to find ways to cooperate on solutions that can benefit a range of involved parties. Similarly, Metcalfe (1994) has developed a nine-point scale of coordination outcomes, extending from independent decision-making by ministries—via information exchange, consultation[3] and arbitration of policy differences—to the development of coherent government strategies. These steps are cumulative in the sense that higher levels of coordination depend on the existence of lower ones (Metcalfe, 1994, p. 281).

The scholarship also distinguishes between different *types or forms of coordination*. Peters (1998), for instance, underlines the distinction between horizontal and vertical coordination. The former occurs across organisations at the same level, while the latter takes place between organisations at different levels (or within single organisations but across different hierarchical levels; see Thompson, 1967).

A related approach is to emphasise the different *stages or actors in coordination processes*. At the broadest level, Peters (1998) separates administrative and political actors, while Davies (1997) contrasts the coordination of policy across sectors and domains with the coordination of politics across the interests of different parties in multi-party cabinets. From a core executive stance, although administrative and political actors might be closely intertwined at different stages of coordination it is analytically important to distinguish between them in order to answer the fundamental question: 'Who does what?'—especially given that the 'under-involvement of political actors in co-ordination' has been identified as a paradox (Peters, 1998, p. 295). In short, the extent to which different actors are engaged in coordination remains an empirical question, one we pursue throughout this book.

Furthermore, it is possible to separate out different *coordination mechanisms*. Mintzberg (1979) talks about coordination mechanisms or liaison devices: that is, certain positions, instruments (such as task forces and committees) and meetings (and in particular the rules and procedures governing these). Anticipated reactions—the process whereby actors volitionally adjust their actions if they know they will be reviewed and possibly punished by more influential actors—can also be considered a coordination mechanism (Friedrich, 1963). Insofar as there has been empirical work undertaken on the phenomenon, anticipated reactions have been found to be important in the Scandinavian countries, both between ministries, and between cabinet and parliament (Larsson, 1994; Olsen, 1983; Sundström & Lemne, 2016; Rasch & Tsebelis, 2011; see also Russell and Cowley (2016) on the UK case).

The concept of the core executive speaks to both formal institutional settings and the sorts of looser, informal relational networks through which coordination takes place. In this regard it echoes Chisholm's (1992) distinction between *formal and informal coordination*. According to Chisholm, informal channels of communication, relationships and networks, and informal bargains and agreements can all contribute directly or indirectly to processes of coordination (1992, p. 12).

The references to 'final arbiters' (Rhodes, 1995, p. 12) and to 'tie-breakers in deadlocked conflicts' (Dunleavy & Rhodes, 1990, 16) is an acknowledgement that there are circumstances in which certain core executive actors need to take final decisions. Put another way: when the coordination mechanisms deployed by various actors have failed to solve disputes, someone has to step in. Prime ministers and cabinet ministers will be central to the resolution of disagreements over government policy. However, the core executive framework also directs the focus towards people outside of meetings of the full cabinet or its committees. Guidance on this comes from coalition scholars, who note that conflict resolution mechanisms might have members from both within and outside the cabinet (including parliamentary leaders; see Andeweg, 1997; Andeweg & Timmermans, 2008).

Core Executives: Structuring Contemporary Environments

Part of the point of stressing the importance of coordination was to shift the academic gaze away from something Dunleavy and Rhodes saw in the long-running debate over the power of the prime minister vis-à-vis the cabinet, which was a certain normative anxiety regarding Britain's 'unbalanced constitution, party structured legislature and an inadequate rational policy process inside the executive' (1990, p. 3). In that context they proposed the notion of the core executive not as a means of addressing concerns regarding the state of particular governing arrangements, but as a neutral framework which would focus attention on the functioning of the government machine (Dunleavy & Rhodes, 1990, p. 4).

Today's societies look very different to those that existed when the concept was unveiled. To take just one example, in recent years the sense that established understandings of and practices associated with democracy are under pressure has become palpable. Economic discontent, anger at élites and a lack of trust in experts (a matter that has become even more contentious in the advent of the COVID-19 pandemic) have led to the emergence of anti-establishment parties—and individual political chief executives—which have challenged normative and institutional settlements long considered fundamental in developed societies, raising a new clutch of questions about the functioning of the government machine. In this section, then, and by way of providing a context for the chapters that follow, we elaborate on several of the most significant of these developments, which encompass both larger societal changes and shifts in the composition and distribution of resources within core executives. We place particular emphasis on developments in the media, the recentring of the government apparatus, coalition dynamics and the rise of populism, as well as large scale crises such as the global pandemic. Each of these is an instance of what Alisdair Roberts has called a 'large force'; an example of the 'conditioning factors that give public administration its peculiar stamp in each country' (Roberts, 2013, p. 16). They are part of the context that throws up the coordination challenges and conflicts which core executives must respond to, and we neglect them at our peril.

Developments in the Media

Changes in media technology—and subsequently in the media industry—have transformed modern societies. The internet has seemingly affected everything: where people work and the work they undertake; how and when communication takes place; the ways in which news is produced, read and digested; and how election campaigns (and changes in political administrations) unfold. Driven by intensified competition and commercialisation, interventionist news media have emerged (Asp, 2014), with increased production pressures and forms of reporting that both focus on the personal and emotional aspects of 'news' and highlight strategic aspects of contemporary politics (Holtz-Bacha et al., 2014; Mazzoleni, 2000). Accentuated by the emergence of online news outlets and social media, in which environments user-generated content promotes emotional evaluations and the personalisation of interactivity (Klinger & Svensson, 2015; Van Dijck & Poell, 2013), these developments have created 24/7, instantaneous news cycles (Chadwick, 2017). The relentless pressures this places on both politicians and the wider government apparatus are difficult to overstate.

In some contexts this has triggered institutional responses within core executives, including the creation of communications units both in ministries and within ministers' and prime ministers' offices (Heffernan, 2006; Karvonen, 2010; Sanders & Canel, 2013). Such developments can affect models of executive politics and the coordination of (especially) political communication in contemporary government (Negrine, 2008). For example, and this point is illustrated by Van Drop and Rhodes in Chap. 8, media-oriented ministers surrounded by entourages of political appointees and communication professionals may demonstrate less concern for the government's policy projects and agenda than for their own visibility (Helms, 2008). A related issue arises from the fact that, while ministerial advisers are allowed (and often explicitly required) to enter the sphere of party politics, civil servants are formally constrained from—and are in practice often reluctant to—engage with that realm. One possible consequence—as noted in several of the chapters that follow—is the playing out of a tension between political and professional imperatives in the development and delivery of policy.

Typically, as far as relationships with 'old' media are concerned, a traditional division of labour has existed in public bureaucracies. But while civil servants are classically enjoined to be faceless and anonymous, the voracious appetite of contemporary social media for speedy responses challenges Weberian notions of anonymity. Responses to this conundrum vary: in some countries top civil servants and communication professionals communicate on social media themselves and are authorised to publish what they deem appropriate (Grube, 2017), while in other contexts such communication is strongly centralised (Marland et al., 2017).

Recentring of the Government Apparatus

One way or another, in virtually all of the contributions to this volume the point is made that NPM reforms characterised by the division of policy and operations, functional specialisation and marketisation have had negative effects—including institutional fragmentation, the cementation of 'silos' and difficulties in securing cross-government coordination—that have spurred recent efforts at recentring government (Dahlström et al., 2011; Halligan, 2006; Lodge & Gill, 2011).

Recentring has been given different names in the literature, including post-NPM (Christensen & Lægreid, 2007a), whole-of-government (Christensen & Lægreid, 2007b) and joined-up government (Bogdanor, 2005). Whatever the rubric, this trajectory tends to be associated with attempts to strengthen coordination by enhancing centralised and/or collaborative capacity (Lodge & Gill, 2011). Specific initiatives include the merging of departments and the establishment of mega-departments (Craswell & Davis, 1994; Dahlström et al., 2011; Davis et al., 1999), the beefing up of prime minsters' offices or cabinet offices with the establishment of planning and implementation units (Halligan, 2006; Wanna, 2006), and/or the appointment of policy tsars (Kavanagh & Richards, 2001; Smith, 2011).

Moreover, and this specific practice was less prevalent at the time Dunleavy and Rhodes coined their new term (at least in Westminster and Scandinavian contexts; in Napoleonic settings it has been a longstanding tradition), political advisers are increasingly found in ministries and ministers' offices (Dahlström, 2009; Eichbaum & Shaw, 2010; Shaw & Eichbaum, 2018; Yong & Hazell, 2014)—including those noted in Chaps. 4, 6, 8 and 9. Recourse to political appointees can be explained as part of executives' attempts to increase horizontal coordination and to assert political control of both cabinet policy and the standing bureaucracy (Dahlström et al., 2011; Peters, 2004). However, per Roberts' comments above regarding large forces, the institutionalisation of the ministerial (or special) adviser's role is also a response to other imperatives, including the increased media pressures noted above, coalition dynamics (as discussed below; see Dahlström & Pierre, 2011) and Europeanisation. Regarding the latter, scholars have shown how, in an attempt to boost intra-governmental coordination, decision-making in the European Union has also transferred authority and resources to chief executives and their offices (Damgaard, 2000; Johansson & Tallberg, 2010).

These and other developments consistent with the recentring thesis have had various consequences for core executives. For one thing, although the particulars will be context-specific, in a descriptive sense the configuration of the contemporary core executive will likely feature actors and institutions that may not have been present three decades ago. Similarly, and this too is an empirical question touched on in the country cases that follow, in an institutionally distributed environment, not only might the coordination function of government be more challenging than it was, the web of resource interdependencies upon which that function rests might be more tightly woven.

Coalition Dynamics and the Rise of Populism

The principal focus in core executive studies is on the identity of and ways in which actors, organisations and structures draw together and integrate central government policies. The original concept (and, as Chap. 2 explains, much of the subsequent scholarship) was grounded in a constitutional setting with a long history of single-party majority governments. Since then, however, it has travelled to places where multi-party administrations are the norm. And in modern coalition cabinets (as, for that matter, in some single-party administrations) there will be actors that act as centrifugal rather than centripetal forces (Andeweg, 1988). Rivalry between coalition partners can be a constant source of tension—a theme that pops up repeatedly throughout this book, including in Chaps. 4, 6, 10 and 11—and policy-making tends to be more conflictual in coalitions than in single-party cabinets (see also Andeweg & Timmermans, 2008, p. 269; Frognier, 1993). Conflicts in coalitions are often also graver, since disagreements along party lines are arguably more serious than those that take place along department lines (Andeweg, 1997, p. 65), not least because they have the potential to end administrations. In multi-party governments, both ministries and parties constitute 'centrifugal forces'

(Andeweg, 1988), thereby increasing the importance of and challenges associated with both coordination and conflict.

Across Europe there is a current trend towards the formation of multi-party governments comprising parties without a history of governing together (Deschouwer, 2008; Grotz & Weber, 2016). In some countries those governments have included populist parties: examples include the Freedom Party (2000) in Austria, Syriza in Greece (2015), the Five Star Movement in Italy (2018) and the Progress Party in Norway (2013). There is a growing scholarship on what happens to populist parties that enter government: the gains and costs of office, ideological changes, intra-party developments and so forth (Akkerman et al., 2016; Bolleyer et al., 2012; Deschouwer, 2008; Van Spanje, 2011). But rather less is known about how these new parties actually function in government and whether or not executive modes of operating under such circumstances can be explained by orthodox understandings of the concept of the core executive (but see Askim et al., 2021). To take just one issue: many populist parties are sceptical of the public bureaucracies they lead, and their governing demeanour (rhetorically, in particular) might not fit well with the norms and conventions of collegial decision-making required to make coalition cabinets work.

Neither coalition governments nor populist partners in office were necessarily at the centre of the initial thinking regarding the concept of the core executive. At different times and in different contexts, however, both have been and/or remain features of the political operating environment—and therefore need to feature in the contemporary literature on the core executive.

Crises and the Core Executive

Governments are creatures of their time and place: so, too, are the challenges with which they deal and the resources ministers have at their disposal for doing so. The purpose of this section has been to set out, in a necessarily broad fashion, four of Roberts' 'conditioning factors' shaping the context in which contemporary government takes place and which differ, at least to a degree, to the circumstances that applied some 30 years ago. The last of these concerns crises.

It goes without saying, perhaps, that crises can affect the functioning and problem-solving capacities of the government machine (Lodge, 2013; Lodge & Wegrich, 2012, 2014; Lægreid et al., 2015). Over a three-decade span, of course, crises both large and small have had effects on the world's administrations. The 9/11 terror attacks, the global financial crisis in 2008 and the climate emergency are all examples of global upheavals that have and continue to shape executive structures and processes. The most recent of these predicaments, of course, has been the COVID-19 pandemic.

COVID-19 has placed considerable pressure on core executives around the globe. In particular, as Salomonsen and Trangæk explain in the Danish context, the capacity of the core executive to chart and implement a coordinated response to the various health, economic and social consequences of the virus has been well and truly stress-tested. In some country contexts the response appears to have accelerated the (re)assertion of the centre noted earlier in this chapter: that is, in the interests of efficiency of process the core has effectively been pared back to those individuals and agencies directly involved in decision-making. Dostal (2020) provides an example of this, explaining—as do Hundehege and Hustedt in Chap. 7—that decision-making authority has been streamlined at the centre of the German core post-COVID (see also Van der Wal, 2020). In other countries, the centre has chosen not to assume a strong role (as Brinde, Hustedt and Salomonsen show in Chap. 9 on the Swedish executive).

Elsewhere, of course, the centre has not held (at least, not all the time). The UK, the USA, India and Brazil have each stood out at various times as instances in which the core executive has failed to provide the requisite coherence and coordination. Quite what explains this—political culture, leadership; constitutional design, levels of public trust in institutions and so on—will occupy comparativists for years. For present purposes, it is sufficient to draw attention to the complex ways in which responses to the global pandemic have intersected with some of the other 'large forces' mentioned here: the ways in which social media platforms have been used to both spread dis/misinformation but also to communicate governments' strategies comes to mind, as do various attempts to coordinate and centralise control over those responses. It is too soon to say with any degree of confidence whether this interplay has reinforced extant trajectories or, conversely, it has disrupted matters and is taking them in new, unforeseen directions. It is not premature, however, to suggest that the turmoil occasioned by COVID-19 will have determinative consequences for core executives—and for the study thereof.

The Remainder of the Book

One of the challenges associated with pulling together a book of this nature lies in ensuring an appropriate degree of thematic coherence across individual contributions. To that end, and reflecting the direction taken in this chapter, we provided our contributors with a broad framework within which to locate the specifics of their country case (and which we return to in the concluding chapter). Specifically, we asked each to address the following questions:

1. What is the particular configuration of institutions and actors comprising the core executive in your country?
2. How do these key institutions and actors coordinate the various activities of governing (i.e., what specific formal and informal coordinating modes, mechanisms and instruments do they deploy)?
3. How do core executive actors arbitrate conflict within governing institutions?
4. What resources are at the disposal of those actors, and have societal changes had any bearing on the nature or distribution of such resources?
5. Have those societal developments had impacts on the composition and functioning of the core executive, and if so how?
6. To what extent does the concept of the core executive, as originally articulated, descriptively capture circumstances in your country?

Our intention was not to apply an editorial straightjacket, and so we have left it to each author to determine how they go about the task. It is our objective, however, to produce a publication that is both conceptually and empirically substantive. To some extent there is a cult (Dunleavy & Rhodes, 1990, p. 4)—or at least a veil—of secrecy surrounding central government and the inner workings of cabinet, which can make core executives difficult to research. To prise open these 'black boxes', Rhodes in particular has advocated adopting an interpretive approach (one he elaborates on in Chaps. 3 and 4, and which he and Erik-Jan van Dorp deploy in Chap. 8), including ethnographic methods, which provides opportunities to recount scenes and dialogues from the executive court. Others, too—including Bernadette Connaughton (Chap. 5), and Heidi Houlberg Salomonsen and Amalie Trangbæk (Chap. 10)—draw on interviews with political and administrative élites, allowing the views of practitioners to reveal the nature and rhythm of everyday politics. On the other hand, consistent with Elgie's call for 'a more resolutely positivist account of the core executive' (2011, p. 64), some—such as Kristoffer Kolltveit and Jostein Askim (Chap. 11)—have combined qualitative material with quantitative research designs the better to illuminate the relevant issues and challenges in their country contexts. In the end, we think, methodological pluralism produces the richest, most comprehensive analyses.

The structure of the rest of the book is as follows. Chapters 2 and 3 complete the process of theoretical and empirical scene-setting. In Chap. 2 we provide a thematic overview of the core executive literature, particularly as it has developed since the publication of Robert Elgie's (2011) excellent review. R. A. W. Rhodes, in Chap. 3, canvasses developments in core executive studies, tracing the convergence of variants therein on an approach to the study of court politics which combines interpretivism with an ethnographic sensibility.

Part 2 comprises three case studies drawn from the Westminster community of nations. In Chap. 4 Rhodes puts the heuristic of court politics to work in order to make sense of David Cameron's tenure in No. 10 Downing Street. 'Court politics' functions as more than a pretty metaphor here; through the empirical deployment of notions of beliefs, practices, traditions and dilemmas, it enables the teasing out of the material statecraft of élite political actors, situating these practices in the context of various political and departmental courts. Bernadette Connaughton's assessment of arrangements in Ireland in Chap. 5 also refers to the existence of multiple executive courts (the most significant of which are collectively named the 'Holy Trinity', which seems appropriate in the Irish case). Connaughton also illuminates the ways in which the political imperatives associated with multi-party government serve as countervailing forces to prime ministerial power. Coalition government also features in the third Westminster case, that of New Zealand. In Chap. 6 Richard Shaw and Rose Cole assess the impact of electoral system change on the institutional organisation of the core executive in New Zealand; they also argue for a more consistent empirical focus on the ministerial office (the 'core within the core'), an institutional environment within the wider executive ecosystem which has been under-researched.

In Part 3 the focus moves to the Germanic tradition. Anna Hundehege and Thurid Hustedt go in search of the centre of political power in Germany in Chap. 7. The hunt is complicated by the institutional logic of the dispersal of power that has characterised the post-war development of the German state. What they find, therefore, is a complex story of executive dualism in which formal institutional stability co-exists with informal change. In Chap. 8, Erik-Jan van Dorp and R. A. W. Rhodes focus on the office of the prime minister in the Netherlands. It transpires that, contra the orthodox view of an institutionally weak prime minister, contemporary incumbents are increasingly predominant (depending, at least in part, on the skill and craft of individuals), occupying the influential roles of diplomat-in-chief, communicator-in-chief, crisis manager-in-chief and boundary spanner-in-chief.

Three Scandinavian nations are the focus of Part 4. Erik Brinde, Thurid Hustedt and Heidi Houlberg Salomonsen tackle the Swedish case in Chap. 9. Although the Swedish Constitution entails a dualist separation of powers between the executive and the administration, EU membership, increasing media pressure and other developments have necessitated a strengthening of the Government Offices. Unlike other countries, however, during the COVID-19 pandemic the government has shied away from taking central control. In Chap. 10, Salomonsen and Amalie Trangbæk assess the extent to which recent developments within the Danish core executive are consistent with past practice. A feature of their analysis—one they share with several other contributions—is the influence of what they term the 'inner courts of governments', of which the one centred on the prime minister has become the most powerful. In the last of the country cases, Chap. 11, Kristoffer Kolltveit and Jostein Askim also find evidence of a flourishing ecosystem of political courts in Norway. What stands out is the extent to which the contests—for power, for resources, for influence—that take place between these courts reflect the intersection of endogenous features of the Norwegian polity and exogenous developments in the wider political, economic and media worlds.

In the final chapter (Chap. 12) we return to the matters that lie at the genesis of the book. Reflecting on the contents of the substantive case studies, and drawing on the broad framework set out above, we seek to identify and explain changes in core executive arrangements across (and to some extent within) countries and regions, to identify a future research agenda for core executive studies and to reflect generally on the extent to which a term coined in the previous century retains heuristic value. Even at this early point in proceedings it is probably giving nothing away to indicate that, in our view, the concept Dunleavy and Rhodes unveiled three decades ago is likely to remain central to the work of understanding and explaining the work of political executives in the challenging times we live in.

Notes

1. Dunleavy and Rhodes did allow that a more sympathetic and nuanced reading of the literature on the structure and functioning of the prime minister and cabinet is possible using the lens of the core executive. Doing just that they identify six variants of prime ministerial versus cabinet orthodoxy: prime ministerial government (which has monocratic and clique variants), cabinet government, ministerial government, segmented decision-making and bureaucratic coordination (1990, p. 6). Craft (2015) updates that typology to incorporate the agency of political advisers.
2. In its concern with functional rather than locational considerations core executive studies anticipates (and perhaps shaped) an equivalent debate within the scholarship on policy advisory systems (Craft & Halligan, 2017; Craft & Howlett, 2013; Hustedt & Veit, 2017).
3. Metcalfe's concept of consultation resembles Olsen's (1972, p. 273) notion of the sounding-out process, whereby participants indicate their interests and sound out the reactions of others in order to move the final outcome towards the most highly valued end-result.

References

Akkerman, T., de Lange, S. L., & Rooduijn, M. (Eds.). (2016). *Radical Right-Wing Populist Parties in Western Europe: Into the Mainstream?* Routledge.

Andeweg, R. (1988). Centrifugal Forces and Collective Decision-Making: The Case of the Dutch Cabinet. *European Journal of Political Research, 16*(2), 125–151.

Andeweg, R. (1997). Collegiality and Collectivity: Cabinets, Cabinet Committees and Cabinet Ministers. In P. Weller, H. Bakvis, & R. A. W. Rhodes (Eds.), *The Hollow Crown. Countervailing Trends in Core Executives* (pp. 58–83). Macmillan.

Andeweg, R., & Timmermans, A. (2008). Conflict Management in Coalition Government. In K. Strøm, W. Müller, & T. Bergman (Eds.), *Cabinets and Coalition Bargaining. The Democratic Life Cycle in Western Europe* (pp. 269–300). Oxford University Press.

Armstrong, W. (1971). The Civil Service Department and Its Tasks. In R. Chapman & A. Dunsire (Eds.), *Style in Administration* (pp. 318–337). Allen & Unwin.

Askim, J., Karlsen, R., & Kolltveit, K. (2021). Populists in Government: Normal or Exceptional? *Government and Opposition, 1–21*. https://doi.org/10.1017/gov.2021.30

Asp, K. (2014). News Media Logic in a New Institutional Perspective. *Journalism Studies, 15*(3), 256–270.

Bevir, M., & Rhodes, R. A. W. (2008). The Differentiated Polity as Narrative. *British Journal of Politics and International Relations, 10*(4), 729–734.
Bogdanor, V. (Ed.). (2005). *Joined-Up Government*. Oxford University Press.
Bolleyer, N., Van Spanje, J., & Wilson, A. (2012). New Parties in Government: Party Organisation and the Costs of Public Office. *West European Politics, 35*(5), 971–998.
Bouckaert, G., Peters, B. G., & Verhoest, K. (2010). *The Coordination of Public Sector Organizations*. Palgrave Macmillan.
Chadwick, A. (2017). *The Hybrid Media System: Politics and Power*. Oxford University Press.
Chisholm, D. (1992). *Coordination Without Hierarchy: Informal Structures in Multiorganizational Systems*. University of California Press.
Christensen, T., & Lægreid, P. (2007a). Introduction—Theoretical Approach and Research Questions. In T. Christensen & P. Lægreid (Eds.), *Transcending New Public Management. The Transformation of Public Sector Reforms* (pp. 1–16). Ashgate Publishing.
Christensen, T., & Lægreid, P. (2007b). The Whole-of-Government Approach to Public Sector Reform. *Public Administration Review, 67*(6), 1059–1066.
Craft, J. (2015). Revisiting the Gospel: Appointed Political Staffs and Core Executive Policy Coordination. *International Journal of Public Administration, 38*(1), 56–65.
Craft, J., & Halligan, J. (2017). Assessing 30 Years of Westminster Policy Advisory System Experience. *Policy Sciences, 50*(1), 47–62.
Craft, J., & Howlett, M. (2013). The Dual Dynamics of Policy Advisory Systems: The Impact of Externalization and Politicization on Policy Advice. *Policy and Society, 32*(3), 187–197.
Craswell, E., & Davis, G. (1994). The Search for Policy Coordination: Ministerial and Bureaucratic Perceptions of Agency Amalgamations in a Federal Parliamentary System. *Policy Studies Journal, 22*(1), 59–73.
Dahlström, C. (2009). Political Appointments in 18 Democracies, 1975–2007. In *Quality of Government (QoG) Working Paper Series, 18*. Quality of Government.
Dahlström, C., Peters, B. G., & Pierre, J. (Eds.). (2011). *Steering from the Centre: Strengthening Political Control in Western Democracies*. University of Toronto Press.
Dahlström, C., & Pierre, J. (2011). Steering the Swedish State: Politicization as a Coordination Strategy in Western Democracies. In C. Dahlström, B. G. Peters, & J. Pierre (Eds.), *Steering from the Centre: Strengthening Political Control in Western Democracies* (pp. 193–211). University of Toronto Press.
Damgaard, E. (2000). Conclusion: The Impact of European Integration on Nordic Parliamentary Democracies. *Journal of Legislative Studies, 6*(1), 151–169.

Davies, G. (1997). Executive Coordination Mechanisms. In P. Weller, H. Bakvis, & R. A. W. Rhodes (Eds.), *The Hollow Crown. Countervailing Trends in Core Executive* (pp. 126–147). Macmillan.

Davis, G., Weller, P., Eggins, S., & Craswell, E. (1999). What Drives Machinery of Government Change? Australia, Canada and the United Kingdom, 1950–1997. *Public Administration, 77*(1), 7–50.

Deschouwer, K. (2008). *New Parties in Government.* Routledge.

Dostal, J. (2020). Governing Under Pressure: German Policy Making During the Corona Virus. *The Political Quarterly, 91*(3), 542–552.

Dunleavy, P., & Rhodes, R. A. W. (1990). Core Executive Studies in Britain. *Public Administration, 68*(1), 3–28.

Eichbaum, C., & Shaw, R. (Eds.). (2010). *Partisan Appointees and Public Servants: An International Analysis of the Role of the Political Adviser.* Edward Elgar.

Elgie, R. (2011). Core Executive Studies Two Decades On. *Public Administration, 89*(1), 64–77.

Friedrich, C. J. (1963). *Man and His Government: An Empirical Theory of Politics.* McGraw-Hill.

Frognier, A.-P. (1993). The Single Party/Coalition Distinction and Cabinet Decision Making. In J. Blondel & F. Müller-Rommel (Eds.), *Governing Together. The Extent and Limits of Joint Decision-Making in Western European Cabinets* (pp. 43–76). St. Martin's Press.

Grotz, F., & Weber, T. (2016). New Parties, Information Uncertainty, and Government Formation: Evidence from Central and Eastern Europe. *European Political Science Review, 8*(3), 449–472.

Grube, D. (2017). Rules, Prudence and Public Value: Public Servants and Social Media in Comparative Perspective. *Government & Opposition, 52*(1), 75–99.

Halligan, J. (2006). The Reassertion of the Centre in A First Generation NPM System. In T. Christensen & P. Lægreid (Eds.), *Autonomy and Regulation. Coping with Agencies in the Modern State* (pp. 162–180). Edward Elgar.

Hanf, K., & Scharpf, F. W. (Eds.). (1978). *Interorganizational Policy Making.* Sage.

Heffernan, R. (2006). The Prime Minister and the News Media: Political Communication as a Leadership Resource. *Parliamentary Affairs, 59*(4), 582–598.

Helms, L. (2008). Governing in the Media Age: The Impact of the Mass Media on Executive Leadership in Contemporary Democracies. *Government & Opposition, 43*(1), 26–54.

Holtz-Bacha, C., Langer, A. I., & Merkle, S. (2014). The Personalization of Politics in Comparative Perspective: Campaign Coverage in Germany and the United Kingdom. *European Journal of Communication, 29*(2), 153–170.

Hustedt, T., & Veit, S. (2017). Policy Advisory Systems: Change Dynamics and Sources of Variation. *Policy Sciences, 50*(1), 41–46.

Johansson, K. M., & Tallberg, J. (2010). Explaining Chief Executive Empowerment: EU Summitry and Domestic Institutional Change. *West European Politics, 33*(2), 208–236.

Karvonen, L. (2010). *The Personalisation of Politics. A Study of Parliamentary Democracies*. ECPR Press.

Kavanagh, D., & Richards, D. (2001). Departmentalism and Joined-Up Government. *Parliamentary Affairs, 54*(1), 1–18.

Klinger, U., & Svensson, J. (2015). The Emergence of Network Media Logic in Political Communication: A Theoretical Approach. *New Media & Society, 17*(8), 1241–1257.

Lægreid, P., Sarapuu, K., Rykkja, L. H., & Randma-Liiv, T. (2015). New Coordination Challenges in the Welfare State. *Public Management Review, 17*(7), 927–939.

Larsson, T. (1994). Cabinet Ministers and Parliamentary Government in Sweden. In M. Laver & K. Shepsle (Eds.), *Cabinet Ministers and Parliamentary Government* (pp. 169–186). Cambridge University Press.

Lodge, M. (2013). Crisis, Resources and the State: Executive Politics in the Age of the Depleted State. *Political Studies Review, 11*(3), 378–390.

Lodge, M., & Gill, D. (2011). Toward a New Era of Administrative Reform? The Myth of Post-NPM in New Zealand. *Governance, 24*(1), 141–166.

Lodge, M., & Wegrich, K. (2012). *Executive Politics in Times of Crisis*. Palgrave Macmillan.

Lodge, M., & Wegrich, K. (Eds.). (2014). *The Problem-Solving Capacity of the Modern State: Governance Challenges and Administrative Capacities*. Oxford University Press.

Marland, A., Lewis, J., & Flanagan, T. (2017). Governance in the Age of Digital Media and Branding. *Governance, 30*(1), 125–141.

Mazzoleni, G. (2000). A Return to Civic and Political Engagement Prompted by Personalized Political Leadership? *Political Communication, 17*(4), 325–328.

Metcalfe, L. (1994). International Policy Co-ordination and Public Management Reform. *International Review of Administrative Sciences, 60*(2), 271–290.

Mintzberg, H. J. (1979). *The Structuring of Organizations: A Synthesis of the Research*. Prentice Hall.

Negrine, R. (2008). *The Transformation of Political Communication: Continuities and Changes in Media and Politics*. Palgrave Macmillan.

Olsen, J. P. (1972). Voting, 'Sounding Out', and the Governance of Modern Organizations. *Acta Sociologica, 15*(3), 267–283.

Olsen, J. P. (Ed.). (1983). *Organized Democracy: Political Institutions in a Welfare State: The Case of Norway*. Universitetsforlaget.

Peters, B. G. (1998). *Managing Horizontal Government: The Politics of Coordination. Research Paper 21*. Canadian Centre for Management Development.

Peters, B. G. (2004). Back to the Centre? Rebuilding the State. *Political Quarterly, 75*(1), 130–140.
Rasch, B. E., & Tsebelis, G. (Eds.). (2011). *The Role of Governments in Legislative Agenda Setting*. Routledge.
Rhodes, R. A. W. (1980). Analysing Intergovernmental Relations. *European Journal of Political Research, 8*(3), 289–322.
Rhodes, R. A. W. (1995). From Prime Ministerial Power to Core Executive. In R. A. W. Rhodes & P. Dunleavy (Eds.), *Prime Minister, Cabinet and Core Executive* (pp. 11–37). Macmillan.
Rhodes, R. A. W. (2007). Understanding Governance: Ten Years On. *Organization Studies, 28*(8), 1243–1264.
Rhodes, R. A. W., & Salomonsen, H. (2020). Duopoly, Court Politics and the Danish Core Executive. *Public Administration, 99*(2), 72–96.
Rhodes, R. A. W., & Tiernan, A. (2016). Court Politics in a Federal Polity. *Australian Journal of Political Science, 51*(2), 338–354.
Richardson, J., & Jordan, A. (1979). *Governing under Pressure: The Policy Process in a Post-parliamentary Democracy*. Martin Robertson.
Roberts, A. (2013). *Large Forces: What's Missing in Public Administration*. CreateSpace Independent Publishing Platform.
Robson, J. (2015). Spending on Political Staffers and the Revealed Preferences of Cabinet: Examining a New Data Source on Federal Political Staff in Canada. *Canadian Journal of Political Science, 48*(3), 675–697.
Russell, M., & Cowley, P. (2016). The Policy Power of the Westminster Parliament: The 'Parliamentary State' and the Empirical Evidence. *Governance, 29*(1), 121–137.
Sanders, K., & Canel, M. J. (Eds.). (2013). *Government Communication: Cases and Challenges*. Bloomsbury Publishing.
Scharpf, F. W. (1994). Games Real Actors Could Play: Positive and Negative Coordination in Embedded Negotiations. *Journal of Theoretical Politics, 6*(1), 27–53.
Shaw, R., & Eichbaum, C. (Eds.). (2018). *Ministers, Minders and Mandarins: An International Study of Relations at the Executive Summit of Parliamentary Democracies*. Edward Elgar.
Smith, M. (2011). Tsars, Leadership and Innovation in the Public Sector. *Policy and Politics, 39*(3), 343–359.
Sundström, G., & Lemne, M. (2016). Bo Smith-utredningen betraktad från andra sidan bron. *Politica, 48*(4), 455–480.
Thompson, J. (1967). *Organizations in Action: Social Science Bases of Administrative Theory*. McGraw-Hill.
Van der Wal, Z. (2020). Being a Public Manager in Times of Crisis: The Art of Managing Stakeholders, Political Masters, and Collaborative Networks. *Public Administration Review, 80*(5), 759–764.

Van Dijck, J., & Poell, T. (2013). Understanding Social Media Logic. *Media and Communication, 1*(1), 2–14.

Van Spanje, J. (2011). Keeping the Rascals in: Anti-Political-Establishment Parties and their Cost of Governing in Established Democracies. *European Journal of Political Research, 50*(5), 609–635.

Wanna, J. (2006). From Afterthought to Afterburner: Australia's Cabinet Implementation Unit. *Journal of Comparative Policy Analysis, 8*(4), 347–369.

Yong, B., & Hazell, R. (2014). *Special Advisers: Who They Are, What They Do and Why They Matter.* Hart Publishing.

CHAPTER 2

Core Executive Studies in the Wild

Richard Shaw and Kristoffer Kolltveit

INTRODUCTION

The purposes of the previous chapter were to set out the core executive stall and make the case for revisiting the core concept. In this chapter we explore in greater detail the scholarly labour the concept has performed in the 30 years since its inception. In effect, what follows is an extended response to this question: What did Dunleavy and Rhodes, and more particularly Rhodes, expect of their concept when it was coined?

We take Elgie's (2011) systematic review of the core executive literature as our point of departure, concentrating in the main on publications that have come to light since then, although occasionally we refer to earlier work (including those which Elgie did not cite). Our interest is in the formal scholarship—refereed journal articles, monographs or book

R. Shaw (✉)
School of People, Environment and Planning, Massey University, Palmerston North, New Zealand
e-mail: R.H.Shaw@massey.ac.nz

K. Kolltveit (✉)
Department of Political Science, University of Oslo, Oslo, Norway
e-mail: kristoffer.kolltveit@stv.uio.no

chapters—in which the phrases 'core executive' or 'core executive studies' feature in titles or abstracts, or as key words.

We begin by distinguishing two major variants within the core executive literature, and then both assess scholars' empirical foci and explore the various research designs which feature in the literature. Subsequently we comment on the degree to which the core concept has roamed across different constitutional arrangements, and consider whether these travels have occasioned conceptual 'stretching' (Sartori, 1970). We round the chapter off with our views on the extent to which Rhodes' and Dunleavy's initial intent has been realised.

Developments in the Field

In his summation of Rhodes' work on the core executive, Elgie (2011, p. 65) identifies three overlapping, connected facets to that scholarship: (1) the elucidation of the central concept and the subsequent articulation of the resource-dependency approach to core executive studies, (2) the working of the language of the core executive into a broader narrative of the 'hollow state' and (3) the theoretical and empirical elaboration of the non-institutionalist, interpretivist approach with Mark Bevir (see Chap. 3).

Our primary concern in this book is with the first of these. We are certainly not suggesting that debates regarding governance or competing methodological approaches are unimportant (in fact, the contributors to this volume circle back to both at different times). Nonetheless, it is the construct of the core executive that sits at the centre of this work: its travels and evolution, the degree to which it is utile in non-parliamentary contexts and so forth. This is a book about core executive studies—even if it is, of course, nigh on impossible to address that matter without occasionally touching on Rhodes' other concerns.

Two broad camps have emerged within the field, each associated with one or other of Rhodes' fundamental questions. Scholars who tackle the first query ('Who does what?') emphasise the functional facets of the core executive. The standard assumption—and dominant empirical focus—is that coordination is the primary challenge of government. The observation that there may be other equally (or more) important functions was first made (see Andeweg, 1997) shortly after Rhodes struck out alone down the core executive path, although it has taken some time for this to gain purchase. The best recent instance is Corbett et al. (2020), who find that in small states, where politics tends to be characterised by close personal ties, coordination is less of a challenge than are matters related to legitimacy, accountability and capacity. On the matter of functions, coordination has been joined by other concerns.

The literature tackling the second question ('With what resources?') comprises the resource-dependency approach, and it is this avenue of inquiry that has come to dominate core executive studies (Elgie, 2011). The critical insight is that in order to govern, core executive actors must exchange resources. In a world characterised by complexity, bounded rationality and imperfect knowledge no single actor can achieve her goals in their entirety. In the game of governing no one has everything they need and everyone needs something—reputation, trust, authority, influence (or, per Staranova and Rybar (2020), patronage), support bases, human resources (including political staff), networks, detailed policy advice, technical expertise and so on—that someone else has.

Within the broad church of resource dependency a split has opened up between two competing accounts of the nature and bases of perhaps the most significant resource of all: political power. Broadly speaking, the contest is between those for whom power—the capacity to bring about consequences, including for those with whom one might be in disagreement—is inherent in and in large measure a function of structural considerations, and those who consider that it is structured through and wielded within relations.

The latter position underpins the differentiated polity approach, which was first articulated by Rhodes (1988). Chief amongst its proponents are Rhodes and Bevir (Bevir & Rhodes, 2006, 2008; Rhodes, 2011, 2017), for whom political power is fluid and contingent rather than fixed and stable (see also Chap. 3 of this volume). Intentionality and the exercise of ability are what count (Heffernan, 2003). From this view, in the 'free market of the core executive' (Blick & Jones, 2014, p. 508), agency and not structure determines the ebb and flow of interactions between ministerial colleagues. Indeed, Bevir and Rhodes find the very concept of structure 'unhelpfully vague' (Bevir & Rhodes, 2008, p. 730), looking instead to interpretations of the practices, rituals and beliefs of those within the political or departmental courts (and their constituent political, policy and administrative 'sub-courts'; see Rhodes & Tiernan, 2016). In short, there is room here for intent and execution: if not quite the core executive equivalent of a meritocracy, then certainly not the buttoned-down version of the story in which location determines all.

For the protagonists of the asymmetrical power model, however, structure matters—especially an actor's location within a hierarchy. Ontologically, from this view 'power is a function of position' (Royal Holloway Group, 2012, p. 424). Exchange relations and agency certainly count—as does the skill of the players of the game—but locational considerations go a long way to explaining the asymmetrical distribution of power and other resources (including, as Robson (2015) has demonstrated, the size of budgets for political staff). For Heffernan (2003, 2013), Marsh (2011), Marsh et al. (2003) and others the shadow of hierarchy (Jessop, 1997) is always there. And that has led Elgie (2011) to warn that the asymmetric model, and especially the prime ministerial predominance variant thereof, is essentially a reworking of the 'long-running chestnuts' of the prime minister versus cabinet, albeit wrapped in the language of the core executive.

Elgie (2011) also conceded, however, that this hybrid approach—a healthy dose of structure with a dash of player agency—was the dominant school within core executive studies. That remains largely the case. To wit: a recent study testing the relevance of the language of the core executive and court politics in the Danish context (Rhodes & Salomonsen, 2020, p. 74) suggested that the 'PM is the focal point of these networks: the innermost network linking the set of networks that comprise the core executive. ... [T]he PM has more central resources to support the work. These resources increase the power potential of the PM.' In other words, while the power of the political centre may fluctuate depending on personalities and proclivities, location is significant as far as possession of key resources is concerned.

Much the same point has been made by others in the context of analyses of the roles of political appointees (Askim et al., 2016), studies of how membership of executive committees with vetoes over fiscal policy or political strategy is an important structural determinant of power and influence (Dunleavy, 2003; Rhodes & Salomonsen, 2020; Robson, 2015; Royal Holloway Group, 2012), and examinations of the court politics of fiscal policy decision-making (Herzog & Makhaylov, 2019). In such accounts, scarcity (in the form of limited seats at different executive tables) intersects with spatial considerations to account for the asymmetrical distribution of power.

It is possible to overstate the distinction between the asymmetric power and differentiated polity approaches, which in our view is less a chasm than a matter of emphasis. If ontological fundamentalism is put aside these two variants look less like bookends than complementary platforms from which the relevant phenomena can be viewed. Rhodes' own recent work with Salomonsen (Rhodes & Salomonsen, 2020) and Tiernan (Rhodes & Tiernan, 2016) tacitly acknowledges that the chief (political) executive enjoys endowments that are not available to others, while most of those inclined to privilege locational determinants also concede that individual actors' skills and dispositions are critical to understanding whether or not a particular actor makes the most of her structural advantages (see Eichbaum & Shaw, 2012). In short, 'positions and potential influence are merely the starting point for understanding the exercise of power' (Royal Holloway Group, 2012, p. 431). The point, which Allen and Siklodi (2020) also make in their analysis of the efficacy of Dunleavy's (2003) positional-influence measures, is that a structural advantage remains mere potential until it is realised via agency. Equally, executive courts are, by definition, hierarchical assemblages of actors: whether political or departmental, they are the institutional locations in which agency is situated, traditions are established (and troubled) and logics are determined to be appropriate or otherwise.

What Has Been Studied?

Spend too long at the level of broad trajectories and it is easy to lose sight of other ways in which the scholarship has evolved. The obvious place at which to start is with a survey of the empirical application of the central term.

Dunleavy and Rhodes (1990, pp. 19–24) outlined an empirical agenda comprising four broad areas:

1. decisional studies (case-studies of specific executive decision-making processes);
2. differentiated accounts of the central executive (including accounts of coordination, organisational relationship management and resource exchanges);
3. the application of coalition models (within cabinet, cabinet committees and in intra- and inter-departmental contexts); and
4. assessments of leadership influence (including the impact of leadership style and personality on decision-making).

As was the case a decade ago (Elgie, 2011), the second of these categories accounts for the lion's share of empirical studies, the majority of which are consistent with the asymmetric power model rather than Rhodes' differentiated polity approach. There is just a smattering of cases of discrete policy-making episodes or decisions (including Dommett & Flinders, 2015; Dostal, 2020; Mogaki, 2015) and even fewer of the ways in the performance of leadership gives shape and structure to core executive activity (Featherston & Papadimitriou, 2013; Kirkup & Thornton, 2016).

There are, too, an increasing number of studies which while not formal applications of coalition theory do study empirical phenomena under coalition conditions (Askim et al., 2016; Flinders & Tonkiss, 2016; Royal Holloway Group, 2012). Consistent with the differentiated polity approach, these tend to confirm that structural considerations—the internal composition (single- or multi-party) and parliamentary strength (majority or minority) of governments—have a bearing on functional considerations and core executive actors' roles.

On the Matter of the Dependent Variable

One way of classifying these analyses of the differentiated executive is to arrange them according to the dependent variable. Most attention is paid to matters of core executive management and coordination. In fact, coordination—or the lack of it (Zubek, 2001)—dominates to the near-exclusion of everything else (Connaughton, 2015; Craft, 2015; Eichbaum & Shaw, 2012; Flinders & Tonkiss, 2016; Rhodes & Tiernan, 2016; Rhodes & Salomonsen, 2020).

Curiously, given that Rhodes' definition of the core executive explicitly refers to all those institutional arrangements 'which *coordinate* central government policies, and act as final arbiters of *conflict* between different parts of the government machinery' (Rhodes, 1995, p. 12; emphasis added), little direct attention is paid to the causes, contexts and resolution of conflict. Zubek's (2011) comparative study of the ways in which new member states' executives can seek to avoid compliance with European Union directives is an exception (the tension here occurring at the border between states and supra-national institutions rather than between actors within a specific executive). Herzog and Makhaylov (2019), too, explicitly address intra-cabinet conflict in the context of fiscal policy decision-making. Still, the relative paucity of research in which conflict is centre stage rather than positioned as incidental to or consequent upon a failure in coordination is surprising.

Of Functions and Resources

A second means of shuffling the literature is to distinguish between functional and resource-dependence accounts. The former focus on what governments do—and to reiterate the point just made, what they do, overwhelmingly it seems, is coordinate things. Typically, the point of coordination is to bring about 'policy coherence among the wider political system, including networks of bureaucrats, party organizations and civil society' (Corbett et al., 2020, p. 104). The spectrum of 'things' being synchronised extends to political and administrative contributions to the policy agenda (Connaughton, 2015; Maley, 2011), decision-making in the core and implementation on the periphery (Flinders & Tonkiss, 2016; McMahon & Phillimore, 2013), security policy-making (Smith, 2010) and competing policy imperatives within political executives (Eichbaum & Shaw, 2012). From time to time the lens rises above specifics: Craft's (2015) advocacy of a distinction between the procedural and substantive aspects of coordination is a case in point.

The privileging of coordination in functional accounts is starting to irk some. Echoing an earlier call from Andeweg (1997), Corbett et al. (2020) suggest that more attention needs to be paid to other significant government functions. Briefly, the argument is that the close interpersonal relations that tend to inhere between core executive actors in small states often reduce the extent to which coordination is the major governing challenge. Other matters are more pressing, including considerations of accountability, capacity and legitimacy. Andeweg et al. (2020) make a similar case for expanding the functional focus beyond coordination, one which makes good sense if core executive scholars have aspirations to take their conceptual craft out into the 20% or so of the world's nations which are classified as small states (Corbett et al., 2020).

What emerges from these functional studies is the impression that capacity issues (and especially shortages thereof) often go hand-in-hand with coordination challenges. Corbett et al. (2020) and Flinders and Tonkiss (2016) make this point, the former in noting that in small states capacity constraints tend to be more pressing than coordination challenges; the latter simply in observing that to date too little research attention has been paid to identifying the skills required to get the job of governing done.

In the main, those who take the path of resource dependency focus on the nature and deployment of sundry resources within the core executive: political staff, including chiefs of staff (Askim et al., 2016; Garrido & Martinez, 2019); prime ministerial authority (Featherston & Papadimitriou, 2013); policy advisory capacity (Fleischer, 2009) and so forth. Four features of—or rather absences from—this body of work strike us. The first concerns the under-specification of the nature of the resources traded by core executive actors. (Smith's (2010, p. 11) assertion that 'intelligence needs to be understood not as a stream of information but [as] an important power resource' is a welcome exception.) True, there are some studies that are apposite: Herzog and Makhaylov (2019), for instance, analyse the differential leverage actors exert over fiscal decision-making, while Craft (2015) sees political advisers as a resource in the context of coordinating policy and fighting political fires. In the main, though, references to resources tend to be generic allusions rather than tightly focused characterisations.

Second, while Blick and Jones' (2010) astute disentangling of 'power' into its political, personal, constitutive and institutional components is an exception, on the whole typologies of the different sorts of resources are lacking. Moreover, there are no extant means of classifying the temporal determinants of resource exchanges (although see Staranova and Rybar (2020) on the ways in which the use of patronage powers changes over time). There is also a shortage of means of telling apart the exogenous (party political endowments, membership of committees etc.) and endogenous (individual expertise, rhetorical prowess etc.) character of resources. Apropos this, however, Byrne and Theakston (2019) offer a useful critique of the propensity to focus on political leaders' personal attributes at the expense of a contextualised analysis of power resources (see also Heffernan, 2003, 2013), which they attribute to the dominance of leadership models generated in presidential contexts.

Third, there are few available heuristics for quantifying resources. Dunleavy's (2003) formula for assessing the degree of power and influence that attaches to membership of different cabinet committees is an exception (see Allen and Siklodi (2020) and Royal Holloway Group (2012) for applications of the framework). Aside from Robson's (2015) use of public accounts data as a proxy for ministers' preferences regarding the deployment of partisan staff, we found few other means of giving shape and substance to fuzzy constructs such as 'authority', 'treasure' and 'expertise'.

And finally, there is little detail regarding the competencies required to trade these resources to best effect. Locational considerations aside, what distinguishes a truly good player of the core executive game? Flinders and Tonkiss (2016, p. 494) observe that 'there is very little literature that focuses on the issue of sponsorship skills'. Although they offer this in the context of the study of relations between core executive actors and those in arms-length delivery bodies, much the same can be said of the (under) study of those between actors within the political and departmental courts. That said, Rhodes' work, alone or with others, on the manoeuvrings of the baronial court (see also Van Dorp & 't Hart, 2019) stands out, as does Maley's (2011) mapping and analysis of relations between partisan actors in the core. But there is not all that much more, and we could do with greater insights into the art and craft of successfully navigating resource interdependencies.

Research Designs in Core Executive Studies

Part of the point of articulating the concept of the core executive was to shake up a fairly moribund empirical debate. A second important element of the project was to encourage a range of research designs. Following the question: 'What has been studied?', therefore, is the related query: 'How have core executive scholars gone about their work?'

Comparative Research: Are We There Yet?

Dunleavy and Rhodes held high hopes regarding the generation of a comparative research agenda. Elgie (2011, p. 72), however, found 'precious few genuinely comparative studies that operationalise the concept of the core executive'. That remains largely the case. There are exceptions, of course. In a conceptual piece that sits firmly within the resource-dependency tradition, for instance, Craft (2015) updates Dunleavy and Rhodes' (1990) typology of executive models (see note 1, Chap. 1) to incorporate the agency of political advisers in the executive court (see also Elgie, 1997). Corbett et al.'s (2020) study of six small states in Europe, the Pacific and the Caribbean probes some fundamental assumptions regarding the functions of government, while Stiller and van Gerven (2012) explore the strategic use of European law by core executives to influence domestic employment policy decisions.

Beyond that, however, the comparative pickings remain thin, and the single-country case is still the preferred research design. Perhaps this reflects the challenges inherent in articulating relationships between various independent variables with the requisite degree of methodological precision. Featherstone & Papadimitriou, 2013, p. 524) are useful here: the matrix of indicators they use to 'evaluate the relations between actors within a core executive, facilitating both the location of cases within conventional typologies and international comparison', is an instance of the sort of careful design that should underlie future comparative work. In a different vein, the elaboration of different modes of court politics (Rhodes & Salomonsen, 2020; Rhodes & Tiernan, 2016; 't Hart, 2014) also has comparative potential, although in the case of those working under the umbrella of the differentiated polity approach, such as Van Dorp and 't Hart (2019), access to executive élites can present challenges. (R. A. W. Rhodes addresses both matters in the following chapter.)

Of Parliaments and Presidents

Dunleavy and Rhodes (1990, p. 4) and held that their concept had the 'considerable advantage of being applicable to other countries with radically different systems of government, such as presidential structures', but there is little to suggest that the invitation has been accepted by scholars working in those structures. If anything the conceptual traffic is still heading in the other direction, with researchers in parliamentary contexts continuing to deploy—much to the chagrin of Bevir and Rhodes (2006)— language drawn from presidential systems (see Blick & Jones, 2014 for other instances of influential American imports).

Indeed, we struggled to locate anything to suggest that the lens of the core executive is being used systematically to guide empirical work in non-parliamentary contexts. Zubek (2001, 2011) has studied the Polish presidency, but there is next to nothing coming from new European democracies or the Americas (north, centre and south) that uses the logic and language of the core executive.[1] Presidential scholars appear to be enduringly resistant to Rhodes' and Dunleavy's framing. Considerations of academic habit and practice aside, why that should be is not clear to us, although we do wonder if a concept built on contingent interdependencies has less appeal in contexts in which executive hierarchy is constitutionally codified than in those where the exercise of power is more fluid.

What we did find, however, were clear indications that the core construct is being put to use well beyond its home territory of Westminster (which we tease out further below). In addition, the standard focus on political and administrative élites at the national level is being complemented by analyses of interactions and exchanges that play out at and across different levels of government. Rhodes and Tiernan's (2016) study of the executive court in the Australian state of Queensland, to take one instance (see also McMahon & Phillimore, 2013), illustrates the explanatory utility of the lens of the court in federal polities—and while such accounts have yet to emerge, we see no reason why Rhodes' and Tiernan's logic should not also apply in sub-national contexts in unitary states.

Perhaps the key theme to be taken from studies straddling different governing strata concerns the reassertion of control by the political and administrative centre(s) (see, Dahlström et. al, 2011). Both Dommett and Flinders (2015) and Flinders and Tonkiss (2016) address the state of relations between the core and the legion of arms-length agencies spawned by the structural reforms of recent decades—and both conclude that the core is successfully prosecuting the search for control and order in an institutionally fragmented landscape. Our best guess—and all indications seem to be to this effect (see Dostal, 2020)—is that this dynamic has been accelerated by the global COVID-19 pandemic.

Resolutely Positive?

A decade after it was issued, Elgie's (2011) call for a positive turn in core executive studies (see Byrne and Theakston (2019) for a vigorous rejoinder to this) has only partially been responded to. Askim et al. (2016) are among the few to have used quantitative methods: in this case, data from large N surveys are drawn on to clarify the nature of political advisers' roles. In a finding that devotees of the asymmetric power model are likely to reach for, the authors establish that, at least in the Norwegian case, '[f]ormal structure is the strongest explanatory perspective' (Askim et al., 2016, p. 352) for accounting for advisers' roles.

A handful of others—Allen and Siklodi (2020), Herzog and Makhaylov (2019), Robson (2015), Royal Holloway Group (2012) and Shaw and Eichbaum (2014)—have also sought to assuage Elgie's (2011, p. 74) grumpiness about the lack of 'resolutely positivist' accounts of the core executive. Methodologically, however, these accounts remain firmly in the minority. One of several reasons for this is found in a critique of the utility of Dunleavy's (2003) positional-influence measures (derived from membership of cabinet committees). Dunleavy's framework was felt to be just the sort of 'wonderfully innovative' thing core executive studies needed more of (Elgie, 2011, p. 74). Allen and Siklodi (2020), however, are not convinced, arguing—on the basis of a methodology that marries Dunleavy's positivism with qualitative interviews of core executive insiders—that 'power and influence ... are exogenous to the cabinet-committee system' (Allen & Siklodi, 2020, p. 223), not somehow embedded in it.

This looks like a defence (or at least an echo) of Rhodes' and Bevir's views on the (non)significance of structure. More to the point, Allen and Siklodi are among the few whose scepticism that influence and power are inherently related to positionality derives from a rigorous, methodical research design (rather than hunch, intuition or assertion). We take from this that Elgie's call for resolute positivism needs to be tempered by an acknowledgment that the informal, relational dimensions of power and influence—those of Rhodes' court—are not easily (or perhaps even at all) captured via quantitative metrics. This is not a defence of anti-positivism; rather, it is to acknowledge that a mixed methods approach is the most likely route to a comprehensive appreciation of the exercise of power at the executive centre.

Methodological pluralism is certainly a feature of some of the most interesting research designs in the field. Herzog and Makhaylov (2019), for instance, use quantitative text analysis to explore contests and conflict between Irish prime ministers and their finance ministers in the context of budget allocations. Specifically, they develop quantitative scales of ministers' fiscal preferences on the basis of the parliamentary record. Apart from anything else, this throws fascinating empirical light on the shifting and relative resource endowments of prime ministers and ministers of finance in response to changes in the macro-economic environment. Featherston and Papadimitriou (2013), too, use both quantitative and qualitative data to challenge classical interpretations of prime ministerial power in Greece and to articulate a new descriptive category of the Greek core executive.

As to the sorts of data, and their sources, featuring in the recent published record, it is worth reflecting on Dunleavy and Rhodes' (1990, pp. 4–5) complaints regarding the 'meagre and largely anecdotal evidence'—the 'memoires, diaries and platitudinous observations by ex-ministers'—that in their view marked orthodox studies of prime ministers and cabinets. (Diamond and Richards (2012) mount a vigorous defence of the legitimacy of political biography as a source of data; Rhodes himself also draws on such sources in Chaps. 3 and 4.) Clearly, the expectation was that studies framed by the logic of the core executive would have recourse to data generated through systemic research designs. That has certainly come to pass. The prevalence of data generated via surveys and other quantitative methods has already been noted. Elite interviews comprise the primary source of data for many of those undertaking qualitative research in single-country contexts (Maley, 2011; Rhodes & Salomonsen, 2020; Rhodes & Tiernan, 2016; Stiller & van Gerven, 2012; Van Dorp & 't Hart, 2019), and sensibly so, given the centrality of these sorts of empirical materials to getting 'any grip on the question of how generic institutional norms such as the "politics–administration dichotomy" or container notions such as "public service bargains" (Hood & Lodge, 2006) are understood, applied and negotiated by the people performing these roles on a day-to-day basis' (Van Dorp & 't Hart, 2019, p. 878). Researchers are also drawing on various other repositories of data: observations of departmental workshops (Flinders & Tonkiss, 2016), the parliamentary record (Kirkup & Thornton, 2016) and public accounts data (Robson, 2015) increasingly feature in the published record.

How Far Has the Core Concept Travelled?

Alongside the focus and design of empirical studies, consideration needs to be given to the routes taken and distances travelled by the concept of the core executive.[2] The term emerged out of a debate that was particular to parliamentary contexts (and, more specifically, to the Westminster variant of that form) but the clear expectation was that it would migrate into presidential (and by implication semi-presidential) contexts. By design the core construct is institutionally non-denominational: the political and administrative actors, institutions and mechanisms that feature in the core executive—the bits and pieces from which the machinery of government is built—also exist in other types of democracies. All that needs changing are the nouns.

The point was made in the earlier discussion on research design that there has been limited success on this front: Elgie's (2011) assessment that the language of the core executive was largely missing in studies of presidential systems still holds. (Ironically, given his own expertise, Elgie did not explicitly refer to semi-presidential systems, but Zubek's (2011) analysis remains one of the few to speak to such arrangements, at least in English language publications.) Moreover, although the number of studies from Europe is slowly climbing (Askim et al., 2016; Dostal, 2020; Featherston & Papadimitriou, 2013; Garrido & Martinez, 2019; Herzog & Makhaylov, 2019; Van Dorp & 't Hart, 2019), the bulk of the scholarship continues to emerge from the UK and other Westminster parliamentary jurisdictions (although see Mogaki, 2015).

And therein lies a challenge. Dunleavy and Rhodes (1990, p. 3) rightly criticised previous framings of executive studies as ethnocentric. However, while their own conceptual contribution has partially escaped the gravitational pull of empire, European studies aside, the core executive scholarship has overwhelmingly been undertaken in what might be called 'white Westminster' (that is, the former Dominions). 'Westminster' is often invoked as the generic category, but in practice the same small set of nations (the UK, Australia, Canada, New Zealand and the Republic of Ireland) dominates to the exclusion of other former UK colonies such as Bangladesh, Belize, the Cook Islands, Malaysia, Nauru, Nigeria and Samoa. Corbett et al. (2020) aside, there are few or no studies of executive arrangements in the many former British colonies that did not achieve Dominion status.

This has nothing to do with the concept itself: the whole point is that its institutional agnosticism allows it to be deployed far and wide (although Hustedt's (2019) thoughtful comments on the ways in which Westminster's empirical dominance can shape theorising are worth reflecting on). Rather, our sense is that it is a specific instance of a more general issue—one which also applies to cognate approaches, including the literature on policy advisory systems (see Howlett, 2019 for this critique)—which has to do with the relative institutional and academic capital stored in Europe, North America and Australasia, and the dominance of research and publishing that is attendant upon that imbalance. Whatever the reasons, one of the challenges confronting core executive studies is to bring a wider and more diverse range of nations into the fold.

Contemporary Core Executive Studies: Theories and Frameworks

The final matter we tackle in this chapter has to do with the various theoretical traditions that inform studies of the core executive. Core executive studies is a field of enquiry, not a theory (Dommett & Flinders, 2015; Marsh, 2011). The construct is essentially spatial, directing attention to the relational and locational architecture of governing arrangements. Put another way, the core executive is a 'neutral term … [which] … emphasises that the full range of actors within the central government territory need to be included in any study of power in that context, but it does not tell us anything about the power of those actors themselves or the relations between them' (Elgie, 2011, p. 72).

Sketching the Contemporary Core Executive

The better part of the literature is given over to explaining, comparing and contrasting the particulars of different executive arrangements. As such, the construct is often used as an explanatory heuristic, used to frame, explain or illuminate distributed executive arrangements (Eichbaum & Shaw, 2012; Kirkup & Thornton, 2016), the motives and conduct of court actors (Rhodes & Salomonsen, 2020; Rhodes & Tiernan, 2016; Shaw & Eichbaum, 2014), and relations both within the political executive (Garrido & Martinez, 2019) and between policy sectors (Smith, 2010).

There are several matters thrown up by this usage which merit reflection. One concerns whether or not the core term has undergone conceptual elaboration (Sartori, 1970)—and, if so, whether this has sharpened its explanatory utility or produced a sort of intellectual flabbiness. This largely depends on whether scholars define and then operationalise the term 'core executive'. As it happens, most do neither.[3] Only a third of the sources we reviewed explicitly defined the term. In every case bar one the definition is from either Dunleavy and Rhodes (1990) or Rhodes (1995): the exception is Borrás and Peters (2011, p. 529), whose definition of the core executive as the 'Prime Minister, cabinet office, and the set of organizations directly depending on the Prime Minister' is unorthodox in its omission of other ministers and departments.

In a further third of cases a definition was implied (generally via citing the 1990 or 1995 articles), and the remainder did not define the term at all. The third of these practices, in particular, bears out Elgie's (2011,

p. 64) point that the core executive is now part of the 'new orthodoxy'. Where once people might have referred to 'the executive branch' or the 'government' (safely *sans* explicit definition) they now use 'the core executive' a sort of 'container notion' (Van Drop & 't Hart, 2019, p. 878), the meaning of which is taken as given. Used like this the term serves as academic wallpaper: as has been written with respect to Kuhn's phrase 'paradigm shift', sometimes it seems as if references to the core executive are 'embarrassingly everywhere' (Hacker, 2012, p. xix).

Even when it is defined the concept is often used when, in fact, some other dependent variable is at issue. Elgie's (2011, p. 72) 'wonderful flag of linguistic convenience' is still flying high. The core executive provides the context for Diamond and Richards (2012) epistemological analysis of the merits of political biographies; Stiller and van Gerven (2012) use it as a synonym for ministers; for Flinders and Tonkiss (2016) the term describes one party to the tussle for control between ministerial departments and the arms-length bodies they sponsor; and so on and so forth. In these sorts of cases the construct tends to be engaged without reference to resource interdependencies, court politics and so on. This does not derogate from the merits of the work in question: what it does demonstrate, however, is the extent to which we are all core executive scholars now.[4]

One particular manifestation of this tendency occurs when the core executive serves—wittingly or otherwise we cannot say—as a smokescreen for continuing the debate about the relative powers of the prime minister and cabinet. To some extent this is probably inevitable: as long as there are prime ministers and cabinets to study scholars will study them, and they will employ the language *du jour* when doing so. There is an obvious irony, of course, that the term is being used to continue a conversation it was supposed to end. The idea of the core executive was fashioned in the hope that it would usher in a very different discussion about the chestnuts of the British constitution; instead, there are plenty of instances in which—suitably shorn of its context—it appears simply to have been parachuted into that long-running conversation.

Towards a More Explicit Theorisation

The relative absence of theorising is wholly consistent with the Kuhnian (1962) notion of intellectual puzzle-solving, in the sense that the 'normal (social) science' of those who study core executives lies in solving the puzzle of complexity in contemporary governance. But once the descriptive particulars have been established, the term has to be nestled within some over-arching theoretical account or wider conceptual framework if progress is to be made.

And there have been conceptual developments. In the main, these are instances of what Kuhn (1962) would describe as the 'mopping up' that follows on the heels of the introduction of new ideas, theories or constructs. The term is not one of diminishment, but refers to the ongoing empirical and theoretical specification that ensures new additions to the intellectual toolkit are sharpened and their explanatory utility expanded. Thus, 't Hart's (2014) typology of executive courts has been expanded to include the notion of the duopoly (Rhodes & Salomonsen, 2020), while Rhodes and Tiernan (2016) propose conceptions of the court as ceremony, myth and siege. Relatedly, in the following chapter Rhodes elaborates a theoretical architecture of court politics which builds on the cognate literatures on prime ministerial predominance, the statecraft thesis and high politics (and which he then deploys in Chap. 4).

For their part, Askim et al. (2016) have joined Craft (2015, p. 57) in calling for 'the core executive "gospel"' to be updated by including political appointees amongst the membership of the core executive. Doing so has consequences not least for understandings of the nature and deployment of executive resources, for as Shaw and Eichbaum (2014, p. 604) point out, such advisers can 'constitute a resource both in and of themselves (insofar as they possess specialist expertise, knowledge of policy networks and other forms of political capital), and in the sense that they can be strategically deployed to leverage resources located elsewhere within and beyond the core executive'.

So much for studies that address conundrums and quandaries within core executive studies. Increasingly there are also fruitful collisions between the conceptual architecture of core executive studies and proximate theoretical approaches. These contributions are enabled by Rhodes' and Dunleavy's emphasis on resource interdependencies, which takes matters past normative models of the political–administrative dichotomy into the material particulars of 'political–administrative interdependence' (Van Dorp & 't Hart, 2019, p. 879). Dichotomies tend towards states of *in*dependence rather than *inter*dependence; erase that binary and it becomes much easier to explore positive-sum possibilities with cognate approaches.

There are, for instance, analyses combining insights from core executive studies and public value management (Shaw, 2015), meta-governance (Dommett & Flinders, 2015), rational choice/principal-agent models

(Robson, 2015) and political-administrative relations (Connaughton, 2015). Some of these attempts to bring together 'islands of theorizing' (Hooghe and Marks 2003; cited by Dommett & Flinders, 2015, p. 5) engage with contemporary theories of the state. A case in point is Dommett and Flinders' (2015, p. 2) study of the centripetal tendencies of the British Cabinet Office, which is expressly located in the context of 'the changing role, capacity, and reach of the state in an era of proliferating networks and increasingly decentred structures' (and which language and logic resonates with Rhodes' early work on network governance). In this framing, the core executive is a meso-level construct connecting the macro of meta-governance and the micro of specific institutions and actors.

Some of this more overtly theoretical work interrogates contemporary orthodoxies: the logic of resource dependency, for example, 'implicitly rejects overly-simplistic principal–agent accounts and in its place offers a more complex account of bargaining and game-playing' (Dommett & Flinders, 2015, p. 4; although see Robson (2015) for a rejoinder to that claim). And all of it provides useful insights into—and sometimes challenges to—the nature of core executive studies that might otherwise be missed. For instance, public value management's focus on citizens' engagement in policy decision-making and implementation challenges core executive studies assumptions regarding the locus of executive authority and of executive resources (Shaw, 2015). Not all of those conundrums have been fully addressed, but the point is that core executive scholars are increasingly engaging in theoretical discussions that extend well beyond the fundamental business of puzzle-solving.

Conclusion: Mind the Gap

Standing back from the detail, several things seem fairly clear to us. The first is that the core executive has not travelled as far as its creators might have liked: the growing number of forays into continental Europe notwithstanding, it continues to beat a well-worn path around parts of the (federal and unitary) Westminster world, rarely venturing further afield into non-parliamentary jurisdictions. Second, the concept has not undergone a great deal of conceptual elaboration. These two things are likely to be connected: the fact that it has not travelled all that far from home may negate the need for further elucidation. Of course, that the construct retains its original shape can also be read as evidence that it is fundamentally well designed: it is not in need of additional work because it is doing its job.

Neither conclusion means that the concept of the core executive is exhausted. Rather, in our view there are several areas that hold further potential. Empirically, that part of the research agenda set out by Dunleavy and Rhodes (1990) speaking to coalition studies is only just starting to bear fruit. There has been some work on coalition governments (see, e.g., Royal Holloway Group, 2012) but as we noted in Chap. 1 the bridge across to the formal coalition literature—much of which is rooted in European country contexts in which the core executive lens is also utilised—remains under construction.

In addition, temporal considerations have yet to be fully factored into research designs. Elgie was calling for this as far back as 1997, and while some (Byrne et al., 2017; Dommett & Flinders, 2015; Featherston & Papadimitriou, 2013) have responded, core executive studies is still some way from having systematically addressed the evolution of core executive institutions, and the practices and rituals of actors, across time. On this count there is much to be learnt from the attention given in historical institutionalism to the 'different aspects of temporality which constitute … reform processes as sequences of mechanisms that link institutional arrangements and actor choices' (Di Mascio & Natalini, 2013, p. 331).

There is at least one other matter that core executive scholars might usefully sink their teeth into, and it concerns the boundaries of the core executive. Bluntly, how do we know when we have left the core and entered the periphery? At one level, references to the political and administrative executives in Rhodes' and Dunleavy's seminal definitions answer that question. But we think the issue has been problematised by the advent of a fragmented post-NPM landscape in which any answer to Rhodes' question: 'Who does what?' necessarily includes: 'A lot of agencies and organisations not classically considered part of the core'. And in these disaggregated institutional environments it is difficult to precisely determine whose actions have consequences for coordination (or for conflict resolution) and whose do not.

That issue would sharpen up considerably if core executive scholars were to rise to Blick and Jones' (2014) challenge to pay closer attention to the material outcomes of exchanges that occur within the executive court. Charting endogenous goings-on is all well and good, but linking them to exogenous material states would require modelling the contributions of non-core executive actors (civil society individuals and groups, the media, economic actors etc.). Clarity around boundaries would be useful in such circumstances but care would also be needed, because it is not difficult to see the risk that, in Sartori's (1970) terms, the amount of stretching this could require need might snap the concept entirely.

To turn this matter entirely around, a persuasive argument can be made that in the advent of the COVID-19 pandemic pressures on the boundary of the core have taken on a centripetal rather than centrifugal character (a dynamic Dahlstrom et al., 2011) addressed well before the virus erupted). To take just one instance: Dostal (2020) explains that in its pandemic response the German core executive has 'downscale[d] the procedures of political life' (pp. 547–548) and 'succeeded in rapidly concentrating decision-making power at the top of the pyramid' (p. 549).

We don't imagine the German state has been alone in this sort of consolidation. This, too, is about the location—and direction of travel—of the boundaries of the core executive, and it prompts us to wonder whether the nature of our times requires that we must now define the core executive more tightly than Dunleavy and Rhodes did 30 years ago. Perhaps what was 'all those organizations and procedures which coordinate central government policies' in a pre-COVID world has become 'all of those key organizations and procedures which coordinate central government policies'. In short, it may be that for functional purposes there is now, within the core as conventionally understood, an inner core. That matter is one that several of our contributors attend to.

Contra Elgie (2011), for whom core executive studies was at risk of stagnating in the absence of a significant methodological step-change, we think there remains much to be done. (Moreover, in our view Rhodes' ongoing work on interpretivism—see Chap. 3—represents just the sort of epistemological and methodological change in gear Elgie was after.) Along with his observations regarding the importance of solving the puzzles created by new paradigms, Kuhn (1962, p. 24) also ventured that people tend to underestimate 'quite how fascinating such work can prove in the execution'. We agree. There is much yet to learn about the executive landscape Rhodes and Dunleavy opened up three decades ago, all of it intriguing. We make no claim to completing the puzzle set by Dunleavy and Rhodes, but the chapters which follow contain insights into eight different core executives that collectively comprise a significant step towards that end.

Notes

1. We are conscious that our reliance on English language publications is such that there may well be an extant body of work that we are not cognisant of.
2. It would also be of interest—but beyond our scope—to explore the extent to which the construct has found its way into cognate academic disciplines such as history (e.g., see Rogers, 2011).
3. Russell and Serban (2020) use a four-part filter (no definition, implicit definition, partial definition, full definition) to assess the different scholarly conceptions of 'Westminster', and find that in a high proportion of cases the term is either not defined at all or its meaning is taken as given (Russell & Serban, 2020, p. 7). Using the same method we found much the same thing in our own search.
4. Perhaps it also raises a moot point as to whether these sorts of studies should be considered part of the oeuvre.

References

Allen, N., & Siklodi, N. (2020). Objectivity and Falsehood: Assessing Measures of Positional Influence with Members of David Cameron's Cabinets. *British Journal of Politics and International Relations, 22*(2), 220–237.

Andeweg, R. (1997). Collegiality and Collectivity: Cabinets, Cabinet Committees and Cabinet Ministers. In P. Weller, H. Bakvis, & R. A. W. Rhodes (Eds.), *The Hollow Crown* (pp. 58–83). Macmillan.

Andeweg, R., Elgie, R., Helms, L., Kaarbo, J., & Müller-Rommel, F. (Eds.). (2020). *Oxford Handbook of Political Executives*. Oxford University Press.

Askim, J., Karlsen, R., & Kolltveit, K. (2016). Political Appointees in Executive Government: Exploring and Explaining Roles Using a Large-N Survey in Norway. *Public Administration*. https://doi.org/10.1111/padm.12272

Bevir, M., & Rhodes, R. A. W. (2006). *Governance Stories*. Routledge.

Bevir, M., & Rhodes, R. A. W. (2008). The Differentiated Polity as Narrative. *British Journal of Politics and International Relations, 10*(4), 729–734.

Blick, A., & Jones, G. (2010). *Premiership: The Development, Nature and Power of the Office of the British Prime Minister*. Imprint Academic.

Blick, A., & Jones, G. (2014). The Contingencies of Prime-Ministerial Power in the UK. In R. A. W. Rhodes & P. 't Hart (Eds.), *The Oxford Handbook of Political Leadership* (pp. 503–516). Oxford University Press.

Borrás, S., & Peters, B. G. (2011). The Lisbon Strategy's Empowerment of Core Executives: Centralizing and Politicizing EU National Co-ordination. *Journal of European Public Policy, 18*(4), 525–545.

Byrne, C., & Theakston, K. (2019). Understanding the Power of the Prime Minister: Structure and Agency in Models of Prime Ministerial Power. *British Politics, 14*(4), 329–346.

Byrne, C., Randall, N., & Theakston, K. (2017). Evaluating British Prime Ministerial Performance: David Cameron's Premiership in Political Time. *British Journal of Politics and International Relations, 19*(1), 202–220.

Connaughton, B. (2015). Navigating the Borderlines of Politics and Administration: Reflections on the Role of Ministerial Advisers. *International Journal of Public Administration, 38*(1), 37–45.

Corbett, J., Veenendaal, W., & Connell, J. (2020). The Core Executive and Small States: Is Coordination the Primary Challenge? *Public Administration, 99*(1), 103–117.

Craft, J. (2015). Revisiting the Gospel: Appointed Political Staffs and Core Executive Policy Coordination. *International Journal of Public Administration, 38*(1), 56–65.

Dahlström, C., Peters, B. G., & Pierre, J. (Eds.). (2011). *Steering from the Centre: Strengthening Political Control in Western Democracies.* University of Toronto Press.

Di Mascio, F., & Natalini, A. (2013). Analysing the Role of Ministerial Cabinets in Italy: Legacy and Temporality in the Study of Administrative Reforms. *International Review of Administrative Sciences, 79*(2), 328–346.

Diamond, P., & Richards, D. (2012). The Case for Theoretical and Methodological Pluralism in British Political Studies: New Labour's Political Memoirs and the British Political Tradition. *Political Studies Review, 10*(2), 177–194.

Dommett, K., & Flinders, M. (2015). The Centre Strikes Back: Meta-governance, Delegation, and the Core Executive in the United Kingdom: 2010–2014. *Public Administration, 93*(1), 1–16.

Dostal, J. (2020). Governing Under Pressure: German Policy Making During the Corona Virus. *The Political Quarterly, 91*(3), 542–552.

Dunleavy, P. (2003). Analysing Political Power. In P. Dunleavy, A. Gamble, R. Heffernan, & G. Peele (Eds.), *Developments in British Politics 7* (pp. 338–359). Palgrave Macmillan.

Dunleavy, P., & Rhodes, R. A. W. (1990). Core Executive Studies in Britain. *Public Administration, 68*(1), 3–28.

Eichbaum, C., & Shaw, R. (2012). Political Staff in Executive Government: Conceptualising and Mapping Roles within the Core Executive. *Australian Journal of Political Science, 46*(4), 583–600.

Elgie, R. (1997). Models of Executive Politics: A Framework for the Study of Executive Power Relations in Parliamentary and Semi-presidential Regimes. *Political Studies, 45*(2), 217–231.

Elgie, R. (2011). Core Executive Studies Two Decades On. *Public Administration, 89*(1), 64–77.

Featherstone, K., & Papadimitriou, D. (2013). The Emperor Has No Clothes! Power and Resources within the Greek Core Executive. *Governance, 26*(3), 523–545.

Fleischer, J. (2009). Power Resources of Parliamentary Executives: Policy Advice in the UK and Germany. *West European Politics, 32*(1), 196–214.

Flinders, M., & Tonkiss, K. (2016). From 'Poor Parenting' to Micro-management: Coalition Governance and the Sponsorship of Arm's-Length Bodies in the United Kingdom, 2010–13. *International Review of Administrative Sciences, 82*(3), 490–515.

Garrido, A., & Martinez, M. (2019). The Gatekeepers and the Hidden Face of Government: Spain in a Comparative Perspective. *European Politics and Society, 21*(5), 587–602.

Hacker, I. (2012 [1962]). Introduction. In T. Kuhn (Ed.), *The Structure of Scientific Revolutions*. University of Chicago Press.

Heffernan, R. (2003). Prime Ministerial Dominance? Core Executive in the UK. *British Journal of Politics and International Relations, 5*(3), 347–372.

Heffernan, R. (2013). There Is No Need For–Isation: The Prime Minister Is Merely Prime Ministerial. *Parliamentary Affairs, 66*(3), 634–645.

Herzog, A., & Makhaylov, S. (2019). Intra-cabinet Politics and Fiscal Governance in Times of Austerity. *Political Science Research and Methods.* https://doi.org/10.1017/psrm.2019.40

Hood, C., & Lodge, M. (2006). *The Politics of Public Service Bargains: Reward, Competency, Loyalty—And Blame*. Oxford University Press.

Howlett, M. (2019). Comparing Policy Advisory Systems beyond the OECD: Models, Dynamics and the Second-Generation Research Agenda. *Policy Studies, 40*(3–4), 241–259.

Hustedt, T. (2019). Studying Policy Advisory Systems: Beyond the Westminster-bias? *Policy, 40*(3–4), 260–269.

Jessop, B. (1997). Capitalism and Its Future: Remarks on Regulation, Government and Governance. *Review of International Political Economy, 4*(3), 561–581.

Kirkup, J., & Thornton, S. (2016). 'Everyone Needs a Willie': The Elusive Position of Deputy to the British Prime Minister. *British Politics, 12*(4), 492–520.

Kuhn, T. (1962). *The Structure of Scientific Revolutions*. University of Chicago Press.

Maley, M. (2011). Strategic Links in a Cut-throat World: Rethinking the Role and Relationships of Australian Ministerial Staff. *Public Administration, 89*(4), 1469–1488.

Marsh, D. (2011). The New Orthodoxy: The Differentiated Polity Model. *Public Administration, 89*(1), 32–48.

Marsh, D., Richards, D., & Smith, M. (2003). Unequal Plurality: Towards an Asymmetric Power Model of British Politics. *Government and Opposition, 38*(3), 306–332.

McMahon, L., & Phillimore, J. (2013). State and Territory Government Strategic Plans: Exercises in Managing, Monitoring and Marketing. *Australian Journal of Public Administration, 72*(4), 404–418.

Mogaki, M. (2015). The Evolving Powers of the Core Executive: A Case Study of Japan's ICT Regulation after the 1980s. *Pacific Affairs, 88*(1), 27–49.

Rhodes, R. A. W. (1988). *Beyond Westminster and Whitehall*. Routledge.

Rhodes, R. A. W. (1995). From Prime Ministerial Power to Core Executive. In R. A. W. Rhodes & P. Dunleavy (Eds.), *Prime Minister, Cabinet and Core Executive* (pp. 11–37). Macmillan.

Rhodes, R. A. W. (2011). *Everyday Life in British Government*. Oxford University Press.

Rhodes, R. A. W. (2017). *Network Governance and the Differentiated Polity*. Oxford University Press.

Rhodes, R. A. W., & Salomonsen, H. H. (2020). Duopoly, Court Politics and the Danish Core Executive. *Public Administration*. https://doi.org/10.1111/padm.12685

Rhodes, R. A. W., & Tiernan, A. (2016). Court Politics in a Federal Polity. *Australian Journal of Political Science, 51*(2), 338–354.

Robson, J. (2015). Spending on Political Staffers and the Revealed Preferences of Cabinet: Examining a New Data Source on Federal Political Staff in Canada. *Canadian Journal of Political Science, 48*(3), 675–697.

Rogers, C. (2011). Economic Policy and the Problem of Sterling under Harold Wilson and James Callaghan. *Contemporary British History, 25*(3), 339–363.

Royal Holloway Group PR3710. (2012). A Partnership of Unequals: Positional Power in the Coalition Government. *British Politics, 7*(4), 418–442.

Russell, M., & Serban, R. (2020). The Muddle of the 'Westminster Model': A Concept Stretched Beyond Repair. *Government and Opposition*. https://doi.org/10.1017/gov.2020.12

Sartori, G. (1970). Concept Misformation in Comparative Politics. *American Political Science Review, 64*(4), 1033–1063.

Shaw, R. (2015). Raising the Bar: Core Executive Studies, Public Value and a Changing World. *Political Studies Review, 13*(4), 520–533.

Shaw, R., & Eichbaum, C. (2014). Ministers, Minders and the Core Executive: Why Ministers Appoint Political Advisers in Westminster Contexts. *Parliamentary Affairs, 67*(3), 584–616.

Smith, M. (2010). Intelligence and the Core Executive. *Public Policy and Administration, 25*(1), 11–28.

Staranova, K., & Rybar, M. (2020). Personal or Party Roots of Civil Service Patronage? Ministerial Change Effects on the Appointments of Top Civil Servants. *Administration & Society, 53*(5), 651–679.

Stiller, S., & van Gerven, M. (2012). The European Employment Strategy and National Core Executives: Impacts on Activation Reforms in the Netherlands and Germany. *Journal of European Social Policy, 22*(2), 118–132.

't Hart, P. (2014). *Understanding Political Leadership*. Palgrave.

Van Dorp, J.-E., & 't Hart, P. (2019). Navigating the Dichotomy: The Top Public Servant's Craft. *Public Administration, 97*(4), 877–891.

Zubek, R. (2001). A Core in Check: the Transformation of the Polish Core Executive. *Journal of European Public Policy, 8*(6), 911–932.

Zubek, R. (2011). Core Executives and Coordination of EU Law Transposition: Evidence from New Member States. *Public Administration, 89*(2), 433–450.

CHAPTER 3

Court Politics: From Metaphor to Theory

R. A. W. Rhodes

INTRODUCTION

Cherie Blair, the wife of Prime Minister (PM) Tony Blair, purchased two flats in Bristol using Peter Foster, the lover of her friend Carole Caplin, for the negotiations. He was a convicted con man. On 1 December 2002, The *Mail of Sunday* ran the story, which Cherie Blair denied. Her denial created a media firestorm because the *Mail on Sunday* had emails between her and Foster. She had to make a speech admitting her mistakes. 'Cheriegate' ran for two weeks and to the PM it was 'ridiculous', 'nonsense' and he resented the diversion from his priority of Iraq. It was not only an unwelcome distraction, but it soured his relationship with one of his closest advisers, Alastair Campbell, because he had briefed against Cherie. Thereafter, it became a question of when, not if, Campbell departed, and he did so in August 2003 (see Blair, 2010, pp. 518–9; Campbell, 2007, pp. 646–53).

Welcome to the world of court politics and to an exploration of who did what to whom, when, how, why and with what consequences. This

---

R. A. W. Rhodes (✉)
University of Southampton, Southampton, UK
e-mail: r.a.w.rhodes@soton.ac.uk

© The Author(s), under exclusive license to Springer Nature Switzerland AG 2022
K. Kolltveit, R. Shaw (eds.), *Core Executives in a Comparative Perspective*, Understanding Governance,
https://doi.org/10.1007/978-3-030-94503-9_3

chapter explores theoretical approaches to *realpolitik* or the 'court politics' of executive government and the starting point is the notion of the core executive.[1]

Executive studies form a broad church and the various denominations include rational choice, new institutionalism and political psychology.[2] This chapter focuses on the core executive approach. The first section discusses three developments since the idea was put forward in 1990: the 'prime ministerial predominance' thesis, the 'statecraft' thesis and 'high politics'. In the second section, I argue that these several contributions converge on the study of court politics. In the third, I discuss how an interpretive approach combined with an ethnographic sensibility provides an analytical approach to the study of court politics that moves beyond mere metaphor. Finally, I summarise the strengths and weaknesses of this focus on court politics and its advantages over other approaches to studying executive government.

Approaches to the Study of Core Executive Government

I begin with a summary of the core executive approach before describing recent developments.

Core Executive Studies

Dunleavy and Rhodes (1990) proposed the concept of the core executive and it was developed and refined over the next decade.[3] The idea recognises that the institutions of the executive are not limited to the prime minister and cabinet, but also include ministers in their departments. It includes 'all those organizations and procedures which coordinate central government policies, and act as final arbiters between different parts of the government machine'. Thus, the core executive comprises 'the complex web of institutions, networks and practices surrounding the prime minister, cabinet, cabinet committees and their official counterparts, less formalised ministerial "clubs" or meetings, bilateral negotiations and interdepartmental committees' (Rhodes, 1995, p. 12). Twenty years on, as Elgie (2011, p. 64) notes, the 'core executive' is well established in the political science literature (see also Vercesi, 2020). Apart from the study of British central government, it has travelled well to other Westminster systems such as Australia, to European countries and, on occasion, beyond. So, it has also travelled widely.[4] However, much of this work is single-country case studies rather than fully comparative and it does not cover presidential systems (see the discussion by the editors in Chaps. 1 and 2).

Core executive studies challenged mainstream analyses of the British executive, which were 'positional'—assuming power inhered in key positions (the prime minister and the cabinet) and their incumbents. Rather, it focused on resource dependence, asking such questions as: 'Who does what?' and 'Who has what resources?' The core executive approach argues that power is fluid; it is not fixed by, and does not accrue to, a specific position. It varies according to the relative power of other actors and to prevailing circumstances. Power relations vary because all core executive actors have some resources, but no one consistently commands all the resources necessary to achieve their goals. So, they exchange such resources as, for example, money, legislative authority or expertise. These exchanges take the form of games in which actors manoeuvre for advantage. Resource dependence thus characterises relationships within the core executive. Elgie (2011, p. 64) claims that the ideas of the core executive and resource dependence have become the 'new orthodoxy' in executive studies, but there are significant variants, most notably prime ministerial predominance.

Prime Ministerial Predominance

This thesis is associated with the work of Richard Heffernan and Mark Bennister. For Heffernan (2003, p. 348) the proposition that power is relational and based on dependency is 'only partially accurate. Power is relational between actors but it is also locational. It is dependent on where actors are to be found within the core executive, and whether they are at the centre or the periphery of key core executive networks.' He agrees the core executive is segmented, but disputes that power is as fragmented and dispersed as Rhodes and others have suggested. An inherently unequal distribution of resources affords leaders unique advantages, creating the potential for prime ministerial predominance.

Since power-dependence is a recurrent feature of core executive relationships, it follows that attention should focus on the distribution and dispersal of resources and shifting patterns of dependence between multiple actors. Prime ministers command many 'institutional resources', including patronage, prestige, authority, political centrality and policy reach, knowledge, information and expertise, Crown Prerogative (e.g., to delegate powers and responsibilities to ministers and departments) and control of the agenda (Heffernan, 2003, pp. 356–357). They also have 'personal resources' such as reputation, skill and ability, association with actual or anticipated political success, public popularity and high standing in the party (Heffernan, 2003, p. 351, 2005, p. 16). It follows that the more resources a prime minister has, or can accumulate, the greater their potential for predominance. But ministers also have access to many resources that are not available to the prime minister, including 'a professional, permanent and knowledgeable staff, expert knowledge and relevant policy networks, time, information and, not least, an annual budget' (Heffernan, 2005, p. 614).

So, the unit of analysis in core executive studies cannot be solely the prime minister, nor can it be just the cabinet; power is more widely dispersed. Prime ministers remain key actors who, because of their access to institutional and personal resources and their position at the centre of key networks, have the *potential* to exercise significant power (Heffernan, 2003, 2005). Tony Blair in the UK and Australian Prime Ministers John Howard and Kevin Rudd were all predominant until fate intervened. Unpredictable forces shape, constrain and sometimes undermine leaders' ability to get their own way. Therefore, we must examine the relations between leaders and their colleagues in cabinet, the party room and other 'followers' on whom they also depend.

Indeed, both Bennister and Heffernan agree the core executive approach need not necessarily abandon the idea of a strong executive government; the two approaches are not mutually exclusive (Bennister, 2007, p. 328; Heffernan, 2005, p. 607). Even Heffernan's initial version of the argument had many qualifications. He suggests that prime ministerial authority is 'contingent and contextual'. Prime ministers have the 'potential' to be predominant, 'but only when personal resources are married with institutional power resources, and when the prime minister is able to use both wisely and well'. The prime minister's personal resources are 'never guaranteed. They come and go, are acquired and squandered, are won and lost' (Heffernan, 2003, p. 350, 356). Moreover, 'there is ... a vast and sprawling system of networks, committees and taskforces where most work is undertaken' (Bennister, 2007, p. 335). Later versions of the prime ministerial predominance argument introduce more significant qualifications:

> Prime ministers can be sure-footed or clumsy, be associated with policy success or failure, have a low or a high party standing, a solid or a weak parliamentary reputation, become electorally popular or unpopular. He or she can

preside over a happy or unhappy parliamentary party and can face weak or powerful intra-party rivals. Prime ministers can be lucky or unlucky and face strong or weak inter-party opponents. Often, an underperforming economy, or some other such record of policy failure, can prove the instrument of the prime minister's downfall. (Heffernan, 2005, pp. 616–617)

Proponents of the core executive approach never abandoned the idea of strong executive government. Rather, they opened the debate about the power of the prime minister to the limits imposed by contingency and context and identified the variety of core executive practices. For example, Elgie identifies six patterns of core executive practices in prime ministerial and semi-presidential systems ranging from, for example, monocratic government where prime ministers predominate, to ministerial government where the political heads of major departments decide policy, to bureaucratic government where non-elected officials in government departments and agencies decide policy (Elgie, 1997; see also 't Hart, 2014).

The advantage of this formulation is that it gets away from bald assertions about the fixed nature of executive politics. While one pattern of executive politics may operate at any one time, there can still be fluidity as one pattern is succeeded by another. Take, for example, the rapid decline in public support for Kevin Rudd that followed his decision to abandon his commitment to an emissions trading scheme. This policy change created an opportunity for those angered by Rudd's domineering leadership style to harness discontent among ministers and the Labor caucus. Allegiances, including those of Rudd's former supporters, shifted to his deputy, Julia Gillard. Overnight, Rudd was ousted in a party-room challenge which, lacking support, he did not contest.

Unintended consequences and the effect of one damn thing after another concentrate the mind on contingencies and on the question of which pattern of executive politics prevails. When, how and why did it change? Focusing solely on the power of the prime minister and cabinet is limiting, whereas these questions open the possibility of explaining similarities and differences in the court politics of the core executive (Elgie, 1997, p. 23 and citations). Indeed, 'predominance can ... ebb and flow' (Bennister, 2007, p. 340). Few would have difficulty accepting that the prime minister is the 'principal node of key core executive networks' (Heffernan, 2005, p. 613; and see Burch & Holliday, 1996).

So, I read the later work of Heffernan and Bennister as an important set of caveats to the prime ministerial predominance argument (Bennister &

Heffernan, 2011; Heffernan, 2005). It is significant that they wrote their first version during the heyday of the Blair 'presidency', while their qualifications reflect his later decline. In his most recent article, Heffernan emphasises that prime ministers can have 'more or less political capital' and their 'power waxes and wanes' (Heffernan, 2013, p. 642, 643; see also Dowding, 2013). These qualifications bridge the gap between their approach and proponents of the core executive approach. By downplaying prime ministerial predominance, Heffernan opens the way for a convergence on the notions of statecraft and court politics (Heffernan, 2005, pp. 616–617).

Statecraft
The ideas of high politics and statecraft crept into political science from history, most notably in the work of James Bulpitt. For Bulpitt, 'The court is … the formal Chief Executive, plus his/her political friends and advisers' (Bulpitt, 1995, p. 518). Members of the court, the political élite, have an 'operating code', which is 'less than a philosophy of government and yet more than a specific collection of policies. It refers to the accepted rules of "statecraft" as employed over time by political elites' (Bulpitt, 1983, p. 68, n. 23). The statecraft of the court comprises a set of governing objectives (or 'beliefs'); a governing code (or 'practices'); and a set of political support mechanisms, for example, for party management (Bulpitt, 1995, p. 519). 'Statecraft is about the relationship between ideas and political practice. It is about short-term politicking or tactical manoeuvring' (Buller, 1999, p. 695). It is about gaining and keeping office, creating an image of governing competence and creating government autonomy over high politics. It is an exercise in *realpolitik*.

The approach rests on three assumptions. First, Bulpitt assumes that the court will 'behave in a unitary (united) fashion'. Second, he assumes the court possesses a 'relative autonomy' from structural factors. Finally, he assumes the court is rational, that it will 'develop strategies which will enable them to attempt to pursue consistently their own interests' (Bulpitt, 1995, p. 517, 518, 519).

Bulpitt is well served by several followers, most notably Jonathan Bradbury, James Buller and Toby James, who claim him for the new institutionalism and the realist school of political philosophy. The criticisms that follow apply to the statecraft thesis, not just to Bulpitt's version.

First, a persistent criticism of the statecraft thesis 'has been its indifference to empirical refutation' and, indeed, to methods more generally

(Buller, 1999, p. 704). Bulpitt (1983, p. 239) concedes the point; 'the supporting data for many of these arguments is much less than perfect'. As Buller (1999, p. 704) notes, 'acquiring knowledge about governing codes is a task beset with analytical problems'. I suggest below that students of high politics address these matters more satisfactorily.

Second, Buller (1999, pp. 699–705) argues that Bulpitt neglects ontological and epistemological questions. This observation is undoubtedly accurate, and the muddles that ensue can be clearly seen in Bulpitt's three assumptions about the court, none of which are necessary, and each of which betrays a lingering positivism. Indeed, Bulpitt (1995, p. 517) considered all his assumption to be 'operating assumptions, something to guide the analysis until it becomes unsatisfactory'. He qualified the first assumption straight away, considering the question of who the principal actor is 'a very real problem' (Bulpitt, 1995, p. 518). For the analysis of court politics, it is less important to ask when the court is united than to ask when there are factions, and with what consequences. Bevir (2010, p. 443) concluded that Bulpitt was unusual in combining positivism with Tory historiography. I suggest it is more profitable to employ the notion of 'situated agency' (see below) and ask what traditions shape the courts beliefs and practices (i.e., its statecraft).

Buller seeks to resolve many of these issues by appealing to critical realism. This creates a new set of problems, mainly because critical realism and Bulpitt's work are uneasy bedfellows. As Bevir (2010, p. 445) suggests, Bulpitt's work owes a 'debt to a Tory Tradition ... in particular ... historians such as Lewis Namier and Jack Plumb'. Bulpitt treats 'their portrait of the eighteenth-century court as an ideal type applicable to the whole of British history'. This 'Tory moment' is the source of Bulpitt's distinctions between court and country, and high and low politics. There is also a clear overlap with the work of the latter-day Tory historian, Maurice Cowling; both share a concern with the political élite, high politics and *realpolitik*.

Bulpitt's modernist empiricism has led commentators to assimilate him to the new institutionalism and critical realism but 'that is only half the story' (Buller, 1999, pp. 705–719; Bevir, 2010, p. 446). Bulpitt was ambivalent about the ideas of institutions and structure when used to explain élite actors' behaviour. Rather, he leaves the definition of structure 'to the designated principal actors' because 'they will be able to choose which structural features preoccupy them and in what sequence they will be tackled' (Bulpitt, 1995, p. 518). This constructivist view of structure fits uneasily with the claim by critical realists of 'necessity' and 'emergent properties'; it simply does not admit structures that have 'causal powers' (Buller, 1999, p. 706).

At this point we can see the overlap between Buller's views on structure and Heffernan's analysis of prime ministerial predominance. Heffernan argues that the exchange of resources occurs 'under the structures imposed by the political system'. He makes the strong claim that 'institutional *imperatives decide* the arrangement of relations between, say, the executive, the legislature and the judiciary. These imperatives also *determine* intra-executive, legislative and judicial configurations' (Heffernan, 2005, p. 610; emphasis added). Both Buller and Heffernan reify and overstate the effect of 'structure'. Instead, I suggest below that we focus on traditions, beliefs and practices. Most discussions of 'structure', when looked at critically, dissolve into 'traditions' and 'practices', and if they do not, they have not been looked at critically enough.

High Politics

Although there is no defining statement, no manifesto, Craig (2010) draws together the ideas in the high politics approach and provides a helpful overview of the main contributors to the study of high politics. The founder of this approach is Maurice Cowling.

For Cowling (1971, pp. 3–4), the high politics approach meant studying the intentions and actions of a political leadership network that consisted of 'fifty or sixty politicians in conscious tension with one another whose accepted authority constituted political leadership'. High politics was 'a matter of rhetoric and manoeuvre' by statesmen. Cowling explores the tension between 'situational necessity and the intentions of politicians using the letters, diaries and public speeches of this network of élite leaders. His people behave 'situationally' but Cowling never deploys such reified notions as institution or class. Such 'structures' are defined by the élite; they choose which ones they will pay attention to. Instead he asks: 'What influences played upon, what intentions were maintained, what prevision was possible and what success was achieved by the leading actors on the political stage' (Cowling, 1967, p. 322). In short, Cowling analyses the *realpolitik* of the governing élite.

His approach is characterised by 'relativistic individualism' and an emphasis on historical contingency (Ghosh, 1993, p. 276, n. 76). As Williamson (2010, p. 131, 141) observes, Cowling's 'most noted and notorious contribution to political history' was high politics and his insistence that political leaders had 'relative autonomy, with substantial independence in taking decisions'. The study of high politics moves away from structural and class-based explanations of politics to politics as 'an enclosed rule bound game' and to the 'intellectual setting' of that game. The focus is on the study of political leaders, political practices and political ideas.

A fine present-day example of high politics for political scientists is historian Philip Williamson's biography of Stanley Baldwin. Williamson (1999, pp. 12–18) argues two approaches are necessary to understand major politicians. First, there is the interpretive study of high politics; 'the narrative is not of one politician nor even of one party, but rather of the whole system of political leadership'. So, the biographer must place individuals in 'the full multi-party and multi-policy contexts'. Second, there is biography, where it is necessary to go beyond chronological narrative to examine 'the nature and practice of political leadership'. This approach explores 'the remorseless situational and tactical pressures, the chronic uncertainties, and the short horizons which afflict all political leadership'. It looks for 'the qualities that really distinguish and explain a politician's effectiveness'. This focus on the patterns in high politics and the practices of political leaders leads to the study of Baldwin's statecraft and to the analysis of his use of political rhetoric because 'politicians are what they speak and publish'.

Williamson's (2010, pp. 119–120) craft lies in his analysis of Baldwin's personal papers, speeches, publications and film appearances. Like Cowling, he shows we can explore the beliefs and practices of the governing élite by studying their letters, diaries and speeches (and see Cowling 1967, pp. 311–340 for a discussion of his sources). The study of high politics demonstrates the importance of historical methods for political scientists. Thus, Kavanagh (1991, p. 480, 483) argues that 'the contribution of history, as the systematic study of the past, to political science has been more as a body of knowledge than as a set of methods'. He identifies several uses of history in political science: for example, history as a database for testing theories and as a source of lessons. In effect, he reduces historians to collectors of facts for political scientists. It is scarcely a surprise that historians do not agree. Lawrence and Taylor (1997, pp. 15–16) are only two of the dissenting voices. They reject the historian's role of 'furnishing anecdotal material and suggestive counter evidence for the [models of] political scientists'. Rather, they argue 'the proper task of the historian should be to render theory problematic ... because many theories simply do not time-travel very well'. Archival research using the private papers and speeches of élite actors is an essential tool for uncovering the beliefs and practices of the governing élite and understanding their actions. Cowling and Williamson exemplify the skills that political scientist could use in the service of their own questions and concepts. And political scientists need the help. For example, I noted earlier a persistent criticism of the statecraft thesis that it has little to say about evidence and methods. The historians of high politics surmount these problems and take us inside the black box. In short, to turn Kavanagh on his head, history is less a body of knowledge and more a set of methods; tools we can use to explore beliefs and practices in context.

ONWARDS TO COURT POLITICS

The overlap between the ideas of court politics, high politics and statecraft is substantial. All these ideas focus on the *realpolitik* of the governing élite; on 'the relationship between ideas and political practices' and on 'short term politicking or tactical manoeuvring' (Buller, 1999, p. 695). Court politics have existed throughout the ages (see, e.g., Campbell, 2010; Duindam, 2018; Elton, 1976; Starkey, 1987). By long historical association, the term is used to refer to the interactions of a leader and his or her immediate entourage.

The phrase court politics is clearly analogous to the idea of a royal court. It is an updated version of *curia regis* (Adams, 1907). In his discussion of pre-modern élites, Duindam (2018, pp. 161–162, 166) distinguishes between spouses, concubines and servants as the domestic court, 'the upper layers of pen and sword elites' (soldiers and administrators) and inner and outer domains. These terms have their contemporary equivalents in such notions as the PM's inner and outer circles of confidants and advisers.

I do not suggest that PMs are directly equivalent to monarchs—they are not. PMs regularly come and go whereas monarchs abide. However, we are now in Humpty Dumpty's world of words meaning what we choose them to mean. I use the term court politics to mean the internal politics of the political leadership networks at the heart of the government and treat it as a synonym for 'high politics'. Court politics is an evocative metaphor for describing the actions of political leaders and their courtiers. I prefer it to 'kitchen cabinet' or the more prosaic inner circle or inner cabinet or the cumbersome 'intra-executive politics' (Bennister & Heffernan, 2011, p. 778). I did not invent it. I am not the first to use it for either

American presidents or the skulduggery of British prime ministers (see, e.g., Campbell, 2010; Dexter, 1977; Rawnsley, 2010). It pervades television drama and the examples are legion, including *House of Cards* (1990 and 2013), *Borgen* (2010), *The Game of Thrones* (2011) and *The White Queen* (2013). Metaphors are about seeing things anew. So, the dark arts of today's courts resemble the activities of the historical courts they evoke. I suspect that Thomas Cromwell would be at home with the machinations of today's courts even if his methods would be deemed a tad extreme.[5]

Unsurprisingly in a country with a monarchical tradition, the analogy can be extended to the grace and favour heritage buildings PMs occupy. The PM's 'palaces' are No. 10 Downing Street in town and Chequers, a sixteenth-century manor house in the country. No. 10 is a 'great building' (Cameron, 2019, p. 196). Neither matches the grandeur of the Elysée Palace, residence of the French President, but they are not to be sniffed at. The changes in, and the uses of, the buildings have been documented as if they were royal palaces (see Brown, 2019; Major, 2001; Seldon, 1999). Favours extend to individuals. When it comes to the honours list, PMs resemble the princes of yesteryear by acting as 'fountains of honour' (Duindam, 2018, p. 167) dispensing gongs to the most loyal if not most deserving.

PMs also have bodyguards, although not the monarch's Yeomen of the Guard. It is much more prosaic. The personal bodyguard is now the Specialist Protection Group of the Metropolitan Police Service, referred to more as 'the detectives'. They have laid aside their swords and partizans (or pole arms) for Glock 17s. The carriage has been replaced with a Jaguar XJ Sentinel with drivers skilled in anti-hijack and evasive driving skills accompanied by motorcycle outriders. The cars are lined with titanium and Kevlar armour.

Like the kings of yore, PMs must deal with their barons or ministers. Nick Clegg, deputy prime minister in the UK's Coalition government (2010–2015), reports that his role was to counter Balkanisation by Whitehall departments and baronial rivalries (Clegg, 2016, pp. 115–116; see also Norton, 2000, pp. 116–117; Riddell, 2019, Chap. 6). The counterweight to the barons is the court, which is the organisational glue holding the centre together. It coordinates the policy process by filtering and packaging proposals. The court contains and manages conflicts between ministerial barons. It acts as the keeper of the government's narrative and as the gatekeeper and broker for internal and external networks. And its power ebbs and flows with that of the prime minister. Studies of the court exist as journalists' reportage, and in the autobiographies, biographies, diaries and memoirs of politicians. There are many useful books, too many for a listing here (but see Chap. 4).[6] Among political scientists, the most important contribution is by Donald Savoie.

Savoie defines the court as 'the prime minister and a small group of carefully selected courtiers'. It covers also the 'shift from formal decision-making processes in cabinet … to informal processes involving only a handful of actors' (Savoie, 2008, p. 16). He suggests that: 'Court government provides quick and unencumbered access to the levers of power to make things happen and to pick and choose those political, policy and administrative issues that appeal to prime ministers or that need resolution because the media are demanding immediate answers' (Savoie, 2008, p. 231).

It suits the prime ministers and his courtiers:

> Because it enables them to get things done, to see results, and to manage the news and the media better than when formal cabinet processes are respected. Written documents can be kept to a minimum, minutes of meetings do not have to be prepared, records of decisions are not necessary, formal processes can put aside, and only the most essential interdepartmental consultations have to be undertaken. (Savoie, 2008, p. 232)

There are two problems with Savoie's conception of court government. First, it is too narrow. I accept there is often an inner sanctum but participants in high politics are rarely so few. I prefer Cowling's more expansive definition. The number of participants is still limited. But, as well as the core network or inner circle, we can also talk of circles of influence—a notion that accords with political folklore (see Hennessy, 2000, pp. 493–500; Seldon & Newell, 2020, pp. 58–69). In the more formal language of political science, the court is a set of interlocking, interdependent networks. For example, Burch and Holliday (1996, pp. 105–106) suggest that the prime minister is at the centre of the core networks supported by enhanced central capacity that increases the power potential of the prime minister. However, 'the enhancement of central capacity within the British system of government reflects contingent factors, including the personalities of strategically placed individuals (notably, but not only, the PM)' (Burch & Holliday, 2004, p. 17). They note that such changes are 'driven by prime ministerial whim' and 'if they so desire, [prime ministers] try to shape the core in their own image'. However, the extent to which they can do so 'depends on the motivation and skill of key actors, and on the circumstances in which they find themselves at any given moment in time' (Burch & Holliday, 2004, p. 20). PMs' courts are nothing if they are not the core network sitting at the heart of a set of interlocking networks

Second, Savoie pays too little attention to the contingencies that beset PMs and their court. Baronial ministers persist, and prime ministers are dependent on senior colleagues. It is hard to see how a prime minister can be predominant when his or her authority is continuously challenged, even undermined, by an ambitious finance minister whether it is Gordon Brown in Britain or Paul Martin in Canada. No prime minister can intervene continuously in everything. They are defeated by the complexity of government and the massive demands on their time not only from the international arena, but also from the more prosaic need to make speeches and media appearances, and to manage the party caucus and question time in the House of Commons—the list is endless, the diary is packed. He or she must be selective. Moreover, intervention may not have the desired effect, and it is important to distinguish between intentions and outcomes. Prime ministers are quickly distracted, so incrementalism characterises the overwhelming bulk of government policy-making, not dramatic interventions by the prime minister.

It helps to distinguish between the electoral, policy-making and implementation arenas. Prime ministerial predominance is most obvious in media management and electioneering. In the policy-making arena, there is some evidence to support the claim of centralisation on the prime minister's office. However, for Australia and Canada, as well as Britain, this claim applies to selected policy areas only, with the equally important provisos that the PM's attention is selective, and intervention is intermittent. Arguably, the continuous search to improve coordination by central agencies speaks of the failure of such coordination, not its success. The prime minister's influence is most constrained in the policy implementation arena. Here, other senior government figures, ministers and their departments, other agencies, state or provincial government and even local governments can be key actors. Prime ministers are nodal actors, but they are still only one actor among many interdependent ones in the networks that crisscross central, state and local government, and beyond.

As most proponents of the predominant PM thesis concede, there is much ebb and flow. For every Clement Atlee and Margaret Thatcher there is an Anthony Eden or Alex Douglas Hume. Moreover, such judgements are often not shared widely: for example, avowedly predominant prime ministers do not do well in the reputational rankings of prime minister (Strangio et al., 2013, Part III).

So far, I have used the phrase court politics as a metaphor. Metaphors help us to look at old problems from a new angle. They create new ways of seeing things. But once we have opened the window, we must analyse what we see afresh. I suggest that an interpretive approach and its central notion of situated agency, and the associated concepts of beliefs, traditions, practices and dilemmas, provide the tools for such an analysis.

An Interpretive Ethnography

An interpretive approach represents a shift of focus from institutions and positions to individuals and their everyday practices. It focuses on the beliefs and practices of core executive actors. Practices are actions that display a stable pattern; they are what a group of people do. So, a government department or a core executive network or the court is a set of embedded practices. We interpret these actions by ascribing beliefs to them. Practices presuppose apt beliefs, and beliefs do not make sense without the practices to which they refer.

Beliefs and practices are passed on through inherited traditions. At the heart of this analysis of tradition is the notion of *situated agency*; of individuals using local reasoning consciously and subconsciously to reflect on and modify their beliefs and act for reasons of their own. So, analysis shifts to people's beliefs and practices, the traditions in which they are located and the games interdependent people play to resolve the dilemmas they confront (see Bevir & Rhodes, 2003, 2006). This shift to the practices of the court captures the intense rivalry between, for example, Tony Blair and Gordon Brown in the UK, or Kevin Rudd and Julia Gillard in Australia. It also rejects any notion of dominance by any one actor or set of actors. As Allen and Siklodi (2020) show, the formal structure is a poor indicator of ministerial influence. Rather, analysis should focus on the informal networks of the core executive. Such networks are the focus of interpretive analysis, which is an actor-centred approach that explains what people do by exploring their reasons, conscious and unconscious. However, their beliefs and actions are inherited, and these traditions constrain their actions—hence situated.

I focus on the practices of élites; that is, on 'a set of actions, often a set of actions that exhibit a pattern, perhaps even a pattern that remains stable across time' (Bevir & Rhodes, 2010, pp. 75–76). Similarly, Pouliot (2016,

p. 49) defines practices as 'socially meaningful and organized patterns of activities; in lay parlance, they are ways of doing things'. We can learn about the élite's ways of doing things from biographers because they probe the reasons underlying the actions of their subject. We can learn from journalists because their exposé tradition probes actions to show 'all is not as it seems'. Both focus on individual actors; both are important sources of data on beliefs and practices. If the metaphor of court politics is to have any explanatory power, it must analyse the beliefs and practices of the courtiers, and the traditions of government within which they act—because 'no understanding of a world is valid without representation of those members' voices' (Agar, 1996, p. 27). Thick descriptions provide those members' voices.

So, to explore court politics is to seek to understand the webs of significance that people spin for themselves and to provide 'thick descriptions' in which the researcher writes his or her construction of the subject's construction of what the subject is doing (Geertz, 1973, p. 9, 15). The task is to unpack the disparate and contingent beliefs and practices of individuals through which they construct their world; to identify the recurrent patterns of actions and related beliefs; and to explore the contingencies that bear down on the actions of governing élites.

The phrase 'thick descriptions' implies that the court politics approach is ethnographic. It is possible to observe British élites in action, although such access is rare. This study of court politics is not ethnographic as conventionally understood. It is not based on participant observation, deep immersion or unstructured soaking. Immersive observation was not an option, but I still seek to understand the webs of significance that people spin for themselves. I bypass the problems of access and secrecy by acting as a *bricoleur* (Levi-Strauss, 1966, pp. 16–17; see also Denzin & Lincoln, 2011, p. 4; Hammersley, 1999). My aim is to be a Jack and Jill of all trades investigating problems with whatever resources are available; what works is best. For example, Shore's (2000, pp. 7–11) cultural anthropology of how EU élites sought to build Europe defines ethnography to include participant observation, historical archives, textual analysis of official documents, biographies, oral histories, recorded interviews and informal conversations as well as statistical and survey techniques. In a similar vein, Boswell, Corbett, Flinders et al. (2019) identified the following methods in the *bricoleur's* toolkit: hit-and-run ethnography, memoirs and other insider accounts, focus groups, para-ethnography and visual ethnography. Whatever the tools, whatever the sources of data, interpretive ethnographers are united by their *ethnographic sensibility*. This phrase encompasses:

- The search for meaning: the aim is to 'glean the meanings that the people under study attribute to their social and political reality' (Schatz, 2009, pp. 5–6).
- Focusing on '"complex specificness" in context' (Wolcott, 1995, p. 174).
- Positionality or 'a critical awareness on the part of the researcher of what they bring to the field, their beliefs and predispositions and how that might be affecting the research process' (Killick, 2020, p. 27).

In short, an ethnographic sensibility does not require either deep immersion in the field or non-participant observation (see also Pader, 2006; Simmons & Smith, 2017). Ethnography is a broad ecumenical church united around the idea of meaning. It is about recovering and recounting complex specificity in context irrespective of the methods used to collect the data. I provide an ethnographic reading of insider accounts; of interviews and considered writing (Oakeshott, 1996, p. x).

What lessons can we learn from interpretive ethnography for the study of court politics? The most obvious lesson is that thick descriptions (as in Chap. 4) are an essential method in the political scientists' toolkit, one currently conspicuous mainly for its absence. Thick descriptions normally rely on observation but there are many ways to observe other than deep immersion. *Bricolage* makes fieldwork on secretive governments possible. It supplements the opportunities for observation with opportunities for indirect observation through, for example, the considered writing of participants. No matter whether we employ direct or indirect observation, ethnography opens new windows for analysis—moments of serendipity, epiphany and surprise. Finally, the approach helps to draw out the negotiated, symbolic and ritual elements of political life. Ethnographic analysis draws attention to deeper principles of organisation that are not visible to empiricist or positivist approaches.

Conclusions

My use of the phrase court politics allied to interpretive theory and an ethnographic method not only expands the available approaches to the study of executive government, it also brings together previously separate approaches such as the core executive and prime ministerial predominance. For example, Bennister (2007, p. 337) cites with approval Bevir and Rhodes on court politics. It also provides the ontological and epistemological foundations missing from earlier uses of the term high politics by, for example, Bulpitt and Cowling (see Craig, 2010, pp. 470–474). So, court politics is more than a metaphor because the notions of beliefs, practices, traditions and dilemmas are effective tools for unpacking the statecraft of élite actors and their networks. It marries the analysis of individual actors, such as the prime minister, to the broader context of the court and its traditions. It explores a world of situated agents.

When the toolkit of political science also includes the skills of the historian, biographer and ethnographer, we can open the black box of executive government. Documentary evidence in its many forms is the bedrock for the analysis of court politics. It is not plausible to claim that governmental secrecy precludes studying court politics. Not only are there too many examples of direct ethnographic fieldwork on governing élites for this claim to stand (see note[7]) but also, as Chap. 4 will show, there are many indirect ways to substitute for fieldwork. Of course, the study of court politics poses practical challenges, but they should not be overstated. Perhaps we are too concerned to comment on the present-day; much private and official documentation of, for example, the Thatcher era is now available. Perhaps we underestimate just how much is out there. The volume of 'private information' reported by insider accounts is impressive and supports the analysis of the membership and practices of courts. If we are dedicated *bricoleurs*, we need to mine all publicly available information, irrespective of discipline or profession.

The advantage of a court politics approach compared with the other denominations of executive studies is that it reaches parts they do not reach. It explores the reasons underpinning people's actions but it does not assume they act rationally to maximise their goals. It does not assume that institutions are stable but explores how they are made and remade in everyday practices. It focuses on individual actors and their understandings of the world, but in contrast to the psychological approach it locates these understandings in the historical context of inherited traditions. Cesare Borgia and Machiavelli are centre stage, not Adam Smith or Sigmund Freud.

The analysis of court politics matters because it asks key questions about the positive and adverse consequences of those politics. Do courts help prime ministers to govern or do they lead to group think? What are the personal, electoral and governmental consequences of court politics? The approach raises important questions about the effectiveness and accountability of core executives.

The focus on court politics also opens new avenues of comparative analysis. The unit of analysis is no longer an institution (the executive) or a position (the prime minister) but the beliefs, practices, traditions and dilemmas of the courts. At first glance, comparing—for instance—the French president with a village chief in India might seem a pointless exercise. But if we focus on the dilemmas each confronts there is much common ground; how to mobilise supporters, how to ensure the loyalty of allies, how to manage a crisis or survive a scandal (Boswell et al., 2019, pp. 1–3; Bailey, 1969, pp. vii–xi). The focus on the practices and dilemmas of situated agents provides a novel unit of analysis that bypasses many of the longstanding problems of comparative institutional analysis whether we are talking cross-country comparison or comparisons between courts in a single country (see Rhodes & Salomonsen, 2020; Rhodes & Tiernan, 2016; Weller et al., 2021).

Court politics are ubiquitous and to focus on its games is to focus on *realpolitik*. We can move beyond the metaphor to study systematically the beliefs, practices, traditions and dilemmas of governing élites. This chapter shows that the historical and ethnographic study of high politics will open a Faustian world to public scrutiny. In Chap. 4, I provide an example of a court 'in action'.

Notes

1. This chapter draws on Rhodes (2014, 2016; Rhodes, 2017). I would like to thank the editors, Jenny Fleming, Jack Corbett and Erik-Jan Van Dorp, for their advice on the first draft.
2. For comprehensive surveys see Andeweg et al. (2020) on political executives; Best and Higley (2018) on political élites; and Rhodes and 't Hart (2014) on political leaders.
3. On subsequent extensions and applications see Burch and Holliday (1996); Elgie (1997); Marsh et al. (2001); Rhodes and Dunleavy (1995); and Smith (1999, 2010).
4. On Australia see, for example, Davis (1997); Eichbaum and Shaw (2012); Rhodes and Tiernan (2016). On European countries see, for example, Eymeri-Douzans et al. (2015); Featherstone and Papadimitriou (2013); Goetz (1997); Helms (2005); Rhodes and Salomonsen (2020); 't Hart and Wille (2006); and Zubek (2001). On

other countries see, for example, Corbett et al. (2020); Heilman (2017); Mogaki (2015); and Xu and Weller (2016).
5. See MacCulloch (2018, Chap. 14) for an account of the court politics that led to the death of Anne Boleyn; and Chap. 20 for an account of the Exeter (White Rose) conspiracy. The singular feature of these plots is that the traitors were executed, a fate that did not befall Michael Gove after his treachery (see Chap. 4 below).
6. My favourite recent UK examples include Blunkett (2006); Bower (2016, 2020); Cameron (2019); Campbell (2007); Laws (2016); Rawnsley (2001, 2010); Seldon and Lodge (2010); Seldon and Newell (2020); Seldon and Snowdon (2015); and Shipman (2016, 2017).
7. They include Heclo and Wildavsky (1981 [1974]) on the Treasury and public expenditure; Burns (1977) on the BBC; Crewe (2005, 2015) on the House of Lords and House of Commons respectively; Faucher-King (2005) on party conferences; Geddes (2020) on the select committees of the House of Commons; Rhodes (2011) on British government departments and Rhodes et al. (2007), which covers various government élites in European countries.

References

Adams, G. B. (1907). The Descendants of the Curia Regis. *The American Historical Review, 13*(1), 11–15.
Agar, M. (1996). *The Professional Stranger* (2nd ed.). Academic Press.
Allen, N., & Siklodi, N. (2020). Objectivity and Falsehood: Assessing Measures of Positional Influence with Members of David Cameron's Cabinets. *British Journal of Politics and International Relations, 22*(2), 220–237.
Andeweg, R. B., Elgie, R., Helms, L., Kaarbo, J., & Muller-Rommel, F. (Eds.). (2020). *The Oxford Handbook of Political Executives*. Oxford University Press.
Bailey, F. G. (1969). *Stratagems and Spoils*. Blackwell.
Bennister, M. (2007). Tony Blair and John Howard: Comparative Predominance and Institution Stretch in the UK and Australia. *The British Journal of Politics and International Relation, 9*(3), 327–345.
Bennister, M., & Heffernan, R. (2011). Cameron as Prime Minister: The Intra-executive Politics of Britain's Coalition Government. *Parliamentary Affairs, 65*(4), 778–801.
Best, H., & Higley, J. (Eds.) (2018). *The Palgrave Handbook of Political Elites*. London: Palgrave Macmillan.

Bevir, M. (2010). Interpreting Territory and Power. *Government and Opposition, 45*(3), 436–456.
Bevir, M., & Rhodes, R. A. W. (2003). *Interpreting British Governance.* Routledge.
Bevir, M., & Rhodes, R. A. W. (2006). *Governance Stories.* Routledge.
Bevir, M., & Rhodes, R. A. W. (2010). *The State as Cultural Practice.* Oxford University Press.
Blair, T. (2010). *A Journey.* London: Hutchinson.
Blunkett, D. (2006). *The Blunkett Tapes. My Life in the Bear Pit.* Bloomsbury.
Boswell, J., Corbett, J., Flinders, M., Jennings, W., Rhodes, R. A. W., & Wood, M. (2019). What Can Political Ethnography Tell Us About Anti-Politics and Democratic Disaffection? *European Journal of Political Research, 58*(1), 56–71.
Boswell, J., Corbett, J., & Rhodes, R. A. W. (2019). *The Art and Craft of Comparison.* Cambridge University Press.
Bower, T. (2016). *Broken Vows. Tony Blair. The Tragedy of Power.* Faber & Faber.
Bower, T. (2020). *Boris Johnson: A Biography.* W.H. Allen.
Brown, J. (2019). *No. 10: The Geography of Power at Downing Street.* Haus Publishing.
Buller, J. (1999). A Critical Appraisal of the Statecraft Interpretation. *Public Administration, 77*(4), 691–712.
Bulpitt, J. (1983). *Territory and Power in the United Kingdom: An Interpretation.* Manchester University Press.
Bulpitt, M. (1995). Historical Politics: Macro, In-Time, Governing Regime Analysis. In J. Lovenduski & J. Stanyer (Eds.), *Contemporary Political; Studies 1995, Volume II* (pp. 510–520). Political Studies Association.
Burch, M., & Holliday, I. (1996). *The British Cabinet System.* Prentice Hall/Harvester Wheatsheaf.
Burch, M., & Holliday, I. (2004). The Blair Government and the Core Executive. *Government and Opposition, 39*(1), 1–21.
Burns, T. (1977). *The BBC: Public Institution and Private World.* Macmillan.
Cameron, D. (2019). *For the Record.* William Collins.
Campbell, A. (2007). *The Blair Years. Extracts from the Campbell Diaries.* London: Hutchinson.
Campbell, J. (2010). *Pistols at Dawn. Two Hundred Years of Political Rivalry from Pitt and Fox to Blair and Brown.* Vintage.
Clegg, N. (2016). *Politics: Between the Extremes.* The Bodley Head.
Corbett, J., Veenendaal, W., & Connell, J. (2020). The Core Executive and Small States: Is Coordination the Primary Challenge? *Public Administration.* https://doi.org/10.1111/padm.12682
Cowling, M. (1967). *1867, Disraeli, Gladstone and Revolution: The Passing of the Second Reform Bill.* Cambridge University Press.
Cowling, M. (1971). *The Impact of Labour 1920–1924.* Cambridge University Press.

Craig, D. (2010). "High Politics" and the "New Political History". *The Historical Journal, 53*(2), 453–475.

Crewe, E. (2005). *Lords of Parliament: Manners, Rituals and Politics*. Manchester University Press.

Crewe, E. (2015). *The House of Commons: An Anthropology of MPs at Work*. Bloomsbury.

Davis, G. (1997). The Core Executive. In B. Galligan, I. McAllister, & J. Ravenhill (Eds.), *New Developments in Australian Politic* (pp. 85–101). Macmillan.

Denzin, N. K., & Lincoln, Y. S. (2011 [1994]). Introduction: The Discipline and Practice of Qualitative Research. In N. K. Denzin & Y. S. Lincoln (Eds.), *Handbook of Qualitative Research*, 4th ed. (pp. 1–19). Sage.

Dexter, L. A. (1977). Court Politics: Presidential Staff Relations as a Special case of a General Phenomenon. *Administration & Society, 9*(3), 267–283.

Dowding, K. (2013). The Prime Ministerialization of the British Prime Minister. *Parliamentary Affairs, 66*(3), 617–635.

Duindam, J. (2018). Pre-modern Power Elites: Princes, Courts and Intermediaries. In H. Best & J. Higley (Eds.), *Palgrave Handbook of Political Elites* (pp. 161–179). Palgrave Macmillan.

Dunleavy, P., & Rhodes, R. A. W. (1990). Core Executive Studies in Britain. *Public Administration, 68*(1), 3–28.

Eichbaum, C., & Shaw, R. (2012). Political Staff in Executive Government: Conceptualising and Mapping Roles Within the Core Executive. *Australian Journal of Political Science, 46*(4), 583–600.

Elgie, R. (1997). Models of Executive Politics: A Framework for the Study of Executive Power Relations in Parliamentary and Semi-Presidential Regimes. *Political Studies, 45*(2), 217–231.

Elgie, R. (2011). Core Executive Studies Two Decades On. *Public Administration, 89*(1), 64–77.

Elton, G. R. (1976). Presidential Address: Tudor Government: The Points of Contact: III. The Court. *Transactions of the Royal Historical Society (Fifth Series), 26*(December), 211–228.

Eymeri-Douzans, J., Bioy, X., & Mouton, S. (Eds.). (2015). *Le règne des Entourages: Cabinets and Conseillers de l'exécutif*. Presses de Sciences Po.

Faucher-King, F. (2005). *Changing Parties: An anthropology of British political conferences*. Palgrave Macmillan.

Featherstone, K., & Papadimitriou, D. (2013). The Emperor Has No Clothes! Power and Resources Within the Greek Core Executive. *Governance, 26*(3), 523–545.

Geddes, M. (2020). *Dramas at Westminster: Select Committees and the Quest for Accountability*. Manchester University Press.

Geertz, C. (1973). Thick Description: Toward an Interpretive Theory of Culture. In C. Geertz (Ed.), *The Interpretation of Cultures* (pp. 3–30). Basic Books.

Ghosh, P. (1993). Towards the Verdict of History: Mr Cowling's Doctrine. In M. Bentley (Ed.), *Public and Private Doctrine: Essays in British History Presented to Maurice Cowling* (pp. 273–321). Cambridge University Press.

Goetz, K. H. (1997). Acquiring Political Craft: Training Grounds for Top Officials in the German Core Executive. *Public Administration, 75*(4), 753–775.

Hammersley, M. (1999). Not Bricolage but Boat Building. Exploring Two Metaphors for Thinking about Ethnography. *Journal of Contemporary Ethnography, 28*(5), 574–585.

Hart, P. (2014). *Understanding Political Leadership*. Palgrave Macmillan. Relevant insertions made to body of text.

Heclo, H., & Wildavsky, A. (1981 [1974]). *The Private Government of Public Money* (2nd ed.). Macmillan.

Heffernan, R. (2003). Prime Ministerial Predominance? Core Executive Politics in the UK. *British Journal of Politics and International Relation, 5(3*, 347–372.

Heffernan, R. (2005). Exploring and Explaining the British Prime Minister. *The British Journal of Politics and International Relations, 7*(4), 605–620.

Heffernan, R. (2013). There's No Need for the "-isation": The Prime Minister Is Merely Prime Ministerial. *Parliamentary Affairs, 66*(3), 636–645.

Heilman, S. (2017). China's Core Executive. In V. Shue & P. Thornton (Eds.), *To Govern China: Evolving Practices of Power* (pp. 57–81). Cambridge University Press.

Helms, L. (2005). *Presidents, Prime Ministers & Chancellors*. Palgrave.

Hennessy, P. (2000). *The Prime Ministers*. Allen Lane and The Penguin Press.

Kavanagh, D. (1991). Why Political Science Needs History. *Political Studies, 39*, 479–495.

Killick, A. (2020). *Rigged. Understanding 'the Economy' in Brexit Britain*. Manchester University Press.

Lawrence, J., & Taylor, M. (1997). Introduction: Electoral Sociology and the Historians. In J. Lawrence & M. Taylor (Eds.), *Party, State and Society. Electoral Behaviour in Britain since 1820* (pp. 1–26). Scolar Press.

Laws, D. (2016). *Coalition. The Inside Story of the Conservative-Liberal Democrat Coalition*. Biteback Publishing.

Levi-Strauss, C. (1966). *The Savage Mind*. Weidenfeld and Nicolson.

Major, N. (2001). *Chequers: The Prime Minister's Country House and its History*. Little, Brown and Company.

MacCulloch, D. (2018). *Thomas Cromwell: A Life*. London: Allen Lane.

Marsh, D., Richards, D., & Smith, M. J. (2001). *Changing Patterns of Governance in the United Kingdom*. Palgrave.

Mogaki, M. (2015). The Evolving Powers of the Core Executive: A Case Study of Japan's ICT Regulation after the 1980s. *Pacific Affairs, 88*(1), 27–49.

Norton, P. (2000). Barons in a Shrinking Kingdom: Senior Ministers in British Government. In R. A. W. Rhodes (Ed.), *Transforming British Government. Volume 2. Changing Roles and Relationships* (pp. 101–124). Macmillan.

Oakeshott, M. (1996). *The Politics of Faith and the Politics of Scepticism*. Edited by Timothy Fuller. New Haven: Yale University Press.

Pader, E. (2006). Seeing with an Ethnographic Sensibility: Explorations Beneath the Surface of Public Policies. In D. Yanow & P. Schwartz-Shea (Eds.), *Interpretation and Method: Empirical Research Methods and the Interpretive Turn* (pp. 161–175). M.E. Sharpe.

Pouliot, V. (2016). *International Pecking Orders: the politics and practice of multilateral diplomacy*. Cambridge: Cambridge University Press.

Rawnsley, A. (2001). *Servants of the People: The Inside Story of New Labour* (Rev. ed.). Penguin Books.

Rawnsley, A. (2010). *The End of the Party: The Rise and Fall of New Labour*. Viking.

Rhodes, R. A. W. (1995). From Prime Ministerial Power to Core Executive. In R. A. W. Rhodes & P. Dunleavy (Eds.), *Prime Minister, Cabinet and Core Executive* (pp. 11–37). Macmillan.

Rhodes, R. A. W. (2011). *Everyday Life in British Government*. Oxford University Press.

Rhodes, R. A. W. (2014). Core Executives, Prime Ministers, Statecraft and Court Politics: Towards Convergence. In G. Davis & R. A. W. Rhodes (Eds.), *The Craft of Governing: Essays in Honour of Professor Patrick Weller* (pp. 53–72). Allen and Unwin.

Rhodes, R. A. W. (2016). Executive Governance: An Interpretive Approach. In N. Turnbull (Ed.), *Interpreting Governance, High Politics and Public Policy: Essays Commemorating Interpreting British Governance* (pp. 79–96). Routledge.

Rhodes, R. A. W. (2017). Interpretive Political Science. *Selected Essays*, Volume II. Oxford: Oxford University Press.

Rhodes, R. A. W., & Dunleavy, P. (Eds.). (1995). *Prime Minister, Cabinet and Core Executive*. Macmillan.

Rhodes, R. A. W., & Salomonsen, H. H. (2020). Duopoly, Court Politics and the Danish Core Executive. *Public Administration*. https://doi.org/10.1111/padm.12685

Rhodes, R. A. W., & 't Hart, P. (Eds.) (2014). *The Oxford Handbook of Political Leadership*. Oxford: Oxford University Press.

Rhodes, R. A. W., & Tiernan, A. (2016). Court Politics in a Federal Polity. *Australian Journal of Political Science*, 51(2), 338–354.

Riddell, P. (2019). 15 Minutes of Power. *The Uncertain Life of British Ministers*. London: Profile Books.

Savoie, D. (2008). *Court Government and the Collapse of Accountability in Canada and the United Kingdom*. University of Toronto Press.

Schatz, E. (2009). Ethnographic Immersion and the Study of Politics. In E. Schatz (Ed.), *Political Ethnography: What Immersion Contributes to the Study of Power* (pp. 1–22). University of Chicago Press.

Seldon, A. (1999). *10 Downing Street. An Illustrated History*. HarperCollins.

Seldon, A., & Lodge, G. (2010). *Brown at 10*. Biteback Publishing.
Seldon, A., & Newell, R. (2020). *May at 10. The Verdict*. Biteback Publishing. Updated Paperback Edition.
Seldon, A., & Snowdon, P. (2015). *Cameron at 10. The Inside Story 2010–2015*. William Collins.
Shipman, T. (2016). *All Out War. The Full Story of How Brexit Sank Britain's Political Class*. William Collins.
Shipman, T. (2017). *Fall Out. A Year of Political Mayhem*. William Collins.
Shore, C. (2000). *Building Europe: The Cultural Politics of European Integration*. Routledge.
Simmons, E. S., & Smith, N. R. (2017). Comparison with an Ethnographic Sensibility. *Political Science & Politics, 50*(1), 126–130.
Smith, M. J. (1999). *The Core Executive in Britain*. Palgrave Macmillan.
Smith, M. (2010). Intelligence and the Core Executive. *Public Policy and Administration, 25*(1), 11–28.
Starkey, D. (1987). Introduction: Court History in Perspective. In S. Starkey (Ed.), *The English Court: From the Wars of the Roses to the Civil War* (pp. 1–24). Longman.
Strangio, P., 't Hart, P., & Walter, J. (Eds.). (2013). *Prime Ministerial Leadership: Power, Party and Performance in Westminster Systems*. Oxford University Press.
't Hart, P. (2014). *Understanding Political Leadership*. Palgrave Macmillan.
't Hart, P., & Wille, A. C. (2006). Ministers and Top Officials in the Dutch Core Executive: Living Together, Growing Apart? *Public Administration, 84*(1), 121–146.
Vercesi, M. (2020). Cabinet Decision-Making in Parliamentary Systems. In R. B. Andeweg, R. Elgie, L. Helms, J. Kaarbo, & F. Muller-Rommel (Eds.), *The Oxford Handbook of Political Executives* (pp. 438–459). Oxford University Press.
Weller, P., Grube, D., & Rhodes, R. A. W. (2021). *Comparing Cabinets: The Dilemmas of Collective Government*. Oxford University Press.
Williamson, P. (1999). *Stanley Baldwin*. Cambridge University Press.
Williamson, P. (2010). Maurice Cowling and Modern British Political History. In R. Crowcroft, S. J. D. Green, & R. Whiting (Eds.), *Philosophy, Politics and Religion in British Democracy: Maurice Cowling and Conservatism* (pp. 108–152). I.B. Tauris.
Wolcott, H. F. (1995). *The Art of Fieldwork*. Walnut Creek, CA: Altamira Press.
Xu, Y.-c., & Weller, P. (2016). The Challenges of Governing: The State Council in China. *The China Journal, 76*, 1–23.
Zubek, R. (2001). A Core in Check: The Transformation of the Polish Core Executive. *Journal of European Public Policy, 8*(6), 911–932.

PART II

Core Executives in Westminster Contexts

CHAPTER 4

Court Politics in an Age of Austerity: David Cameron's Court, 2010–2016

R. A. W. Rhodes

INTRODUCTION

This chapter focuses on the 'backstage' politics of decision-making in élite networks rather than the more common focus on the 'front stage' politics in the media spotlight (Klijn, 2014, pp. 404–405). Court politics are commonplace but rarely analysed. This chapter focuses on the court of David Cameron, UK Prime Minister (2010–2016). It describes systematically the practices of the court 'in action'. It explains why court politics matter by looking at the consequences of those actions. First, I describe my method—the thematic analysis of inside dopester accounts. Second, I describe the membership, and analyse the practices, of David Cameron's court. Finally, I explore the consequences of his court's practices.[1]

In Chap. 3, I reviewed the field of core executive studies and suggested that a focus on court politics would be productive. The aim of this chapter

---

R. A. W. Rhodes (✉)
University of Southampton, Southampton, UK
e-mail: r.a.w.rhodes@soton.ac.uk

© The Author(s), under exclusive license to Springer Nature Switzerland AG 2022
K. Kolltveit, R. Shaw (eds.), *Core Executives in a Comparative Perspective*, Understanding Governance,
https://doi.org/10.1007/978-3-030-94503-9_4

is to show that the term is more than an evocative metaphor and that it can explain why courts matter. To do that, I marry a description of court politics with an interpretive analysis. I treat the court élites as 'situated agents'; that is, they are agents who can adapt their beliefs or act for reasons of their own (see Bevir & Rhodes, 2003, 2006; see also Chap. 3). I focus on the informal networks of the core executive and the practices of its members. Practices refer to 'a set of actions, often a set of actions that exhibit a pattern, perhaps even a pattern that remains stable across time' (Bevir & Rhodes, 2010, pp. 75–76). If the metaphor of court politics is to have any explanatory power, it must analyse the beliefs and practices of the courtiers, and the traditions of government within which they act. I show also that court politics matter because they have personal, electoral and governmental consequences.

As well as these analytical ambitions, there is an underpinning message. The public curse present-day politicians as knaves for their duplicitous politicking, *but it was ever thus*. Politics is the pursuit of power in which rivalry, intrigue, backstabbing, conspiracy and lying are perennial practices. Too much political science fails to grasp that today's politics are just another version of Macbeth, with smartphones instead of swords, resignations not beheadings. My stories are of wild treachery among the courtiers and weirdness in the court. Same as it ever was.

Methods

I seek to develop a 'thick description' of the practices of the court system (Geertz, 1973; Chapter 3). Whenever possible, I do so in the words of the courtiers. I tell my story of their stories about how things work around here. In an ideal world, I would compare 'the pattern of practice, talk, and considered writing' (Oakeshott, 1996, p. x). Participant observation of the everyday practices of prime ministers and cabinets was not possible for the obvious reason of government secrecy. So, my primary sources are considered writing in the guise of the biographies, memoirs and autobiographies of key participants. David Cameron has published his version of events as have several other key participants. They are listed in the references.

Distinctively, I use the 'inside dopester' accounts of journalists and contemporary historians. Inside dopesters are the savvy figures who 'know a great deal about what other people are doing and thinking in the important or "great-issue" spheres of life'. They know the 'inside story' of political deal-making. I intend no pejorative connotations with the term. It refers to 'political newsmen and broadcasters who, after long training, have succeeded in eliminating all emotional response to politics and who pride themselves on achieving the inside-dopesters goal: never to be taken in by any person, cause, or event' (all quotes in this paragraph are from Riesman et al., 1961, pp. 181–182).

Such written sources were many and long. The volume of 'private information' reported in the work of biographers like Anthony Seldon and journalists like Andrew Rawnsley and Tim Shipman is impressive. Brexit was 'the worst example of ill-discipline in cabinet in British political history' (Smith, 2019), which made the life of journalists and interviewers alike much easier. Leaks were the rule, not the exception.

A subsidiary objective of this chapter is to show that these inside dopester accounts and other sources provide valuable data that will bear secondary analysis. I am a dedicated *'bricoleur'* (Levi-Strauss, 1966, pp. 16–17) convinced we should mine all publicly available information, irrespective of discipline, profession or format.

As the first step, I subjected all sources to thematic analysis (Braun & Clarke, 2006). The codebook drew on my previous work on ministers and civil servants (see Rhodes, 2011; Weller et al., 2021). There were regular iterations of themes and their associated topics. I do not tell a chronological story beyond the minimum necessary for clarity. My task is to identify and describe themes, not write a biography or a contemporary history. Those tasks are done by the insiders on whom I draw.

All methods have their strengths and weaknesses and the sources used here are no exception. All politicians, special advisers (SpAds) and civil servants tell you their version of the story, more or less embellished, more or less accurate, but never 'the truth'. Many of the topics are 'delicate' and have everyone scrambling for deniability. Ministers and civil servants work hard to build and protect their reputations. A picture of the dirty deals done dastardly will not be to their taste. There is the ever-present risk that I read rationalisations after the event (see Diamond & Richards, 2012; Richards & Mathers, 2010). The danger with thematic analysis of élite interviews is that the researcher highlights the vivid quote that dramatises the point. And I do. However, I also provide a handful of more ordinary supporting quotes. For all the limits of the data, I insist that inside dopester accounts are invaluable for understanding the inner workings of government. As the Thomas Theorem suggests, they are necessary but not sufficient evidence for understanding court politics because when 'men (sic) define situations as real, they are real in their consequences' (Thomas & Thomas, 1928, pp. 571–572).

To ensure that my account was plausible, I cross-checked the data whenever possible both with documentary sources, biographies, autobiographies and memoirs. With insider accounts, there will always be questions about their reliability. To increase the plausibility of my account, whenever possible I have not relied either on any one insider or on any one source. I compare memoirs with insider accounts with other inside accounts. Inevitably, there are conflicting accounts. I note the disagreements and exercise my judgement about which account is the more plausible. My judgements were swayed by the details in the story. As a rule of thumb, the greater the detail, the more plausible the story. Because I compare accounts, my ambition is to provide a better description of the court than is currently available but, distinctively, I aim to complement this description with an analysis of court practices.

DAVID CAMERON'S COURT, 2010–2016

My example of the court in British politics is the prime ministership of David Cameron. First, I show that both insiders and outsiders recognise there was a court and I describe the core members of the court. Second, drawing on my thematic analysis of insider accounts, I describe the practices of the court covering such themes as informality, bargaining, loyalty, lying, betrayal and leaking. Finally, I discuss the governmental, electoral and personal consequences of court politics.

Courtiers

The press latched on to Cameron's court long before he came to office (The Telegraph, 2006). It was referred to variously as his inner circle, the chumocracy, the Notting Hill Set, the Chipping Norton set, the Old Etonians, Team Cameron and the Cameroons. Rachel Whetstone, who was married to Steve Hilton and godparent to Ivan Cameron, the deceased son of David Cameron, wrote:

> The political and social lives of the Notting Hill Tories are more closely entwined than any other Westminster set I can think of, either current or historical. They eat at each other's houses, are godparents to each other's children, share the school runs, co-edit church magazines, holiday

together—all between discussing the next stage in the politics of the post-bureaucratic age. (Cited in Elliott & Hanning, 2012, p. 419)

Insiders and their wives also talk about the court and its courtiers (Fall, 2020, p. 6; Swire, 2020, p. 77). Cameron (2019, p. 501) dismissed talk about 'Cameron's chumocracy', claiming his team came 'via job interviews' or were 'poached' from elsewhere and he 'resented any implication that they weren't there on merit'. The problem with these various labels is that they imply Cameron's inner circle was made up of an élite group of friends. It contained some friends and there was the common denominator of working at the Conservative Research Department. But they were in Cameron's team on merit and they stayed because they were good at their jobs. I prefer the description court because it focuses on working for the leader and it is used by insiders. Kate Fall (2020, p. 2, p. 6) observes 'there is always an inner circle' and she notes that 'Kings and Queens had similar coteries of advisers or courtiers' (see also Ashcroft & Oakeshott, 2015, pp. 216–217; D'Ancona, 2013, p. 1; Seldon & Snowdon, 2016, p. xxxiv; Swire, 2020, p. 77, p. 87, p. 89). Letwin (2017, p. 219, p. 224) talks of the 'high politics' of the Coalition. Cameron (2019, p. 678, p. 689) admitted he had a 'core team'.

The court was built on his loyal advisers when in Opposition. It comprised George Osborne (Chancellor of the Exchequer), Ed Llewellyn (Chief of Staff), Kate Fall (Deputy Chief of Staff, trusted confidant and self-confessed 'gatekeeper'), Oliver Dowden (Deputy Chief of Staff and firefighter for daily crises), Steve Hilton (Director of Strategy), Andy Coulson (Director of Communications), Liz Sugg (Head of Operations) and Rupert Harrison (Osborne's Chief of Staff to 2015). Two left: Coulson (in 2011) to be replaced by Craig Oliver, and Hilton (in 2012) to be replaced by Ameet Gill as Head of Strategic Communications. Both remained with Cameron until his resignation in 2016. There was more turnover in the Heads of the Policy Unit (Paul Kirby, Jo Johnson and Camilla Cavendish). Yet, over six years, there was little churn in this core team, which displayed 'a ferocious degree of unity'.[2] As Elliott and Hanning (2012, p. 419) report, 'Tory MPs who do not have a gold swipe card that accesses the inner circle—which is nearly all of them—grumble about his [Cameron's] remoteness and arrogance'.

There was a second circle of key political and administrative allies, notably William Hague (Foreign Secretary), Michael Gove (Secretary of State for Education) and Oliver Letwin (Minister of State for Government

Policy). Thus, Michel Gove was not only initially a friend but also a key mover in the Conservative's modernisation programme. Oliver Letwin had 'huge' influence; 'he was another deputy prime minister' (Cameron, 2019, p. 205) while Michael Gove was a 'soulmate' (Cameron, 2019, p. 218). Only Letwin (2017, pp. 231–232, p. 253) survived to 2016 as Cameron's 'odd job man', fighting fires and overseeing implementation.

The Quad was created to manage the coalition. It was composed of the most senior politicians of the two parties: Cameron, Osborne, Nick Clegg (Deputy Prime Minister and leader of the Liberal-Democrats) and the Liberal-Democrat David Laws who served from 12–29 May 2010 before he was replaced by Danny Alexander (Chief Secretary to the Treasury). So, the meetings were literally quadrilaterals and, on occasion, it looked as if they were dancing Lewis Carroll's (1970, p. 134) Lobster Quadrille of 'will you, won't you, will you, won't you, will you join the dance'. The Quad was the buckle holding the coalition together. Its remit extended way beyond the budget. It was used to 'navigate all the central issues of the government' (Fall, 2020, p. 116; Seldon & Snowdon, 2016, p. 39). It was 'the real inner Cabinet of the coalition'; it was 'the ultimate policy arbiters of the government' (Laws, 2016, p. 67, p. 525, p. 561). It lasted well beyond any other coordinating arrangements.[3] On occasion the membership expanded, and its work was regularly complemented with bilaterals (Heywood, 2021, p. 379). As well as regular meetings between Cameron and Clegg, with occasional advice from Oliver Letwin and David Laws when he returned in September 2012,[4] there were meetings between Clegg and Osborne and between Letwin and Alexander to resolve matters before taking them to Cameron and the Quad (Laws, 2016, p. 529; Hazell, 2012, p. 57). According, to D'Ancona (2013, p. 111), there was a 'caucus' of Cameron, Osborne and Hague. The Quad, bilaterals and caucus were permutations of the same tiny group. If these meetings could not resolve an issue, it could be referred to the Coalition Committee. Although there were occasional meetings, only two matters were formally referred to the committee (Letwin, 2017, p. 179).

The Quad was not a cabinet committee, no formal minutes were taken and it would meet in Cameron's flat for dinner (Laws, 2016, p. 105, p. 398). Of course, its decisions were formalised afterwards by the civil service by either taking them to a cabinet committee or by official correspondence (Hazell, 2012, p. 58). Clegg (2016, p. 81, p. 90) later claimed that this 'theatre of power' was orchestrated to 'obfuscate' what is going on. It was a private world and informality underpinned its practices.

The lead civil servant was Jeremy Heywood (first as PPS, then as Downing Street Permanent Secretary and finally Cabinet Secretary) who was the 'chief courtier' or 'consigliere of the No. 10 court' and attended Quad (D'Ancona, 2013, pp. 200–203; Laws, 2016, p. 67; Moore, 2021). Other key actors included Chris Martin (Principal Private Secretary to the PM after Heywood), Simon Case (Principal Private Secretary to the PM after Martin) and Nicholas Macpherson (Permanent Secretary, Treasury). According to Fall (2020, p. 91), the officials and SpAds quickly become one team.

There was an outer circle of civil servants and SpAds who advised on specific policies and who came and went.[5] They encompassed, for example, Lawrence Mann, political private secretary; Simon Case, foreign policy adviser; Clare Foges, his speech writer; Tom Fletcher, adviser on Foreign Policy and Northern Ireland; Tom Scholar, adviser on the European Union (EU); Colonel Jim Morris, the first military adviser in No. 10, Kim Darroch, national security adviser; Andy Hood, legal adviser and Lynton Crosby, who advised on election strategy.

Practices

Craft

Media commentators described Cameron's leadership style as 'chillaxed' (Elliott & Hanning, 2012, p. 419). Cameron took umbrage at the description: 'He hated that. Enough to let my boss at the time know just how much he hated that' (Francis Elliott, quoted in Saul, 2016). Others criticised him for a lack of strategic grasp. He was seen as a short-term, reactive prime minister, more interested in holding office than implementing a specific policy agenda; he had a 'laissez-faire approach' (Ashcroft & Oakeshott, 2015, p. 525). For David Laws, he was the 'quicksilver politician', ducking and diving to get favourable press coverage but 'he travels lightly in terms of core beliefs and ideology'. Travelling lightly had advantages. It made him an 'ideal figure' to lead the coalition and the personal bond with Clegg was the 'the glue that held the entire coalition together' (Seldon, 2015, p. 15).

As Cabinet chair, Cameron was 'business-like and slightly impatient', 'rarely wrong-footed', 'very well briefed' and 'there was never any question of who was in charge' (Laws, 2016, p. 312, p. 191). He let a meeting rehearse the arguments before concluding with a clear decision (Letwin,

2017, p. 2). Cameron liked routine and his work practices and working day reflect that preference. He created and chaired the National Security Council, which was greeted as 'brilliant' by the intelligence community (Iain Lobban, Head of GCHQ, cited in Seldon, 2015, p. 21). He was self-aware about his craft, adducing some practical lessons for being prime minister such as 'if it's all kicking off at home, come home' (Cameron, 2019, p. 134, pp. 199–200, p. 301; Seldon & Snowdon, 2016, p. 79).

There are other interpretations. Ashcroft and Oakeshott (2015, p. 378) argue that Cameron acted as the conciliator to provide cover for the reforming zeal of Michael Gove and Steve Hilton. Seldon and Snowdon (2016, p. 537) point out that there were issues on which Cameron displayed much commitment and zeal. He was willing to spend his political capital on gay marriage (see Cameron, 2019, Chapter 32). Cameron and Osborne were immoveable on austerity (see the following section). David Laws refers to Cameron's 'don't give me any reasons why I can't do this stuff moods' (Laws, 2016, p. 353). Much of the craft of a prime minister is to 'sail a boundless and bottomless sea' where 'there is neither harbour for shelter nor floor for anchorage, neither starting-place nor appointed destination'. The craft is 'to keep afloat on an even keel' (Oakeshott, 1967, p. 127). Cameron was at the tiller of a ship whose passengers wanted to sail to different destinations so, temporise as he might, an even keel was an unrealistic ambition. Much of the criticism of his leadership craft has its roots in the irreconcilable divisions of the party he sought to lead.

The contrast with George Osborne is instructive. According to Kate Fall (2020, p. 116), 'David is the leader, and strong decision taker, while George is the creative intellect who always want to push the boundaries'. Cameron is compared unfavourably with the 'tactical' and 'flexible' Osborne (Seldon & Snowdon, 2016, pp. 487–488, pp. 537–538). To the partners in the Coalition, Osborne is a 'fully paid up political carnivore' (Laws, 2016, p. 530). But contrasting Cameron and Osborne courts the danger of overlooking the centrality of their partnership to the court.

The court was small and tight and at its heart was the relationship between Cameron and Osborne. There was a high level of trust (Ashcroft & Oakeshott, 2015, p. 394). Osborne deferred to Cameron. He accepted he was the junior partner in, not rival for, the premiership. Osborne was embedded in the heart of No. 10. There was to be no repetition of the Blair-Brown heebie-jeebies (Seldon & Snowdon, 2016, p. 35, p. 498). Cameron and Osborne had a routine. They spoke every Sunday evening and held at least one bilateral a week (Seldon & Snowdon, 2016, p. 541).

Osborne went to a daily 0830 meeting with Cameron in the latter's office in No. 10. Llewellyn, Fall, Coulson (later Oliver), the Press Secretary and the Chief Whip attended, although the pressure from other members of the government to increase numbers grew with the increasing 'fame' of the meeting. In Cameron's absence, Osborne chaired the meeting. Osborne returned to No. 10 at 1600 for a second daily meeting of the court that was restricted to the 'core team' (Fall, 2020, p. 108). Both meetings continued for six years (Cameron, 2019, p. 134; Heywood, 2021, p. 314; Seldon & Snowdon, 2016, p. 79). In short, Osborne's day started and finished with Downing Street. Nick Clegg (2016, p. 187) complains about the 'increasingly presidential style of British politics' and the 'hyper-personalisation of politics'. His characterisation may be accurate for media coverage and elections, but it does not accurately describe the workings of government. The court was built and sustained on a duopoly or dual premiership.[6] It worked because they had complementary attributes—that is, because of their differences—and because they recognised their interdependence and put policy success before personal advancement (Walter & 't Hart, 2014).

Storytelling
Prime ministers craft and own the narrative for their government. Nick Clegg (2016, p. 180) argues, 'people follow stories, not policies, in politics and leaders who have a clear story … will generally be rewarded'. Cameron and Osborne had a clear story known as 'austerity'. It was also known as deficit reduction, cuts and Plan A, which mutated into the Long-Term Economic Plan (LTEP) for the 2015 election' (Cameron, 2019, p. 430). Before the 2010 election, Osborne made it clear that 'Britain faces a debt crisis' and 'real spending will have to be cut, whoever is elected' (Osborne, 2009). In his speech to the 2009 Conservative Party Conference, Cameron claimed 'the age of irresponsibility is giving way to the age of austerity', and he used the word 'austerity' 11 times in his speech (Cameron, 2009). Fiscal rectitude was the order of the day. Reducing the deficit would create macroeconomic stability and provide opportunities for private sector growth.

Plan A was a non-negotiable condition of the Coalition with the Liberal-Democrats. Osborne wrote the rules of the game (D'Ancona, 2013, p. 340). It involved major cuts in public spending. Critics claimed austerity was too harsh, invoking images of a return to the 1930s. The government claimed the cuts were as necessary as they were overdue. Despite implementation problems, most famously the omnishambles budget of 2012 and the 'pasty tax', which imposed VAT on hot take-away food, Plan A remained the cornerstone of Coalition policy.[7] It 'forms the central impetus of the Coalition government. It is the glue that binds us, giving common sense of purpose' (Fall, 2020, p. 74).

The debate about the merits of the policy of austerity continues. For Kate Fall, the 'double act' of David and George 'turned Britain around'. Others are more sceptical, arguing that Plan A delayed economic recovery while yet others argue that 'the big fiscal and economic questions remain unanswered' (Johnson & Chandler, 2015, p. 192). Whatever the economic results, it was a remarkable achievement to make austerity the dominant narrative accepted by both the Coalition and the electorate. The big loser was Steve Hilton and the 'Big Society' narrative.[8] Cameron and Osborne were consistent and persistent in supporting Plan A: 'I was determined to stick to the plan' (Cameron 2019, p. 430, Chapter 31). There was nonstop criticism and some wavering between 2011 and 2013 but there never was an alternative economic strategy. The Quad supported Plan A; they were 'pretty sure ... that we had got it right and would be vindicated' (Osborne aide, quoted in Seldon & Snowdon, 2016, p. 253). The public agreed. People 'found themselves in the uncomfortable position of having to trust that the government knew what it was doing'. They accepted that 'Cameron and Osborne seemed competent and ready to make tough decisions', and the Labour Party offered no credible alternative.[9] Cameron argues that the British people understood 'the simple logic of our position, given that it mirrored the tough choices they were having to make in their own businesses or household budgets' (Cameron, 2019, p. 435). The narrative was in a language people could understand. One reason Cameron's court was tight was the unifying force of the austerity narrative, its comprehensibility and the absence of a competing story.

Reshuffles, Resignations and Leadership Challenges
Alastair Campbell (2007, p. 621) records that when it came to reshuffles 'pain had no memory ... [and] until a new one starts you forget how awful the process is'. While the power to dismiss ministers is one of the bedrocks of prime ministerial power, 'you also know with absolute certainty that today's broadly loyal minister is tomorrow's bitter and backbiting back bencher'. Reshuffles come at high political cost.

Fall (2020, p. 183) would agree; a reshuffle 'makes a few people happy (the ones promoted); a small number very angry (the ones fired); and leaves a large number extremely disappointed (the ones who have been passed over yet again)'. Cameron (2019, p. 384) wanted reshuffles that improved his government, helped him to manage the party and gave new MPs experience of government. However, he believed reshuffles should be minimised because they created more problems than they solved (Seldon & Snowdon, 2016, p. 407). He considered the reshuffle process a 'nightmare' (Cameron, 2019, p. 136). Interviews with colleagues were, by turn, 'soul-destroyingly awful', 'very difficult' and some exchanges 'you never forget' (Cameron, 2019, p. 389, p. 390, p. 391). In the words of Ken Clarke, reshuffles were 'the usual comic shambles' (quoted in D'Ancona, 2013, p. 292).

Resignations were also 'difficult' because 'they destabilise the government, take up time, distract from the agenda and reduce politics to … a soap opera' (Cameron, 2019, p. 396). However, some resignations have momentous consequences. For example, Ian Duncan Smith was Secretary of State for Work and Pensions (known respectively as IDS and DWP). George Osborne 'does not rate IDS intellectually'. Osborne believes 'he's just not clever enough' (Fall, 2020, p. 238; Shipman, 2016, p. 199). Dominic Cummings agrees, calling IDS 'incompetent' and referring to working with him as 'the nightmare of the living dead' (BBC Two, 2020, 18 March). 'Universal Credit' is the moniker for IDS's reform of welfare, which is the largest spending programme. It is Osborne's prime target for cuts but 'he [IDS] opposes every cut' (D'Ancona, 2013, p. 90). The relationship 'reaches a new low—their SpAds are at each other's throats' (Fall, 2020, p. 238; Letwin, 2017, pp. 203–204). For the 2016 Budget, there was yet another disagreement, once again over welfare cuts. IDS sent Cameron a letter of resignation (Cameron, 2019, p. 661; Fall, 2020, p. 284) but he was expected to stay because he 'had tossed around threats to resign in the past as others discuss the weather' (Shipman, 2016, p. 202). However, during discussions between IDS and Cameron about remaining in the Cabinet, *Sky News* announced that 'IDS resigns'. Cameron 'went absolutely ballistic' about being blindsided. There was 'an explosive conversation' in which IDS accused Cameron of not supporting his welfare reforms: 'you cannot expect me to put up with being undermined any longer'. Allegedly, Cameron called IDS a 'shit' but No. 10 counter that he used every expletive except that one (Shipman, 2016, p. 203).

Resignations can be one-time, single-issue affairs, but they can be the result of enduring personal and policy disagreements. IDS's feud with Osborne and the Treasury over Universal Credit was longstanding (Seldon & Snowdon, 2016, pp. 299–301, pp. 303–304, p. 550). Craig Oliver (2016, pp. 147–148) opines 'IDS was given the pretext to resign and portray himself as a martyr', and he took it. In the media, he presented himself as the voice of modern, compassionate Conservatism. A 'bloodbath' ensued in the papers (Oliver, 2016, pp. 147–148). No. 10 believed that IDS was trying to inflict 'maximum damage to the party leadership in order to further his campaign to get Britain to leave the EU'. To others, it looked like revenge for years of belittlement; 'his longstanding feud with Osborne was decisive' (Shipman, 2016, p. 204). I see no reason to make a choice—both reasons are plausible.

Compared to the record of his successor, Theresa May, Cameron had relatively few resignations. There were also few challenges to his leadership. His most senior allies were Osborne, Gove and Hague. They would never stand against him. Indeed, Craig Oliver (2016, p. 150) reports that Cameron could not imagine Gove 'ever being left in charge of the country'. Boris Johnson was a credible threat. There was 'jealousy and resentment at Boris's high profile and his effortless playing to the gallery'. But he was Mayor of London, not in the House of Commons, and in no position to mount a challenge (Seldon & Snowdon, 2016, p. 219). That left Theresa May, who had stepped outside her brief to give a wide-ranging speech on her 'three pillars of Conservatism' (Prince, 2017, Chapter 16; May, 2013). Cameron 'dismissed' the speech, but Gove weighed in at political cabinet, accusing an unnamed minister of 'disloyalty by seeking to burnish their leadership credentials' (*Daily Telegraph* 13 March 2013, quoted in Prince, 2017, Chapter 16). May assured Cameron that 'I've always been loyal, and I would never stand against you' (Letwin, 2017, p. 26; Cameron, 2019, p. 445). But in politics, 'it is the anonymous plotters you have to watch out for, and I could never quite shake the feeling of vulnerability' (Cameron, 2019, p. 445). There may have been no single challenger for the leadership, but such feelings were not paranoia. There was a major challenge from the European Research Group (ERG), a faction within the Parliamentary Conservative Party lobbying for the UK to leave the EU, and it was to bring Cameron down (see Oliver, 2016; Shipman, 2016).

Resignations, reshuffles and leadership challenges are the front-page drama of a continuous political game that takes many forms in the courts of prime ministers and ministers. They are not the only game in town.

The Political Game: Coalition, Barons and Lying

When an interviewer put it to Bill Shankly, the former manager of Liverpool FC, that 'football's a matter of life and death to you', he replied 'it's more important than that'. Much the same can be said about the political games of Westminster and Whitehall. By repute, David Cameron and George Osborne were good game players. For Cameron, 'it's almost as if anything outside his family is just an exercise yard for political skills. It's as if it's just a game of chess, and he wants to come top' (cabinet minister, cited in Ashcroft & Oakeshott, 2015, p. 375). Osborne was likened to Machiavelli because he treated politics as 'gamesmanship and stratagems'. Ed Miliband (Leader of the Labour Party Opposition) considered it 'a deplorable way of reducing statesmanship to a poker night'. The Chancellor did not wilt under such criticisms because he saw no reason to apologise for his style of politics. He regarded 'Miliband as insufferably sanctimonious—ill equipped for the rough and tumble of real politics' (both cited by D'Ancona, 2013, p. 340). In a similar vein, Nick Clegg thought Osborne was 'reducing politics to a great game' and Osborne's response was 'absolutely and watch me win it' (cited by D'Ancona, 2013, p. 339). The three most visible examples of the game were the Coalition Agreement, baronial politics and scandals.

The Coalition Agreement

Despite the initial agreement reached by the two parties,[10] the Coalition experienced several crises and Jeremy Heywood 'spent most of his time resolving Coalition rows' (Heywood, 2021, p. 403). Perhaps the biggest crisis was the referendum on the Alternative Vote (AV) referendum, the spillover effects on the reform of the House of Lords and changes to the boundaries of parliamentary constituencies. The AV crisis pushed the Coalition to breaking point.

Electoral reform was an article of faith for the Liberal-Democrats and AV was the specific reform written into the Coalition Agreement. It was never going to be an easy reform to swallow for many Conservative backbenchers. During the referendum campaign, Graham Brady, chair of the 1922 backbench committee, told the PM that the committee feared the

Conservatives would never have a majority again. So, Cameron and Osborne became much more vigorous campaigners for the 'No' vote. The Liberal-Democrats were infuriated not only by personal attacks on Clegg but also by Cameron leading the 'No' campaign. They believed there was an 'understanding' that he would remain aloof from the campaign. There was a resounding defeat for the Liberal-Democrats in the referendum. The trust between the two parties became a thing of the past as did the notion of the two parties forming one team. From now on, it was tit-for-tat bargaining (Seldon & Snowdon, 2016, p. 122).

Reform of the House of Lords was an important policy on the Liberal-Democrats' reform agenda, but the Conservatives were reluctant, and their MPs in the Commons were employing delaying tactics against the Bill (Laws, 2016, p. 147, pp. 149–150). There was one (of only two) meeting of the Coalition Committee at which the discussion became bad-tempered (Laws, 2016, p. 151). Clegg told Cameron, 'If you do not deliver on the Lords, we will not deliver on the boundary changes' (cited in Seldon & Snowdon, 2016, p. 236; see also Cameron, 2019, p. 362). Cameron rejected the proposition that there was a link between the two policies. Clegg withdrew his Bill from the Commons and instructed his party to oppose the changes to the boundaries of parliamentary constituencies. Anger was the emotion of the moment with Conservative MPs believing the Liberal-Democrats had 'pulled a fast one' and Clegg insisting that 'a deal's a deal' and the Conservatives had reneged on AV (Seldon & Snowdon, 2016, pp. 237–238). There are angry private exchanges between Cameron and Clegg (Seldon & Snowdon, 2016, p. 240; Clegg, 2016, p. 138). The disagreements 'brought us to the brink of divorce' but led to 'a renewal of our vows' through a Midterm Review of the first agreement (Cameron, 2019, p. 367; Laws, 2016, p. 158). Respected trusties Laws for the Liberal-Democrats and Letwin for the Conservatives, reporting to the Quad, came up with an agreed narrative.

It had been a gruesome year but after the Midterm Review there was renewed confidence on both sides, until the next time. And there was always a next time, big and little. On each occasion, the crisis went right to the top, even such 'small stuff' as the policy on free school meals. When Clegg told Cameron that he would go public about his disagreements with Gove, Cameron protested 'I really don't want big rows in the Coalition over small stuff like this'. He told Gove there would be legislation and 'Michael was far from pleased' (Laws, 2016, p. 364, p. 368).

Baronial Politics

If the Coalition Agreement was strictly for the court, baronial politics were the preserve of departments. For Nick Clegg (2016, p. 114, p. 115, p. 118), 'the Balkanisation' of Whitehall is 'dysfunctional', leading to 'a chess game of complex manoeuvres between different departments'. He saw his role as 'to avoid getting sucked into their baronial rivalries' and to reform a Whitehall that 'is congenitally disposed to hoarding power'. 'Departmentalitis' or silo government is rife and refers to a preoccupation with the minister and his or her department to the exclusion of all else (Kaufman, 1980, p. 29). It is a way of life in Whitehall (and for more examples, see Riddell, 2019, Chapter 6).

For Theresa May politics was not a game, and she was 'squeamish about deploying the "black arts" herself'. But baronial politics are inescapable. She employed her SpAds 'to perform a little dark magic on her behalf' (Prince, 2017, p. 139). She had feuds with Cameron, Osborne, Gove, Clarke and the Liberal-Democrat ministers in the Home Office (on which see Baker, 2015, Chapter 22). For example, on immigration, the 'briefing and counter-briefing between the Treasury and the Home Office rose to unedifying levels' (Seldon & Snowdon, 2016, p. 458; Bennett, 2019, p. 287). The flashpoint with Osborne came when he gave her a 'rollicking' in Cabinet over the strip search of a Chinese billionaire at Heathrow (Prince, 2017, Chapter 14). For Osborne, it was all part of the political game. For May, it fuelled a resentment that underpinned her callous dismissal of Osborne from the cabinet when she became Prime Minister (Seldon & Newell, 2020, pp. 76–78).

Cameron's involvement in the legion of inter-ministerial and inter-departmental disputes varied from initiator to referee to judge. The Treasury will always have a dispute with one or other department, especially when it requires spending cuts. Thus, Vince Cable (Secretary of State for Business, Innovation and Skills) had a long-running stand-off with the Treasury over both Plan A and cuts. These spats were one of 'the worst-kept secrets in Whitehall' (Laws, 2016, pp. 167–168). Other conflicts were less predictable, especially the one between the PM and Eric Pickles, Secretary of State for Communities and Local Government.

Cameron chaired the Migrants Access to Benefits and Public Services cabinet committee. Its brief was to get every department to find policy changes that limited illegal migrants' access to public services. Cameron favoured a proposal that private landlords should check the papers of every migrant who wanted to be a tenant and refuse them a tenancy if their papers were not in order. Eric Pickles pushed back: 'I think this is a seriously bad idea. Checking immigration papers is really hard. Many of them … are frankly forged. What are we asking private landlords to do—act as an arm of the immigration service?' Few others on the committee agreed with the prime minister. Pickles was 'willing to face down the Prime Minister … and go on fighting when he clearly took a different view from them'. Without summing up the discussion, the PM called the meeting to an end and walked out. 'Had the PM really just walked out in a strop? Yes, he had' (Laws, 2016, p. 354).

But he had not given up. Cameron told Oliver Letwin to get the Conservative ministers onside, which he did, but the Liberal-Democrats were still offside, and the Home Affairs Committee attached conditions to the proposal. The PM told Nick Clegg, 'tell your people to take their tanks off my lawn'; Clegg refused and eventually vetoed the proposal. As Ken Clarke remarked, the proposal was 'nonsense'; 'Eric is clearly opposed. I doubt even Theresa thinks it will work. It's all about UKIP, I fear' (cited in Laws, 2016, p. 356). When told of the veto, Cameron 'was furious and very difficult' (cited in Laws, 2016, p. 356). Cameron's memoirs do not mention the incident. It was a sideshow in the twisted story of the UK's immigration policy.

Such disagreements are the stuff of everyday life in Westminster and Whitehall. They damage careers and reputations, cost people their jobs and lead to both policy changes and delays.

Lying

Political lying covers not only direct lies but mendacity in all its forms including smears, being 'economical with the truth', disingenuous replies to questions, evasions, sleights of hand and different versions of the 'truth' for different audiences. All are endemic to Westminster, Whitehall and the court. Peter Oborne is blunt: 'lying, cupidity and lack of integrity have become essential qualities for ambitious ministers'. His target is mainly Boris Johnson. However, David Cameron was 'capable of being devious' even if he was not a habitual liar (Oborne, 2021, pp. 5–6).

Political lying aims to deceive by knowingly making factually inaccurate statements, and the examples were legion during the Brexit referendum. The lies included the claims that Britain paid £350 million a week to the EU; that Turkey would become a member of the EU and Britain would receive 15 million migrants within ten years; and that health tourism, or people coming to the UK to use the NHS, cost the country billions.

Leaking by anonymous sources is a common way of getting a lie into the public domain. Cameron was convinced that Gove and Boris Johnson had behaved 'appallingly' and become 'ambassadors for the expert-trashing, truth-twisting age of populism' (Cameron, 2019, p. 687; Bennett, 2019, pp. 285–287). Oborne considers both Gove and Johnson 'habitual liars' (Oborne, 2021, p. 117). Thus, Johnson denied that he had said anything about Turkish immigration when, in a joint letter to the PM, he said 'the only way to avoid having common borders with Turkey is to Vote Leave' (Gove et al., 2016). Perhaps Gove's most notorious leak—allegedly—was the lie that the Queen backed Brexit (Oliver, 2016, pp. 126–127, pp. 132–133; Shipman, 2016, pp. 191–192; Bennett, 2019, pp. 326–327). And the Leave side were not the only sinners. Few accepted the economic predictions underpinning the Remain campaign's 'Project Fear'.

Scandals attract political lying in all its forms, not just direct lies. Evasion was a characteristic of the evidence given by Cameron to the Leveson inquiry. The inquiry's roots lie in the phone hacking by *The News of the World* journalists. Andy Coulson was the paper's editor and he resigned denying any personal involvement but, as editor, accepting responsibility for the actions of the paper's journalists. At the same time, Cameron and Osborne were looking for a director of communications for the Conservative Party. Coulson reassured Cameron that he knew nothing about phone tapping, and he was appointed. Within two years Coulson was a member of Cameron's court (Seldon & Snowdon, 2016, p. 83).

However, the phone tapping scandal refused to go away. The Culture, Media and Sport Select Committee concluded it was 'inconceivable' that *News of the World* executives—that is, Coulson—did not know. It was a polite way of saying that Coulson had lied. Despite several warnings that Coulson was unsuitable (Elliott & Hanning, 2012, p. 453), Cameron stood by him—'I believe in giving people a second chance'—and Coulson became Director of Communications in No. 10 (cited in Seldon & Snowdon, 2016, p. 83). But the scandal rumbled on and Coulson's credibility was slowly shredded. In January 2011, the *New York Times* published an exposé and Coulson resigned saying 'When the spokesman needs a spokesman, it is time to move on' (cited in D'Ancona, 2013, p. 261; Fall, 2020, p. 167).

The problem escalated when the *Guardian* reported that the *News of the World* hacked the phone of a murdered schoolgirl. Its owner, Rupert Murdoch, closed the paper. The editor Rebekah Brooks resigned. Coulson and Brooks were arrested and bailed. Disception abounded. Cameron returned early from a visit to South Africa to make an emergency statement in the Commons, answering 138 questions. A week later he announced an inquiry chaired by Lord Justice Leveson. When Cameron gave evidence, he endured a gruelling grilling. He claimed that he did not have a close relationship with Rebekah Brooks, Coulson's successor as editor, saying they texted each other only once or twice a week. In fact, he stayed in touch with her during the inquiry. She was a member of the Chipping Norton set and both attended the same social gatherings (Ashcroft & Oakeshott, 2015, pp. 466–467; Swire, 2020, p. 334). He was embarrassed and humiliated when emails between himself and Brooks were dissected in court (D'Ancona, 2013, p. 269.) The BBC political editor Nick Robinson said the PM looked 'tense, edgy, uncomfortable and again and again said he couldn't recall events (BBC, 2012, 24 July). Cameron admits that it was 'mildly embarrassing' (Cameron, 2019, p. 261).

I have merely sketched a convoluted story because my concern is less the substantive issue and more about what it tells us about Cameron and his court. Brute fact: Coulson lied repeatedly to his boss, his colleagues and in court. He did know about the phone hacking. He was found guilty of perjury and sentenced to 18 months. Brute fact: Cameron was evasive about cosying up to Rupert Murdoch and his News International empire. Eventually he admitted that 'his party was guilty of the "allied vices" of anonymous briefings, manipulation of the media by politicians and favouritism' (Channel 4, 2012, 14 June). Despite all the brouhaha, and clear evidence that the links between media and politicians were unhealthy, he did not accept the Leveson recommendation for statutory regulation of the press. It was Cameron's 'worst episode' with many consequences (Seldon & Snowdon, 2016, p. 94). As Cameron observes, 'it brought the coalition close to collapse—and my premiership to the precipice' (Cameron, 2019, p. 250; also, see section on Government consequences below). For Cameron's court, guilt or innocence was beside the point. Their overwhelming concern was to protect the prime minister's reputation—the truth was a bystander.

Informality
Initially, there was the Procedural Agreement, which provided for the Deputy Prime Minister to be consulted on all policies and envisaged a central role for cabinet and its committees.[11] Cameron 'was minded to

restore Cabinet government' but after the first flush of enthusiasm he turned to other means (Ashcroft & Oakeshott, 2015, p. 350; D'Ancona, 2013). Cabinet deliberations were 'ever more squeezed' by information briefings and there 'was little serious discussion' (Clarke, 2016, p. 461, p. 477). As Jeremy Hunt observed: 'In David Cameron's cabinet meetings, after George Osborne had spoken, you basically knew what David Cameron and George Osborne thought and the matter was broadly over' (cited in Durrant, 2020).

In short, decisions were not taken in cabinet (see also Clarke, 2016, p. 462). There were formal settings other than full cabinet.[12] Clegg was chair of the Home Affairs Cabinet Committee, which was responsible for all domestic policies apart from the budget. There were formal procedures—for example, circulating 'write around' memos that detailed policy proposals (Clegg, 2016, p. 77). At first, 'fresh life was breathed into cabinet committees' (D'Ancona, 2013, p. 37; Heywood, 2021, p. 315) and they were central to decision-making, but their 'purple patch soon faded' (Clegg, 2016, p. 78; but see Laws, 2016, p. 510). Lynne Featherstone (2015) described them as 'a complete waste of time'. Informality prevailed (Hazell, 2012, p. 51). Table 4.1 lists the common formal and informal meetings.

Table 4.1 The forums of the UK core executive

Chequers: meeting of all ministers; ministerial retreats
Full cabinet meetings: ministers, officials plus advisers as observers
Cabinet committee as preparatory forum with recommendations (sometimes as a formality) to full cabinet meetings: ministers, advisers and officials
Cabinet committees with decision-making powers: NSC, ministers, officials and advisers
Political cabinet: ministers from one party meet, sometimes with advisers and other party notables, to discuss the political conditions; there are no officials present and no minutes or records are kept
Coalition Committee: ministers, equal numbers from Conservatives and Liberal-Democrats. Remit: to handle issues referred to it about the Coalition Agreement.[a]
Quad: membership decided by the PM and Deputy PM, deliberately separate from and not reporting to the cabinet. At first focused on managing public expenditure and the economy but its remit was extended to managing the Coalition.
Sofa government (also known as bilaterals, and one-to-ones): meetings of PMs with individual ministers and advisers to discuss specific issues.

Source: Adapted from Weller et al. (2021)

[a]There was also provision for the Coalition Operation and Strategic Planning Group comprising Oliver Letwin, Danny Alexander, Francis Maude and Jim Wallace but it never met

For the Coalition, there was the innovation of the political cabinet, which was 'a meeting of ministers—and sometimes other politicians from the governing party—that is held to discuss political matters' (Durrant, 2020). The PM's SpAds attended the meetings (Oliver, 2016, p. 34, p. 150, p. 191) but civil servants did not and there were no official minutes (Laws, 2016, p. 314). Increasingly, the political cabinet involved more briefings on the latest polls and less on substantive policy (Clarke, 2016, p. 477), but internally contentious issues such as gay marriage received an airing (Cameron, 2019, p. 440).

One-to-one meetings were a regular way for PMs to do business both before Blair's sofa government and afterwards. There were a plethora of such meetings between all members of the court and between court members and their coalition counterparts (Hazell, 2012, p. 57), many in settings other than No. 10. For example, Kate Fall (2020, p. 105) records her informal briefings with Rupert Harrison (George Osborne's chief of staff) on morning drives into work. David Laws (2016, p. 445) records meetings at airports, on phones and in the car. Oliver Letwin (2017, p. 180) had regular Sunday evening calls with Danny Alexander, and regular Tuesday morning calls with David Laws. Even formal meetings had an informal stripe with the 'real' meetings of Civil Contingencies Committee (COBR) held in Cameron's den (Fall, 2020, p. 132).[13]

A key actor in both formal and informal networks was Jeremy Heywood. D'Ancona argues the circumstances of the Coalition provided the opportunity for a civil servant of Heywood's 'intellect and guile' to act as a 'referee'. He was the 'chief courtier and choreographer of the Coalition' (D'Ancona, 2013, pp. 200–201). This description is a tad too forceful for the man himself:

> I would not use the word 'referee'. I am a civil servant; I don't arbitrate between elected politicians. They have to come to agreements themselves. Obviously, the Deputy Prime Minister, the Prime Minister and other Ministers ask the civil servants occasionally to help them try and find areas of common ground, to filter through issues and pinpoint the issues that really do need to be resolved at a political level, so I do get involved a lot in issues that divide them, but frankly I also get involved equally in issues that divide Departments from one another, not just splits that break down along Coalition lines but Departmental lines. (Heywood, 2012)

Ever the diplomat, Heywood would never dominate the conversation but 'he is always in the room' from the daily meeting at No. 10 onwards, and a 'mainstay' for Oliver Letwin (Fall, 2020, p. 108; Letwin, 2017, p. 192). Some claim Cameron was 'too dependent' on his advice (Seldon & Snowdon, 2016, p. 34). He advised on an array of difficult policies (Heywood, 2021, Chapter 47) and was an important, if softly spoken, voice of authentic dissent (Nemeth et al., 2001, p. 708).

The Whitehall SpAd network typifies informality even down to the clothes that, for example, Hilton wore to work. When Cameron is pondering how to respond to the Saville Report about Bloody Sunday, he consults 'a trusted special adviser' whom he and Llewellyn had embedded in the Northern Ireland Office (Seldon & Snowdon, 2016, p. 49). David Laws (2016, p. 264) reports that the 'special advisers' grapevine' alerted the Lib-Dem leadership to an article that Vince Cable was seeking to publish disowning Plan A. Not all ministers welcomed the attention of the SpAd network. Ken Clarke (2016, p. 450) 'put an immediate stop' to policy aides from No. 10 visiting the department to develop policy proposals with civil servants. He 'ended all talk of direct supervision of my department'. Since 1964, both within departments and across Whitehall, the SpAds network has become a characteristic of modern British government. Unquestionably, it helps the PM and ministers to manage the political context of policy-making, but there are costs. It is a network that can ease cooperation; for example, Cameron's SpAds worked to save David Laws over his parliamentary expenses (Cameron, 2019, p. 240). However, often, the SpAds were a source, even cause, of political infighting because the line between speaking for the PM and acting on their own initiative became blurred. SpAds can and do go rogue.

Infighting

Historically, ministers had an inclination to fight that, in earlier days, included duelling—William Pitt and the Duke of Wellington both fought duels when prime minister. Latter-day politicians are equally pugnacious but less violent. The rivalries between Asquith and Lloyd George, Bevan and Gaitskell, Macmillan and Butler, Heath and Thatcher and Brown and Blair are all well documented (see Campbell, 2010). Here, I focus on the dark arts as practiced by SpAds who step in when the minister does not want a public fight but who also pursue their own agendas and vendettas. So many stories, too many weak stomachs.

Steve Hilton was Cameron's blue-sky thinker with few diplomatic skills. He was energetic and, for Cameron, charismatic. He arrived in the office wearing cycle shorts and walked about in bare feet, the antithesis of power dressing. None of which mattered because he was also impatient and bad-tempered. D'Ancona (2013, p. 185) reports Hilton saying, in an 'incandescent rage', 'You fucking lied' to the Head of the Home Civil Service. A No. 10 staffer said Hilton 'can be astonishingly childish and emotional' (cited in Kavanagh & Cowley, 2016, p. 44). Such bullying behaviour mattered because, to get anything done, he needed colleagues and civil servants to cooperate. His main preoccupation rapidly became the inability of No. 10 to influence the behaviour of departments. As if in a Terry Pratchett (2009, p. 214) Discworld novel, he believed that 'reality was lying'. He repeatedly stressed the need to focus on the policy agenda in the Coalition Agreement. He fumed at the fact that departments spent only 30 per cent of the time on No. 10's reforming agenda while spending 40 per cent on departmental work—referred to as 'stuff'—and 30 per cent on new problems. He claimed ministers had not seen policy proposals coming forward from their departments for approval by No. 10 and in cabinet committees. He also claimed that departments had captured the new business plans, using them to get approval for preferred departmental policies. Central agencies in disputes with departments are an age-old story in Whitehall. Hilton was railing against it and what was most notable was that he had no grasp of what it was like either to work in a department or with the civil service machine. He 'couldn't adapt to government' (Ashcroft & Oakeshott, 2015, p. 386). He thought the ministers' 'contracts' with the prime minister were binding, and that ministers were in a line relationship with the prime minister. He did not grasp that ministers were in competition with one another and, on occasion, with the prime minister, for standing in parliament, in the party and with the public. Cameron (2019, p. 385) later recalled:

> Steve Hilton's ideas continued to be one-part brilliant to several parts bonkers. … However, his relationships with people in government weren't working. He was no longer excused as a free spirit. … His antagonistic style was no longer helping him to advance his cause in Whitehall—it had started to hurt it. I knew that to be a successful radical you have to play the game. And he wasn't interested in playing the game.

Seldon and Snowdon (2016, p. 155) report that Hilton fell out with George Osborne, who refused to let Hilton attend his joint meetings with Cameron, denied him access to key papers and refused to let him attend the Quad (see also Heywood, 2021, p. 337). Hilton also fell out with Paul Kirby, head of Cameron's Policy Unit, and began to excuse himself from the twice-daily meetings in the prime minister's room. He fell out with everybody so ran out of allies (Ashcroft & Oakeshott, 2015, p. 387; D'Ancona, 2013, p. 186; Seldon & Snowdon, 2016, pp. 155–161). The gulf between Hilton and the rest of the inner circle became 'unbridgeable' (Seldon & Snowdon, 2016, p. 161). He became the 'shoeless ghost' (Fall, 2020, p. 127). There was an ever-widening rift with the PM who lost patience. Hilton went.

Dominic Cummings was not paying attention to the saga of Hilton because he followed him down the same path to the political wilderness. Cummings' Wikipedia entry states:

> From 2007 to 2014, he was a special adviser to Michael Gove, including the time that Gove served as Education Secretary, leaving when Gove was made Chief Whip in a cabinet reshuffle.

This summary does not capture his chequered history in government. He was not appointed Gove's adviser in DfE in May 2010 because Andy Coulson vetoed his appointment (Bennett, 2019, p. 225; D'Ancona, 2013, p. 136; Seldon & Snowdon, 2016, p. 400). Informally, he continued to provide advice but, formally, he was not appointed until after Coulson resigned over the phone hacking scandal in January 2011 (Bennett, 2019, p. 234; Swire, 2020, p. 155). As Swire (2020, p. 155) notes, teaming Cummings 'with the single most volatile member of the government was always an explosion waiting to happen'. There were several explosions until pressure from No. 10 led again to Cummings leaving government in December 2013. He did not leave only because Gove was made Chief Whip but also because Cameron thought him a 'bad SpAd' and a 'career psychopath' (Cameron, 2019, p. 507; Oliver, 2016, p. 17). Cummings was equally flattering in return. In an article in *The Times*, he dismissed Cameron as 'a sphinx without a riddle' who 'bumbles from one shambles to another without the slightest sense of purpose' (Hurst et al., 2014; see also Seldon & Snowdon, 2016, p. 404; and Ashcroft & Oakeshott, 2015, p. 377, note 350).

Such exchanges were unedifying and mattered because Cummings created significant chaos and division and angered No. 10. One illustration must suffice. There was a 'Trojan Horse' plot by Islamic extremists to take over schools in Birmingham. Gove blamed May, claiming the Home Office had failed to 'drain the swamp of extremists'. May retorted, 'why did nobody act' from DfE. The spat went public as 'anonymous sources' and 'sources close to' briefed the media. Cameron believed that Cummings, although ostensibly gone, was 'still dripping his poison in Michael's ear'. He demanded that the 'mudslinging' stop and Theresa May's SpAd, Fiona Cunningham, played the role of sacrificial lamb (Bennett, 2019, pp. 287–290; Cameron, 2019, p. 507; Seldon & Snowdon, 2016, p. 404). It is one instance of 'a flow of briefings allegedly from Michael's operation' that created 'a barrage of furious complaints' from Cabinet colleagues (Fall, 2020, pp. 192–193). After leaving DfE, Gove admitted that he 'never realised just how much Downing Street hated him [Cummings] and how much damage he did to me' (cited in Laws, 2016, p. 434).

Loyalty, Betrayal, Leaks and Revenge
Collective responsibility is a key notion in Britain's cabinet government. It stipulates that once a decision is made, then all those in the government are committed to support it in public whether they were party to the decision or not. The Coalition led the Cabinet Office to adapt its definition: 'All government ministers are bound by the collective decisions of Cabinet and Cabinet Committees, *save when it is explicitly set aside*' (Cabinet Office, 2011; emphasis in original).

The condition in italics recognised that Cameron had to manage the political forces that might split his government: his Coalition partners, putative successors and parliamentary rebels, notably the ERG. So, Cameron suspended collective responsibility for the referendum on the EU but not during the negotiations about the terms of British membership that preceded the referendum (Oliver, 2016, pp. 17–18, pp. 25–26, pp. 34–35, p. 44, p. 61). However, various members of the Cabinet lined up to resign so they could campaign for leaving the EU. Cameron finessed their threats by giving the party a free vote in the House of Commons on the results of his negotiations (Fall, 2020, p. 277). He kept a precarious collective unity. It evaporated as quickly as water on the surface of Venus once the referendum campaign began.

Like his predecessors before him Cameron expected loyalty from his ministers if not necessarily his party. Cameron's court was an exclusive group: a 'wigwam of trust' (Steve Hilton, cited in Ashcroft & Oakeshott, 2015, p. 422). For example, Cameron's loyalty to Coulson was 'in character'; it was a 'deeply entrenched aspect of his personality'; 'it was the cement of his political life' (D'Ancona, 2013, p. 273; see also Seldon & Snowdon, 2016, p. 549). He was, to use Nicholas Soames' phrase, 'dog loyal!' (cited in Ashcroft & Oakeshott, 2015, p. 460). He did not want to lose any of his inner circle, so he protected them.

Unanimity is the flip side of the coin of loyalty and an important side effect was that it created outsiders. A senior backbencher commented; 'He seems to think that if you are not a 100 per cent Cameron supporter then you're a dangerous bastard, whereas that's not how political parties work' (Conservative MP, cited in Ashcroft & Oakeshott, 2015, p. 422). Even an ostensible supporter (at the time), Michael Gove, attacked the PM for the 'ridiculous' and 'preposterous' number of Old Etonians in the cabinet (cited in Parker & Warrell, 2014). Such exclusivity was interpreted as privilege and remoteness, underpinning an 'us and them' mind-set.

If loyalty was the expectation, Cameron and his court had to confront wild treachery and weirdness: 'he and his team faced betrayal, lies and political bloodletting on an epic scale' (Oliver, 2016, p. 10). The EU was a constant bone of contention throughout the life of parliament; it was an 'existential threat' to the PM (Conservative Whip, cited in Kavanagh & Cowley, 2016, p. 49). Accusation and counter-accusation abounded during the referendum campaign (see Shipman, 2016). There was many a lie (see section on Lying above). For Craig Oliver (2016, p. 344, p. 339, p. 359, p. 370, p. 396), Michael Gove was 'a disgrace' for standing by the claim about Turkish migrants. He was 'angry' with him for rubbishing experts, and he accused him of talking 'fatuous nonsense'. He saw Gove as crucial to the victory of the Leave campaign with his 'intoxicating cocktail' of 'brilliance and poison' (views supported by Letwin, 2017, p. 23). He gave the Leave campaign 'a veneer of intellectual credibility' (Seldon & Snowdon, 2016, p. 549). In a light-hearted moment, Cameron had told Nick Clegg: 'The thing you have to remember about Michael is that he is at times quite genuinely mad' (cited in Laws, 2016, p. 512). Others opine that he is 'ever so slightly bonkers' (Swire, 2020, p. 58). He was Cameron's 'court jester', his 'charming eccentric' (Bennett, 2019, p. 323; Cameron, 2019, p. 506; Oliver, 2016, p. 69). Oliver (2016, p. 399) is witheringly scornful.

The deteriorating relationship between Cameron and Gove had its roots in the cabinet reshuffle of 2014. Gove's style contributed to undermining his position in the court. There is no shortage of lurid phrases. He has been described as a 'demented Dalek on speed', a 'political street fighter', 'Dr Gove and Mr Hyde' and 'a cross between Jeeves and Che Guevara', who developed a 'pugilistic and mistrusting style' (Laws, 2016, p. 213; Parker & Warrell, 2014; Tory MP, cited in Laws, 2016, p. 213; Smithers, 2015, p. 288). 'Michael ... seemed to be in conflict with just about everyone, from bitter enemies to former close allies' (Bennett, 2019, pp. 274–275; Laws, 2016, p. 421). Laws records that Gove 'regarded anything cross-departmental as an unproductive waste of time'. Cummings did not like Clegg and thought Cameron was a 'complete muppet'. His policy was 'to tell No. 10 absolutely nothing about what we are doing' (Laws, 2016, p. 214, p. 216). But the noise around Gove and education reform was getting louder.

Education reform was a key part of the Conservative's modernisation programme and Cameron trusted Gove to deliver it. However, discontent grew in No. 10 because Gove 'had become so unpopular that there wasn't just a danger to the policy but to the politics' (Cameron, 2019, p. 506). Not only had he alienated the actors whose support he needed to implement his reforms but, in the process, he had become electorally 'toxic' (Lynton Crosby, cited in Seldon & Snowdon, 2016, p. 403; Bennett, 2019, p. 291, p. 294). Also, 'he frequently and unhelpfully ranged well beyond his brief' and, despite being told to pull his head in, continued to do so (Cameron, 2019, pp. 506–507; Clegg, 2016, p. 92; Fall, 2020, p. 193). He admitted he was 'over-opinionated and mouthy about issues outside my brief' (Parker & Warrell, 2014). As well as Nick Clegg, there were spats with Theresa May (Home Office), Eric Pickles (Communities and Local Government), Philip Hammond (Defence) and the PM on free school meals (Laws, 2016, p. 421; Seldon & Snowdon, 2016, p. 404). Although Gove had earlier offered to become Chief Whip, and Cameron believed from previous conversations that Gove understood the reasons for the move, it was a 'humiliating demotion' (Bennett, 2019, pp. 291–292; Fall, 2020, pp. 194–195; Seldon & Snowdon, 2016, p. 393).

Gove's loyalty to Cameron became strained by this demotion. Yet Cameron 'found it hard to believe' that Gove would join the Leave campaign. However, Cameron claims Gove promised that, if he opted for Brexit, 'I'm going to take a back seat. I'll be on their side, but I won't be involved' (Shipman, 2016, p. 153; Bennett, 2019, p. 322). Cameron believed he would play a low-key role (Cameron, 2019, p. 651; Fall, 2020, p. 285; Shipman, 2016, p. 153). This notion was rapidly dispelled. Gove was 'disastrously unclear' about campaigning (Bennett, 2019, pp. 316–317, p. 322; Oliver, 2016, p. 397; Shipman, 2016, p. 147, p. 154). Letwin (2017, p. 21) refers to his 'susurrations' that you had to learn to interpret. Cameron recognised the enormity of the split when he found out the Leave campaign had a 'parallel cabinet' and its leader was Michael Gove (Cameron, 2019, p. 657). Gove 'had broken with his friends and supporters, while taking up positions that were completely against his political identity'. Cameron had a 'very deep sense of personal betrayal' and 'no one else—other than George—could have landed him such a blow as Michael Gove' (Fall, 2020, p. 282; Cameron, 2019, p. 689). There was no possibility of a rapprochement after Gove and Johnson attacked Cameron in an open letter to *The Sunday Times* on immigration policy. They accused him of 'corroding public trust'. Cameron was 'furious and still more hurt' (see Shipman & Harper, 2016; Fall, 2020, p. 285; Oliver, 2016, pp. 257–258). For Craig Oliver (2016, pp. 160–161, p. 398), Gove was trashing the government, and 'out of control'. He was a 'political suicide bomber', a 'political serial killer' who is indulging in 'destructive game-playing'. Cameron's staff had an 'unshakeable loathing of Gove' (Shipman, 2016, p. 154). What Cameron could not live with was the belief that Gove had lied to him personally; he is 'dead to me' (Cameron, cited in Bennett, 2019, p. 358).

There is another interpretation of this piece of theatre—revenge. It was Gove's payback for the demotion—loyalty is meant to be reciprocal but in government 'loyalty is always a one-way street' (Swire, 2020, p. 226). It was not only about the demotion. It was also about the years as 'the performing monkey' at dinner parties, where he was never accepted as one of them (Shipman, 2016, p. 152). Fall (2020, p. 282) hears the 'whispers' about revenge and tries to shut the 'chatter' down as 'unhelpful'.

For the losers in court politics, there is always the next round in the game. There are many instances of petty reprisals. Steve Hilton intervened in the referendum campaign claiming Cameron had been warned years ago that the immigration targets could not be achieved (Fall, 2020, pp. 290–291; Seldon & Snowdon, 2016, p. 553). Dominic Cummings, who had lost his special adviser job twice thanks to interventions from No. 10, briefed regularly against the government, and developed a fondness for abusing Cameron in public. Resignations and reshuffles often have a subtext of revenge—the most spectacular example in recent years being Theresa May's sackings of both George Osborne and Michael Gove.

The prime means for manipulating, embarrassing, extracting revenge and punishing colleagues is the leak. Leaking is covert and refers to both an 'unauthorised source giving information to a journalist' and 'an authorised source with political power and high status using the media to their advantage' (Tiffen, 1989, p. 97). Leaking is no longer confined to the broadcast and print media. It now encompasses the internet, especially social media. As a result, centralised efforts to control government communication are futile: PMs 'do not have enough hands to cover all the holes in the information colander' (Grube, 2019, p. 31). Both Gove and Cummings garnered a reputation for leaking—allegedly. One insider claimed, 'Michael has done this over and over again—had a row internally and then leaked it' (Seldon & Snowdon, 2016, p. 405; D'Ancona, 2013, pp. 138–139). Gove denied his team were 'out of control' (Helm, 2013). The Information Commissioner ruled that Gove's team could not use private email accounts or text messages for official business (Bennett, 2019, pp. 246–248). It made no difference (D'Ancona, 2013, p. 137; Doward, 2013). And if Gove and Cummings were the arch-practitioners, they were not the only ones. The spate of leaks mounted to the point where Sir Jeremey Heywood wrote to officials demanding an end to a 'spate of corrosive leaks' (Civil Service World, 2016). Of course, his memo was leaked; 'perfectly appropriate—Sir Jeremy had proved his point, the leaker(s) had proved theirs' (Mance, 2017). When David Cameron suspended collective responsibility for the referendum, he heralded an era of ill-discipline and leaking that encompassed not only the rest of his premiership but also that of Theresa May.

Rituals, Language, Gossip, Humour and Bullying
Leaks do not only take the form of news stories. Gossip is leaking by another name. It is one of the currencies of the court, which is a private world with its own languages and rituals. For example, No. 10 is 'the House'. The rest of Whitehall is 'the System'. The No. 10 switchboard is 'the Switch'. Inner circle refers to PM as 'Dave' in private. The detectives call him 'the boss'. Officials call him PM or prime minister (Fall, 2020, pp. 87–88, pp. 90–91; Laws, 2016, p. 367). The men use 'power language'. For example, George Osborne does not have 'ideas'; but 'creates narratives'. Fall admits it is tough for women in such male dominated

environments unless 'you learn to take them on using some of their techniques' (Fall, 2020, p. 111; see also Slocock, 2018).

The House, like other government departments, had its rituals. Rhodes describes the roles of the diary secretary and the tea woman in three government departments; No. 10 differed only in detail (Rhodes, 2011, pp. 166–167, pp. 168–170). However, austerity ended the supply of tea, coffee and biscuits at meetings. The hierarchy of phone calls was a shared ritual between No. 10 and the rest of Whitehall (Fall, 2020, p. 89). The junior caller is kept waiting until the senior caller is ready to accept the call. Some prime ministers' calls are monitored with the listener 'patched in'; that is, not speaking. On others, the monitor is free to speak (Fall, 2020, p. 88).

The House has its own traditions. Humphry was the House cat for three prime ministers: Thatcher, Major and Blair. He became a national celebrity with his own Wikipedia page. After he died, David Cameron did not want a pet but, under pressure from Andy Coulson, he agreed the House could have a mouser. Courtesy of Battersea Cats & Dogs Home, Larry was installed as 'Chief Mouser to the Cabinet Office', and he too became a celebrity. Such traditions and practices may not be intrinsically important, but they are markers of the cocoon that is No. 10 (Fall, 2020, p. 106).

Both the PM's cocoon and the Westminster and Whitehall village of which they are a part are hotbeds of gossip, understood as idle chitchat and rumourmongering, even scandalmongering. More formally, gossip is 'the process of informally communicating value-laden information about members of a social setting' (Noon & Delbridge, 1993, p. 25). Some gossipers, for example Gavin Williamson, acquire standing because of their 'network of spies' who are 'lurking in stairwells'. He was a hoover of gossip and a man of 'dextrous charm', with an 'extraordinary font of knowledge—some of which is entirely scurrilous' (Fall, 2020, pp. 110–111). Reputedly, he had a black book of Tory MPs' 'vulnerabilities' (Bower, 2020, p. 372). There was endless scurrilous gossip not only about Boris Johnson and his affairs (see Bower, 2020; Williams, 2017) but also about his wife Marina Wheeler in a 'drunken clinch' with another man. *The Sun* made it clear the story was false, but it did not stop the story doing the rounds of Westminster parties (Bennett, 2019, p. 329, citing *The Sun* 18 May 2016). Indeed, the less believable the story, the greater its circulation. At best, there is only hearsay evidence to support the allegation that David Cameron took part in an initiation rite that involved inserting his penis in the mouth of a hog (Ashcroft & Oakeshott, 2015, pp. 73–74; Cameron, 2019, pp. 592–593). Yet the story made the headlines in tabloid newspapers and was still being repeated in 2020 with continuing speculation about both its possible source and the existence of a photograph of the event (Swire, 2020, p. 204). However, some gossip is accurate; for example, the speculation about the state of George Osborne's marriage (Swire, 2020, p. 230).

Gossip is often malicious and with a smutty and at times scatological sense of humour. Thus, expressions such as 'another turd to polish' are used to describe difficult jobs. Officials wanting to know how to describe a Chinese state visit are advised it can be anything golden provided it is not a golden shower. As Kate Fall (2020, pp. 92–93) observes there is a cultural clash with officials struggling with David's 'boyish sense of humour'. This 'boyish' quality emerges again in stories about Cameron staying up 'to admire Keira Knightley's nipples when she comes out of the fountain in *Atonement*' (Swire, 2020, p. 52). On another occasion, Cameron is in fits of laughter when comparing the size of colleague's penises. Seemingly, Michael Gove's member is impressive; 'like a slinky that comes downstairs before the rest of the body' (Swire, 2020, p. 126). I give these examples because all are a form of humour that is male, public school and further evidence of the social cohesion of Cameron's court. However, on occasion the tone was more elevated with cabinet experiencing a wry sardonic humour. For example, Michael Gove announced to cabinet that 'entries to physics, maths and chemistry are up. But it is with great personal sadness that I have to report to Cabinet a 10 per cent decrease in entries to … media studies. Cue general hilarity' (recounted in Laws, 2016, p. 301).

Social cohesion was also sustained by the parties at which Cameron could unwind at weekends. Cameron had a penchant for 'firing up the karaoke machine'. It was a 'very particular narrow tribe'. Of course, this tribe is not only an example of the persistence of class in British society, but it is also about the élite's need for the 'reassurance of tangible relationships, about organic personal bonds' in face of the 24/7 media. But such 'exclusive hedonism' sits uneasily with the austerity narrative and claims that we are all in it together (Elliott & Hanning, 2012, p. 438, pp. 448–449; Swire, 2020, p. 77).

The downside of this male culture is a macho streak that reveals itself in bullying. Cameron was accused of being a public school bully at PMQs, and of patronising female MPs. Cameron's reply was 'It's a bear pit so you have to be a bear. If you want different behaviour, put me in a different habitat' (Fall, 2020, p. 114). In other words, the practices of the House of Commons reinforced early male socialisation. Yet Cameron was not the worst example of bullying in his government.

When he was Gove's SpAd in DfE, Cummings was 'nonplussed by notions of politeness and civility' (Bennett, 2019, p. 248; Laws, 2017, pp. 25–26). Supported by Gove, Cummings built a macho culture at DfE. A senior civil servant complained of 'intimidation, favouritism and "laddism"' in the communications department headed by James Frayne. Cummings was 'widely known to use obscene and intimidating language' and instilling fear (Lambert, 2020). An internal review concluded disciplinary action was not warranted, although the review also noted that the conduct of Cummings and Frayne was 'perceived as intimidating'. Rather than go to a public tribunal, the DfE agreed a settlement of £25,000. Of course, Gove knew nothing (Jowitt, 2013). Journalists were also subject to 'explosions', aka rants, and Gove 'was not averse to provoking some incoming enemy fire' (Bennett, 2019, pp. 249–251; see also BBC Two, 18 March). The result was a bunker mentality in DfE which complicated relations with Cameron's court.

Consequences

This focus on the court and the PM's courtiers is not an example of academic whimsy. Gordon Brown began his term of office committed to a return to cabinet government after the sofa government of the Blair premiership. In his memoirs, he records that in the era of 24/7 media coverage, it 'was simply not possible'. Rather the 'process of government came to rely even more on a close-knit team at the centre'. There was an 'inner circle' which the critics referred to as 'courtiers', a 'cabal' or a 'clique'. These advisers 'became among Britain's most important decision makers', in effect 'acting as a kind of unelected cabinet' (Brown, 2017, pp. 226–227). The question is not whether court politics is a plausible account of executive government because for at least one prime minister it was a brute fact of his everyday life. This chapter shows that Brown's practices persisted under the successor PM. And these practices had important personal, electoral and governmental consequences.

Personal

The personal consequences of court politics are obvious from my account of the practices. The most dramatic breakup was the breach between the husband and wife teams of David and Samantha Cameron, and Michel Gove and Sarah Vine; 'when the wives get nasty, you know the men have a problem'. It was a bitter personal rift. Sarah Vine was 'furious' and 'snarling', tweeting it was 'a shabby day's work which Cameron will live to regret' (Ashcroft & Oakeshott, 2015, p. 510; Cameron, 2019, p. 510; Fall, 2020, pp. 194–195). Vine may have supported Samantha Cameron and ferried the children around and 'got on brilliantly with Sam' (Cameron, 2019, p. 506). She may have thought the Camerons were 'not acting like grown-ups'; that it was political not personal. She may have approached Kate Fall to broker a rapprochement. But these former close friends indulged in public spats; 'Sarah and Sam, fur flying, have a set-to at the party, with everyone watching and listening in'. The Camerons were furious and hurt. Fall (2020, p. 194, p. 285, p. 313) remarks that friendship and politics 'do not always go together in lock step' and there are 'personal rifts that may never heal' (see also Swire, 2020, p. 227). Craig Oliver (2016, p. 152) finds it hard to be in the same room as Gove.

For members of the court, the effect of these personal fallings-out is the noise they produce. They are a major diversion from the main issues. When Cameron was accused of tax evasion, Oliver thought they had not 'handled it well' and 'we had looked on the run'. They experienced a few difficult days, yet there was no evidence of any wrongdoing by the prime minister (Oliver, 2016, pp. 162–169). Major scandals such as Coulson and hacking followed by the Leveson inquiry were a major distraction. Cameron was 'greatly unsettled and traumatised' by the scandal (Seldon & Snowdon, 2016, pp. 93–94). It was a 'hugely time-consuming distraction for him and a string of senior aides and ministerial colleagues' (Ashcroft & Oakeshott, 2015, p. 460). Nick Clegg thought Cameron was 'in a total panic' and 'incapable of thinking of anything else at the current time' (Laws, 2016, p. 161). Cameron's Deputy Chief of Staff thought the scandal's effect was to 'undermine David's authority and credibility' (Fall, 2020, p. 170; Cameron, 2019, p. 260). The decision to appoint Coulson in the face of warnings from colleagues, and the 'personal humiliation' (Seldon & Snowdon, 2016, p. 91) of his appearance at the Leveson inquiry, eroded his leadership capital by casting doubt on his political skills and depleting his party and public support (Bennister et al., 2017, pp. 1–2, pp. 4–6).

Electoral

The electoral consequences of court politics are not confined either to general elections or to the majority party. Such consequences can be both dramatic and damaging, as they were for Theresa May in the 2017 General Election. Court politics also impact the leadership elections within political parties.

The politics of the Coalition and court politics were inextricably entwined, and the Liberal-Democrats were the losers. In the 2015 election, the party went from 57 to 8 seats. Cutts and Russell concluded this dismal result was caused by:

> loss of trust and competence, the failings of leadership, the focus on issues which lacked salience with voters, the incoherent presentation of the party's role in the coalition and the party's attempts to rectify the problems by adopting the failed equidistance stance of the early 1990s all contributed to the party's woeful performance in 2015. Mistakes made during the campaign added to this. (Cutts & Russell, 2015, p. 84; see also Kavanagh & Cowley 2016; Ross, 2015)

Court politics were a contributory factor because the loss of trust and competence were caused by the high-profile U-turns on student fees, the VAT increase and by their support for austerity. All these policies were negotiated in Quad. All were central to preserving the Coalition.

Court politics were integral to the standing of leadership contenders (see section on Leadership challenges above). Theresa May's speech setting out her political agenda and Gove's criticisms of her disloyalty are illustrations of such political manoeuvring to climb the greasy pole. If this instance did not damage May's credentials, later displays of 'disloyalty' by Gove over the Leave referendum damaged his political reputation with sections of the party. George Osborne was Cameron's natural successor. However, IDS's resignation letter was an attack on Osborne about the welfare cuts in the 2016 Budget, and it had a 'damaging effect' on his standing in the party (Shipman, 2016, pp. 203–205). It gave his enemies a platform from which to attack him. The brand was damaged only to be irreparably tarnished when he became the voice of 'Project Fear' during the referendum (see section on the Political game above).

Governmental

Court politics can have specific consequences for the government of the day. The phone hacking scandal and the Leveson inquiry opened Cameron's dealings with the 'media-political complex' to public gaze and they were 'deeply unedifying' (D'Ancona, 2013, p. 262; Ashcroft & Oakeshott, 2015, pp. 466–467). In Cameron's own words, 'we all did too much cosying up to Rupert Murdoch' (Cameron, cited in D'Ancona, 2013, p. 267; see also Cameron, 2019, p. 258). Crucially, Leveson is another instance of groupthink. It reinforced the image of the Cameroons as an incestuous social and political élite: 'It was incredible to see all these people letting their hair down. But something felt wrong. There were just too many people in too many powerful positions too close to each other. Rebekah Brooks and David Cameron were there' (Ashcroft & Oakeshott, 2015, pp. 466–467).

It portrayed Cameron as a short-term, reactive prime minister focused on holding office. Cameron admits it is a 'story of messy muddling through' (Cameron, 2019, p. 266). So, the 'the PM's primary objective was not to be swept away in the storm of revelation and retribution' (D'Ancona, 2013, p. 264). The strategy was 'to survive Leveson and then try to quickly rebuild his relationship with the press, shelving any significant proposals' (Laws, 2016, p. 161). Finally, it cast doubt on Cameron's judgement. Cameron admits to 'stubbornness'. He believed Coulson's assurances and confesses 'I very much wanted to believe them. … And that always affects your judgement' (Cameron, 2019, p. 256). In other words, he was loyal to a fault and that loyalty was the bedrock of the us and them mentality of the court.

Politicians and civil servants recognise groupthink but more commonly refer to it as living in a 'cocoon'. Few use the word groupthink (on which see Janis, 1982; 't Hart, 2014). However, for Nick Clegg (2016, p. 85), it was revealing 'how fixed groupthink can become in all institutions'. For Kate Fall (2020, p. 106), the critical environment in which politicians work is unpleasant, so 'those who work at No. 10 often revert to a smaller and smaller group of trusted friends. … It is a protective mechanism' but it 'creates a bubble—which can be a bad thing'. And the bad things she alludes to are the characteristic insular features of groupthink. Thus, the court displayed little interest in policies whose supporters were not in the inner circle. Andrew Lansley was the Secretary of State for Health and his health reforms were, along with Gove's education reforms, central parts of the modernisation programme. But Lansley was not a member of the court, so his policy developed without either the court's interest or oversight. It became a 'debacle' and the leading contender for the 'biggest cock up of Cameron's premiership' (Seldon & Snowdon, 2016, p. 181). Warnings about phone hacking and the pitfalls of referenda were also ignored. Opponents were stereotyped most notoriously when Cameron called UKIP a party of 'fruitcakes and loonies and closet racists'. And although the efforts to suppress dissent over Brexit eventually failed, there were many attempts to prevent dissent by members of cabinet. The calls for loyalty were an attempt to impose unanimity. Groupthink stemmed from Cameron's tradecraft; he 'goes into lockdown with a small group' (Cheryl Gillan, Welsh Secretary, cited in Ashcroft & Oakeshott, 2015, p. 421).

In part, the omnishambles budget of 21 March 2012 came about because its roots lay in small group decision-making; 'its contents were known only to the Quad'. The following day the budget fell apart in several ways, including phasing out the age-related tax allowance for pensioners, cutting the top rate of income tax and imposing VAT on pasties. 'No one in the Treasury had raised the problem [with pasties] with the Quad' and 'they should have done'. Cameron notes ruefully 'the more eyes on a controversial policy, the better' (all quotes from Cameron, 2019, p. 355, p. 359).

Groupthink is not the only consequence of court politics. There is also inter-court politics. Confusion and conflict are common by-products. David Laws commented that Cameron was 'fed up' with the 'endless rows' involving DfE. The court politics were 'significant' because 'the chaos and division caused by Dom Cummings' provoked 'real anger' in No. 10. Such politics also created confusion about whom said what and who agreed to what (all quotes from Laws, 2016, p. 434, p. 402). Groupthink, confusion and conflict lead to 'muddling through' as the dominant pattern of decision-making (Lindblom, 1959).

Firefighting and muddling through for issues big and little take up time, distracting attention away from important policies. They also create 'distance' from the public. Actors become cut off from everyday life. The game is played backstage by and for the players, not the public. The media may welcome politics as soap opera for the easy stories it provides. Their readers may find salacious pleasure in tawdry tribulations. But by trivialising politics, it is corrosive of trust; 'it added to the decline of trust in the current system' (Cameron, 2019, p. 250; Bennett, 2019, p. 331).

Conclusions

While Steve Hilton walked the corridors of No. 10, Cameron's court had an 'anarchic and ill-disciplined' streak (Seldon & Snowdon, 2016, p. 542). There were significant stresses and strains arising from, for example, the omnishambles budget and the Leveson inquiry. The EU referendum created some major rifts, notably with court soulmate Michel Gove. But the most distinctive feature of Cameron's court was not that it had difficulties—no court in recent history has cruised on a calm sea—but that despite the various storms it remained unified and many of its core personnel were there at the end. In the sixteenth century, Machiavelli enjoined his princes to have a flexible disposition, varying 'as fortune and circumstances dictate' (Machiavelli, 1961, p. 101). Cameron had a flexible disposition and quality people around him. Court government supplanted cabinet government. It is all too clear that the constitutional conventions of cabinet government were and remain convenient fictions for masking *realpolitik* until they were and are no longer convenient.

No matter which parliamentary democracy is being studied, this chapter has several analytical messages that travel well. The overall message is that the study of the core executive should embrace an interpretive approach with its focus on situated agency. The court is the core network at the heart of the core executive. This court can be systematically unpacked by focusing on its everyday practices. The chapter has an underlying message; the focus of court politics reveals the *realpolitik* of government decision-making in which 'scientific' methods of policy-making take second place to the practice of power. It has an explanatory message; it explains that court politics matter because of their many consequences. It has a methodological message; that for the *bricoleur*, the thematic analysis of insider sources is an invaluable way of exploring governmental practices. It has a comparative message that focusing on the court—on the practices and dilemmas of situated agents—provides not only an operational concept but also a pair of edifying spectacles; we have a more fruitful way of looking at the core executive. Finally, the chapter has a general message for any citizen; temper your expectations. Today's politicians are no more and no less venal, no more and no less statesman-like, no more and no less altruistic than their predecessors over the centuries. Politics was ever an evil trade.

Notes

1. I would like to thank the editors for their comments on the first draft. As ever John Boswell, Jack Corbett and Jenny Fleming (all University of Southampton) provided helpful advice. A new addition to my list of 'informal' referees is Tim Bale (Queen Mary) and I am most grateful for his assistance.
2. This paragraph is based on Cameron (2019); and Seldon and Snowdon (2016, p. xxxiv, p. 4, p. 7, p. 30, p. 213, p. 226, p. 239, p. 313, p. 452, p. 522, p. 542), supplemented with Ashcroft and Oakeshott (2015, pp. 315–316, p. 329, p. 333, p. 372, p. 413); and D'Ancona (2013, p. xii, pp. 3–5, p. 78).
3. Cameron (2019, p. 186); Clarke (2016, p. 461); Clegg (2016, p. 79); D'Ancona (2013, p. 47); Seldon and Snowdon (2016, p. 128, pp. 190–91, pp. 205–206, p. 240, p. 502).
4. Clegg (2016, p. 79); Fall (2020, p. 117); Laws (2016, p. 45, p. 336, p. 525). Laws returned as Minister of State for Schools in the Department for Education, and Minister of State in the Cabinet Office. He was not a full Cabinet minister, but he attended Cabinet.
5. See Seldon and Snowdon (2016, pp. xvii–xix) for a list of No. 10's personnel and their positions.
6. Ashcroft and Oakeshott (2015, opposite p. 179, p. 350); D'Ancona (2013, p. 86); Fall (2020, p. 8, p. 84); Letwin (2017, p. 251); Seldon and Snowdon (2016, p. 35, pp. 498–499, p. 539, p. 542).
7. On the omnishambles budget of 2012, see Cameron (2019, Chapter 25); D'Ancona (2013, Chapter 12); Laws (2016, pp. 121–129); and Seldon and Snowdon (2016, Chapter 17).
8. The other big loser was Vince Cable, Liberal-Democrat, Secretary of State for Business, Innovation and Skills (2010–2015), who spoke consistently against austerity. See Laws (2016, pp. 262–264, pp. 342–344).
9. Ashcroft and Oakeshott (2015, Appendix A, p. 532). The conclusion is based on survey data collected by Lord Ashcroft Polls. See https://lordashcroftpolls.com/about/. Last accessed 7 September 2020. On the public's ambivalent acceptance of austerity, see Killick (2020, pp. 55–56, pp. 59–60).
10. On the negotiations over the initial agreement, see Adonis (2013); Dorey and Garnett (2016); Finn (2015); Hazell (2012); Kavanagh and Cowley (2010, Chapter 10); and Laws (2010).
11. It is available at https://assets.publishing.service.gov.uk/government/uploads/system/uploads/attachment_data/file/78978/coalition-agreement-may-2010_0.pdf. Last accessed 19 July 2021.

12. This summary does not cover May 2015–October 2016 when the Conservatives had a majority, and as a result many of the forums for resolving issues used by the Coalition were no longer necessary (see Letwin, 2017, pp. 233–234; Heywood, 2021, p. 441).
13. COBR is the acronym for the Cabinet Office Briefing Rooms where the Civil Contingencies Committee holds its meetings. Sometimes it is referred to as COBRA because the meetings are held in Committee Room A.

References

't Hart, P. (2014). *Understanding Political Leadership*. Palgrave.
Adonis, A. (2013). *5 Days in May. The Coalition and Beyond*. Biteback Publishing.
Ashcroft, M., & Oakeshott, I. (2015). *Call Me Dave. The Unauthorised Biography of David Cameron*. Biteback Publishing.
Baker, N. (2015). *Against the Grain*. Biteback Publishing.
BBC. (2012). Leveson Inquiry: 10 key witnesses. 24 July. https://www.bbc.co.uk/news/uk-18899085
BBC Two. (2020). Taking Control: The Dominic Cummings Story. Broadcast on Wednesday, March 18.
Bennett, O. (2019). *Michael Gove. A Man in a Hurry*. Biteback Publishing.
Bennister, M., 't Hart, P., & Worthy, B. (2017). Understanding Political Leadership: The Leadership Capital Approach. In M. Bennister, B. Worthy, & P. 't Hart (Eds.), *The Leadership Capital Index: A New Perspective on Political Leadership* (pp. 1–26). Oxford University Press.
Bevir, M., & Rhodes, R. A. W. (2003). *Interpreting British Governance*. Routledge.
Bevir, M., & Rhodes, R. A. W. (2006). *Governance Stories*. Routledge.
Bevir, M., & Rhodes, R. A. W. (2010). *The State as Cultural Practice*. Oxford University Press.
Bower, T. (2020). *Boris Johnson: A Biography*. W. H. Allen.
Braun, V., & Clarke, V. (2006). Using Thematic Analysis in Psychology. *Qualitative Research in Psychology, 3*(2), 77–101.
Brown, G. (2017). *My Life, Our Times*. Brown Bodley Head.
Cabinet Office. (2011). *The Cabinet Manual: A Guide to Laws, Conventions and Rules on the Operation of Government*. Cabinet Office.
Cameron, D. (2009). Speech to the Conservative Party Conference. Retrieved September 7, 2020, from https://www.politics.co.uk/comment-analysis/2009/04/27/tory-spring-conference-speeches-in-full
Cameron, D. (2019). *For the Record*. William Collins.
Campbell, A. (2007). *The Blair Years. Extracts from the Campbell Diaries*. Hutchinson.
Campbell, J. (2010). *Pistols at Dawn. Two Hundred Years of Political Rivalry from Pitt & Fox to Blair & Brown*. Vintage.

Carroll, L. (1970). *The Annotated Alice. Edited by Martin Gardner* (2nd rev ed.). Penguin Books.

Channel 4. (2012). Brooks to Cameron: 'We're definitely in this together. 14 June. https://www.channel4.com/news/david-cameron-takes-the-stand-at-leveson

Civil Service World. (2016). Sir Jeremy Heywood Vows Crackdown on Civil Service Leaks, as Union Urges Same Rules for Ministers. 5 December. Retrieved October 1, 2020, from https://www.civilserviceworld.com/professions/article/sir-jeremy-heywood-vows-crackdown-on-civil-service-leaks-as-union-urges-same-rules-for-ministers

Clarke, K. (2016). *Kind of Blue: A Political Memoir*. Macmillan.

Clegg, N. (2016). *Politics: Between the Extremes*. The Bodley Head.

Cutts, D., & Russell, A. (2015). From Coalition to Catastrophe: The Electoral Meltdown of the Liberal Democrats. *Parliamentary Affairs, 68*(1), 70–87.

D'Ancona, M. (2013). *In it Together. The Inside Story of the Coalition Government*. Vintage.

Diamond, P., & Richards, D. (2012). The Case for Theoretical and Methodological Pluralism in British Political Studies: New Labour's Political Memoirs and the British Political Tradition. *Political Studies Review, 10*(2), 177–194.

Dorey, P., & Garnett, M. (2016). *The British Coalition Government 2010–2015. A Marriage of Inconvenience*. Palgrave Macmillan.

Doward, J. (2013). Michael Gove Advisers Face Claims of Smear Tactics Against Foes. *The Guardian*, February 2. https://www.theguardian.com/politics/2013/feb/02/gove-advisers-claims-smear-tactics

Durrant, T. (2020). Explainers: Cabinet. At https://www.instituteforgovernment.org.uk/explainers/cabinet

Elliott, F., & Hanning, J. (2012). *Cameron: Practically a Conservative*. Fourth Estate.

Fall, K. (2020). *The Gatekeeper*. HQ.

Featherstone, L. (2015). Transcript of Interview with the Liberal Democrat Minister of State for Crime Prevention, Home Office, 7 July 2015, Ministers Reflect Archive, Institute for Government, Online. Retrieved January 26, 2021, from https://www.instituteforgovernment.org.uk/ministers-reflect/person/lynne-featherstone/

Finn, M. (2015). The Coming of the Coalition and the Coalition Agreement. In A. Seldon & M. Finn (Eds.), *The Coalition Effect 2010–2015* (pp. 31–58). Cambridge University Press.

Geertz, C. (1973). Thick Description: Toward an Interpretive Theory of Culture. In C. Geertz (Ed.), *The Interpretation of Cultures* (pp. 3–30). Basic Books.

Gove, M., Johnson, B., & Stuart, G. (2016). Letter to the Prime Minister and Foreign Secretary – Getting the Facts Clear on Turkey. Vote Leave 16 June. Retrieved February 11, 2021, from http://www.voteleavetakecontrol.org/

letter_to_the_prime_minister_and_foreign_secretary_getting_the_facts_clear_on_turkey.html

Grube, D. (2019). *Megaphone Bureaucracy. Speaking Truth to Power in the Age of the New Normal*. Princeton University Press.

Hazell, R. (2012). How the Coalition Works at the Centre. In I. R. Hazell & B. Yong (Eds.), *The Politics of Coalition. How the Conservative-Liberal Democrat Government Works* (pp. 49–70). Hart.

Helm, T. (2013). Michael Gove "misled parliament" over claims of bullying by advisers. *The Guardian*, February 9. Retrieved October 7, 2020, from https://www.theguardian.com/politics/2013/feb/09/michael-gove-bullying-claims-payout1

Heywood, Sir J. (2012). Oral Evidence to the Select Committee on Public Administration, 24 May 2012. Retrieved September 21, 2020, from https://publications.parliament.uk/pa/cm201213/cmselect/cmpubadm/c133-i/c13301.htm

Heywood, S. (2021). *What Does Jeremy Think? Jeremy Heywood and the Making of Modern Britain*. William Collins.

Hurst, G., Thomson, A., & Sylvester, R. (2014). Ally of Michael Gove savages David Cameron for "bumbling". *The Times*, June 16. Retrieved September 25, 2020, from https://www.thetimes.co.uk/article/ally-of-michael-gove-savages-david-cameron-for-bumbling-cw9tqtgdbjt

Janis, I. L. (1982). *Groupthink: Psychological Studies of Policy Decisions and Fiascos*. Houghton Mifflin.

Johnson, P., & Chandler, D. (2015). The Coalition and the Economy. In A. Seldon & M. Finn (Eds.), *The Coalition Effect 2010–2015* (pp. 159–193). Cambridge University Press.

Jowitt, J. (2013). Michael Gove Defends Himself Over Bullying Accusations Against Adviser. *The Guardian*, March 13. Retrieved February 19, 2021, from https://www.theguardian.com/politics/2013/mar/13/michael-gove-defends-bullying-adviser

Kaufman, G. (1980). *How to be a Minister*. Sidgwick & Jackson.

Kavanagh, D., & Cowley, P. (2016). *The British General Election of 2010*. Palgrave Macmillan.

Killick, A. (2020). *Rigged. Understanding 'The Economy' in Brexit Britain*. Manchester University Press.

Klijn, E.-H. (2014). Political Leadership in Networks. In R. A. W. Rhodes & P. 't Hart (Eds.), *The Oxford Handbook of Political Leadership* (pp. 403–417). Oxford University Press.

Lambert, H. (2020). Dominic Cummings: The Machiavelli in Downing Street. *New Statesman*, September 25. Retrieved March 9, 2020, from https://www.newstatesman.com/politics/uk/2019/09/dominic-cummings-machiavel-downing-street

Laws, D. (2010). *22 Days in May: The Birth of the Lib Dem-Conservative Coalition.* Biteback Publishing.
Laws, D. (2016). *Coalition. The Inside Story of the Conservative-Liberal Democrat Coalition.* Biteback Publishing.
Laws, D. (2017). *Coalition Diaries: 2012–2015.* Biteback Publishing.
Letwin, O. (2017). *Hearts and Minds: The Battle for the Conservative Party from Thatcher to the Present.* Biteback Publishing.
Levi-Strauss, C. (1966). *The Savage Mind.* Weidenfeld and Nicolson.
Lindblom, C. E. (1959). The Science of Muddling Through. *Public Administration Review, 19*(2), 79–88.
Machiavelli, N. (1961) [1532]. *The Prince.* Translated by G. Bull. Penguin Classics.
Mance, H. (2017). Five Types of Political Leak and How to Spot Them. *Financial Times,* May 12. Retrieved September 21, 2020, from https://www.ft.com/content/4c6ee0f6-36f8-11e7-bce4-9023f8c0fd2e
May, T. (2013). Speech to Conservative Home's Victory 2015 conference. Retrieved September 8, 2020, from https://www.conservativehome.com/platform/2016/07/full-text-of-theresa-mays-speech-we-will-win-by-being-the-party-for-all.html
Moore, C. (2021). Inside the World of the Extraordinary Man Who Rules Number 10. *The Telegraph,* January 30. Retrieved February 8, from https://www.telegraph.co.uk/news/0/inside-world-extraordinary-man-ruled-number-10/
Nemeth, C., Brown, K., & Rogers, J. (2001). Devil's Advocate Versus Authentic Dissent: Stimulating Quantity and Quality. *European Journal of Social Psychology, 31*(6), 707–720.
Noon, M., & Delbridge, R. (1993). News from Behind My Hand: Gossip in Organizations. *Organization Studies, 14*(1), 23–36.
Oakeshott, M. (1967). *Rationalism in Politics and Other Essays.* Methuen University Paperback.
Oakeshott, M. (1996). *The Politics of Faith and the Politics of Scepticism.* Edited by Timothy Fuller. Yale University Press.
Oborne, P. (2021). *The Assault on Truth, Boris Johnson, Donald Trump and the Emergence of a New Moral Barbarism.* Simon & Schuster.
Oliver, C. (2016). *Unleashing Demons. The Inside Story of Brexit.* Hodder & Stoughton.
Osborne, G. (2009). It's Ridiculous to Pretend to Pretend There Won't Be Cuts. *The Times,* June 15.
Parker, G., & Warrell, H. (2014). How Far Will Michael Gove Go. *The FT Magazine,* March 14. Retrieved September 29, 2020, from https://www.ft.com/content/ebe8018c-aa45-11e3-8497-00144feab7de
Pratchett, T. (2009). *Soul Music.* Corgi.
Prince, R. (2017). *Theresa May: The Enigmatic Prime Minister.* Biteback Publishing.

Rhodes, R. A. W. (2011). Everyday Life in British Government. Oxford: Oxford University Press.

Richards, D., & Mathers, H. (2010). Political Memoirs and New Labour: Interpretations of Power the "club rules". *British Journal of Politics International Relations, 12*(4), 498–522.

Riddell, Peter (2019). 15 Minutes of Power. The Uncertain Life of British Ministers. London: Profile Books.

Riesman, D., Glazer, N., & Denney, R. (1961). *The Lonely Crowd*. Yale University Press.

Ross, T. (2015). *Why the Tories Won: The Inside Story of the 2015 Election*. Biteback Publishing.

Saul, H. (2016). David Cameron: The Surprising Description of Him That He "hated" Enough to Call and Complain. *The Independent*, July 13. Retrieved September 4, 2020, from https://www.independent.co.uk/news/people/david-cameron-chillax-chillaxing-chillaxed-description-complain-francis-elliot-times-angry-birds-a7134361.html

Seldon, A. (2015). David Cameron as Prime Minister, 2010–2015. The Verdict of History. In A. Seldon & M. Finn (Eds.), *The Coalition Effect 2010–2015* (pp. 1–28). Cambridge University Press.

Seldon, A., & Newell, R. (2020). *May at 10. The Verdict*. Biteback Publishing. Updated Paperback Edition.

Seldon, A., & Snowdon, P. (2016). *Cameron at 10. The Verdict*. William Collins. Updated Paperback Edition.

Shipman, T. (2016). *All Out War. The Full Story of How Brexit Sank Britain's Political*. William Collins.

Shipman, T., & Harper, T. (2016). Boris and Gove Lash Cameron on Immigration. *The Sunday Times*, May 29. Retrieved September 30, 2020, from https://www.thetimes.co.uk/article/boris-and-gove-lash-cameron-on-immigration-5kjl329mx

Slocock, Caroline (2018). *People Like Us: Margaret Thatcher and Me* London: Biteback.

Smithers, A. (2015). 'The coalition and society (II): Education'. In Seldon, A. and Finn, M. (Eds.) The Coalition Effect 2010–2015. Cambridge: Cambridge University Press, pp. 257–89.

Smith, J. (2019). Government Chief Whip (2017–2019). Interviewed in *The Brexit Storm: Laura Kuenssberg's Inside Story*', BBC Four. Broadcast 1 April 2019.

Swire, S. (2020). *Diary of an MP's Wife: Inside and Outside Power*. Little. Brown.

't Hart, P. (2014). Understanding Political Leadership. London: Palgrave.

The Telegraph. (2006). Cameron's Inner Circle. 1 October. Retrieved June 18, 2020,romhttps://www.telegraph.co.uk/news/uknews/1530258/Camerons-inner-circle.html

Thomas, W. I., & Thomas, D. S. (1928). *The Child in America: Behavior Problems and Programs*. Knopf.
Tiffen, R. (1989). *News and Power*. Allen & Unwin.
Walter, J., & 't Hart, P. (2014). Distributed Leadership and Policy Success: Understanding Political Dyads (July 21). Australian Political Studies Association, The Australian Political Studies Association Annual Conference, University of Sydney. Available at SSRN: https://ssrn.com/abstract=2469597
Weller, P., Grube, D., & Rhodes R.A.W. (2021). *Comparing Cabinets: The Dilemmas of Collective Government*. Oxford University Press.
Williams, H. (2017). *Boris Johnson: The Beast of Brexit*. London Review of Books.

CHAPTER 5

Ireland's Core Executive at One Hundred Years of Self-government: Navigating Coalition, Crisis and Complexity

Bernadette Connaughton

Glossary
Bunreacht na hÉireann   Constitution of Ireland
Dáil Éireann   Lower House of Parliament
Fianna Fáil   Soldiers of Ireland
Fine Gael   Irish Race
Taoiseach   Prime Minister
Taoisigh   Prime Ministers
Tánaiste   Deputy Prime Minister

B. Connaughton (✉)
Department of Politics and Public Administration, University of Limerick, Limerick, Ireland
e-mail: Bernadette.Connaughton@ul.ie

© The Author(s), under exclusive license to Springer Nature Switzerland AG 2022
K. Kolltveit, R. Shaw (eds.), *Core Executives in a Comparative Perspective*, Understanding Governance,
https://doi.org/10.1007/978-3-030-94503-9_5

Introduction

A centenary of Irish self-government is a perfect juncture for reflecting on how executive actors work together and attempt to address the coordination challenges of present-day governance. In 1922 the transition from 'Castle Government' to an independent Irish administration was advanced by revolution, and yet a continuity in traditions underpinned the establishment of native institutions. Ireland adopted the Westminster model of prime ministerial-led parliamentary government affiliated with a centralised executive and a weak legislature (Hogan & Murphy, 2021)—whereas the Whitehall conventions of a generalist, apolitical and impartial civil service typified the administration, along with the inheritance of a modern imperial structure that was extremely hierarchal (Maguire, 2008). A divisiveness fuelled by disagreements over signing the Anglo-Irish Treaty in 1921 led to a bitter civil war (1922–1923) and resulted in two dominant political parties, Fianna Fáil (Soldiers of Ireland) and Fine Gael (Irish Race), representing the opposing sides, along with a smaller Labour Party.

Ireland's post-colonial adaptation is also shaped by its depiction as a small state. Although it is not typically 'small' in comparison with the demographic or socio-economic features of micro island states within the Commonwealth or the Baltic states in the EU, several descriptors of the Irish polity fit well with how the international literature identifies small states (see Katzenstein, 1985). Traits such as informal policy coordination, personalism, localism and limited capacity are used to describe features influencing how the Irish political-administrative system works in practice, and how reform is mediated (Connaughton, 2016; Laffan & O'Mahony, 2007). Such traits contour the practices modifying the formal executive processes in institutions inherited from large states (Corbett et al., 2021), and the interplay between who does what, where and with what resources in the core executive.

This chapter analyses the core executive in Ireland by identifying the formal structures—cabinet, cabinet committees and departments—and the formal and informal roles, networks and relationships between the principal actors at the centre of government. The compositions and functioning of the core executive are explored through the prisms of (a) coalition government and (b) the contemporary challenges of managing crisis and complexity. Since 1989, government formation in the aftermath of a general election has resulted in the proliferation of coalition governments which have required new structures and political actors to enable working together and the harmonisation of government work. Dominating issues in the twenty-first century, such as COVID-19, Brexit and economic and financial crises, have placed significant pressures on the capacity of the Irish government and administration, and dealing with an increasing number of 'wicked problems' has exposed the need for upgrading how the core executive functions through facilitating both vertical and horizontal coordination across government and securing consensus at the centre. In approaching 100 years of self-government the Taoiseach and ministers around the cabinet table remain the focal point for formal decision approval. But an understanding of how contemporary government works involves exploring the orbiting supporting structures and exchanges between actors addressing politics and policy challenges.[1]

Configuring the Core Executive

Prior to 1922 the 'Irish Court' was identified physically and symbolically by its location at Dublin Castle and the occupancy of the Lord Lieutenant. Its contemporary counterpart is Government Buildings on Upper Merrion Street in Dublin, which developed into a 'Whitehall writ small' (Moody & Martin, 2011, p. 291) and became the site for weekly cabinet meetings of the newly established Irish Free State Executive Council (1922–1937). This Edwardian-inspired quadrangle of buildings accommodates the key offices of the Irish government: the Department of the Taoiseach, Department of Finance, Department of Public Expenditure and Reform, the Office of the Attorney General and the Cabinet Room. Government Buildings also houses the inner court of the Taoiseach (PM), Tánaiste (Deputy PM), secretary generals, assistant secretaries of the Department of the Taoiseach and chiefs of staff for the party leaders in government. Beyond this compound are ministers of other departments of state and junior ministers in various locations, their senior civil servants and political advisers, as well as the institutional structures within which they convene. Any consideration of government is incomplete without their contribution and an acknowledgement that the core executive is not a unified actor but rather 'a collection of power centres' (O'Malley & Martin, 2018, p. 243).

In terms of understanding power and control in the Irish executive the role of Taoiseach is critical. The position of Taoiseach ('chief'), as instituted by Bunreacht na hÉireann 1937, is the most powerful role in the Irish political system, being both head of government and leader of a political party. The incumbent chairs cabinet and is expected to perform a lead policy coordination role (Farrell, 1971; O'Malley & Martin, 2018). Cabinet is the principal formal decision-making forum and its membership is provided for by Article 28 of the constitution and by the Ministers and Secretaries Act 1924 (and amendments). The Taoiseach and cabinet business are supported by the Department of the Taoiseach which for several decades was a small administrative secretariat, diligently following protocol, and performing 'post-office' type tasks as opposed to being directly engaged in policy-making (O'Malley, 2012, p. 45). In contrast, the Department Finance was regarded as the hub of government in the post-independence period given its inheritance of the treasury function and its minister's authority to make regulations to control the civil service, as stipulated in the Civil Service Regulation Act 1924. Taoiseach and Finance formed a 'duopoly' in a distinctive type of court politics given that new and major policy developments needed their approval (MacCarthaigh, 2020). Both departments, and in addition the Department of Public Expenditure and Reform (DPER), created in 2011, remain integral to how the centre of government works but must be viewed within a framework of a wider array of departmental configurations, structures and agents introduced to deal with government complexity and its political management.

Cabinet business is managed by the Department of the Taoiseach and its Government Secretariat, which is the point of contact between the Office of the President and the departments of state. The Government Secretariat services all government meetings, drawing up the agenda, circulating documentation to ministers and communicating decisions to government departments. Since the 1980s the department has structurally diversified and enlarged considerably to an additional six divisions and two units dealing with EU, international and key social and economic policy to maintain a whole of government perspective (Hardiman et al., 2012, pp. 106–107). In addition, the influence of the department emanates from the formal position of the Taoiseach, which yields political resources and the Secretary General (SG) of the department, who is viewed as the most senior civil servant in the administration. In 2001 the SG role was merged with the position of Secretary General to the Government (SGG) and this renders the incumbent as not only senior but an exceptionally powerful civil servant. The SGG is the only civil servant to attend cabinet meetings and records the decisions taken there. This combined SG/SGG role and that of the assistant secretaries who run the cabinet committee system positions the Department of the Taoiseach as a principal interlocutor. Each party leader in government also has a chief of staff who is a politically appointed senior adviser and works directly with the party leader and on their behalf from the base of Government Buildings. Ireland's civil service remains apolitical and the routinised appointment of 'special advisers' who assist ministers in departments and serve them in the political sphere largely dates to the formation of the Fine Gael and Labour coalition government in 1973 and concerns about civil service impartiality, given their long service to Fianna Fáil led governments (Connaughton, 2010).

As noted, the core executive actors and their relationships span beyond the Government Buildings quadrangle and its inner courts. This is illustrated in Ireland's engagement with the EU policy-making process, which is much more pervasive since membership in 1973, including more ministers and their departments and requiring a blend of informal and distinctly formalised processes to tackle not just coordination but also accountability and capacity challenges within the core executive. For example, Ireland's rejection of the Nice Treaty referendum in 2001 prompted changes in managing relations between the executive and legislature, but it also consolidated what is regarded as a 'holy trinity' of the departments of Taoiseach, Finance and Foreign Affairs as an 'inner core' that manages internal preparation and outward facing relations between Ireland and the EU (Laffan & O'Mahony, 2007). What is important to glean from this short overview is that the Taoiseach is central to the networks in and out of Government Buildings, both politically and through the Department of Taoiseach. However, while powerful, the Taoiseach is also subject to constraints and this will be explored within the circumstances of coalition government which has motivated arrangements, both formal and informal, outside of cabinet meetings. Further, no one actor prevails or is immune when operating in a complex environment of either crisis or 'routine' policy-making.

Coordination: Moving and Shaping Policy Proposals

This section presents features of both vertical processual approaches and the more informal management styles that serve to 'oil the machine' in a relatively small administration. Formally, the operation of cabinet government is underpinned by the internal guidelines set out in the 91 pages of the Cabinet Handbook (2006) and the process for bringing a memorandum to government is overseen by the Government Secretariat. The Department of the Taoiseach's coordination role is emphasised in its strategy statement which refers to supporting 'work at the centre' and engagement with other departments 'to implement policy primarily through the cabinet committee structure' (Department of the Taoiseach, 2021, p. 5). The substantive policy-making role takes place in the line departments, however, whereby Bunreacht na hÉireann refers to ministers as 'in charge' of their departments (Article 12.12). Cabinet remains a final arbiter and these decisions are influenced by the culmination of a lengthy process involving junior ministers, senior officials and advisers participating in a variety of fora.

Formally, the coordination of policy recommendations to advance the programme for government is reflected in the work of cabinet committees and senior officials' groups, particularly where cross-government collaboration is critical (Department of the Taoiseach, 2021). In the 32nd government formed on 27 June 2020, the Taoiseach, Tánaiste, Green Party leader and the Minister for Finance are members of all cabinet committees. The secretary of each of the committees is a senior official of the Department of the Taoiseach. Each cabinet committee is supported by a senior officials' group (SOG), bringing together senior civil servants from departments represented on the cabinet committee. The SOGs can be quite effective working in sequence with cabinet committees (e.g., via the undertaking of preparatory work for the EU climate package in 2014), though the line departments develop the policy substance. Departmental officials must attempt to sort out differences regarding policy, administration and staffing, legal and constitutional implications prior to the discussion in cabinet (Connaughton, 2012, p. 75). Special advisers attend both SOGs and cabinet committees. The cabinet committees generally make policy recommendations that are followed up by a formal memo to government and expire at the end of a government's term in office.

The experience of cabinet committees was weak prior to the early 2000s, when an expansion took place under a Fianna Fáil Taoiseach, Bertie Ahern. Various Taoisigh have viewed their operation differently and cabinet committees can be difficult to schedule, whereas a fixed point in every minister's calendar is cabinet on a Tuesday when the Dáil (lower house) is sitting. A Fine Gael Taoiseach, Enda Kenny, dealt with this by holding marathon back-to-back cabinet committee meetings once a month. This is reflected in the meeting statistics for the 29th government (2011–2016) where, for example, the Economic Recovery and Jobs committee met 33 times (with 37 SOG meetings), and European Affairs met 20 times (with 118 SOG meetings). In contrast, meetings of individual cabinet committees in the 31st government (June 2017–June 2020) are in single figures, with a larger number of SOG meetings. An exception is the COVID-19 committee, which was established on 3 March 2020 and had met six times, supported by 12 SOG meetings, by June of that year. The effectiveness of this system is debatable since the volume of meetings or a pro forma management style does not indicate added value. Cabinet committees were described in personal interviews with the author as 'rattling through agendas', 'awful wind-bagging', and 'death by powerpoint'. But they endure as a coordination device or at least as a forum for discussion.

Memoranda may be submitted as a memorandum for information to signal issues to government, or as a memorandum for decision requiring government authorisation due to new policy developments. The requisites of collective responsibility oblige ministers to inform, and potentially secure approval from their government colleagues, to proceed with policy proposals. Both Department of Finance and DPER have input into all proposals with expenditure implications, and any significant policy departures require prior consultation with the Taoiseach's department. All the party leaders in a coalition government also need to be conferred with in advance, typically through their chiefs of staff. In general, the 'system kind of works as it is meant to for 90% of issues' so 'no surprises' arise on circulation (personal interview). Rarely does an issue get to cabinet that has not been approved and cleared through the system since ministers do not want to bring a memo that they know will be defeated. But informal relationships and practices also underpin how business is conducted and at times ministers bring 'under the arm' memos to cabinet. There is more leeway given to Ministers for Finance and Public Expenditure and Reform given their position in the departmental hierarchy. The 'under the arm' memos are also a feature of crisis: for example, during the pandemic memos came to cabinet from the Department of Health with contents that other ministers were not aware were under discussion.

Other forms of coordination that are not captured in details of constitutional relationships or the cabinet handbook lie in political management. This is where chiefs of staff and special advisers contribute, and O'Malley and Martin (2018, p. 365) sanguinely comment that 'the advisers collectively operate in effect as a lower-level cabinet'. As a team or 'collective' they have the potential to be an effective management tool while collectively helping to ensure that the government remains focused on political priorities (Connaughton, 2010, p. 363).

Since the mid-2000s advisers have met on Mondays before cabinet to go through the agenda and flag up any problems needing 'fixing' or further coordination. It is questionable how effective this is with greater numbers of advisers and online meetings becoming the norm in the pandemic. The online conduct of this fora was described as 'a very prosaic meeting' and 'nothing politically sensitive' (personal interview). Political and press advisers also meet the day before cabinet to coordinate the communications strategy.

A further layer to add is a political meeting whereby party leaders may meet with ministers and senior advisers before cabinet. Many issues are deemed in hand before cabinet and interventions are made to alleviate tensions. For example, the minority 31st government serving between 2017–2020 included independents (non-party) who were supported by a full-time 'Political Coordinator for Independent Ministers in Government', and if problems arose senior ministers would step in to assist with conflict resolution. Apropos, occasions may arise when other members of the government may feel blindsided by decisions taken by core executive actors within the inner court at Government Buildings.

Ultimately, it is the cabinet's remit to legitimate decisions taken within the core executive and meetings are typically held on Tuesday mornings when the Dáil is in session (and on Wednesdays when it is in recess), and the main agenda is available to ministers from the previous Friday. Meetings are attended by cabinet ministers, along with the Chief Whip, Attorney General and the SGG. Table 5.1 indicates the number of meetings and memoranda submitted in 2008, 2018 and in 2020 which was marked by a general election and the beginning of the pandemic.

Table 5.1 Numbers of government meetings and memoranda (information and decision)

	Government meetings (n)	Memoranda submitted (n)
2008	57	1001
2018	52	1011
2020	82	893

Source: Department of the Taoiseach

How decisions are arrived at in cabinet meetings is unclear, since discussions are shrouded in the conventional veil of cabinet confidentiality. The unanimity principle, given constitutional weight through Article 28.4, ensures that once government takes a decision then all ministers are required to support it regardless of their position in the discussions. It is argued that this has a significant impact on how government works since it may push ministers to bring forth politically contentious issues to cabinet meetings, regardless of whether there is a legal imperative to do so (O'Malley & Martin, 2018, p. 250). Cabinet decisions and minutes are recorded by the SGG. This official role was described in interviews as 'the leading force in continuity', 'pen holder in chief' and 'immensely powerful because they are the ones who tell the system, their colleagues, what happened'. This is alluding to the general debrief of cabinet meetings provided from the SGG to the secretaries general on Wednesday mornings before the issuing of the 'pink slips' after a cabinet meeting, which are circulated to departments for comment. Despite the aura of secrecy, it is apparent that ministers do brief officials and advisers on cabinet business to facilitate coordination (see Walshe, 2014). Media frequently report in advance on what is up for discussion in cabinet and leaks are an ongoing challenge for government in a media-charged environment. For example, regarding one cabinet meeting there were 'no fewer than three stories on the front page of the Irish Times, each one based on a memorandum going to government that day!' (personal interview).

Managing communications, briefing the press and defending media content have become a full-time activity, leading to an increased investment in such resources within the core executive. It is also evident in prime ministerial/ministerial styles: witness the personalisation of messaging, such as Taoiseach Leo Varadkar's St. Patrick's Day address to the nation on COVID-19 in 2020, and the pervasive use of social media platforms like Twitter, Instagram and TikTok by certain ministers. The general public, or the civil servants for that matter, are not always receptive to efforts to 'shake up comms' and boost numbers of 'spin doctors'. This is demonstrated in Taoiseach Leo Varadkar's short-lived and controversial Strategic Communications Unit linked to the Department of the Taoiseach in 2018. The unit aimed to streamline and deliver government communications/campaigns but was publicly accused of promoting the Fine Gael party. A review of the unit by the Taoiseach's SG exonerated it from claims of politicisation but recommended its disbandment.

Developments in the Irish Core Executive

The remainder of this chapter explores developments that have influenced and required responses that are evident in the functioning of the core executive and resource exchanges between actors. Firstly, the impact of coalition government is discussed, since this has characterised government formation since 1989 and shaped relations within the core executive. Secondly, the challenges of governing in an era of crisis and increasing policy complexity (e.g., Brexit, COVID-19 and climate change) place more pressure on the core executive in a small state, both functionally (apropos the integration of central government policies) and as the final arbiter of conflict between various components of the government machine.

Coalition Dynamics at the Centre of Government

General elections no longer produce clear-cut outcomes for government formation in Ireland. The time taken to negotiate government agreements has increased from two to three weeks in the late 1990s to a total of 128 days after the general election in 2020. The 33rd government was formed on 27 June 2020 and is referred to as a coalition signifying the 'end of civil war politics', given its composition of Fianna Fáil, Fine Gael and the Green Party. For the first time in the state's history a 'rotating Taoiseach' is introduced, commencing with the Fianna Fáil party leader, and reverting to the Fine Gael party leader on 15 December 2022 (Little, 2021). Coalition, where smaller parties tend to be overrepresented in cabinet, changes the rules of the game and the distribution of power. While it was suggested that coalition management stuck closely to the Westminster model with relatively few adjustments (Seyd, 2002, p. 104), it is evident that the centrality of party politics, and balancing party identity with stable government, influences relational processes, constraints and interdependencies between core executive actors. This is reflected in a Taoiseach's management style and the likelihood of him acting as a 'chairman' rather than a 'chief' (Farrell, 1971). The 'rotating Taoiseach' arrangement of the 33rd government adds to this by placing the office holder in a less commanding position compared to previous incumbents. This highlights that a prime minister's authority can be a 'moveable feast', a consequence of the shifting political environment in which core executive actors find themselves (Heffernan, 2012).

Earlier coalition governments in the 1980s were paralysed by the lack of mechanisms to deal with coordination and conflict resolution in the core executive, and in their absence long, unproductive cabinet meetings took place. Between 1983 and 1989 the cabinet agenda was pragmatically divided into parts one, two and three, with part three being a graveyard of items that the governing parties agreed were intractable but needed to be retained on the agenda for external optics (Connaughton, 2005, p. 264).

The mark of coalition politics on core executive actors and structures largely dates from the Fianna Fáil-Labour government of 1993–1994, whereby Labour Party strategists were determined to restructure the central government machine. This resulted in the introduction of increased numbers of special advisers and a new adviser variant called a programme manager. Programme managers were tasked with tracking and eliminating impediments to the effective delivery of the government's ambitious legislative programme (O'Halpin, 1997). Although they facilitated horizontal coordination within the core executive, the programme manager 'collective' was opposed by the civil service, since they were viewed as a lower-level cabinet. But their ability to diffuse sensitive issues and strive to find compromise between ministers was helpful in preparing the ground for consensus in government meetings (Connaughton, 2018, p. 120). After 1997 the system was largely disbanded and only party leaders included programme managers in their teams, now referred to as chiefs of staff.

The contours of the core executive have also been shaped by specific structures introduced to boost the position of party leaders in coalition, particularly in the role of Tánaiste. Formally, the title is largely honorific, since Bunreacht na hÉireann does not confer additional powers on the office holder. An Office of Tánaiste was created for Tánaiste Dick Spring (Labour), who served from 1993–1997. This enlarged the core executive by providing the support of a junior minister, assistant secretary and a team of advisers. It was designed to shadow the work of the Department of the Taoiseach in that the Labour leader received all government papers, and not just those relating to his own portfolio. The public view of the office, however, was of the Tánaiste posing as a 'mini-Taoiseach' and successive coalition governments did not retain this resource.

But programme managers/chiefs of staff working to a party leader or Tánaiste in coalition have occupied a physical presence in the Taoiseach's Department, albeit with few resources. In 2020 an Office of the Tánaiste returned with staffing support within the Department of the Taoiseach, along with a new Office of the Green Party Leader based in Government Buildings to help coordinate and implement policy within government. The Tánaiste serving in 2020–2022 is the former Taoiseach *and* the Taoiseach in waiting, by virtue of the new rotation which gives this inner court—based directly under the Taoiseach's office—'an extra dynamic and everyone is wired to that because for the first time we know exactly who the next Taoiseach is and what day he will take up the role' (personal interview).

In 2020 the Fianna Fáil, Fine Gael and Green Party coalition appointed over 60 advisers, including 17 working directly to the party leaders. This is a large adviser cohort by Irish standards, and its profile reflects a sizeable recruitment of former media personnel and journalists who are focussed on press and communications. The adviser profile itself waxes and wanes with ministerial appointments, some of whom have been selected from within the civil service. Leahy (2013, p. 112), commenting on the contrasting styles between these actors in the 2011–2016 government, presents a view from an inside informant that the 'Fine Gael guys think it's "The West Wing" and the Labour guys think it's "The Sopranos"'. But the principal influence belongs to the chiefs of staff, whose role and exchanges with each other increase in importance the more complex the government structure, given the need to manage internal parliamentary party business and the government agenda. The inclusion of the improvised political structures discussed here, and the senior adviser appointments, fosters centralisation, coordination and control within government—but may not match with circumstances downstream at the operational level of administration.

Dealing with Crisis and Complexity

A traditional response to dealing with complex cross-cutting issues is the setting up an interdepartmental committee. Line ministers tend to be strongly focused on the business of their own departments, however, and further upstream there is no standing cabinet committee structure in place. The cabinet committees 'derive their authority and privileges from government', are expected to have a cross-cutting dimension and are dissolved at the end of every government's term (Department of the Taoiseach, 2006, p. 25). Nonetheless, 'perhaps the most significant organisational change aimed at improving cross-departmental coordination has been the growing reliance on the cabinet committee system' (Hardiman et al., 2012, p. 120). This section discusses three areas where crisis and complexity have required a coherent and cross-cutting response from the central government machine.

Europeanisation and Brexit
Although relatively small, the Irish system has built up considerable expertise in engaging with the Brussels machine by identifying clear national priorities, displaying flexibility in negotiations and building constructive working relationships with the European Commission. In terms of core executive studies, much of the focus has been on a functional approach to coordination (Laffan & O'Mahony, 2007), given the ongoing and permanent capacities required for managing policy preparation, inter-ministerial engagement and the sheer volume of work undertaken by officials. Key characteristics of this approach are personalism, less *lourdeur administrative* and informal policy coordination within departments, all of which is complemented by the work of the Permanent Representation in Brussels.

There are intervals when formal coordination structures—such as inter-departmental committees—are introduced to upgrade strategic responses or address concerns that departments may be drifting down the scale of effectiveness at EU level (O'Mahony, 2012). This is an area where political staff are less directly involved unless a domestic controversy arises (personal interview). The increased significance of 'summitry' and the primacy of the European Council, however, brings the Taoiseach as head of government more centre stage in EU affairs, and by default also the Department of the Taoiseach. It has developed significant capacity in the EU area relative to the department's size, and this is evident in the appointment of a second secretary general encompassing EU affairs in 2011 and an EU and International Division headed by an assistant secretary. An explanation for this lies in the proliferation of crises and complexity over the past decade, whereby the EU/IMF programme and Brexit have intensified the relationship with EU institutions and communications with other heads of state.

The UK's referendum decision to leave the EU on 23 June 2016 sent shockwaves throughout the Irish government. The ensuing Brexit process, its potential impact for Ireland and attendant intricacies with the Northern Ireland Protocol have ensured that Brexit remains on the political-administrative agenda. Between 2016 and 2020 the triumvirate of ministers within the 'holy trinity' for EU affairs was actively engaged in Brexit business, with the minister for foreign affairs, Simon Coveney, holding special responsibility. While much of the substantial work and diplomacy was conducted by the Department of Foreign Affairs, an EU Strategic Planning Unit also supported the Taoiseach and strategic engagement with EU partners. Brexit was characterised by urgency and stalemate, depending on the negotiation progress, and a highly centralised approach evolved to accommodate this within the core executive. This was representative of a concentration in official work and bilateral meetings with EU counterparts, including the Commission's Brexit Taskforce. Cabinet sub-committees were less involved in Brexit and this is evident in that only three meetings and three SOGs were held under 'Cabinet Committee C' (EU including Brexit). The sensitive issues were dealt with either in full cabinet—based on 'under the arm' memoranda brought directly by Simon Coveney—or else periodically by a small informal group drawn from the 'holy trinity' departments (personal interview). In general, the conduct of EU affairs within the core executive raises questions about executive-legislative relations but it does not appear to be contested by coalition parties in office to date. An exception—or at least a strain on this consensus—is in dealing with the full rigours of an economic crisis.

Enduring Economic Crisis and Navigating the Bailout

Economic crisis presents strong political pressures for central authority and a tendency for more politicised decision-making within executives (Parrado, 2012). After floundering in the initial phases of the global financial crisis, the resultant EU/IMF ('Troika') bailout in November 2010 demanded a coherent response and the Fine Gael-Labour coalition taking office in March 2011 reconfigured core structures. Central to the government's approach in securing the success of the assistance programme was an avoidance of paralysis in decision-making processes, both at home and abroad, and nurturing coalition relations to avoid political instability (Connaughton, 2016, p. 172). Although the Troika visits were primarily managed by officials in the Department of Finance, the Taoiseach and Tánaiste's staff were pivotal in setting up a much more formalised cabinet committee system supervised by the Taoiseach's programme manager, splitting the Department of Finance to accommodate a new Department of Public Expenditure and Reform (DPER), and creating a 'super' cabinet committee called the Economic Management Council (EMC) that was coordinated by advisers rather than civil servants.

The EMC was composed of a select membership of party leaders (Taoiseach and Tánaiste) and their senior advisers, and the ministers and secretaries general for finance and public expenditure and reform. Once created it assumed a different routine to other cabinet sub-committees and it was not supported by a parallel SOG. Between March 2011 and May 2016, the EMC met 153 times, which far exceeded the meetings of any other medium outside of cabinet. In several respects the EMC represented a forum for resource exchange between parties and decision-making which served to facilitate the communication between the two finance ministers who were central to driving the requirements of the Troika programme (Connaughton, 2018, p. 123). It could also be likened to the clearing house nature of the 'Quad' which served as a forum for resolving coalition issues and avoiding conflict at the cabinet table in the UK's coalition government in 2010 (Hazell & Yong, 2012; see also Chap. 4 in this volume).

An important feature of the EMC's operation was that the Fine Gael and Labour parties participated on equal terms in economic policy-making (Gilmore, 2016; personal interviews). Overall, the EMC was a very tight structure that did not leak but it inevitably drew criticism from those orbiting outside its domain. It considered proposals a week ahead of the government meeting, even though it was formally a committee that was not 'empowered to reach decisions on its own' (Leahy, 2013, p. 112). It could be argued that what was offensive to those outside the EMC was the reality it mirrored, since it brought together the most powerful actors in government in an inner cabinet. Or, as expressed in interviews, 'One of the things that is not understood very well about how the government functions is that ultimately it is made up of a few key individuals' and 'at any given time you couldn't include more than half a dozen people in that group between politicians and civil servants' (personal interviews). As the Troika exited the crisis subsided and the EMC's role diminished, though it continued to provide a template for arbitration and strategy on sensitive economic issues with sizeable political implications. Between 2016 and 2020 the disposition was towards more informal arrangements in managing the minority Fine Gael government with Independents.

The COVID-19 Era

In considering how economic and societal change affects the functioning of government, the COVID-19 pandemic stands out as a crisis 'in extremis rather than sui generis' (Ansell et al., 2021, p. 949). The governance of the pandemic has projected more attention on how specific policy decisions are reached and how public health guidance is made. From March

2020 a caretaker government steered the COVID response until the programme for government was agreed on 26 June, at which point the entire leadership base for the pandemic shifted in the new Fianna Fáil, Fine Gael and Green Party administration. The structures remained largely intact, however, and from 2020 they consisted of a governance apparatus encompassing a range of advisory groups feeding into a National Public Health Emergency Team (NPHET) chaired by the Chief Medical Officer (CMO) who, along with several of his colleagues, became a household figure, much to the grievance of some of the political actors. NPHET's advice is channelled upwards to the core executive through the Minister of Health and a cabinet sub-committee on COVID-19 (serviced by a SOG whose chair acts as secretary to the cabinet committee) which assesses impacts and oversees a cross-government response in advance of recommendations to the government. Further, briefings are organised with the CMO, SG (Taoiseach) and chiefs of staff to give ministers outside the inner core an opportunity to engage.

Two developments are worth noting. Firstly, the pervasiveness of the pandemic has placed scientific and public health advice centre stage, which has at times led to tensions between the advisory role of NPHET and the political-administrative leadership with decision-making responsibility. Instances arose whereby senior government figures felt blindsided by recommendations from NPHET 'coming out of the blue' or without 'any preparatory [ground] work' (Chambers, 2021, p. 186). A particular example of this occurred in October 2020, when NPHET recommendations to reintroduce lockdown were leaked to national media before the cabinet sub-committee met or before the Taoiseach was informed. This resulted in pushback from senior figures in the core executive and commentary from ministers to the effect that 'cabinet was being usurped' and 'there was a sensitivity in the political system because we were responding to media rather than a report and analysis' (Chambers, 2021, pp. 179–180).

Secondly, aside from any discombobulation resulting from leaks and missteps outside Government Buildings, the coalition itself did not opt for a tight coordination mechanism—such as the EMC—to arbitrate conflict or work strategically, despite the more extreme circumstances of the COVID crisis. The closest to this is a cabinet sub-committee on government coordination which meets on Monday evenings in advance of cabinet, but which appears to be an informal structure that does not have a secretariat supporting it in the way senior advisers worked within the EMC. The coalition party leaders attend, as does the SGG and the chiefs of staff. The ministers for Finance and DPER may attend on occasion but given the centrality of their positions that is not optimal for communications flow. Arguably, the number of parties to this government leads to greater complexity and presents a rationale for having clearer political structures within the core executive (personal interview).

Conclusion

This chapter began by referencing a centenary of Irish self-government that, despite its tumultuous start, has endured with stable democratic institutions. Through the lens of the concept of the core executive it proceeded to explore the landscape of Government Buildings and observe the inner networks of those residing within. In the case of Ireland, the 30-year period during which the core executive studies literature has been evolving aligns with distinctive developments in executive politics and policymaking: the shift to coalition and/or minority governments, the increased impact of Europeanisation, and complex, multiple and interrelated crises. The latter is most evident in the 'war footing' status imposed by COVID-19, which places considerable pressure on the capacities of the actors, structures and procedural norms in a small state. While it remains the case that cabinet is the final arbiter, a probing of 'who does what' and 'with what resources' both within and outside the confines of the cabinet room provides a fuller account of how government operates in Ireland. Although coalition places constraints on the Taoiseach as 'chief', the incumbent remains the most significant figure within executive politics and the Department of the Taoiseach plays a primary role in supporting the office and coordinating the government agenda. Government business is advanced in multiple fora, dissected in the inner courts—selectively populated by party leaders, senior ministers, elite bureaucrats and chiefs of staff—and scrutinised by an omnipresent media.

Note

1. The author would like to thank those who participated in interviews for their helpful insights and commentary.

References

Ansell, C., Sørensen, E., & Torfing, J. (2021). The COVID-19 Pandemic as a Game Changer for Public Administration and Leadership? The Need for Robust Governance Responses to Turbulent Problems. *Public Management Review, 23*(7), 949–960.

Chambers, R. (2021). *A State of Emergency: The Story of Ireland's Covid Crisis*. Harper Collins Ireland.

Connaughton, B. (2005). The Impact of Coalition Government on Politico-administrative Relations in IRELAND 1981–2002. In B. G. Peters, T. Verheijen, & L. Vass (Eds.), *Politico-administrative Relations under Coalition Governments* (pp. 247–272). NISPAcee.

Connaughton, B. (2010). Glorified Gofers, Policy Experts or Good Generalists: A Classification of the Roles of the Irish Ministerial Adviser. *Irish Political Studies, 25*(3), 347–369.

Connaughton, B. (2012). Ministers and Their Departments: Inside the 'black box' of the Policy-Making Process. In E. O'Malley & M. MacCarthaigh (Eds.), *Governing Ireland: From Cabinet Government to Delegated Governance* (pp. 61–87). IPA.

Connaughton, B. (2016). Confronting Interrelated Crises in the EU's Western Periphery: Steering Ireland-EU Relations Back to the Centre. In J. M. Magone, B. Laffan, & C. Schweiger (Eds.), *Core periphery Relations in the European Union* (pp. 166–178). Routledge.

Connaughton, B. (2018). Ireland: Steps Towards a Political Coordination Role for Ministerial Advisers. In R. Shaw & C. Eichbaum (Eds.), *Ministers, Minders and Mandarins: An International Study of Relationships at the Executive Summit of Parliamentary Democracies* (pp. 110–128). Edward Elgar.

Corbett, J., Veenendaal, W., & Connell, J. (2021). The Core Executive and Small States: Is Coordination the Primary Challenge? *Public Administration, 99*(1), 103–117.

Department of Taoiseach. (2021). *Strategy Statement 2021–2023*. Department of the Taoiseach.

Department of the Taoiseach. (2006). *Cabinet Handbook*. Department of the Taoiseach.

Farrell, B. (1971). *Chairman or Chief: The Role of Taoiseach in Irish Government*. Gill and Macmillan.

Gilmore, E. (2016). *Inside the Room: The Untold Story of Ireland's Crisis Government*. Merrion Press.

Hardiman, N., Regan, A., & Shayne, M. (2012). The Core Executive: The Department of Taoiseach and the Challenge of Policy Coordination. In E. O'Malley & M. MacCarthaigh (Eds.), *Governing Ireland: From Cabinet Government to Delegated Governance* (pp. 106–127). IPA.

Hazell, R., & Yong, B. (2012). *The Politics of Coalition: How the Conservative-Liberal Democrat Government Works.* Hart Publishing.

Heffernan, R. (2012). There's No Need for the '-isation': The Prime Minister is Merely Prime Ministerial. *Parliamentary Affairs, 66*(3), 636–645.

Hogan, J., & Murphy, M. (Eds.). (2021). *Policy Analysis in Ireland.* Policy Press.

Katzenstein, P. (1985). *Small States in World Markets.* Cornell University Press.

Laffan, B., & O'Mahony, J. (2007). Managing Europe from an Irish Perspective: Critical Junctures and the Increasing Formalisation of the Core Executive in Ireland. *Public Administration, 85*(1), 167–188.

Leahy, P. (2013). *The Price of Power—Inside Ireland's Crisis Coalition.* Penguin Ireland.

Little, C. (2021). Change Gradually, Then All At Once: The General Election of February 2020 in the Republic of Ireland. *West European Politics, 44*(3), 714–723.

MacCarthaigh, M. (2020). The Role of the 'centre' in Public Service Reform. *Administration, 68*(4), 27–40.

Maguire, M. (2008). *The Civil Service and the Revolution in Ireland, 1912–38: Shaking the Blood Stained Hand of Mr Collins.* Manchester University Press.

Moody, T. W., & Martin, F. (2011). *The Course of Irish History.* Mercier Press.

O'Halpin, E. (1997). Partnership Programme Managers in the Reynolds/Spring Coalition, 1993–4: An Assessment. *Irish Political Studies, 12*(1), 78–91.

O'Mahony, J. (2012). When Europe Hits Home: Government and the European Union. In E. O'Malley & M. MacCarthaigh (Eds.), *Governing Ireland: From Cabinet Government to Delegated Governance* (pp. 190–214). IPA.

O'Malley, E. (2012). The Apex of Government: Cabinet and Taoiseach in Operation. In E. O'Malley & M. MacCarthaigh (Eds.), *Governing Ireland: From Cabinet Government to Delegated Governance* (pp. 35–60). IPA.

O'Malley, E., & Martin, S. (2018). The Government and the Taoiseach. In J. Coakley & M. Gallagher (Eds.), *Politics in the Republic of Ireland* (6th ed., pp. 243–269). PSAI/Routledge.

Parrado, S. (2012). The Executive at Work During Times of Crisis. In M. Lodge & K. Wegrich (Eds.), *Executive Politics in Times of Crisis* (pp. 197–216). Palgrave Macmillan.

Seyd, B. (2002). *Coalition Government in Britain: Lessons from Overseas.* Constitution Unit, UCL/Nuffield Foundation.

Walshe, J. (2014). *An Education: How an Outsider Became an Insider—and Learned what Really Goes on in Irish Government.* Penguin Ireland.

CHAPTER 6

New Zealand: The Core Within the Core

Richard Shaw and Rose Cole

INTRODUCTION

Arend Lijphart once described Aotearoa New Zealand as 'more Westminster than Westminster' (Lijphart, 1987, p. 97), such was the Pacific nation's fidelity to the original parliamentary template. Things have since changed, notably as a consequence of the adoption of a decidedly un-Westminster proportional representation electoral system in the mid-1990s, and because of state sector reforms which have both fragmented administrative arrangements and generated subsequent incentives to (re)centralise control.

This chapter will unfold at two levels. Broadly, we explore the implications for the New Zealand core executive of the twin processes of electoral

---

R. Shaw (✉)
School of People, Environment and Planning, Massey University,
Palmerston North, New Zealand
e-mail: R.H.Shaw@massey.ac.nz

R. Cole
School of Business and Government, Victoria University of Wellington,
Wellington, New Zealand
e-mail: rose.cole@vuw.ac.nz

© The Author(s), under exclusive license to Springer Nature
Switzerland AG 2022
K. Kolltveit, R. Shaw (eds.), *Core Executives in a Comparative Perspective*, Understanding Governance,
https://doi.org/10.1007/978-3-030-94503-9_6

law reform (which has institutionalised policy moderation, if not Lijphartian consensus) and public sector restructuring (which has complexified the business of coordinating government activity). Other imperatives have been in play, but in our view these two have had the most significant impact on the institutional organisation of the core executive and the trading of resources therein in recent decades.

To gain a more focused sense of what all of this means, we also examine interactions and arrangements within a specific core executive location: the ministerial office. New Zealand cabinet ministers' offices are critical executive nodes: information flows through them and consequential strategic and tactical conversations take place within them. They are one of the places where attempts to coordinate politics and administration occur: what goes on in them reveals a good deal about the state of the core executive.

The structure of the chapter is as follows. We begin by describing two sets of institutional changes that have created particular challenges for the New Zealand core executive and set out the modes, mechanisms and instruments deployed in response. We then zero in on the ministerial office as an important (and understudied) location of efforts to coordinate political and administrative resources in the pursuit of ministers' objectives. We bring to this section a focus on the role of the departmental private secretary, for if the ministerial office has received relatively little attention in the core executive literature, so too has the role of the public servant who connects that institution with the standing bureaucracy. Finally, we reflect on the ongoing utility of the concept of the core executive given the contemporary condition of the New Zealand state. Throughout, we draw on primary research undertaken with ministers, ministerial advisers and public servants—particularly in the context of the ministerial office—in New Zealand.

The New Zealand Core Executive: Changes and Challenges

Rhodes' definition of the core executive as all those '*organizations and procedures which coordinate central government policies, and act as final arbiters of conflict between different parts of the government machine*' (Rhodes, 1995, p. 12; original emphasis) suggests an institutional ecosystem comprising three elements: actors, forums and rules-in-play.

The primary actors in the New Zealand core executive are prime ministers, ministers, public servants of various stripes and ministerial (or political) advisers. The formal arenas in which these players of the game interact include cabinet and its committees, cross-ministerial teams, the (prime) ministerial office and central agencies including the Treasury, Department of the Prime Minister and Cabinet (DPMC) and the Public Service Commission. Structuring relationships within and across those institutions are sundry formal and informal rules-of-the game, encompassing principles for the operation of cabinet government (found in the Cabinet Manual), the political agreements upon which multi-party and/or minority governments rest and the miscellaneous statutory requirements regarding strategic and financial planning in the public sector.

The difficulty with this sort of description is the same as that which attaches to any organisational chart: it tells you where everything is but reveals little of the actual workings of the core executive, and nothing at all regarding the degree to which these arrangements are historically contingent. To get at those matters requires an examination of two political-administrative processes that have significantly shaped the way in which things are done down-under.

Chronologically, the first of these was the re-engineering of the public sector. In its initial iteration that process, which has been bubbling away since the mid-1980s, was informed by an *ex ante* theoretical diagnosis of bureaucratic distemper based on new institutional economics, public choice, agency theory and transaction cost economics (Boston et al., 1996). The corresponding prescription for structural reform included the corporatisation of public trading departments (and the subsequent privatisation of many of these), the institutional division of policy and operations (and the devolution of the latter to non-departmental providers) and a tightening of the accountability regime applied to public servants (through the introduction of time-limited employment contracts for top civil servants, performance-based budgeting and a shift from relational to classical forms of contracting for services rendered).

The New Zealand version of the hollowing out of the state (Rhodes, 2007) created a public sphere in which networks of purchasers, providers, interests and actors jostled for resources on a jumbled landscape of '[c]ontracts, partnerships, franchising and private financial arrangements' (Dahlström et al., 2011, p. 5). It also threw up significant coordination challenges and, on the political demand side, a corresponding need for additional advisory capability regarding, for instance, the purchase of outputs from competing providers. To a significant degree, subsequent change processes (more on which shortly) have amounted to a series of attempts to address, if not ameliorate, these challenges.

The second part of the story concerns changes made to New Zealand's electoral rules in the mid-1990s. Briefly, in 1993, and largely in response to executive arrogance on both the centre-left and centre-right, New Zealand's voters opted—via two referenda—to adopt the mixed-member proportional (MMP) system as the basis for the election of the national legislature.

In the context of this chapter, the major consequence has been the demise of single-party majority governments. With the exception of the administration formed after the 2020 general election, which was the first single-party majority government since the adoption of MMP, the shift has consistently produced the sorts of minority and/or multi-party administrations more familiar to the parliamentary democracies of Western Europe than to those of Westminster.

This has various implications for the business of governing. For one thing, securing and maintaining a single government agenda in multi-party and/or non-majority governments is more demanding. The seams of a government stitched together from different parties are subject to particular pressures, particularly if one accepts Kam and Indriðason's reflection that 'cabinet members, the PM included, are at once colleagues and rivals' (2005, p. 332). The challenges associated with achieving coherence and cohesion play out in other ways, including when a portfolio is split between ministers from different parties. In these sorts of contexts the incentives and opportunities for 'individual ministers … to "drift" from the overall government policy in their departments' (Bäck et al., 2019, p. 150) are perhaps greater than when ministers are members of a single party.

Minority governments, which have become the norm in New Zealand, confront particular challenges. Those administrations have to seek, secure and actively maintain the support of other parliamentary parties, and the development of various procedural and substantive means of doing so (see below) has been a particular characteristic of the adaptation of the New Zealand core executive to the governing environment ushered in by the new electoral rules.

Rising to the Occasion: Modes, Mechanisms and Instruments

Some of the responses to these challenges have long been part of the governance toolkit in New Zealand and have simply been adapted to the new settings. Where the necessary implements were not to hand, however, they had to be created, and so several of the mechanisms detailed below are innovations triggered by the new institutional 'architectonics' (Hood, 2011) that have emerged from a refashioned electoral and administrative state.

Partly as a rejoinder to the centrifugal effects of the first generation of state sector reforms a second tranche of changes has recently been implemented via legislation intended to enable the public service to function as 'a single system by [creating] new organisational forms, leadership arrangements, and a modernised framework for public service employment' (Hughes, 2019, p. 3). The critical initiatives, at least as far as the business of coordination is concerned, are:

- the Public Service Leadership Team, which comprises all departmental chief executives and provides strategic leadership across the public service;
- the Public Service Leaders Group (effectively a senior executive service), membership of which is drawn from across the sector and comprises senior and other influential officials; and
- interdepartmental (or joint) ventures, a distinct form of public service organisation headed by a board comprising several chief executives and whose purpose is to strategically combine resources in attempts to tackle cross-cutting policy challenges.[1]

Writ large, these and other initiatives (the broader suite encompasses the statutory codification of principles and expectations and machinery of government changes) are part of the seemingly perennial attempt to better coordinate policy, planning, budgeting and delivery.

Reactions to the challenges posed by MMP fall loosely into three clusters. The first contains the different forms of political agreement developed to underpin multi-party and/or non-majority governments. Formal coalition agreements are decided between partners in a multi-party executive; confidence and supply agreements are negotiated by a governing party (or parties) requiring the support of another parliamentary party (or parties) to secure the Treasury benches; and cooperation agreements and memoranda of understanding are used to lock in parliamentary support beyond the level required for securing the confidence of the House (see Boston, 2009).

Twenty-five years ago none of these governance implements existed in New Zealand, but they are now central to the construction and functioning of administrations. Specifics vary, but in general terms such instruments set out parties' and government's policy aspirations; identify areas in which governing partners will cooperate (and those in which they might maintain distinctive stances); specify the allocation of portfolios and distinguish cabinet from non-cabinet ministers; describe the procedures for managing the business of governing and resolving conflict; determine who receives cabinet papers; provide for consultation between government ministers and support parties' spokespeople and so on. They are, in effect, political bargains which structure the coordination of political parties' executive, legislative and political resources (Boston, 2011).

The second category concerns the codification of cabinet decision-making as it has evolved in the post-MMP era. From a core executive perspective, the main items of interest are those related to the conventions and practices associated with collective cabinet responsibility. Collective responsibility continues to apply but has been modified in two key respects. First, the Cabinet Manual's 'agree-to-disagree' provisions permit parties to a coalition government, in certain circumstances, 'to agree to take different policy positions in public and in Parliament, including on legislative matters' (Boston & Bullock, 2009, p. 40). Second, in an arrangement characterised by a former prime minister (Palmer, 2006, p. 34) 'selective collective responsibility', ministers from parliamentary support parties who sit outside of cabinet are bound by collective responsibility only in relation to their portfolio areas.

Finally, the advent of the ministerial adviser can also be considered an institutional response to the miscellaneous challenges associated with new executive configurations. In political terms ministerial advisers take on 'the "backroom" stuff' (Eichbaum & Shaw, 2010, p. 125)—negotiations around government formation, ironing out policy differences between partners, discussing parliamentary tactics with support parties and so on—that now underpins executive politics and policy-formation but which is well beyond the public service pale. That type of political labour was generally not a requirement before the mid-1990s; it is now institutionalised.

The Core Within the Core: Who Does What and with Which Resources?

Thus far, we have focused on the sorts of core executive arenas and arrangements that conventionally feature in responses to Rhodes' questions, 'Who does what, and with what resources?' (Rhodes, 2007, p. 1247). But we are conscious that while there is a substantial literature—including several of the chapters in this volume—regarding the resources of political and administrative leaders and the various institutional markets in which these are traded (Burch & Holliday, 2004; Dahlström et al., 2011; Lindquist, 2006), much less has been written about those core executive actors further down the chain of command. Furthermore, while we subscribe to the standard position on prime ministerial predominance (Heffernan, 2003), it strikes us that captains always get more attention than their teammates. At the risk of mixing metaphors, a focus on the highest executive court risks overlooking goings-on within those smaller retinues that cluster around the courtiers themselves, whose entourages may be less glamorous but no less pivotal to the achievement of political objectives. In other words, in our view the ministerial office—the core within the core—has not received the attention from core executive scholars it merits, and so it is to that place that we now go.

The Ministerial Office

The ministerial office in New Zealand comprises a combination of impartial public servants and political appointees. Staff usually number a Senior Private Secretary (who provides personal, political and administrative support, including day-to-day management of all office staff); at least one Press Secretary to manage media and communications; one or more political advisers who furnish political and policy advice; one or more private secretaries seconded from departments; and a receptionist. While it may be that New Zealand ministers' offices now approximate what Maley (2018) characterises as a 'partisan' ministerial office (i.e., one dominated by political staff) rather than a neutral (dominated by civil servants) or hybrid (both partisan and professional advisers) type, nonetheless both political and professional advisers co-exist, and it is the relationship between the two we wish to delve into.

The Private Secretary

Private secretaries have been a resource in ministers' offices since the introduction of Westminster-style governance in New Zealand in the nineteenth century. The Cabinet Manual states that ministers are required to engage with the public service through departmental chief executives (DPMC, 2017); this engagement is achieved through the services of a private secretary seconded from the relevant portfolio department, who is the channel for advice and information between the minister's office and the department. 'Advice' broadly includes making recommendations on departmental briefings; providing subject matter expertise related to the minister's portfolio; clarifying issues for the minister; the coordination and delivery of departmental policy advice and providing policy advice and analysis (Cole, 2020a).

Prior to the introduction of ministerial advisers (see below), private secretaries were the minister's preeminent adviser with the associated level of access. The advent of the former, however, has crowded out the advisory function so that, these days, on a day-to-day basis private secretaries' attention is focussed on the flurry of administrative activities such as commissioning and checking departmental advice for quality and risk … coordinating departmental input into responses to parliamentary questions, ministerial correspondence and media releases. As a resource for the minister, the private secretary is expected to be a perambulating compendium of in-depth and up-to-date knowledge of all matters pertaining to departmental advice: formally, they are important conduits between those core executive actors who propose and those who dispose. Unsurprisingly, therefore, the capacities traditionally associated with a departmental 'mandarin'—notably discretion, impartiality and possession of sufficient 'nous' to navigate the ambiguities of the political-administrative milieu—are critical.

As conduits for advice and information between the minister's office and the department there is a duality in the nature of the role, insofar as the private secretary both represents the authority of the minister to the department and maintains the position of the department in the minister's office. In the former capacity a good private secretary can furnish insights regarding the minister's preferences and direction of thinking that enhance a department's ability to effectively respond to the needs of the political principal. In the latter they are expected to have a solid understanding of the machinery of government and of how their department works, so as to ensure that information is sourced for the minister efficiently. A background in policy advice is not essential, and private secretaries may be selected with skills that meet the minister's needs (e.g., data analysis or expertise in the portfolio area). Ironically, a private secretary with specific expertise may find their ability to provide advice is minimised by being cast in the role of administrator, and at the lowest level in the informal office hierarchy (Cole, 2020b).

As far as the ebb and flow of daily work is concerned, private secretaries engage most frequently with ministerial advisers, who act as a proxy for a busy and preoccupied minister. Immersion in the politicised environment that is the contemporary ministerial office means that private secretaries must be clear about their role as neutral public servants. In most situations they are supported by their political colleagues: they may, for example, be asked to absent themselves physically or mentally if political matters are being discussed (Cole, 2020c).

The relationship between private secretaries and ministerial advisers is significant for policy coordination. Departmental advice is processed by the private secretary and then is distributed to the adviser for review and to the minister for consideration. That intermediate step institutionalises the possibility for the politicisation of public service advice, and tensions can arise when there is disagreement about the quality or sufficiency of advice provided by the department. In effect, it falls to private secretaries to manage the risk of administrative politicisation (Eichbaum & Shaw, 2008), taking on the role of departmental gatekeeper by defending the integrity of departmental advice rather than changing it in response to pressure from ministerial advisers to render it more politically palatable (Cole, 2020b).

Moreover, as the last politically neutral reviewer in the departmental advice delivery chain, private secretaries must also manage the risk of functional politicisation (Eichbaum & Shaw, 2008), which arises when departmental advice is perceived as overly responsive and insufficiently responsible. The personal resources of private secretaries, such as relationship management skills, resilience and political-tactical acuity, are critical to being effective in this particular role (Cole, 2020c).

Finally, somewhat unusually, in New Zealand ministerial offices are physically located away from departments in an executive wing known as the Beehive. From a departmental perspective (and perhaps also from the point of view of those who value contestable policy-making), the physical proximity of the private secretary to the minister makes them a key resource, able to provide insights into and potentially to influence the minister's thinking and needs. In this respect private secretaries are an important counterweight to the advantage ministerial advisers tend to enjoy by virtue of their physical and institutional proximity to ministers. And as the following section demonstrates, the countervailing presence of the cadre of departmental private secretaries is no small thing given the institutionalisation of partisan advisers in the contemporary executive court.

The Ministerial Adviser

These days, those advisers are key members of the ministerial court, where they are deployed to various ends and in multiple contexts. Perhaps most immediately, ministerial advisers help ministers manage the demands of the job. If the institution of cabinet government is under pressure (Bevir & Rhodes, 2006; Laughrin, 2009), that load is felt most keenly in the ministerial office, whose incumbents confront an unrelenting media environment, an electorate that is intolerant of uncertainty and ambiguity and an adversarial political climate in which changes of mind are seen as weakness and there is little time for careful consideration of or genuine debate on complex policy issues. Ministerial advisers are an important source of support with this, including by taking on the role (for some ministers) of confessor or confidante and by coordinating with other staff both within the office and in other ministers' demesnes (Shaw & Eichbaum, 2014).

They also expedite tactical and strategic political leadership. Ministers turn to their advisers for counsel on and assessments of what is politically feasible. An adviser can 'think the unthinkable, challenge accepted orthodoxies, propose alternatives and review the Government's overall strategy and priorities' (Elcock, 2002, p. 2). Advisers, then, are one of the ways in which political executives seek (with varying degrees of success) to 'impose more direction, control and coordination over policy through less unwieldy mechanisms than the traditional line departments' (Aberbach & Rockman, 1988, p. 9).

They are also important resources in the context of political–administrative relations. The assumption is often that ministers are leery of the motives of civil servants and duly deploy their political staff as part of the process of 'reasserting the primacy of democracy over bureaucracy' (Aucoin, 1990, p. 115). An adviser's job, from this perspective, is to insulate ministers' political imperatives against the cold water of bureaucratic obfuscation dressed up as impartial advice. However, while the orthodox view may be that political advisers threaten the impartiality of the civil service (Aucoin, 2012; Dahlström, 2009)—principally through interventions against which the private secretary is seen as an important bulwark—a different proposition is that by taking care of the partisan function they (a) enable public servants to concentrate on the provision of responsible competence and (b) add an element of contestability to the policy process that would otherwise be missing (Shaw, 2020).

All of which suggests that ministerial advisers require a broad range of competencies. A little counter-intuitively, the evidence suggests that ministers prioritise policy-related skills over those associated with more obviously partisan functions. In a study of current and former New Zealand ministers, for instance, participants placed the highest premium on those advisers who had the procedural and substantive policy-related skills needed to work effectively within a contingent executive environment (Shaw & Eichbaum, 2014). A commitment to the minister's priorities and the government's policy agenda were taken as givens, but most participants did not attach great significance to the party political affiliation of their advisers and little emphasis was given to the need for ideological compatibility. In the ministerial court in New Zealand, it seems, solving problems and clearing policy and political logjams are more important than doctrinal orthodoxy.

Collegial Cooperation or Trouble in the Office?

In Chap. 2 of this volume the point was made that surprisingly little attention is paid in the literature to that part of Rhodes' (1995) standard definition of the core executive that refers to the arbitration of 'conflict between different parts of the government machinery'. In earlier sections we described the range of political instruments used to structure political relationships and resource exchanges and to defuse or manage conflict, within the executive court (coalition and cooperation agreements, the Cabinet Manual and so forth). Within the confines of the ministerial office, however, things are often less clear cut.

To be sure, the formal picture seems straightforward enough. The Public Service Act (2020) requires private secretaries to adhere to a series of public service principles, including political neutrality, the provision of free and frank advice, the fostering of a culture of open government and the proactive stewardship of the public service. Ministerial advisers are also included in the scope of the Act, with the obvious exception of the provisions regarding merit appointments. In addition, a series of behavioural expectations are designed into the dedicated Code of Conduct for Ministerial Staff issued in 2017, which enjoin ministerial advisers to act fairly, lawfully, ethically and honestly; to demonstrate respect for the role of Parliament and to recognise the duty of public servants to provide free, frank and impartial advice to ministers.

It is important to acknowledge that interactions between advisers and private secretaries within the office ecosystem are often collegial and cooperative. Much of this stems from the fact that both sorts of administrative agents serve the same principal. Thus, both parties are engaged to support the minister achieve their policy goals—the ministerial adviser approved by the minister and engaged by Ministerial and Secretariat Services within the Department of Internal Affairs, and the private secretary supplied by the department and approved directly by the minister. To a degree, too, the functional roles of advisers and private secretaries mirror and complement each other. Both have a gatekeeping function, for example, controlling the flow of information to the minister. Ministerial advisers assess the extent to which advice might enhance or impact negatively on the minister's policy goals, while the private secretary ensures the provision of high quality, 'free and frank' departmental advice to the minister. In a sense, both also act as ministerial minders, ensuring—from their respective institutional vantages—that policy and reputational risks are managed. For the private secretary this entails ensuring that administrative matters are efficiently managed so that departmental advice and ministerial correspondence are well commissioned and processed within agreed timeframes (such that the minister is seen as effective and responsive).

Therefore, when the relationship is a collaborative one, the demarcation between the political and bureaucratic spheres is clear and public service advice proceeds to the minister with complementary comment or input from the ministerial adviser. But things do not always work that way. For one thing, formal role descriptions may or may not exist (see Cole, 2021), and it is far from clear that agreed understandings regarding the rules of engagement across the professional–partisan divide are the norm in most ministerial offices. Indeed, one study (Shaw & Eichbaum, 2014) found that only a quarter of ministers had expressly established protocols governing contact between ministerial advisers and departmental officials. In other words, institutional arrangements within many (if not most) ministerial offices are as likely to permit conflict as they are to foster collegiality.

Furthermore, while the structure of the ministerial office formally recognises ministerial advisers and private secretaries as equals in supporting the minister, in practice an informal functional hierarchy privileges the former at the expense of the latter. Thus, communication between the private secretary and minister is more often than not via the ministerial adviser—as the minister's closest adviser, advisers are often also responsible for relaying the minister's instructions or requests to private secretaries. This delegated authority suggests an asymmetrical power relationship in which the ministerial adviser (who has greater cachet as the primary driver of policy coordination and delivery) sits above the private secretary (whose primary responsibilities are for administrative matters).

The demands of a 24/7 media cycle and the relentless scrutiny of caucus, the opposition and the public are such that the working environment in a ministerial office is highly demanding. In these testing conditions private secretaries, as departmental proxies, are sometimes viewed as obstructive and bear the brunt of negative reactions from the minister or their political advisers. All the same, the traffic is not all one way. For one thing, despite the challenges they face by virtue of occupying a subordinate role in an intensely partisan environment, private secretaries are not without both personal and institutional resources. In addition, while ministerial advisers' proximity to and relationship with ministers may afford them significant power and influence, they rely upon private secretaries for the smooth, efficient and constant supply of advice from departments.

THE CONTEMPORARY STATE OF PLAY

Stepping out of the ministerial office and back into the wider environment, what can be said regarding the broader socio-cultural context within which the New Zealand core executive is located, and of the extent to which the concept of the core executive continues to make sense of that executive landscape?

To our eyes, the synchronous ebb and flow of centralising and decentralising currents is perhaps the most prominent feature of the New Zealand context. It is not uncommon for centralisation and decentralisation to be treated if they are zero-sum ontological points: things are either one thing or the other. In fact, 'things' are much more likely to be differentiated, and to exist in flux if not outright tension.[2]

In New Zealand this is manifest in a process of political consolidation (a gathering of various resources into the core and to particular actors therein) that plays out in a political-administrative context which—the best efforts of institutional engineers notwithstanding—remains stubbornly disaggregated. In that context the recent batch of statutory changes described above might best be thought of not as attempts to (re)centralise within the bureaucracy (there has not been, for instance, any wholesale merging of departments, nor much suturing back together of the policy and delivery functions) but as evidence of the scope and magnitude of the coordination challenges created by decades of New Public Management reformist orthodoxy. True, there are some indications of the (at least partial) rehabilitation of centralisation as a credible and legitimate policy response, not least in the April 2021 decision to abolish twenty separate regional health authorities and to establish a single national authority (which will work in tandem with a parallel organisation for the indigenous Māori people). On balance, however, the New Zealand core executive continues to grapple with coordination challenges out on the administrative periphery, and the search for more robust alternatives to Bevir and Rhodes' (2006, p. 59) 'rubber levers of control' continues.

In that context, to what degree does the concept of the core executive still make sense of things? Certainly the classical focus on the top tables—the prime minister, ministers and senior civil servants, especially those in central agencies—remains utile (the more so following a decision in mid-2021 to establish an implementation unit in the DPMC, led by the deputy prime minister and tasked with overseeing policy delivery in key areas). In particular, in our view the asymmetric power variant of core executive studies (Marsh et al., 2003), which posits that power is contingent on the deployment of both personal resources and those which derive from institutional location, retains considerable explanatory salience.

That said, the environment in which those asymmetries play out has altered over recent decades. Structural changes have splintered institutions, generated a proliferation in principal-agent relationships and placed discretionary policy-making authority well beyond the immediate reach of state bureaucracies and their political bosses. We are not suggesting that there has been a fundamental transformation in the contours of the core executive: if anything, there is an inverse relationship between institutional disaggregation and attempts to accrete power at the centre. There has, however, been some diminution in the capacity of the centre to steer the policy process since the mid-1980s/early-1990s; at the very least, that process has become more challenging.

A similar but less publicly prominent process of political attenuation has taken place within the political executive. The New Zealand prime minister remains predominant, but in the post-MMP environment that predominance sits alongside the additional complexity that has been baked into the interdependent relationships on which the core executive rests. Under conditions of non-majority single-party government, especially, there exists the potential for countervailing, non-prime ministerial centres of power to emerge. Similar states of affairs can occur in single-party governments, of course (especially between prime ministers and their ministers of finance), but quite apart from intra-party politics New Zealand prime ministers—particularly those who lead multi-party governments—now routinely need to negotiate a more complex and sometimes fractious court. From time to time, the courtiers can be seen loitering around more than one crown.

Something is going on, too, apropos the nature of the resources needed to govern from the centre. There is a view (see Shaw & Eichbaum, 2020) that the exchange value of the responsible competence traditionally furnished by an impartial public service is depreciating as political demand grows for responsive competence. Insofar as the currency of the latter is appreciating, that may suggest that the relevant resources (itemised in earlier sections) are being traded in historically significant volumes.

To return to the central concern of core executive studies: insofar as this change is occurring, is it helping or hindering coordination? One view—prevalent in a recent survey of officials (Shaw & Eichbaum, 2020)—is that there has been a partisan turn which is hindering the business of good governance: advice flows between departments and their ministers are interrupted; political intrusions into the administration of freedom of information legislation are routine; and there is a counter-productive tension between abrasive ministerial advisers and public servants protective of their impartiality and operational autonomy. In other words, the core executive may be functioning but it is not in the best of health and its capacity to coordinate, much less resolve conflict, is compromised.

There is a second view (including amongst senior civil servants) which is rather more sanguine on the matter. This perspective has it that what is occurring is less inappropriate politicisation than legitimate contestation; that the emergence of a critical voice in the form of the ministerial adviser is simply one element of the wider 'transition from government to governance and the changing patterns of demand [which] jointly constitute the preconditions for a more or less competitive market for the supply of advice' (Shaw, 2020, p. 6). Contestability is now designed into the institutional fabric, and the challenge for the bureaucracy is not the spectre of politicisation so much as the need to sharpen its policy game in order to compete—with the attendant benefits that would produce for the core executive's net policy capability and capacity.

Conclusion

Three decades on from the introduction of the term 'core executive', in New Zealand the relevant particulars may have changed but the classificatory thrust of the concept remains relevant. Indeed, if Dunleavy and Rhodes hadn't coined it in 1990 someone would need to invent it now, particularly as its primary contribution—the admonition to scholars of executive government to look beyond what Bagehot might have called the dignified elements of the executive to the efficient ones—is probably more apposite in a post-COVID, post-NPM world than it was then.

Nonetheless, the implications of certain elements of the contemporary context for the explanatory capability of the core construct should not be glossed over. Chief amongst these is the opacity of the boundaries (if such they can any longer be called) between state and non-state entities. The first chapter of that story is one of executive actors attempting to wrangle a sprawling delivery landscape under some sort of control in the interests of improving the coordination of policy delivery. But the second is an epistemological one. These days Rhodes' invitation to focus on 'who does what' and 'with what resources' seems to produce an ever-expanding cast of characters. In other words, the borders between state and non-state actors are not the only ones that have become tricky to spot: the efforts of the centralisers notwithstanding, the frontier between the core executive and the rest is also increasingly difficult to locate.

Beyond such considerations, there is the more prosaic fact of the size and scope of the challenges faced by those who would join the executive court. Several of these have been discussed in this chapter. In addition there are the sundry 'large forces' (Roberts, 2013) that shape the environments that core executives must now navigate: 'masses of media' (Aucoin, 2012, p. 181) and a rising tide of public expectation are only some of the things contributing to a complex job. Perhaps it is no bad thing that the number and size of executive courts may also be expanding. More courtiers, rather than fewer, would seem sensible given the magnitude of the challenge—assuming, that is, that the resultant courtly behaviour is well coordinated.

NOTES

1. For details of the Public Service Act (2020) see https://www.publicservice.govt.nz/our-work/reforms/
2. We would like to thank R. A. W. Rhodes for this insight.

REFERENCES

Aberbach, J. D., & Rockman, B. A. (1988). Image IV Revisited: Executive and Political Roles. *Governance, 1*(1), 1–25.

Aucoin, P. (1990). Administrative Reform in Public Management: Paradigms, Principles, Paradoxes, and Pendulums. *Governance, 3*(2), 115–137.

Aucoin, P. (2012). New Political Governance in Westminster Systems: Impartial Public Administration and Management Performance at Risk. *Governance, 25*(2), 177–199.

Bäck, H., Teorell, J., & Lindberg, S. (2019). Cabinets, Prime Ministers, and Corruption: A Comparative Analysis of Parliamentary Governments in Post-War Europe. *Political Studies, 67*(1), 49–70.

Bevir, M., & Rhodes, R. A. W. (2006). Prime Ministers, Presidentialism and Westminster Smokescreens'. *Political Studies, 54*(4), 671–690.

Boston, J. (2009). Innovative Political Management: Multi-party Governance in New Zealand. *Policy Quarterly, 5*(2), 52–59.

Boston, J. (2011). Government Formation in New Zealand under MMP: Theory and Practice. *Political Science, 63*(1), 79–105.

Boston, J., & Bullock, D. (2009). Experiments in Executive Government Under MMP in New Zealand: Contrasting Approaches to Multiparty Governance. *New Zealand Journal of Public and International Law, 7*(1), 39–76.

Boston, J., Martin, J., Pallot, J., & Walsh, P. (1996). *Public Management: The New Zealand Model*. Oxford University Press.

Burch, M., & Holliday, I. (2004). The Blair Government and the Core Executive. *Government and Opposition, 39*(1), 1–21.

Cole, R. (2020a). Public Service Bargains and Non-partisan Ministerial Advisors: Servants of Two Masters. *International Review of Administrative Sciences.* https://doi.org/10.1177/0020852320955217

Cole, R. (2020b). The Public Servant in the Ministerial Office: A 'Ghost in the Machine'? *ECPR General Conference Comparing Core Executives: Actors, Processes, and Change*, August, 1–16. https://ecpr.eu/Events/Event/PaperDetails/54318

Cole, R. (2020c). Maintaining Neutrality in the Minister's Office. *Australian Journal of Public Administration.* https://doi.org/10.1111/1467-8500.12419

Cole, R. (2021). Non-Partisan Advisors in the Minister's Office—Ghosts in the Core Executive Machine? *Parliamentary Affairs.* https://doi.org/10.1093/pa/gsab050

Dahlström, C. (2009). *Political appointments in 18 Democracies, 1975–2007.* Quality of Government Institute.

Dahlström, C., Peters, B. G., & Pierre, J. (Eds.). (2011). *Steering from the Centre: Strengthening Political Control in Western Democracies.* University of Toronto Press.

Department of the Prime Minister and Cabinet. (2017). *Cabinet Manual.* Retrieved October 13, 2021, from https://www.dpmc.govt.nz/our-business-units/cabinet-office/supporting-work-cabinet/cabinet-manual

Dunleavy, P., & Rhodes, R. A. W. (1990). Core Executive Studies in Britain. *Public Administration, 68*(1), 3–28.

Eichbaum, C., & Shaw, R. (2008). Revisiting Politicization: Political Advisers and Public Servants in Westminster Systems. *Governance, 21*(3), 337–363.

Eichbaum, C., & Shaw, R. (2010). New Zealand. In C. Eichbaum & R. Shaw (Eds.), *Partisan Appointees and Public Servants: An International Analysis of the Role of the Political Adviser* (pp. 114–150). Edward Elgar.

Elcock, H. (2002). The Proper and Improper Use of Special Advisers. *Public Policy and Administration, 17*(4), 1–4.

Heffernan, R. (2003). Prime Ministerial Predominance? Core Executive Politics in the UK. *British Journal of Politics and International Relations, 5*(3), 347–372.

Hood, C. (2011). Risk and Government: The Architectonics of Blame Avoidance. In L. Skinns, S. Scott, & T. Cox (Eds.), *Risk* (pp. 62–84). Cambridge University Press.

Hughes, P. (2019). Public Service Legislation and Public Service Reform. *Policy Quarterly, 15*(4), 3–7.

Kam, C., & Indriðason, I. (2005). The Timing of Cabinet Reshuffles in Five Westminster Parliamentary Systems. *Legislative Studies Quarterly, 30*(3), 327–363.

Laughrin, D. (2009). Swimming for Their Lives: Waving or Drowning? A Review of the Evidence of Ministerial Overload and of Potential Remedies for It. *The Political Quarterly, 80*(3), 339–350.

Lijphart, A. (1987). The Demise of the Last Westminster System? Comments on the Report of New Zealand's Royal Commission on the Electoral System. *Electoral Studies, 6*(2), 97–103.

Lindquist, E. (2006). Organizing for Policy Implementation: The Emergence and Role of Implementation Units. *Journal of Comparative Policy Analysis, 8*(4), 311–324.

Maley, M. (2018). Understanding the Divergent Development of the Ministerial Office in Australia and the UK. *Australian Journal of Political Science*. https://doi.org/10.1080/10361146.2018.1450356

Marsh, D., Richards, D., & Smith, M. (2003). Unequal Plurality: Towards an Asymmetric Power Model of British Politics. *Government and Opposition, 38*(3), 306–332.

Palmer, G. (2006). The Cabinet, the Prime Minister and the Constitution: The Constitutional Background to Cabinet. *New Zealand Journal of Public and International Law, 4*(1), 1–36.

Rhodes, R. A. W. (1995). From Prime Ministerial Power to Core Executive. In R. A. W. Rhodes & P. Dunleavy (Eds.), *Prime Minister, Cabinet and Core Executive* (pp. 11–37). Macmillan.

Rhodes, R. A. W. (2007). Understanding Governance: Ten Years On. *Organization Studies, 28*(8), 1243–1264.

Roberts, A. (2013). *Large Forces: What's Missing in Public Administration*. CreateSpace Independent Publishing Platform.

Shaw, R. (2020). Ministerial Advisers, Contestability and Politicisation in the Core Executive in Westminster Systems. In H. Sullivan, H. Dickinson, & H. Henderson (Eds.), *The Palgrave Handbook of the Public Servant*. Palgrave Macmillan. https://doi.org/10.1007/978-3-030-03008-7_10-1

Shaw, R., & Eichbaum, C. (2014). Ministers, Minders and the Core Executive: Why Ministers Appoint Political Advisers in Westminster Contexts. *Parliamentary Affairs, 67*(3), 584–616.

Shaw, R., & Eichbaum, C. (2020). Still Friends? Revisiting New Zealand Public Servants' Perceptions of Ministerial Advisers. *Political Science*. https://doi.org/10.1080/00323187.2020.1742073

PART III

Core Executives in Continental Countries

CHAPTER 7

On a Wild Goose Chase? The (Core) Executive in Germany

Anna Hundehege and Thurid Hustedt

INTRODUCTION

Searching for the centre of power in the German political system can be a cumbersome endeavour, as the institutional grammar of post-war Germany follows a strong logic of decentralisation and dispersion: 'No concentration of power' was the narrative or baseline of the constitutional architects convening in the castle Herrenchiemsee, located on an island in the Bavarian Chiemsee, in 1948. Federalism (which institutional path goes back to the end of the 30-years' war in 1648) avoids the concentration of power on one level of governance. And the federal government was embedded in a trilateral governance framework resulting in dispersed power and bureaucratic capacity, as detailed in the course of this chapter.

We provide an up-to-date account of the dynamics in the German core executive at the end of the 'era Merkel'. The chapter seeks to paint the contours of the distribution of power and investigate the current shape of

---

A. Hundehege (✉) • T. Hustedt
Hertie School, Berlin, Germany
e-mail: a.hundehege@phd.hertie-school.org; Hustedt@hertie-school.org

© The Author(s), under exclusive license to Springer Nature Switzerland AG 2022
K. Kolltveit, R. Shaw (eds.), *Core Executives in a Comparative Perspective*, Understanding Governance,
https://doi.org/10.1007/978-3-030-94503-9_7

the core executive. Looking at the core executive or the overall governance system in formal terms, there have been no crucial changes for the last several decades. Yet, when taking informal developments into account, the picture becomes more complex. This duality structures the remainder of the chapter.

Accordingly, the next section explores the institutional setting, focusing on the role of the chancellery, the key features of politico-administrative relations and the key mechanisms of government coordination. Then follows a discussion of recent developments that, firstly, look into crisis management dynamics; secondly, into Europeanisation and summitry; and thirdly, into personalisation. The chapter ends with a conclusion on how best to characterise the current state of the core executive in Germany.

INSTITUTIONAL SETTING: THE CORE EXECUTIVE IN GERMANY

The Role of the Chancellor and the Chancellery Within the Federal Government

The German chancellor (*Bundeskanzler*) has a strong role in the German politico-administrative system, due to the nature of the constitutionally defined role and the degree of political control it gives the chancellor over her party (Busse & Hofmann, 2019, pp. 48 f.; Fleischer, 2011a, p. 55). According to Article 64 Basic Law, the chancellor chooses the ministers that form the cabinet, which consists of the chancellor and her ministers (Art. 62 Basic Law). In practice, coalition parties negotiate the division of portfolios and personnel choices during the process of coalition formation that follows federal elections. In a continuation of the pre-war constitution of the Weimar Republic, the Basic Law defines three principles guiding federal government operations: the *chancellor principle, the departmental principle and the cabinet principle*. The chancellor has the right to define the political guidelines (*Richtlinien*) of the government (Art. 65 Basic Law). This competence provides the chancellor with political discretion over when and how to intervene in policy-making and ensure policy coherence across departments (Busse & Hofmann, 2019, pp. 52 f.). However, this so-called *chancellor principle (Kanzlerprinzip)* is at odds with the *departmental principle (Ressortprinzip)*, which states that ministers are responsible and independent within their area of competence

(Art. 65 Basic Law). The departments have the right to participate in all decision-making processes related to their jurisdiction. Each department takes the lead (*Federführung*) on policy proposals within their area of competence and involves other ministries through consultation and co-signature (*Mitzeichnung*).

The chancellery (*Bundeskanzleramt*) supports the chancellor in her duties and prepares the cabinet meetings. The organisational structure of the chancellery serves strategic planning and the monitoring of policy-making in the ministerial departments. The chancellor and the chancellery's chief of staff (*Chef des Bundeskanzleramts* or *ChefBK*) have staff and communication units to prepare their meetings and advise them on public relations.

Three departments in the chancellery serve the inter-ministerial coordination of policy-making. The sections (*Spiegelreferate, mirror units*) in these departments monitor important developments in the ministerial departments, coordinate cross-cutting issues and inform the chancellor about politically salient policy proposals. Civil servants in these sections are usually seconded from ministerial departments on a rotational basis to improve coordination and to prepare for promotion in their home ministry (Fleischer, 2011b, 2021, p. 69). This monitoring does not involve hierarchical instruction and the loyalty of the civil servants often remains with their home ministry. In addition, one department is responsible for European affairs, one for internal administration and cross-cutting issues like relations with the parliament and the federal states (*Länder*) and one for the intelligence service (*Bundesnachrichtendienst*). A special task force prepares the G7 and G20 summits. In 2017, a new department for political strategy, innovation and digital policy was created to centrally coordinate digital policy and to strengthen planning and innovation capacity in the federal government. This tendency to centralise cross-cutting policy issues in the chancellery has, however, not led to strengthened clout in these areas (for better regulation, see Jantz & Veit, 2011).

Except during crisis management (see below), the departmental principle prevails in administrative practice (Fleischer, 2011a, pp. 59 f., 2021, p. 62). However, the departments anticipate that the chancellor principle will become relevant when inter-ministerial coordination is unsuccessful (Fleischer, 2011b, p. 201).

Due to limited resources and capacity, the chancellery cannot and is not supposed to be involved in the technical detail of policy proposals. The chancellery employs 716 staff (2020; agencies excluded), which is the smallest number among the ministries (followed by the Ministry for Family, Senior Citizens, Women and Youth with 750 staff). The budget of the chancellery is similar to the budget of a small German ministry (€100 Mio. in 2020).[1] On an administrative level, the chancellery does not exercise strong political control over the ministerial departments. Rather, the political influence of the chancellor is transmitted through party leadership and coalition politics. The strong political position of the chancellor is not backed with administrative capacity in the chancellery. The chancellery must therefore rely in the main on the political power of the chancellor within her party and the governing coalition to influence policy, rather than on policy expertise or administrative capacity. Although the *Richtlinienkompetenz* (§§ 1, 3 GOBReg) formally gives the chancellor the right to get involved in politically salient policy issues (to make them a *Chefsache*) such as high-level international summits, the chancellery relies on the cooperation of the lead ministry for technical expertise (Fleischer, 2011a, p. 60). Because of limited administrative resources in the chancellery, ministerial departments are quite autonomous within their jurisdiction and within the political framework set by the coalition agreement (see also Fleischer, 2011a).

With regards to policy-making, the ministerial departments are the most important actors in the German government. Most policy proposals are initiated in the departments, not the chancellery, because that is where policy expertise and administrative resources lie. Inter-ministerial conflicts are usually resolved at lower levels of the hierarchy prior to cabinet meetings (see below). The departments inform the chancellery of politically relevant developments (§ 3 GOBReg), and in cases of inter-departmental conflict the chancellor can use the *chancellor principle* for conflict resolution. In practice, however, German chancellors use this measure only in exceptional cases. Ministers rarely deviate publicly from cabinet decisions and the coalition agreement: they are bound by the *chancellor principle* and the *cabinet principle* (*Kabinettsprinzip*) which requires consultation of the cabinet (§ 15 GOBReg).

On a political level, inter-party conflicts between departments are resolved in the coalition committee, although cabinet meetings can serve as a conflict resolution mechanism of last resort if policies cannot be coordinated between the ministerial departments beforehand. It is an established practice, however, to avoid conflicts in the cabinet and to resolve them at the lowest level of hierarchy if possible (§17 GOBReg; see also Fleischer, 2011a, p. 60). This subsidiary approach to conflict resolution protects the strong role of the departments in policy-making and prevents political interference from the chancellery. Due to the strong rule of law tradition (*Rechtsstaatstradition*) (Sommermann, 2021), the informal practice of policy initiation and coordination generally follows the provisions laid down in the Joint Rules of Procedures of the Federal ministries (*Gemeinsame Geschäftsordnung der Bundesministerien, GGO*) and the Rules of Procedure of the Federal Government (*Geschäftsordnung der Bundesregierung, GOBReg*), which further specify the constitutional principles of government.

Although the departments are generally independent within their area of responsibility, some ministries are more influential than others. The ministers for Finance, Justice and Defence are mentioned in the German Basic Law and, therefore, these ministries can only be terminated via a constitutional reform. The Finance Minister has a qualified veto regarding unbudgeted expenses (Art. 112 Basic Law) and on budgetary matters when she/he is not present in the cabinet meeting (§26(1) GOBReg). The Ministries of Justice and the Interior have the same right to object on legal grounds (§26(2) GOBReg). Furthermore, legislative drafts are checked for legal compliance by the Ministry of Justice (§§45, 46 GGO) and the Ministry of Finance is involved in the drafting process when the budget is affected (§51 GGO) (Fleischer, 2021, p. 65).

Traditionally, the ministries are also unequal in terms of administrative resources (budget and personnel).[2] The most well-resourced departments in 2020 are the Federal Foreign Office, the Ministry for Economics, the Ministry of Home Affairs and the Ministry of Finance. When including subordinate agencies, the Ministry for Labor and Social Affairs, the Ministry of Defense and the Ministry for Infrastructure have the largest personnel and budgets in 2020. These departments are usually among the most desired in coalition negotiations and their ministers tend to sit close to the chancellor in cabinet meetings. Besides administrative capacities, the perceived political power of the minister plays a role in coordination. Civil servants consider the chances of administrative and political success when investing in inter-ministerial coordination (for the Ministry of Environment see Müller, 1986; Pehle, 1998). The differences in political influence become relevant only in contentious cross-cutting issues that require coordination and conflict resolution. The scope of the portfolio also determines the number of legislative drafts that a ministry has the lead responsibility for and how often it is involved in coordination processes (Fleischer, 2021, p. 72).

The role of the federal chancellery is further limited by administrative federalism in Germany (see Behnke & Kropp, 2021). Although the German federal states (*Länder*) have just a few exclusive competences (most importantly, education, police and cultural policy), they have many important shared competences with the federal level where they participate in federal decision-making in the second chamber (*Bundesrat*). Competences are separated by function rather than policies, which means that the Länder implement federal legislation and bear the associated administrative costs (administrative connectivity—*Verwaltungskonnexität*) (Behnke & Kropp, 2021, p. 37). Consequently, the federal level and the Länder are closely intertwined in horizontal and vertical coordination structures for joint decision-making (Behnke & Kropp, 2021, p. 37): 'This consensual culture of decision-making in multilevel structures was illustratively described as entangled or interlocking politics (a more or less clumsy translation of Politikverflechtung as coined by Fritz W. Scharpf)' (Behnke & Kropp, 2021, p. 36). Administrative federalism is deeply rooted in German administrative history (Behnke & Kropp, 2021, p. 36) and cannot easily be circumvented. While Europeanisation has strengthened the role of executives, it has also strengthened administrative federalism in Germany (Behnke & Kropp, 2021, p. 46).

The formal role of the chancellor and the chancellery in Germany has not changed in recent years (see also Busse & Hofmann, 2019) and their steering capacity remains limited (see also Fleischer, 2011a). The strong departmental principle and the consensual character of the politico-administrative system are such that the chancellery is no clear centre of power in the German federal government. Although the chancellor and chancellery can situationally and informally assume a leadership role on politically salient issues (see below), the departments have a central role in policy-making, thanks to the formal setup of the German government and the concentration of policy expertise and administrative resources in those departments.

Politico-administrative Relations

Turning to political-administrative relations, it is possible to identify several key properties to the relationship between politics and administration in German federal government. First, formal politicisation at the top is key: the two top layers of hierarchy (administrative state secretaries and heads of division) are so-called political civil servants (*politische Beamte*) who can be dismissed at any point in time and without further notice according to the Civil Service Law (§ 54 BBG). This rule goes back to Prussia and serves to strengthen the political responsiveness of the bureaucracy. The core rationale behind this instrument is that the two top layers are crucial for ensuring that ministers can both translate their preferences into programmes and fully trust the bureaucratic position holders. If they lose trust, they can replace the person.

The instrument is pivotal after elections and in particular after a change of government. For instance, after the election in 2013 when the previous conservative-liberal government was replaced by a coalition of the conservative and the social democratic parties, 96% of administrative state secretaries and 65% of division heads were replaced by the incoming government (Ebinger et al., 2018, p. 398). This mechanism allows the minister to handpick their political civil servants, and research shows that they increasingly appoint individuals with a background outside the federal government, often linked to party politics (Bach & Veit, 2017). As important, however, the civil service below the two top layers is based on merit and tenure.

Second, functional politicisation is also characteristic for the federal bureaucracy—and has always been (Mayntz & Derlien, 1989). Functional politicisation refers to strengthening 'political responsiveness by anticipating and integrating politically relevant aspects in the bureaucracy's day-to-day functions' (Hustedt & Salomonsen, 2014, p. 750, see also: Aberbach et al., 1981; Mayntz & Derlien, 1989). According to survey-based research, federal bureaucrats acknowledge and appreciate the political nature of their job and generally consider it part of their role to include considerations of political feasibility alongside their technical expertise when providing advice to the minister (Ebinger & Jochheim, 2009; Veit et al., 2018).

Third, the organisation and role of the units directly supporting the minister have changed considerably over the last two decades. While many other countries have established and expanded the positions of special advisers who come and go with the minister, an observation offered in several other contributions to this volume, developments in Germany have been different. No new formal position has been established, but the formerly small offices of the ministers have developed into full-fledged staff units (*Leitungsstäbe*) with the head of the unit (*Leiter Leitungsstab*) often evolving into the most important and intimate adviser to the minister. Hence, these units are functionally equivalent, but formally different from developments in, for example, Denmark (Chap. 10), New Zealand (Chap.

6), or the UK (Chap. 4). The staff units comprise communication, press and public affairs functions, units coordinating with the chancellery and the Parliament, the private office of the minister and often speech-writing or a unit dedicated to a particular policy project. This functional differentiation from what traditionally had been just a small secretariat making sure the minister was at the right location at the exact point in time with the correct files under their arm has gone hand in hand with an increase in staff numbers and, perhaps more important, an increasing internal significance. The staff unit—and particularly their head—is today considered the eyes and ears of the minister. This change happened almost unnoticed from the outside (Hustedt, 2013, 2018).

The chancellery manages chancellor, governmental, departmental, party political, coalition and media logics (Grunden, 2011; Korte, 2011). Recruitment based on party political and personal networks is a mechanism for the chancellery to enhance steering capacity and to receive relevant information on time (Korte, 2011). Because of the various veto players in the German system, to form a centre of power the German chancellery must assume informal steering, control and coordination functions for the ministers and departments, majoritarian parliamentary group and coalition partner(s) and the governing party, as well as build reliable networks with relevant stakeholders and the media (Grunden, 2011, p. 250). A small circle of personal advisers to the chancellor meets for a daily briefing (*Morgenlage*) (Korte, 2011, p. 131). The ChefBK, press officer and chancellor's office manager are usually part of this group (Grunden, 2011, p. 266). Based on personal loyalty and their ability to represent one of the institutional logics personal advisers are recruited to assume a mediating role on behalf of the chancellor (Grunden, 2011).

All in all, both in the ministerial departments and in the chancellery, personal loyalty has increased in relevance and shapes the interaction of those at the political top with the bureaucratic line organisation. Through closely working with their 'inner circles', ministers emphasise the political nature of 'their' bureaucracies' work as their close aides serve as political filters or watch-dogs for the advice ministers receive from the civil service.

Inter-ministerial Coordination and Conflict Resolution

Inter-ministerial coordination in the German federal government follows the logic of negative coordination (Scharpf, 1993, 1994) and is often characterised by a strong policy logic (Hustedt & Danken, 2017). In contrast to positive coordination, processes of negative coordination are dominated by the lead unit preparing a proposal to be sent to other involved ministries. These other parties check the proposal for potential negative implications for their area of responsibility. If they find such implications, they report their objection to the initiating lead ministry. Through this process, the scope of the initial proposal is often rather narrow because for the process to proceed agreement by all involved ministries is required. Hence, the output represents the lowest-common denominator. As importantly, the perspective of the lead ministry usually keeps prevailing throughout the process and shapes the final proposal because other ministries predominantly check for 'what needs to go' (as opposed to what they would want to add). Thus, the division of competences across federal government is crucial for the coordination output (Hustedt & Danken, 2017). Two formal instruments, laid down in the *GGO*, reinforce the key significance of this division: the instrument of the lead ministry (*federführendes Ressort*), the one with main responsibility for a certain issue and the instrument of the other involved ministries whose participation and agreement in the process is required (*mitzeichnendes Ministerium*).

Importantly, the lead ministry does not hold a hierarchically superior position. Because of the departmental principle all ministries are considered equally important in formal terms. Also, the chancellery is not formally in a position to instruct other participating ministries in inter-ministerial coordination. Thus, coordination and conflict resolution respectively follow the hierarchy: the bulk of coordination is carried out at the working level, that is, at the level of the policy officials (*Referenten*), who seek to solve all issues possible. Involving the next superior hierarchical level is usually the ultima ratio. This process is often long and complicated because each involved unit strictly defends its own turf from the interference of others. Hence, coordination often escalates into 'co-signing wars' (Murswieck, 2003, p. 129, translation by the authors). The chancellery gets involved as an arbiter when the ministries do not manage to agree on contested issues.

Besides the usual, predominantly procedural inter-ministerial coordination (*Ressortabstimmung*), the federal government sometimes establishes inter-ministerial coordination working groups to develop proposals for certain policy issues. Such working groups have been set up for various cross-cutting policy issues. As there is no official, central documentation on inter-ministerial working groups, providing exact numbers is impossible and empirical data is rare. However, recent case study research on inter-ministerial working groups provides insights into their inner working dynamics (Danken, 2017; Hustedt & Danken, 2017).

Inter-ministerial working groups were often seen to represent typical examples of positive coordination as they usually involve all affected actors and are mandated to agree upon a joint draft for a policy, and this is often a policy 'from scratch'. However, empirical research shows that despite the organisational group setting, the involved ministries retain the pattern of negative coordination: the lead ministry drafts a proposal and the others defend their turfs, again resulting in lowest-common denominator proposals (Hustedt, 2014; Hustedt & Danken, 2017). However, two aspects are crucial. First, not all groups deliver on their mandate and agree on a joint document—whether they do depends on the dominant logic in the group. If they acquire a policy logic—that is, they understand their mutual conditions and want to deliver on the mandate and solve the problem at hand to their best available knowledge—there is a good chance they will agree on a draft. In contrast, if a political logic dominates—that is, the core reference in the group is political gains, elections and power struggles—finding consensus becomes all the more difficult (Hustedt & Danken, 2017).

Second, it does not mean that setting up inter-ministerial working groups has no impact or relevance at all. With the recurrent meetings in group settings over a period of time, participants improve their mutual understanding and can move towards developing a joint understanding of the problem or at least developing an understanding of why the neighbouring ministry insists on a diverging problem definition (Hustedt, 2014).

All in all, the formal rules according to which the federal government coordinates have remained unchanged over recent decades, and while there is an increasing perception by many civil servants that the coordination load has increased and consensus-finding has become all the more difficult, there is no research on that.

Key Developments: Institutional Stability in a Changing Context?

Crisis Management

When Angela Merkel's term(s) in office had come to an end, she was increasingly seen a 'crisis chancellor'. She had to manage three crucial crises: the financial crisis (2008), the migration crisis (2015) and the

COVID-19 pandemic (2020). In all three crises, Merkel was a key figure in formulating and managing the national response—albeit one who was embedded in the decentralised politico-administrative system described earlier.

In particular, the management of the country's response to COVID-19 since March 2020 highlights the interplay of formal and informal mechanisms in coordinating national coronavirus policy. As expected by crisis management research, the public eye turned to the chancellor when it became obvious that COVID-19 would spread in Europe. On 11 March 2020, she publicly announced that Germany would take what became called a 'flattening the curve' approach to fight the pandemic (Bundesregierung, 2020), just a few days later putting in place social distancing measures, closing schools and announcing a mild form of lockdown (with the closure of non-essential shops but allowing citizens to leave their homes for a walk). This approach was complemented by efforts to expand hospital capacity and, over time, by economic stimulus and support packages (see for details Dostal, 2020).

Already in the early periods of the pandemic the chancellor was a key figure in public communication—for instance, through a remarkable speech on TV, in which she exhorted citizens to 'take the situation seriously' and adapt their behaviour, given that her executive power was limited by the division of competences in federalism (see below). This was the only televised speech in response to those events during Angela Merkel's incumbency in which she emphasised that the country was in a situation of severe crisis: regular communication about crisis development was left to others (see below).

In the federal system, the Länder hold the key responsibilities for executing federal pandemic legislation (*Bundesinfektionsschutzgesetz*) and only the Länder have the right to impose significant restrictions on their citizens. The federal government can issue recommendations on what measures to take but cannot instruct the Länder to follow (Kuhlmann et al., 2021). To agree on uniform measures, conferences between the chancellor and the prime ministers of the Länder became the core coordination body of the German COVID-19 response. In the early periods, consensus among the actors on what measures to implement was high, but riffled away over time when some prime ministers started to exploit the situation for their own political profiles—with upcoming elections in sight. However, in particular the chancellor managed to push for some degree of uniformity in measures, although time and again there was substantial variation among the Länder regarding the details of containment measures (Dostal, 2020; Hattke & Martin, 2020; Kuhlmann et al., 2021). And although the chancellor was crucial in the coordination of the pandemic response, the chancellery was not equipped with increasing resources.

However, over the course of the pandemic, the federal government initiated changes to the national pandemic legislation at several stages, effectively equipping the federal level with more powers to make nation-wide binding decisions in the pandemic in a response to what—from the federal-level perspective—was an overly decentralised system. While the Chancellor was the key actor at the federal level, she was not the only relevant figure: the Health Minister was holding weekly press conferences on the pandemic situation together with the Head of the Robert-Koch-Institut (Federal Health Agency), and occasionally together with leading virologists. The health minister was, for example, key in coordinating with the hospitals and in devising and rolling out a testing strategy. A few other ministers, such as the finance minister or the minister for labour, also became important in the coordination of the economic stimulus package or the support scheme for short-term work (*Kurzarbeitergeld*). Importantly, in those instances where federal regulation was enacted, it was prepared by the responsible line ministry (rather than the chancellery).

All in all, the formulation of the pandemic policy in Germany emphasises the limits to centralisation that the federal system and the decentralised federal government system provide for. Despite public demands for uniform responses and high expectations of a leading role for the chancellor, her legal room for manoeuvre was constrained. Nonetheless, this expectation and the high level of public support for restrictions (at least throughout much of the pandemic) allowed her to push for consensus in federal-Länder coordination and to at least partially seize control at the federal level.

Europeanisation and Summitry

The chancellery has a subordinate role in EU policy coordination. EU policy positions for the Council of the European Union are coordinated in the Ministry of Economics regarding COREPER I, in the Federal Foreign Office regarding COREPER II and the Ministry of Finance regarding the Euro Group (Bulmer & Paterson, 2019, pp. 78 ff.; Freudlsperger & Weinrich, 2021, p. 8; Jensen et al., 2016, pp. 639 ff.).[3] The coordination process for EU policy is the same as for domestic affairs (see section 2.2; Beichelt, 2015, pp. 272 f.). Each German ministry has a European affairs department and an EU delegate (*Europabeauftragte*). The lead ministry, as determined by responsibility for the respective policy, develops a draft position which is then coordinated with other concerned ministries in various inter-ministerial coordination structures at the different hierarchical levels. The EU coordination structures are headed by the Ministry of Economics or the Federal Foreign Office, depending on the issue at hand (Jensen et al., 2016, pp. 639 ff.).

The increasing political salience of European affairs and deepened economic integration over recent decades have led to several major redistributions of power and competences between the Federal Foreign Office, the Ministry of Economics and the Ministry of Finance. The strong departmental principle means that Europeanisation has not privileged the chancellery over other departments in EU policy coordination and attempts by the former to take control over coordination for the General Affairs council and the European Council have not been successful (Freudlsperger & Weinrich, 2021, p. 8). Due to the strong coordination requirements in EU policy, the German government tends to speak with various voices to take a position late in the decision-making process and to regularly abstain in the Council of the EU when no inter-ministerial consensus can be reached. This behaviour has informally become known as the 'German vote' (Beichelt, 2015, p. 279).

Regarding EU affairs, the chancellery focuses on strategic questions. The German chancellor traditionally has an important role in EU treaty negotiations and crisis management. Because of the institutional setup of the EU, a Franco-German compromise was often a prerequisite for European integration, although the degree to which the Franco-German tandem acted as a 'motor' for or 'brake' on European integration is subject to debate (Calla & Demesmay, 2013; Cole, 2008; Paterson, 2008). The enlargement of the EU has also shifted the power distribution within the Council of the EU such that Franco-German leadership has become more difficult (Schild, 2010), as has been the case with Brexit. Nevertheless, German chancellors can take a leadership role within the European Council in cooperation with other influential heads of states.

More recently, Angela Merkel has taken a coordinating role in EU crisis management. Together with the German Finance Minister, she had an important part in negotiating the Euro crisis response. In the refugee crisis of 2015–2016, her decisions de facto suspended the EU Dublin III agreement. The efforts to reach a joint EU solution to the distribution of refugees and border protection demonstrated her strong role in crisis management. Merkel also played a leading role in negotiating the EU-Turkey deal to organise a controlled migration of refugees from Turkey to the EU. Her negotiation strategy and conduct with various bilateral meetings, conflict mediation and a strong personal conviction were important enabling factors for the EU responses to the Euro and refugee crises (Helms et al., 2019).

This leadership role of the chancellor in EU crisis management is only possible in close cooperation with the German lead ministry. In crisis management, the chancellery informally takes control over the coordination of German EU policy positions in the European Council and the Council of the EU (Behnke, 2016; Beichelt, 2015, pp. 262 ff.; Freudlsperger & Weinrich, 2021, p. 9). Its limited resources are such that the chancellery cooperates with the lead ministry, which provides the necessary policy expertise and administrative capacity (Freudlsperger & Weinrich, 2021, p. 11) to form a 'dual centre' in EU policy coordination (Fleischer, 2010; Fleischer & Parrado, 2010). To manage the crisis, administrative capacity is increased in the lead ministry, not in the chancellery (Freudlsperger & Weinrich, 2021). According to Freudlsperger and Weinrich (2021), a strengthening of decentralised coordination is the consequence in the long run despite short-term informal centralisation.

In addition, administrative federalism is an important institutional constraint on centralised EU policy coordination. The Länder participate in decision-making when their areas of competence are concerned, which is codified in Art. 23 Basic Law and in the Law on the cooperation of federal and state governments on EU affairs (*EUZBLG, Gesetz über die Zusammenarbeit von Bund und Ländern in Angelegenheiten der Europäischen Union*). Because the Länder are usually responsible for policy implementation, their involvement is the rule rather than the exception in EU policy coordination. Not only have the Länder become increasingly active in EU decision-making throughout the Europeanisation of the German politico-administrative system (Jensen, 2014; Sturm & Pehle, 2012), they provide important policy expertise to the federal government, enabling the latter to take an informed position in the Council of the EU (Bulmer & Paterson, 2019, p. 103).

Overall, deepened European integration with the enhanced role of the European Parliament and the expansion of the Ordinary Legislative Procedure has strengthened the policy perspective and the role of the departments in German EU policy. In 'regular' EU policy-making, the lead ministry has a strong role because of its coordinating function and participation in decision-making at the EU level (Beichelt, 2015, p. 268). Regarding European integration, EU crisis management and issues of high political salience, the German chancellor can informally take control over policy coordination within the German core executive, thanks to the *Richtlinienkompetenz*, which is not, however, a new trend (see also Behnke, 2016; Beichelt, 2015, pp. 262 ff.).

Personalisation and Mediatisation

Although mediatisation is a general trend in the German government, it has not favoured the chancellery over the ministerial departments. The departmental principle prevails. Each department has created their own staff and communication units as well as processes for the internal coordination of public relations. In an age of social media and new media formats, the Federal Press Office (*Bundespresseamt*), which is subordinate to the chancellery, and the regular press conferences (*Bundespressekonferenz*) have become less important compared to interviews, background and panel discussions, or social media statements. Public relations are not strictly coordinated between the ministries, but each department is responsible within their own jurisdiction. Despite informal inter-ministerial meetings of communication units, attempts by the Federal Press Office to streamline governmental communication across departments have not been successful because the departments insist on the departmental principle.

Issues of high strategic importance and political salience such as crisis communication, however, are coordinated between ministries by the lead ministry. The collegial principle and coalition politics usually keep the departments from public conflicts, although press conferences have been used in exceptional instances to portray inter-ministerial conflicts (interviews by the authors).[4] Deviation from this principle is rare and attracts strong public attention. A recent example is the German vote in the Council of the European Union on the glyphosate approval in 2017, where the Minister for Agriculture unilaterally voted in favour—knowing full well that the Minister for the Environment did not approve and that the inter-ministerial coordination process had not been completed.

Personalisation in German executive politics can be observed in the chancellor's leadership role in the management of recent crises. It was only during her third term that Merkel's leadership style became more personalised (Helms et al., 2019). In the management of the Euro crisis and the refugee crisis in the European Union, she insisted on a joint EU solution and acted according to her personal values despite opposition within her own party and parts of the German electorate (Helms et al., 2019). However, personalisation is not a general trend in German executive politics. Bluntly, mediatisation and personalisation have not strengthened the German core executive within the German government.

Due to the recent EU policy crises, which have had broad domestic implications and high political salience (see also Freudlsperger & Weinrich, 2021, p. 1), the privileged role of the chancellor and the political executive in European integration and crisis management have received more public attention. Internationally, Angela Merkel was personally associated with the response to the EU financial crisis and the Greek bailout programme negotiated in 2015. As a consequence, she received a lot of media attention internationally and especially in Greece, where she was publicly discredited for her harsh negotiation style. The domestic media discourse on the Euro crisis, however, was focused on the policy response rather than the chancellor's personal role. A prominent example is the constitutional appeal brought to the German constitutional court against the bailout programme for Greece in the context of the EU financial crisis, which was directed towards questions of democratic accountability and national sovereignty rather than the role of the core executive within the federal government.

Domestically, personalisation could be observed in crisis management as well. In the refugee crisis, the chancellor's decision on 4 September 2015 to suspend the EU Dublin III agreement and to open the German borders to refugees without coordination with the Minister of the Interior or the cabinet was strongly debated in German media. This decision can be interpreted as a measure of personal conviction (Helms et al., 2019) and as a response to rising media pressure related to the humanitarian crisis in refugee camps and casualties in the Mediterranean Sea (Kepplinger, 2019). The credo *Wir schaffen das* ('We can do it') (Bundesregierung, 2015) referring to the management and integration of a rising number of refugees from Merkel's press conference on 31 August 2015 was strongly contested. The public discourse was divided between a 'welcoming culture' and scepticism towards migrants in the aftermath of sexual assaults on New Year's Eve 2015 in Cologne and the terrorist attack on a Christmas market in Berlin in 2016. Similarly, Merkel had an important part in crisis communication during the response to the COVID-19 pandemic when she asked the German population for compliance with the COVID policies via her video blog. Nevertheless, as noted, the main crisis management and communication was left to the ministerial departments and the Robert-Koch-Institut.

The crisis management policies were partially associated with Angela Merkel personally. Among members of the right-wing populist protest movement PEGIDA (*Patriotische Europäer gegen die Islamisierung des Abendlandes*), which was formed in 2014 in reaction to the migration policy, the Chancellor was personally insulted and her resignation demanded (*Merkel muss weg*—'Merkel must leave'). The right-wing party *Alternative für Deutschland* (AfD—Alternative for Germany), founded in 2013 as a Eurosceptic party, has strategically conducted several personalised campaigns against Merkel and individual AfD parliamentarians insulted her during parliamentary speeches. These personalised reactions were, however, not limited to the Chancellor but concerned several individuals involved in the crisis communication.

Despite these tendencies for personalisation and mediatisation, the chancellor and the core executive have not been strengthened in German executive politics—except in controversial crisis management situations where more centralised coordination is required. Due to the strong departmental principle, media communication only serves the chancellery as a governmental steering mechanism to a limited extent.

Conclusion

In Germany, recent developments such as Europeanisation, mediatisation and personalisation have not led to the same degree of government centralisation that has been observed in other countries (including a number of those featured in this book). Although the chancellery can assume a stronger role in crisis situations as a short-term reaction, this is not institutionalised in administrative capacity and processes in the long term. Ministerial departments remain the most important actors in policy-making and the chancellery relies on the cooperation of the respective lead ministry for the provision of expertise and resources.

The German politico-administrative system is historically characterised by a strong division of powers. The steering capacity of the core executive is limited by the strong need for coordination that flows from three main factors. First, administrative federalism puts the German federal states in a strong position. This could be observed in the COVID-19 crisis management, but is equally true for Europeanisation more generally, whenever the Länder are involved in implementation. Second, German governments are coalition governments, which require coordination at the political and administrative levels of government. Third, the departmental principle underpins the strong position of single ministerial departments as the key actors in federal government policy-making and coordination and emphasises the dispersion of power at the federal government level. While other politico-administrative systems such as Denmark have similar coordination requirements, German institutional relations are more competitive than consensual in character (and in comparison). Ministerial departments in Germany defend their respective turf against the chancellery and usually do not welcome central involvement as political support.

The analysis shows that the German chancellor and the chancellery are no strong centre of power despite the international developments that have contributed to centralisation in many countries. Nevertheless, the concept of the core executive, with its focus on institutional configurations, informal processes and resources in coordination and conflict resolution, captures the nuances and developments over time in the distribution of power within the German government, including short-term power shifts in crisis management that cannot be captured by looking at formal institutions alone. However, as the concept directs (almost) all attention to the centre of government, there is a conceptual risk of overstating the role of the centre—in particular, in highly decentralised and dispersed systems in which the crucial governance issues are vertical and horizontal interactions and coordination. Hence, the 'bias towards the centre' might create a misperception overstating the role of the German chancellor and chancellery in the context of important institutional constraints. In systems with a strong separation of powers and institutional interdependence, searching for the core executive might seem like a wild goose chase: the composition of the core executive in Germany varies by policy issue and depends on the political context as well as the interaction with other institutional actors.

At the end of the 'era Merkel', German federal government has remained remarkably stable in formal terms—experiencing no major changes for decades but showing some degree of flexibility in adapting to changing environments in more subcutaneous forms. Thus, in some respects politico-administrative relations have shifted to a personal loyalty basis, providing for a tighter political filtering function at the top of ministries. Crisis management shifts attention and provides for a politically and temporally contingent (but not necessarily formally defined) central role for the chancellor. However, overall, Angela Merkel remained embedded in a web of mechanisms impeding centralisation: the decentralisation of power in German federalism, the dispersion of power through a constitutionally strong role of individual ministerial departments and coalition governance. All these mechanisms restrict centralisation. And because they are deeply institutionalised in German governance it remains questionable if one can reasonably expect the chancellery to willingly seize control and push their own political agenda. The degree to which this would be considered appropriate is very limited. However, whether these limits remain effective barriers to centralisation or if noiseless moves within this web were a particular feature of Merkel's long term in government remain open questions we may be able to discuss when the new Chancellor Olaf Scholz has spent a certain period of time in government.

Notes

1. Calculations by the authors based on the Federal Budget Plan 2021; the numbers are for the ministries only (i.e., they exclude subordinate agencies).
2. Calculations by the authors based on the Federal Budget Plan 2021.
3. COREPER (*Comité des représentants permanents*) is a committee of permanent representatives of the EU member states, which prepares the meetings of the Council of the EU at the administrative level. Depending on the issue at hand, the committee meets in two different constellations: the deputy permanent representatives meet in COREPER I, which deals with the common market and related issues, while the permanent representatives constitute COREPER II for Foreign and Security Policy, Justice and Home Affairs and institutional and budgetary questions.
4. Eleven interviews with civil servants in the communication units of the German federal ministries were conducted by Thurid Hustedt in 2015 as a part of a research project on government communication (with Heidi Houlberg Salomonsen).

References

Aberbach, J. D., Putnam, R. D., & Rockman, B. A. (1981). *Bureaucrats and Politicians in Western Democracies.* Harvard University Press.

Bach, T., & Veit, S. (2017). The Determinants of Promotion to High Public Office in Germany: Partisan Loyalty, Political Craft, or Managerial Competencies? *Journal of Public Administration Research and Theory, 28*(2), 254–269.

Behnke, N. (2016). Effekte der Wirtschafts- und Finanzkrise auf die bundesdeutsche Ministerialbürokratie—Weitere Zentralisierung und funktionale Politisierung. *Zeitschrift für Politikwissenschaft, 26*, 179–194. https://doi.org/10.1007/s41358-015-0013-0

Behnke, N., & Kropp, S. (2021). Administrative Federalism. In S. Kuhlmann, I. Proeller, D. Schimanke, & J. Ziekow (Eds.), *Public Administration in Germany* (pp. 35–51). Springer International Publishing.

Beichelt, T. (2015). *Deutschland und Europa: Die Europäisierung des Politischen Systems*. Springer Fachmedien Wiesbaden GmbH.

Bulmer, S., & Paterson, W. E. (2019). *Germany and the European Union. Europe's Reluctant Hegemon* (The European Union Series). Macmillan International Higher Education.

Bundesregierung. (2015, August 31). *Sommerpressekonferenz von Bundeskanzlerin Merkel*: Mitschrift Pressekonferenz. Montag. https://www.bundesregierung.de/breg-de/aktuelles/pressekonferenzen/sommerpressekonferenz-von-bundeskanzlerin-merkel-848300

Bundesregierung. (2020). *Pressekonferenz von Bundeskanzlerin Merkel, Bundesgesundheitsminister Spahn und RKI-Chef Wieler*. Mitschrift der Pressekonferenz. Berlin, Germany. https://www.bundesregierung.de/breg-de/suche/pressekonferenz-von-bundeskanzlerin-merkel-bundesgesundheitsminister-spahn-und-rki-chef-wieler-1729940

Busse, V., & Hofmann, H. (2019). *Bundeskanzleramt und Bundesregierung*. Nomos Verlagsgesellschaft mbH & Co. KG.

Calla, C., & Demesmay, C. (2013). *Que reste-t-il du couple franco-allemand? (Réflexeeurope)*. Documentation Française.

Cole, A. (2008). Franco-German Relations: From Active to Reactive Cooperation. In J. Hayward (Ed.), *Leaderless Europe* (pp. 147–166). Oxford University Press.

Danken, T. (2017). *Coordination of Wicked Problems: Comparing Interdepartmental Coordination of Demographic Change Policies in Five German States*. Universität Potsdam.

Dostal, J. M. (2020). Governing Under Pressure: German Policy Making During the Coronavirus Crisis. *The Political Quarterly, 91*(3), 542–552.

Ebinger, F., & Jochheim, L. (2009). Wessen loyale Diener? Wie die Große Koalition die deutsche Ministerialbürokratie veränderte. *der moderne staat—Zeitschrift für Public Policy, Recht und Management, 2*(2), 327–345.

Ebinger, F., Lux, N., Kintzinger, C., & Garske, B. (2018). Die Deutsche Verwaltungselite der Regierungen Brandt bis Merkel II. Herkunft, Zusammensetzung und Politisierung der Führungskräfte in den Bundesministerien. *der moderne staat—Zeitschrift für Public Policy, Recht und Management, 11*, 1–23. https://doi.org/10.3224/dms.v11i2.01

Fleischer, J. (2010). A Dual Centre? Executive Politics under the Second Grand Coalition in Germany. *German Politics, 19*(3–4), 353–368.

Fleischer, J. (2011a). Steering from the German Centre: More Policy Coordination and Fewer Policy Initiatives. In C. Dahlström (Ed.), *Steering from the Centre: Strengthening Political Control in Western Democracies* (pp. 54–79). University of Toronto Press.

Fleischer, J. (2011b). Das Primat der Richtlinienkompetenz im politischen Prozess: Zur Bedeutung der Organisation des Bundeskanzleramtes. In M. Florack (Ed.), *Regierungszentralen: Organisation, Steuerung und Politikformulierung zwischen Formalität und Informalität* (pp. 201–224). VS Verl. für Sozialwiss.

Fleischer, J. (2021). Federal Administration. In S. Kuhlmann, I. Proeller, D. Schimanke, & J. Ziekow (Eds.), *Public Administration in Germany* (pp. 61–79). Springer International Publishing.

Fleischer, J., & Parrado, S. (2010). Power Distribution in Ambiguous Times: The Effects of the Financial Crisis on Executive Decision-making in Germany and Spain. *Der moderne staat—Zeitschrift für Public Policy, Recht und Management, 3*(2), 361–376.

Freudlsperger, C., & Weinrich, M. (2021). Decentralized EU Policy Coordination in Crisis? The Case of Germany. *JCMS: Journal of Common Market Studies.* https://doi.org/10.1111/jcms.13159

Grunden, T. (2011). Das informelle Politikmanagement der Regierungszentrale: Vom Sekretariat der Regierung zum Machtzentrum der Regierungsformation. In M. Florack (Ed.), *Regierungszentralen: Organisation, Steuerung und Politikformulierung zwischen Formalität und Informalität* (pp. 249–284). VS Verl. für Sozialwiss.

Hattke, F., & Martin, H. (2020). Collective Action during the Covid-19 Pandemic: The Case of Germany's Fragmented Authority. *Administrative Theory & Praxis, 42*(4), 614–632.

Helms, L., van Esch, F., & Crawford, B. (2019). Politische Führung aus dem Kanzleramt: "Conviction Leadership" statt Pragmatismus? In R. Zohlnhöfer & T. Saalfeld (Eds.), *Zwischen Stillstand, Politikwandel und Krisenmanagement: Eine Bilanz der Regierung Merkel 2013–2017* (pp. 169–194). Springer VS.

Hustedt, T. (2013). *Ministerialverwaltung im Wandel.* Nomos.

Hustedt, T. (2014). Negative Koordination in der Klimapolitik: Die Interministerielle Arbeitsgruppe Anpassungsstrategie. *der moderne staat—Zeitschrift für Public Policy, Recht und Management, 7,* 311–330.

Hustedt, T. (2018). Germany: The Smooth and Silent Emergence of Advisory Roles. In R. Shaw & C. Eichbaum (Eds.), *Ministers, Minders and Mandarins: An International Study of Relationships at the Executive Summit of Parliamentary Democracies* (pp. 72–90). Edward Elgar Publishing.

Hustedt, T., & Danken, T. (2017). Institutional Logics in Inter-departmental Coordination: Why Actors Agree on a Joint Policy Output. *Public Administration, 95*(3), 730–743.

Hustedt, T., & Salomonsen, H. H. (2014). Ensuring Political Responsiveness: Politicization Mechanisms in Ministerial Bureaucracies. *International Review of Administrative Sciences*, 80(4), 746–765.

Jantz, B., & Veit, S. (2011). Steuerung von Querschnittspolitik durch das Bundeskanzleramt: Das Beispiel Bürokratieabbau. In M. Florack (Ed.), *Regierungszentralen: Organisation, Steuerung und Politikformulierung zwischen Formalität und Informalität* (pp. 285–310). VS Verl. für Sozialwiss.

Jensen, M. D. (2014). Game Changing—Tracing the Positions, Strategies and Interaction Modes of the German Länder towards the (Ever Expanding?) European Union. *Regional & Federal Studies*, 24(3), 263–280.

Jensen, M. D., Jopp, M., & Nedergaard, P. (2016). Coordination of EU Policy Positions in Germany and Denmark: A Politics of Institutional Choice Approach. *Journal of Contemporary European Research*, 12(2), 634–652.

Kepplinger, H. M. (2019). Die Mediatisierung der Migrationspolitik und Angela Merkels Entscheidungspraxis. In R. Zohlnhöfer & T. Saalfeld (Eds.), *Zwischen Stillstand, Politikwandel und Krisenmanagement: Eine Bilanz der Regierung Merkel 2013–2017* (pp. 195–217). Springer VS.

Korte, K.-R. (2011). Machtmakler im Bundeskanzleramt: Personelle Faktoren im informellen Entscheidungsprozess. In M. Florack (Ed.), *Regierungszentralen: Organisation, Steuerung und Politikformulierung zwischen Formalität und Informalität* (pp. 123–142). VS Verl. für Sozialwiss.

Kuhlmann, S., Hellström, M., Ramberg, U., & Reiter, R. (2021). Tracing Divergence in Crisis Governance: Responses to the COVID-19 Pandemic in France, Germany and Sweden Compared. *International Review of Administrative Sciences*. https://doi.org/10.1177/0020852320979359

Mayntz, R., & Derlien, H.-U. (1989). Party Patronage and Politicization of the West German Administrative Elite 1970–1987: Toward Hybridization? *Governance*, 2(4), 384–404.

Müller, E. (1986). *Innenwelt der Umweltpolitik: sozial-liberale Umweltpolitik—(Ohn)macht durch Organisation?* Westdeutscher Verlag.

Murswieck, A. (2003). Des Kanzlers Macht: Zum Regierungsstil Gerhard Schröders. In C. Egle, T. Ostheim, & R. Zohlnhöfer (Eds.), *Das rot-grüne Projekt: Eine Bilanz der Regierung Schröder 1998–2002* (pp. 117–135). Westdt. Verl.

Paterson, W. E. (2008). Did France and Germany Lead Europe? A Retrospect. In J. Hayward (Ed.), *Leaderless Europe* (pp. 89–110). Oxford University Press.

Pehle, H. (1998). *Das Bundesministerium für Umwelt, Naturschutz und Reaktorsicherheit: Ausgegrenzt statt integriert?: Das institutionelle Fundament der deutschen Umweltpolitik*. Deutscher Universitätsverlag.

Scharpf, F. W. (1993). Positive und Negative Koordination in Verhandlungssystemen. *MPIfG Discussion Paper (93/1)*. Köln, München. http://hdl.handle.net/10419/125917

Scharpf, F. W. (1994). Games Real Actors Could Play: Positive and Negative Coordination in Embedded Negotiations. *Journal of Theoretical Politics,* 6(1), 27–53.

Schild, J. (2010). Mission Impossible? The Potential for Franco-German Leadership in the Enlarged EU. *JCMS: Journal of Common Market Studies,* 48, 1367–1390. https://doi.org/10.1111/j.1468-5965.2010.02117.x

Sommermann, K.-P. (2021). Constitutional State and Public Administration. In S. Kuhlmann, I. Proeller, D. Schimanke, & J. Ziekow (Eds.), *Public Administration in Germany* (pp. 17–33). Springer International Publishing.

Sturm, R., & Pehle, H. (2012). *Das neue deutsche Regierungssystem: Die Europäisierung von Institutionen, Entscheidungsprozessen und Politikfeldern in der Bundesrepublik Deutschland.* VS-Verl.

Veit, S., Fromm, N., & Ebinger, F. (2018). "NEIN" zu sagen ist eine unserer wichtigsten Pflichten. Politisierung, Rollenverständnis und Entscheidungsverhalten von leitenden Ministerialbeamt*innen in Deutschland. *der moderne staat—Zeitschrift für Public Policy, Recht und Management, 11,* 1–24.

CHAPTER 8

The Netherlands: How Weak Prime Ministers Gain Influence

Erik-Jan van Dorp and R. A. W. Rhodes

INTRODUCTION: THE PUZZLE OF WEAK PRIME MINISTERS

Throughout Western Europe, prime ministers (PMs) come in many shapes and sizes. Some are regarded as 'strong' (e.g., UK and Germany) whereas others are said to be 'weak' (e.g., Italy and Luxembourg). The Dutch PM has always been considered *weak* in terms of formal powers, with a prime minister serving as primus inter pares, not as a proper 'leader' (Van den Berg, 1990). Dutch ministers serve *with* not *under* a prime minister (Daalder, 1955, p. 8). In that vein, Andeweg (1991) characterised the prime minister's position as 'not just chairman, not yet chief'. Prime Minister Jan-Peter Balkenende (2002–2010) echoed this sentiment when

---

E.-J. van Dorp (✉)
Utrecht University School of Governance, Utrecht, The Netherlands
e-mail: g.h.vandorp@uu.nl

R. A. W. Rhodes
University of Southampton, Southampton, UK
e-mail: r.a.w.rhodes@soton.ac.uk

© The Author(s), under exclusive license to Springer Nature Switzerland AG 2022
K. Kolltveit, R. Shaw (eds.), *Core Executives in a Comparative Perspective*, Understanding Governance,
https://doi.org/10.1007/978-3-030-94503-9_8

he observed that 'the expectations about the power of the PM are not matched by his real and by his formal position' (cited in Andeweg & Irwin, 2014, p. 155). However, we suggest that the present-day Dutch PM has become more predominant. Yet this development does not involve an increase in formal competencies (e.g., the right to appoint and fire cabinet ministers) or an increased organisational base (e.g., a larger Prime Minister's Office with many advisers). We address this puzzle and ask: Has the Dutch prime minister become predominant, and if so, how has this impacted the workings of the core executive?

In this chapter, we analyse 28 original interviews with key actors in Dutch executive government, including (prime) ministers and senior civil servants, and identify four trends that have stimulated the rise of the Dutch prime minister: Europeanisation, personalisation, crisis management and the changing party-political landscape. Our findings suggest cabinet ministers and top civil servants see the Dutch PM as pivotal to every important decision: it is nearly impossible to reach a cabinet decision without the PM's support. We describe the influence of a pivotal PM who masters a 'court' of powerful actors and networks. Further, we find that the PM's constitutional and institutional basis barely matters for their functional role and influence. The everyday-life view of the PM is only loosely coupled to the legal competencies that constitute the office (cf: Visser, 2009, pp. 122–123). We also find that cabinet decision-making is a succession of phases, which end with the weekly cabinet meeting. This meeting is best understood as a 'closing ceremony', which legitimises the preceding stages. The PM and the Prime Minister's Office (PMO) are central to understanding this view of 'cabinet-as-process'. In conclusion, we discuss the implications for the craft of PMs.

We make two distinct contributions. First, we provide original empirical evidence that revises the accepted view of Dutch executive government. Interviews with a PM, deputy prime ministers, cabinet ministers and top-level civil servants provide insightful 'voices from the inside', hitherto missing from many other accounts (e.g., Fiers & Krouwel, 2005). Such research has not been conducted in The Netherlands since Andeweg's (1990) landmark volume. Our study contributes to a much-needed update that considers the impact of the significant changes that have taken place in the last 30 years (see also Timmermans & Breeman, 2009). Second, we contribute a novel theoretical perspective by applying core executive theory, most notably the idea of 'court politics', to the Dutch executive (Rhodes, 1995, 2017 and Chap. 3 this volume). We explore how well the concept travels to a non-majoritarian context such as The Netherlands and assess how it improves our understanding of 'weak' core executives.

Weak Prime Ministers in Consensual Democracies: The Netherlands

The 'weak' status of the Dutch PM has its origins in the oft-repeated observation that the Dutch PM has fewer formal competencies and fewer supporting resources than similar offices in for instance the UK, Denmark or Germany (Bäck et al., 2019; Bovend'eert et al., 2005; De Vries et al., 2012; Van den Berg, 1990). The consensus among constitutional scholars is that the PM and the cabinet are central to understanding executive government policy-making, and the cabinet is the most important forum, with the PM as primus inter pares. As first among equals, the PM is slightly elevated above the other ministers (Andeweg, 1991). Since the introduction of parliamentary government there have been important changes, such as recognising formally the position of 'Prime Minister' in the revised constitution of 1983, but little has changed in its formal powers (Belinfante & De Reede, 2009, p. 63; Bovend'eert et al., 2005; Hoekstra, 1983; Rehwinkel, 1991). The main innovations have been the agenda-setting competency for the PM, formal recognition of the PM as head of government when abroad and the instalment of standing cabinet committees. Timmermans and Breeman (2009) argue that the primus inter pares principle normally holds but stress the contingency of the individual characteristics and resources of PMs. Thus, Swinkels et al. (2017) mapped the leadership capital of two Dutch PMs (Kok, 1994–2002 and Balkenende, 2002–2010) over time and underscored the waxing and waning of PM's resources. It is often hard to distinguish between the impact of personal and institutional factors on PMs (Van den Berg, 1990).

Dutch PMs work in a relatively strong cabinet government setting. Historically, Maarseveen (1969) contended that the cabinet, not individual ministers or parliament, characterised Dutch government. Andeweg (1990, 1991) described the cabinet as a 'dual' institution that combined both party-political differences and contending departmental interests. He introduced a 'gearbox' metaphor for conflict management in cabinets: cabinets can decide to change 'gears' by framing a contested issue as political (inter-party conflict) or departmental (interdepartmental conflict). This 'gearbox' interpretation has become standard.

Andeweg (1997, p. 80), using empirical data collected in the 1980s, also characterises the Dutch cabinet as mostly collective and partially fragmented. He argued that segmentation (or committee government) in the cabinet was less important than in other parliamentary systems (Andeweg,

1997, p. 73). More recently, Andeweg and Irwin (2014, p. 157) point to the many hours that ministers spend on the weekly cabinet meetings to highlight their importance. Also, compared to, for example, the UK, the Dutch cabinet is relatively small, allowing 'real' discussion and debate (Timmermans & Breeman, 2009, p. 77). Andeweg did signal (and deplore) the increased prominence of the weekly coalition management meeting of the governing parties and parliamentary group leaders. He saw them evolving into a 'separate and distinct power centre' (Andeweg, 1997, p. 75; see also Andeweg & Irwin, 2014, pp. 160–161; Andeweg & Timmermans, 2008, p. 272).

Our data suggest that these practices of the core executive have changed. The Dutch PM has gained influence, becoming the fulcrum of cabinet coordination, and the predominant public leader and diplomat-in-chief of the government. We ground our interpretation in two concepts: the core executive and court politics, both of which have been introduced in Chaps. 1–3.

Studying Executive Politics in The Netherlands

The Netherlands is a parliamentary democracy, and here we introduce briefly its key institutions. The monarch fulfils mainly a ceremonial role. The legislative branch is a bicameral parliament with a lower house (150 seats) and a senate (75 seats). The Dutch government has been characterised repeatedly as a consociational democracy (Lijphart, 1968). To the present day, cabinets have been multi-party coalition cabinets with usually relatively extensive coalition agreements (Timmermans, 2003). The cabinet consists of cabinet ministers and junior ministers (called 'state secretaries'). Only the former have a permanent seat and voting rights in the cabinet meeting. Ministers and junior ministers answer to the parliament, but they are not members of the parliament. The PM chairs the weekly cabinet meeting and is nowadays the national leader of the biggest political party. Ministers are nominated by their respective party leaders and appointed by the crown. They do not need an electoral mandate. While most ministers have experience in politics, not all are career politicians. They come from various backgrounds, including business, academia and diplomacy.

The core executive approach guided our interviews on Dutch executive government in several ways. First, we did not limit our focus to positions such as the PM, PMO and cabinet. We also interviewed ministers in key departments such as the Ministry of Finance, senior civil servants and journalists. Second, we looked for a court, seeking to identify and talk to the key individuals. Literally, we draw a map of the court (see Fig. 8.2). Third, we asked about the beliefs and practices of members of the core executive, which, as it transpired, led us to provide an account of the *new* practices of the PM and his court.

The data consist of 28 semi-structured elite interviews with 26 informants including a PM, 9 cabinet ministers, 2 political advisers to the PM and 12 civil servants. The latter include (former) permanent secretaries, directors-general and councillors in the PMO. Though some interviewees were still in political or administrative office, all talked about their experience in a past position. Their experiences spanned five decades, but the interviews focused on trends in the past 30 years. We also interviewed two parliamentary journalists as a way of getting an overall picture (see Empson, 2018 for a helpful review of elite interviewing). We interviewed two informants twice. We wrote a formal letter targeted, first, at retired members of the cabinet and senior civil servants (n = 8). At these interviews, we asked the interviewee to recommend us to one or more of their colleagues—'snowballing'. In total, 31 people refused or ignored our request for an interview (response rate 46%). We interviewed 22 men and 4 women.

Given that two of the three interviewers did not speak Dutch, most interviews were conducted in English, although two were in Dutch. They lasted anywhere from one to three hours and the successful interviews resembled conversations. The interviews took place between March and October 2017. We recorded all interviews, and they were transcribed. All transcripts were checked against the recording. We then subjected each transcript to thematic analysis (Braun & Clarke, 2006) which provided the first draft of our codebook for use with NVivo software. We made minor corrections to the English of the authorised quotes.

From Cabinet as Meeting to Cabinet as Process

Based on our interviews, we contend that the weekly cabinet as meeting during the Rutte cabinets (2010–2017) is no longer front and centre to decision-making, but has largely evolved into a rite of passage for decisions made elsewhere and earlier in the process (Weller, 2003). Figure 8.1 shows a schematic and simplified flowchart of core executive decision-making as a process, as understood by our informants in 2017 and widely documented in formal papers (e.g., Rijksoverheid, 2019). The various departments prepare policy proposals. They submit them to an administrative interdepartmental committee, known as 'entry committees' (Dutch: *Voorportaal*). Here, early interdepartmental conflicts are resolved and/or spelled out. Policy proposals that survive the entry committee move on to the relevant standing cabinet committee (Dutch: *Onderraad*). In addition, proposals that can be resolved are pushed 'up' rather than pushed 'down'. Both ministers and civil servants participate in these standing committees. The PM chairs all cabinet committees. The proposals will be discussed, fine-tuned and a preliminary decision will be formulated. Proposals that survive the standing committee get on the agenda of the cabinet meeting in which only cabinet members have a seat. During this meeting, a formal decision will be made, before it is sent to parliament. The progress of proposals is watched, steered and oiled carefully by the PMO, which tries to be informed and involved at every stage.

What Fig. 8.1 obscures is the constant struggle for power, access, budget and closeness to the centre of participants and policies. Struggle is the substance of court politics. Nor does it show the repetitive nature of the process, something of which our informants were all too well aware. A bill may move back and forth between the different forums. There are also regular meetings that do not have any formal standing. They are not in Fig. 8.1, even though their role in the core executive is undoubtedly important.

These informal meetings include a weekly meeting of the PM, the deputy PM(s) and the respective parliamentary leaders of the parties, as well as the party's elite meetings that precede the weekly cabinet meeting on Thursday nights, during which the political parties prepare for the cabinet meeting. Also, many of these 'meetings' are preceded by 'pre-meetings' which in turn may also be prepared by even more private pre-meetings. A Minister of Finance confessed to being 'in session' almost all day (interview March 2017). These meetings are hybrid, including politicians, civil servants and advisers. Still we simplify. This summary excludes impromptu

Fig. 8.1 The cabinet process in Dutch executive government

meetings and the countless phone calls and texts that are exchanged to smooth coordination and resolve conflicts. At times, our informants wondered if PM Mark Rutte (2010–present) is ever off his mobile phone.

Policy-making in The Netherlands is fragmented. Constitutionally, responsibility for policy lies with the individual ministers and their departments. Departments are effectively silos. The effect of this fragmentation on the core executive has been long recognised. It means decision-making is either sucked upwards by the PM or leaked downwards into various informal forums and meetings of politicians and members of the core executive who broker a consensus (Andeweg, 1990, p. 18). The cabinet's role is to legitimate decisions effectively taken elsewhere in the core executive. We found no evidence to suggest any change in the role of the cabinet. On the contrary, the cabinet as meeting is not the most opportune forum for decision-making, especially when the cabinet cannot rely on a solid majority in the parliament or senate. A cabinet secretary reiterated the formal position: 'So, the PM wears two hats: first he is head of a department. Second, the PM has the responsibility for the coordination of cabinet policy' (interview March 2017). He continues to say: 'the ministers are responsible for their domain and the PM is only responsible for the coordination of domains, and only when there is a problem' (interview Cabinet Secretary, March 2017). Still, the informal power of the PM is 'huge: everyone knows in the end the PM can decide' (interview Cabinet Secretary, March 2017; cf.: Visser, 2009). The legal position of the PM has been strengthened in subtle ways, for example, with regard to agenda setting (Andeweg & Irwin, 2014, p. 154). But to insiders 'the informal things are much more important. I would say that the key power is the power to persuade' (interview minister, March 2017).

The prime minister, cabinet and the surrounding meetings are the sole focal point of coordination. As a result, there are more inner cabinet and bilateral meetings, such as the 'turret consultation'—a reference to the location of the PM's office in the '*Torentje*' or turret (Andeweg & Timmermans, 2008, p. 272; Fiers & Krouwel, 2005, p. 135). More and more matters are for the PM. The point of these informal coffee dates is to prevent rude surprises. A minister assured us: 'I have never been faced with any surprise in the formal cabinet meeting on Friday' (interview March 2017). In fact, experienced ministers know the ritual: if there are no surprises, you have done the work. A Minister of Finance: 'A good minister will always try to get into the cabinet meeting without having a disagreement with a colleague' (interview March 2017). If ministers are to navigate the core executive effectively, they need to make sure that their colleagues and their departments—especially the PM—are on board before the cabinet meeting starts. A PMO councillor added: 'if the PM doesn't know about it, he will certainly push it away' (interview March 2017).

A deputy PM explained the persistence of this practice of overcoming hurdles before and outside the cabinet meeting: 'He [PM Rutte] only wants to have issues on the Friday agenda from those meetings that have been resolved, so that the Friday is available for current affairs, events and sometimes the real big things that cannot be solved immediately' (interview March 2017). A cabinet secretary echoed this practice and PM Rutte's preferences: 'If he has to interfere, he will. Then we will organise a smaller meeting for him to preside over, with two or three ministers and a few civil servants' (interview July 2017).

The Dutch core executive has become segmented, proliferating committees of all kinds. Coordination no longer happens in the full cabinet. Andeweg's (1990) 'gearbox' metaphor for conflict management is still apt. Yet, given the fragility, volatility and fragmentation of Dutch parliamentary politics, the gearbox now has as many gears as a Formula 1 racing car, and top gear is the court of the prime minister.

Mapping Dutch Court Politics

A nodal or core network around the PM—the court—supports the pivotal role of the PM. It links to several other core executive networks, which overlap, but only the core network links to all of them (see Fig. 8.2). Of 't Hart's (2014) four types of courts, the PM's court as an arena for bargaining and conflict resolution best captures Dutch practice. We map its 2012–2017 shape.

At the heart of it are the PM and two advisers. PMs chair the cabinet meeting, cabinet committee meetings and every other meeting they attend. They prioritise or postpone issues on the agenda and give the decisive vote where necessary. The PM is increasingly becoming *more* than '*primus inter pares*'—despite a humble legal basis, the PM is becoming 'more equal than others'.

As councillor-in-chief, the permanent secretary of the PMO is also a respected spokesperson for the PM in internal forums such as cabinet committees or bilateral meetings with ministers (Van Dorp & 't Hart, 2019). The prime ministerial adviser is the main partisan adviser and

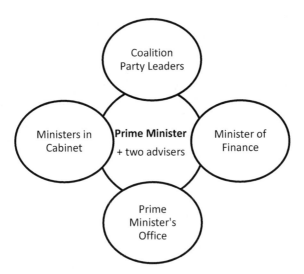

Fig. 8.2 The prime minister's court (2012–2017)

advises on any political matter. Until 2002, this adviser was a relatively low-key actor, performing a liaison function between the PM and his political party—s/he would not interact with the press or the public (Van den Berg, 2018). This is still the norm. One prime ministerial adviser commented about the job: 'Advisers are not allowed to talk to the press, but many of them do' (interview July 2017). The prime ministerial adviser has almost complete freedom because s/he 'has a special position'.

The top circle in Fig. 8.2 is clearly political and informal. It is a widely recognised network of the PM, the deputy PMs (each coalition party nominates one deputy PM) and the respective delegation leaders of the coalition parties in the parliament (cf: Andeweg & Timmermans, 2008). When they all attend, the party leaders of the coalition are in the room. This is where the coalition balance is coordinated, contested and reconciled. Although discussions may be about specific policies, legislation or decision-making, this forum is specifically aiming at consolidating any fragilities of the coalition and keeping it together. The political advisers of the respective members and various digital media, including WhatsApp groups, parallel this forum. A parliamentary journalist identified the importance of this circle during the 2012–2017 government: '[the] cabinet meeting itself lost its significance in a very big way […] all the big decisions were discussions outside of the cabinet. The PM likes to do it that way' (interview July 2017).

The Minister of Finance is a key player in these networks. S/he will often be a deputy PM and leader of one of the coalition parties. No funding can proceed before it is 'cleared' by the Ministry of Finance and few policies do not cost money: 'nothing was flying if he didn't give his seal of approval' (interview minister, July 2017). In a smoothly functioning coalition, the PM and the Minister of Finance work closely together. A Minister of Finance said: 'The finance minister can only play his role if he is at all times backed by the PM' (interview April 2017).

Fourth is the PMO. There are about 15 '*raadadviseurs*' or councillors, each liaising with a department or a major policy portfolio. Some councillors are assisted by a junior adviser, totalling fewer than 25 people, excluding support staff. One of its permanent secretaries commented: '[T]hat is its big advantage. It's small. It's quick. The prime minister is quick. So, it's always ahead of the game. That is at least what the PMO tries. It hates surprises' (interview October 2017). The councillors have direct access to the PM and multiple points of entry into their respective departments at all levels. Councillors are typically high-flying non-partisan civil servants with not only expertise but also sensitive political antennae. They borrow authority because working with the PM confers influence—and everyone knows it—but come without any formal powers. They work in the shadow of the PM's authority. They struck us as energetic, witty and—once you are through security doors—easily accessible.

The final part of the court covers the members of the cabinet. The cabinet is the ultimate formal decision-making forum of the Dutch core executive and it is where decisions need to be approved. It can act as a tiebreaker for deadlocked issues that get pushed upstairs by the committees. Yet, we contend the weekly cabinet meeting is better understood as a closing ceremony that legitimises this process. Of course, it is not merely symbolic because Dutch ministers spend many hours in cabinet meetings (cf: Andeweg & Irwin, 2014, p. 157), and because, like much else in politics, cabinet's role is shaped by the contingencies of the moment. It can weave various disparate strands of decision-making together to make sure they are consistent with the coalition agreement and its narrative.

Although we believe the PM's court captures an essential element of the Dutch executive, that does not mean it is the only existing set of networks. There are other networks—for example, the committee on socioeconomic policy commonly known as 'the triangle'. Nor does it mean that people who are situated in less nodal networks have less influence on Dutch executive government. On the contrary, despite institutional settings and power differences, people make the system work for them by showing political nous, deploying smart power and avoiding rude surprises. During our study, the deputy PM and party leaders were part of the same 'court' but given the contingencies of political life, one or more of them could lead a rival 'court'. When we were interviewing (March–October 2017), few would have been surprised if that were the fate of the unfolding Rutte-III Cabinet.

The Rise of the Prime Minister

Against this backdrop of the everyday workings of the core executive, our interviewees shared the view that the Dutch prime minister (the office, not just the current incumbent) was on the rise (see also Fiers & Krouwel, 2005). Their argument is that the influence of the PM has strengthened incrementally—the PM can interfere with any policy, despite the legal convention of individual ministerial responsibility. More and more issues and policies become framed as '*chefsache*'—a matter for the boss. A long-serving councillor in the PMO illustrated this point: 'There is no way of keeping the PM out. Today, the PM has to answer for what other ministers said or did' (interview March 2017). The increased involvement and centrality of the PM in cabinet decisions and everyday life of the core executive was widely accepted by interviewees. Most of our interviewees claim the PM has become more influential. Those who hesitated claimed that PMs have always been more influential than they seemed: 'Nevertheless, it depends on the person. In the 1980s, we already had a very strong PM Ruud Lubbers who really had much more clout than the office would describe' (interview Permanent Secretary, October 2017).

The beliefs about the office of the PM fit into a tradition of Dutch governance that many interviewees subscribe to. A permanent secretary: 'Dutch history is steeped in a tradition of dividing powers—even ambiguity about who is really in power. That was already the case 400 years ago. Every time someone starts to act like a real sovereign—that will be the end of it' (interview October 2017). To fit this tradition, PMs nourish the idea that they have no real power. They are 'masters the art' of not admitting they are powerful, and there is 'a deliberate ambiguity about who is really in power' (interview March 2017).

Yet our interviewees consistently pointed to the rise of the PM. They provided four partial and overlapping explanations for the increasing prominence of the office of the PM: (1) summitry and Europeanisation; (2) the personalisation of politics; (3) crisis management and (4) the changing party-political landscape (see also Andeweg, 2008, pp. 267–268; De Vries et al., 2012; Van den Berg, 1990).

Summitry and Europeanisation

Our interviewees suggested that the impact of European Union (EU) leadership summits on domestic policy-making led PMs to become more prominent. Much national legislation is impacted by EU decisions. It is discussed mainly by ministers of the respective departments and the Minister of Foreign Affairs and in meetings of Eurocrats (Geuijen et al., 2008). However, at the key summits (e.g., on Brexit and G20) and the European Council, only the PM is invited as 'diplomat-in-chief' (De Vries et al., 2012, p. 161). Here, his prominence is increased at the expense of the ministers. A permanent secretary illustrated this point: 'The EU, and the European Council in particular, have a very important role in that because there's only one guy going to the European Council no matter what the subject is. [...] The Dutch PM has to work on the same level as the French president and the German *Bundeskanzler* and so on. And they don't care about the fact that Dutch PMs have a different mandate' (interview October 2017).

A former PM reiterates the same point: 'For example, on international issues or European issues, well the role of prime ministers and political leaders is becoming more and more important because they, [...] well they represent their country' (interview April 2017). In his memoir, Bernard Bot reminisces this is 'a reality the Minister of Foreign Affairs needs to learn to live with' (Bot, 2015, p. 265). Key policies and legislation are discussed and established in European forums in which only the PM has a seat at the table. Interviewee after interviewee stressed the impact of the EU. A minister noted that before 1970: 'No prime minister had any international experience' (interview March 2017). Today's PMs increasingly walk on an international stage (see also Fiers & Krouwel, 2005, p. 132).

Personalisation of Politics

Second, the interviewees stressed that the growing visibility of the PM and the personalisation of politics have augmented the prominence of the PM in another way (Karvonen, 2010; Poguntke & Webb, 2005). Media images of EU summits and crises depict the PMs as personifications of their government. The EU is not the only factor. The equivalent of international summitry occurs whenever there is a domestic crisis or a security issue. A ministerial adviser to the PM makes this point: 'The media are influencing the activities of the PM. This is because—more than ever before—when there is something going on in parliament, members say: "we want the PM in this debate too"' (interview March 2017). A deputy PM explains: 'Well, I think there is a natural tendency that the press and public opinion want to have one person who is symbolising the government' (interview April 2017).

Politics and elections focus on the PM; they too have become personalised. Paradoxically, Boumans et al. (2011) chart the increased media attention on Dutch and British politicians, noting that less senior politicians have received more attention in recent years. Still, the PM is singled out and receives the most attention. Mediatisation may be all pervasive, but the PM is the focus (De Vries et al., 2012, p. 160). The current incumbent, Mark Rutte, has 'rock star appeal'. While doing our interviews, we watched his arrival at the 'turret' when he was mobbed by a party of schoolchildren on a visit to parliament. He chatted with them, they took selfies and the event was surrounded by a hubbub of excitement. It happens wherever he goes, and he carries it off with a smile and aplomb—we saw a political celebrity working an enthused crowd.

Crisis Management

The PM is increasingly involved in crisis management. The Netherlands faces as many crises as any other country in Western Europe, and they will be a matter for the boss. A permanent secretary in the PMO reflected: 'In crises, and with big things happening in the country, he is—of course—on television. He is the first who has to address it' (interview March 2017). This was illustrated by the COVID-19 crisis. From March 2021 on, when The Netherlands introduced measures against the spread of the virus, the PM was front and centre. He gave two solo addresses to the nation on live television with viewings exceeding most football matches, although for most press conferences he was flanked by ministers of health and experts.

Similarly, three years earlier in March 2017, days before general elections and fresh in our interviewees' memories, the PM played a dominant front stage role in a diplomatic crisis. He publicly denied access to The Netherlands to multiple high-level officials from Turkey. Their presence caused unrest and division, culminating in urban riots and elite police units removing the Turkish official. Although diplomacy, local affairs and law and order are not formally the exclusive prerogative of the PM, Rutte was the only visible minister representing the executive branch. There is a sharp contrast with earlier crises in which the Dutch government had to counter an 'invisible' enemy. In 1986, radioactive material spread over Europe as a result of the Chernobyl explosion, resulting in eating restrictions. A former director-general remembers that PM Lubbers: 'felt so, apparently, comfortable, that he did not cancel his trip to Japan, and went. So, he left it to this group of ministers to handle the thing' (interview March 2017). Few would imagine a present-day PM travelling abroad in such a situation. S/he would instead be front stage.

The Changing Party Landscape

The fourth reason is the growing complexity of the Dutch political landscape. In The Netherlands, there used to be three 'big' parties (Christian-Democrat, Social-Democrat and Conservative-Liberal). After 2002, they were no longer preeminent. There has been an upsurge in right wing populist parties, with Geert Wilders' Freedom Party the most well-known example. At the time of our interviews, 13 parties were elected to parliament, with the biggest having 22% of the seats. The changes in the party system were summarised by Pennings and Keman (2008, pp. 174–176) as 'pendulum consociationalism'—that is, the party system swings between consensual and adversarial styles depending on the electoral climate. If the party landscape has changed, the need for brokering majorities in parliament has increased (Kolltveit, 2014). The PM tries to meet this need. The PM has a decisive role as leader of the biggest political party to work across the aisle and broker majorities for the cabinet's programme. A deputy PM argued: 'The most effective PMs have always been PMs who have had very flexible personal and political opinions. If you have very strong personal views, then you will not survive as PM in the Netherlands' (interview

March 2017). A PM commented on his struggle to balance party interests and lead a coalition government while in office:

> It is always hard to find the balance between serving the interests of your country and serving the interests of your party. As PM you have to serve the interests of the country, whether you like it or not. That means that if compromises are necessary—and quite often they are necessary—then you have to be in a position where people take you seriously irrespective of the political party they come from. (Interview April 2017)

Though we report the rise of the PM, our research was not about individuals or about the 2010–present incumbent Mark Rutte. Rather, we focused on the collective in which multiple actors, including the PM, have a role. We now explore the implications of court politics and the rise of the PM for the craft that its officeholders must master.

Prime Ministerial Craft

The rise of the office of the PM should not be understood as a linear trend towards 'presidentialisation'. As always, the political capital and influence of individual PMs waxes and wanes during their tenures, both in The Netherlands and beyond (Strangio et al., 2016, 2017; Swinkels et al., 2017; 't Hart & Schelfhout, 2016; Weller et al., 2021). For example, Ruud Lubbers (1982–1994) was widely recognised as an effective 'operator' who acted as a spider in the web of collective decision-making, although he lost much of his touch and impact during his third term in office. His successor Wim Kok (1994–2002) had to grow into the role, then played it masterfully for several years, only to suffer one of the most acute losses of standing in Dutch political history in the six months between 9/11 and the 2002 elections. Jan-Peter Balkenende (2002–2010) was regarded initially as inexperienced, although he gained influence later, particularly on the international stage. The social skills and political flexibility of the current incumbent, Mark Rutte (2010–present), were universally recognised, but now governing a complex multi-party minority government even his powers of persuasion are being taxed. Individual officeholders differ in the way they take up their roles, but the expectations that come with the office have increased.

According to a long-serving parliamentary journalist, the craft of the PM concentrates on: 'the ability to make political deals. That's the only way you can work in this system' (interview July 2017). Our interviews echo the observation of De Vries et al. (2012, p. 162) that the predominance of the position of the Dutch PM is 'rooted in subtle process management rather than blunt realities of a direct and personal political mandate'. Prime ministerial craft steers the court. Influence is found not in monocratic office holding or in the wielding of executive orders, but is a reflection of how the Dutch core executive has intensified its focus on the PM. Whereas the argument used to be 'not just *chairman*, not yet *chief*' (Andeweg, 1991; italics added), we see PMs as diplomat-in-chief (summitry and Europeanisation), communicator-in-chief (personalisation of politics), crisis and issue manager-in-chief (crisis management) and boundary spanner-in-chief (changing party landscape). A former PM stressed the paradox of the increased standing when 'you're not the boss' (interview April 2017). They are not monocratic, not even in crises, but demand for policy coordination steers political actors towards them (cf: Van den Berg, 1990, p. 116).

So, PMs are at the centre of information streams, committees and negotiations. To maintain this position, it is vital, as our informants explained, that the PM should be perceived as a 'helper', not as a 'threat'. After all, PMs' standing is not a given—and being PM is a skilful craft (Weller, 2018). To cultivate this craft, PMs need a measure (and varieties) of 'leadership capital', including hard and soft skills, reputational capital and relational capital (Bennister et al., 2017). The following metaphor captures our interpretation of our informants' interpretation.

Imagine a complex policy issue as a house of cards. Each card represents an actor, a promise, a grievance or a deadline, all of which are common for a complex policy. While all cards are neatly stacked, little is needed to tip over the entire house. It is very easy to destroy the game, especially in the Dutch system which is built on interdependency and the willingness to compromise. The task of PMs is to tiptoe around the house of cards. They protect the game of building houses of cards, rather than a single card or even the whole house. An urge they should probably resist is to add more cards to the house. This would make the house yet more complex and prone to collapse. In other words, they should hesitate to add their own ideology, policy whims or ego—instead, they mediate in conflicts and seek to break deadlocks. There is no fixed set of skills for managing the house of cards. No leadership traits are uniquely suited to the task. However, it is all too obvious when the PM's craft does not fit the circumstances in which they play the cards—the house collapses.

In the early 2020s, the four interconnected trends identified by our interviewees mean that more and more is expected of PMs. Keeping the house together is no longer good enough. Such demands make the 'rise-of-the-PM' narrative a cautionary tale. Though elevated standing may provide some levers to realise a cabinet agenda and to get things done, it is also an increasingly vulnerable position. Where the PM used to be held responsible for keeping the multi-party cabinet together, the current view also makes the PM an 'issue-manager-in-chief'—responsible for volatile issues ministers might be eager to buck-pass on. The question of whether the 'weak' office of the PM will be able to sustain its officeholders to keep doing the impossible remains unanswered. They may have more influence than before, but perhaps not enough to meet party and public expectations.

Conclusion: Courts, Influence and Executive Government

In this chapter, we have discussed the position of the Dutch PM and its rise to prominence despite marginal increases in legal or organisational resources, in order to understand how this has impacted the workings of the core executive. We provided elite interview data, updating the existing literature and providing a distinctive interpretation of those data. It is not a static picture but a description of 'everyday politics', the way politics and collective decision-making are done in Dutch executive government on a day-to-day basis.

Without pretending to fully resolve our initial puzzle, we suggest three conclusions. First, four interconnected trends sustain and drive the increased predominance of the office of the PM. The PM is still 'not yet chief', but the recent officeholders are increasingly momentary chiefs: diplomat-in-chief, communicator-in-chief, crisis manager-in-chief and boundary spanner-in-chief. Second, the increased need for coordination underpins a formal and informal 'court' seeking to prevent 'rude surprises'. We have mapped the PM's court, the key individuals and forums and the circles of influence. Third, predominance and the court place a high premium on prime ministerial craft. If more is expected from the office, while that office provides few legal and organisational resources, courtiers may look to the officeholder to compensate.

This, we believe, provides a novel interpretation of Dutch executive government that is helpful for two reasons. First, it encompasses *multiple* actors involved in decision-making, coordination and conflict resolution, not just the PM and the cabinet. Though we foreground the PM, we follow in the footsteps of our interviewees, who included ministers, civil servants and ministerial advisers. Second, we focus on the stated *beliefs and practices* of members of the core executive, so we can identify changes in those beliefs and practices. Above all, the core executive and court politics approach captures the ebb and flow of influence in the core executive, throughout meandering political and administrative seasons. From their origins in the study of the majoritarian Westminster systems we believe these concepts travel well to consensual multi-party systems such as The Netherlands.

References

Andeweg, R. (Ed.). (1990). *Ministers en Ministerraad*. Sdu Uitgevers.
Andeweg, R. (1991). The Dutch Prime Minister: Not Just Chairman, Not Yet Chief? *West European Politics, 14*(2), 116–132.
Andeweg, R. (1997). Collegiality and Collectivity: Cabinets, Cabinet Committees and Cabinet Ministers. In P. Weller, H. Bakvis, & R. A. W. Rhodes (Eds.), *The Hollow Crown. Countervailing Trends in Core Executives* (pp. 58–83). Macmillan.
Andeweg, R. (2008). Coalition Politics in The Netherlands. From Accommodation to Politicization. *Acta Politica, 43*(2–3), 254–277.
Andeweg, R., & Irwin, G. (2014). *Governance and Politics of the Netherlands* (4th ed.). Macmillan Education.
Andeweg, R., & Timmermans, A. (2008). Conflict Management in Coalition Government. In K. Strøm, W. Müller, & T. Bergman (Eds.), *Cabinets and Coalition Bargaining. The Democratic Life Cycle in Western Europe* (pp. 269–300). Oxford University Press.
Bäck, H., Teorell, J., & Lindberg, S. (2019). Cabinets, Prime Ministers, and Corruption: A Comparative Analysis of Parliamentary Governments in Post-War Europe. *Political Studies, 67*(1), 149–170.
Belinfante, A., & De Reede, J. (2009). *Beginselen van het Nederlandse Staatsrecht* (16th ed.). Kluwer.
Bennister, M., 't Hart, P., & Worthy, B. (2017). *The Leadership Capital Index: A New Perspective on Political Leadership*. Oxford University Press.
Bot, B. (2015). *Achteraf bezien*. Promotheus.
Boumans, J. W., Boomgaarden, H. G., & Vliegenthart, R. (2011). Media Personalisation in Context: A Cross-national Comparison between the UK and the Netherlands, 1992–2007. *Political Studies, 61*(1), 198–216.

Bovend'eert, P., Hoekstra, R., & Eppink, D. (2005). *Over de versterking van de positie van de Minister-president.* Ars Aequi Libri.

Braun, V., & Clarke, V. (2006). Using Thematic Analysis in Psychology. *Qualitative Research in Psychology,* 3(2), 77–101.

Daalder, H. (1955). Parties and Politics in the Netherlands. *Political Studies,* 3(1), 1–16.

De Vries, J., 't Hart, P., & Onstein, H. (2012). From Oblivion to Limelight: Stability and Change in Dutch Post-Prime Ministerial Careers. In K. Theakston & J. De Vries (Eds.), *Former Leaders in Modern Democracies* (pp. 161–185). Palgrave Macmillan.

Empson, L. (2018). Elite Interviewing in Professional Organizations. *Journal of Professions and Organization,* 5(1), 58–69.

Fiers, S., & Krouwel, A. (2005). The Low Countries: From 'PMs to President-Minister'. In T. Poguntke & P. Webb (Eds.), *The Presidentialization of Politics: A Comparative Study of Modern Democracies* (pp. 128–158). Oxford University Press.

Geuijen, K., 't Hart, P., Princen, S., & Yesilkagit, K. (Eds.). (2008). *National Civil Servants in EU Policymaking.* Amsterdam University Press.

Hoekstra, R. J. (1983). *De ministerraad in Nederland: Preadvies van de Vereniging voor de vergelijkende studie van het recht van Belgie en Nederland.* Tjeenk Willink.

Karvonen, L. (2010). *The Personalisation of Politics: A Study of Parliamentary Democracies.* ECPR Press.

Kolltveit, K. (2014). Concentration of Power in Cabinets: Exploring the Importance of the Party Political Context. *Acta Politica,* 49(3), 266–285.

Lijphart, A. (1968). *The Politics of Accommodation. Pluralism and Democracy in the Netherlands.* University of California Press.

Pennings, P., & Keman, H. (2008). The Changing Landscape of Dutch Politics since the 1970s. *Acta Politica,* 43(2–3), 154–179.

Poguntke, T., & Webb, P. (Eds.). (2005). *The Presidentialization of Politics: A Comparative Study of Modern Democracies.* Oxford University Press.

Rehwinkel, J. P. (1991). *De Minister-President. Eerste onder gelijken of gelijke onder eersten?* Tjeenk-Willink.

Rhodes, R. A. W. (1995). From Prime Ministerial Power to Core Executive. In R. A. W. Rhodes & P. Dunleavy (Eds.), *PM, Cabinet and Core Executive* (pp. 11–37). Macmillan.

Rhodes, R. A. W. (2017). On Court Politics. In R. A. W. Rhodes (Ed.), *Interpretive Political Science. Selected Essays. Volume II* (pp. 115–129). Oxford University Press.

Rijksoverheid. (2019). *Hoe komt een wet tot stand.* Retrieved November 18, 2019, from https://www.rijksoverheid.nl/onderwerpen/wetgeving/hoe-komt-een-wet-tot-stand

Strangio, P., 't Hart, P., & Walter, J. (2016). *Settling the Office: The Australian Prime Ministership from Federation to Reconstruction*. Melbourne University Press.

Strangio, P., 't Hart, P., & Walter, J. (2017). *The Pivot of Power: Australian Prime Ministers and Political Leadership 1950–2016*. Melbourne University Press.

Swinkels, M., Van Zuydam, S., & Van Esch, F. (2017). Modern Prime-Ministerial Leadership in the Netherlands: Consensus or Confrontation? In M. Bennister, M. Worthy, & P. 't Hart (Eds.), *The Leadership Capital Index: A New Perspective on Political Leadership* (pp. 164–182). Oxford University Press.

't Hart, P. (2014). *Understanding Public Leadership*. Palgrave Macmillan.

't Hart, P., & Schelfhout, D. (2016). Assessing Prime-Ministerial Performance in a Multi-party Democracy: The Dutch Case. *Acta Politica, 51*(6), 153–172.

Timmermans, A. (2003). *High Politics in the Low Countries. An Empirical Study of Coalition Agreements in Belgium and The Netherlands*. Ashgate Publishing.

Timmermans, A., & Breeman, G. (2009). Politieke agendavorming en collegiale besluitvorming in de Ministerraad. In A. Bekke, K. Breed, & P. de Jong (Eds.), *Naar een collegiaal en samenhangend overheidsbestuur* (pp. 75–90). Sdu Uitgevers.

Van den Berg, J. (1990). De Minister-president: aanjager van noodzakelijk beleid. In R. Andeweg (Ed.), *Ministers en Ministerraad* (pp. 97–125). Sdu Uitgeverij.

Van den Berg, C. (2018). The Netherlands: The Emergence and Encapsulation of Ministerial Advisers. In R. Shaw & C. Eichbaum (Eds.), *Ministers, Minders and Mandarins. An International Study of Relationships at the Executive Summit of Parliamentary Democracies* (pp. 129–144). Edward Elgar Publishing.

Van Dorp, E. J., & 't Hart, P. (2019). Navigating the Dichotomy: The Craft of Top Public Servants. *Public Administration, 97*(4), 877–891.

Visser, R. (2009). *In dienst van het algemeen belang*. BOOM.

Weller, P. (2003). Cabinet Government: An Elusive Ideal? *Public Administration, 81*(4), 701–722.

Weller, P. (2018). *The Prime Minister's Craft: Why Some Succeed and Others Fail in Westminster Systems*. Oxford University Press.

Weller, P., Grube, D., & Rhodes, R. A. W. (2021). *Comparing Cabinets*. Oxford University Press.

PART IV

Core Executives in Scandinavia

CHAPTER 9

The Swedish Executive: Centralising from Afar

Erik Brinde, Thurid Hustedt, and Heidi Houlberg Salomonsen

INTRODUCTION

For the avid public administration scholar, Sweden presents a most interesting case when it comes to the organisation of government and the core executive. On the one hand, Swedish state governance is characterised by a dualist tradition whose foundation dates as far back as the seventeenth century (Ehn et al., 2003); one marked by clear boundaries between the core executive and administration, as well as national and local

E. Brinde (✉)
Gothenburg, Sweden

T. Hustedt
Hertie School, Berlin, Germany
e-mail: Hustedt@hertie-school.org

H. H. Salomonsen
Department of Management, Aarhus University, Aarhus, Denmark
e-mail: hhs@mgmt.au.dk

© The Author(s), under exclusive license to Springer Nature Switzerland AG 2022
K. Kolltveit, R. Shaw (eds.), *Core Executives in a Comparative Perspective*, Understanding Governance,
https://doi.org/10.1007/978-3-030-94503-9_9

governance. Yet, on the other, this administrative dualism also appears ripely positioned to successfully embrace the deepening trend of 'steering at a distance' associated with the New Public Management (NPM) practices which have dominated administrative reform policies in many countries in recent decades (Klijn & Koppenjan, 2015, p. 7). This leaves several interesting questions on the table for this chapter to engage with, particularly with regards to steering, coordination and changing power relations. For example, has the long-standing tradition of institutional dualism facilitated a smoother implementation of NPM practices? Does the historical experience of at-distance steering translate into stronger coordination capacities? And finally, what effects have NPM and other relevant phenomena such as mediatisation and politicisation had on the power dynamics across the Swedish state? By the end of this chapter, light will have been shed on these and other relevant matters.

The remainder of the chapter proceeds as follows. The first section provides an outline of the institutional landscape surrounding the Swedish core executive, followed by a discussion of administrative reforms. The subsequent section explores dynamics in Swedish governance regarding central-local relations, politicisation and control at central government level and in Swedish crisis management as well as mediatisation. The chapter concludes by taking stock of Swedish centralisation.

The Executive Landscape[1]

Throughout the years, the Swedish core executive has existed under a variety of names and forms, yet has remained largely true to the structural characteristics discussed herein (Regeringskansliet, 2008). Until the constitutional reforms of 1974, the executive branch went under the name of the Royal Majesty's Office. But when the monarchy abdicated its power, the core executive was renamed as the Government Offices (*Regeringskansliet*), which was now to lead the country together with the Swedish Parliament, known as the Riksdag (Regeringskansliet, 1974). The Government Offices was at the time still separated from the different ministerial departments; this changed with the reform of 1997, whereby all ministries—along with the Office for Administrative Affairs (*Förvaltningsavdelingen*)—merged with the Prime Minister's Office (PMO) (*Statsrådsberedningen*) under one roof, at which point the Government Offices was also declared an official state authority (Jacobsson, 2001). As such, the Government Offices is to be understood as a single public authority including the line ministries, the PMO and the Office for Administrative Affairs.

The purpose of this merger was, first and foremost, to be able to meet the rising demands associated with political internationalisation, European Union (EU) membership and major public-sector change with greater flexibility (see section C1. 'Regeringskansliet m.m' of Sveriges Riksdag, 1996). The centralisation of the executive also served to consolidate power in the Government Offices in lieu of the Parliament, whose sway over governmental affairs has diminished in recent decades. Today, the Swedish Parliament acts as a democratic custodian more than anything else, authorising government formations every fourth year as well as deciding on legislative and budgetary proposals, while also assisting the government in shaping some foreign and EU policy (Sveriges Riksdag, 2021).

Focusing on the core executive in the Government Offices, its function is largely to support the prime minister and his or her government in all matters of governance. This includes various coordination activities on the international, national and subnational levels; preparatory work related to legislative and budgetary proposals going to the parliament; communication and press-related issues; senior public-servant appointments; work of a project- or programme-specific nature; as well as other support tasks internal to the department.

Today there are 21 ministers in total inside the Offices, each responsible for one or part of the 12 ministerial wings of the Government (Regeringskansliet, 2021a). Although the prime minister (PM) is the one that leads the organisation, executive decision-making is made collectively in accordance with the constitution, which requires the attendance of at least a handful of ministers for decisions to be legitimate (Regeringskansliet, 2021b). Aside from the PM having the authority to convene meetings and appoint or dismiss department heads at will, officially at least, power is more or less shared amongst the ministers (Öberg & Wockelberg, 2015, p. 132). In practice, however, ministerial influence can differ depending on the status of a minister in relation to the procedural issue at hand (for instance, the Minister for Finance in discussions regarding the budget). As such, Swedish ministers can be said to wield relatively less power than their European peers, especially under more diverse coalition governments.

There are roughly 4600 civil servants employed across all ministries, including some 200 political appointees working closely with the ministers (Regeringskansliet, 2021c). Recruitment is generally delegated to agencies and conducted according to meritocratic criteria, though the government possesses noteworthy control when it comes to appointing agency heads, other related boardroom and council positions, as well as county governors. While such senior positions are usually publicly advertised, the government still has the final word in selection, based on its own interpretation of appropriate merits (Ehn, 2015; Hysing & Olsson, 2012, p. 61; Sveriges Riksdag, 2017): insiders have emphasised governmental loyalty as a decisive factor (Johansson, 2008, p. 279).

Over the centuries the Swedish core executive has remained comparatively modest in size, largely due to a constitutionally grounded dualism, which together with public transparency, decentralised local governance and stakeholder involvement, comprise the hallmarks of Swedish state administration (for a thorough elaboration, see Hall, 2015). Notwithstanding some modern innovations, the essence of this dualism has and continues to be a separation between policy-making and the bureaucracy in national and local governance: that is, between the Government Offices on the one hand, and both (national and local) state agencies as well as municipalities carrying out the majority of administrative work on the other (see, e.g., Ehn et al., 2003). As such, the role of the executive branch is largely centred around coordination from on high: steering the ship while delegating work on deck, so to speak. Such an arrangement is exemplified by the close to 255,000 employees across what is currently 341 different agencies (down from 1300 agencies in the early 1990s owing to mergers and centralisation) (Statskontoret, 2021, pp. 13, 37).

While agencies are responsible for implementation, the executive has a long history of drawing on commissions for formulating policy (Ehn, 2015). These have been at the heart of the nation's strong labour tradition, and an essential forum for stakeholder compromise and consensual policy-making. Outside the legislative domain, executive steering of agencies officially occurs through ordinances and appropriation letters, the latter containing various guidelines, priorities and aims for the new budget year (Government Offices of Sweden, 2021). Although agencies remain answerable to their respective ministries and the overarching goals of the government, they still enjoy considerable autonomy in their everyday operations under the protection of the constitution—which precludes the parliament, Government Offices as well as presiding ministers from meddling with agency business, as they exercise authority within their given mandate (Andersson, 2004). Still, the Swedish Constitution appears to leave plenty of room for interpretation on a number of issues, including how far this agency independence actually extends (Öberg & Wockelberg, 2015, p. 133). Indeed, it has been argued that the constitutional architecture has been set up to give, again, not individual ministers, but the Government (Offices) as a whole, greater reach on the political input side while also allowing for leeway and tractability in decision-making and procuring policy objectives (ibid.; Öberg, 2015).

Ways and Means of Securing Coordination

Social Democratic one-party leadership was long the rule rather than the exception in Swedish politics. This changed in the mid-1970s as government formation took on an increasingly coalitional tone, which since 2006 has become the normative state of affairs. While the greater bargaining complexity of minority governments appears to have had noticeably little effect on the stability of Sweden's parliamentary democracy (Lindvall et al., 2020), it does seem to have necessitated the greater use of political advisers on behalf of ministers (Noreland, 2019). Still, with the recent establishment of the populist right party Sweden Democrats, a heightened sense of uncertainty lingers over the future of Swedish coalition dynamics and political issue salience. This uncertainty sits alongside the long-established normative understanding of Swedish governance as based on a tradition of negotiated and coordinated compromise and consensus-seeking. Within the executive, this is reflected in a number of different coordination mechanisms (including those relating to government communications, which are dealt with later in the chapter).

Political coordination units staffed with political appointees have been established (Dahlström & Pierre, 2011, p. 200), alongside formal rules prescribing how political coordination and the preparation of policies and strategies should be performed, whether these involve different ministries (*gemensam beredning*) or the entire government (*allmän beredning*) (Ministry of Finance, 2004, p. 112). While critiques of these rather comprehensive procedural rules for coordination have been voiced, they are in general perceived as functioning well, in part due to the relatively high level of trust among the coordinating actors (Jacobsson, 2019, pp. 21–22).

Gemensam beredning can be described as informal meetings on cross-departmental issues, primarily involving ministers concerned with the specific issue(s); the allmän beredning, led by the PM in a slightly more formal manner following each Thursday's cabinet meeting, focuses on the current state of politics, allowing ministers to raise issues before going public

(Ullström, 2011, pp. 231–232). Although minutes are taken at cabinet meetings in case dissenting opinions exist, it is the government which 'determines which specific principles are to apply to the decision-making process at cabinet meetings—for example, whether votes are to be taken, whether the majority rule is to apply or whether the prime minister's and party leader's votes are to carry more weight than those of other ministers' (Sundström, 2009, p. 150).

This suggests that the significance of these different types of formal meetings can vary. Cabinet meetings are described as 'strictly formalised', constituting 'a simple registration of decisions which have already been made' (Larsson, 2002, p. 196). Rather, it is the allmän beredning which constitutes the main forum for the government's collective discussions of political issues (Sundström, 2009, p. 150). The latter are more informal. As described by Larsson:

> The summons to these informal sessions are issued by the Prime Minister's Office, and usually follow directly upon a Cabinet meeting. During these informal sessions a minister will present to his (sic) colleagues the issue at hand, often assisted by civil servants from the relevant ministry. When the reports have been presented, the civil servants leave the room and wait outside while the Cabinet discusses the issue. Votes are extremely rare at such meetings, and the normal procedure is that the Prime Minister summarises the debate after general discussion and establishes the government policy. (2002, p. 196)

Alongside these formal meetings are the more informal lunch meetings (lunch beredningar) which take place each weekday but Friday, and where no minutes are taken (Sundström, 2009, p. 150; Ullström, 2011, p. 230). Described as an 'important forum for collective deliberation' (Sundström, 2009, p. 150), since the 1920s they have been a forum for eating lunch, discussing [issues] but also taking quite an amount of actual decisions (Sundström, 2009, p. 150).

The afore-mentioned central coordination unit under the PMO plays a vital role in government coordination, and is critical to the functioning of the core executive in Sweden: its responsibility is to ensure that there is a formal government decision on all new policies, and that these decisions are communicated. Husted and Salomonsen illustrate this vital role:

[P]olicy coordination is carried out between the political advisers in the central coordination unit and the state secretaries and does not involve the permanent civil servants in the line ministries (SWEPA2, SWEPA5, SWEPA2, SWEHD1). The role of the political advisers in this unit is generally described as relatively powerful for coordinating the political aspects of policy (SWEHD1, SWEPA5, SWEPA4). This unit has the political authority to ensure coordination in the case of disagreement due to 'turf wars' or party-political differences within the coalition—even blocking policy initiatives proposed by ministers and state secretaries if they do not fit with the political goals set by the coalition. Hence, the unit is the ultimate arbiter of the political sphere of horizontal government coordination for ensuring the coordination of policies from the perspective of the government as a whole before the cabinet level, and, indeed, casts a significant hierarchical shadow over the otherwise horizontal self-coordination activities. (2017, pp. 400–401)

At the bureaucratic level, the rather formalised procedures for political coordination provide for a strong civil service norm ensuring coordination at the administrative level (Premfors & Sundström, 2007, Chapter 7). Amongst other things, this is reflected in the civil service practice of anticipating other departments' points of view when preparing policies, in the interests of smoothing subsequent coordination (Premfors & Sundström, 2007, pp. 173–174; see also Sundström & Lemne, 2016, p. 468).

Compromises and consensus-seeking across the executive vis-à-vis the parliament and other important stakeholders are established via strong state-society ties, nurtured through frequent consultations and commissions with stakeholders (Elder & Page, 1998; Lindvall & Rothstein, 2006; Petersson, 2015). Given the rather small and compartmentalised structure of the Swedish state, scholars have attested to the vital role informal communications play in managing such relations—described as a hierarchical yet balanced interplay of teamwork and mutual trust based on normative expectations and foresight (Jacobsson, 1984; Jacobsson & Sundström, 2015, pp. 355–356; Niemann, 2013). In reality, such informality has caused something of a blurring of the lines between the administration and executive politics; and, as per the constitutional vagueness noted above, consensus-making bound by political loyalty seems to take precedence in most cases.

Leading the Way for Performative Governance

While the typical characteristics of Swedish state governance have, to a considerable degree, endured into the twenty-first century, recent decades have also brought notable change to the Government Offices. Over the last 50 years, and especially so in the last 30, Sweden has taken a leading role in the adoption of NPM (Sundström, 2015). Given the long-standing tradition of a bureaucracy that is largely separated from the political realm, the gradual introduction of NPM practices has not required as drastic a change as might have been the case elsewhere. Rather, Swedish NPM appears more as modest adjustments, complementing the tenacious normativity of consensus-making (Öberg & Wockelberg, 2015, p. 133). Perhaps the most relevant example has been the goal-oriented overtone now tied to the budget, which involves a two-way exchange of, on the one hand, additional guidance and performance monitoring from the executive, and on the other, both greater decision making independence as well as accountability requirements on the part of agencies (Grossi et al., 2018; Molander et al., 2002). If anything, this has meant fewer legislative decisions inside the Government Offices, and a heavier leaning towards the arm's length management of the numerous agencies under its watch (Jacobsson, 2001, p. 6).

In line with the broader rationale of the 1997 merger of the Government Offices, the utilisation of performance budgeting has been depicted as a reinforcement of political clout at the executive level as a way of managing the higher pace and demands of modern politics (read internationalisation, EU membership and public-sector complexities), and promoted for the sake of improved public-sector efficiency. Coinciding with these developments has been a substantial increase in the number of political appointees inside the Prime Minister's Office, including various expert advisers and, most relevantly for our chapter, press secretaries and other employees involved in government communication (Johansson & Raunio, 2020, p. 1151; Johansson, 2008).

On the whole, however, these developments should perhaps best be understood as a backdrop for our current discussion, and not necessarily as a particularly active process. And in spite of the supposition of some natural fit between NPM and the Swedish governance model, scholars have nevertheless raised a finger of warning for the added complexity that may follow from merely piling additional obligations on top of already established practices (Grossi et al., 2018, p. 1848; see also Sundström,

2015). As such, even if loyalty and consensus-making continue to prevail as the hard currency within the Swedish administration, an overly cluttered management system runs the risk of muddling the liaison between agencies and the executive (Pollitt, 2005; see also Freivalds & Heckscher, 2018)—a concern that is certainly not new in the Swedish context.

Ever More Control? Dynamics in Swedish Governance

In recent years, four phenomena have characterised Swedish governance: tensions in central-local relations, attempts to increase control through politicisation at central government level, Swedish policy responses to the coronavirus (which received considerable international attention) and, finally, the mediatisation of the Swedish central government. In the following section we address each of these matters in turn.

Central-Local Relations

One central tension in Swedish governance refers to central-local relations: that is, the functions of the municipalities as self-determined democratic units and their ever-increasing role in implementing the welfare state, where they operate as the extended arm of central government. As noted above, local governments have traditionally had a strong position because they are key to public service delivery. Strong local and regional governments are central to the implementation of a welfare state that emphasises equal access to public services—and a key role for local government is to adjust service delivery to local conditions.

The Local Government Act 1991 provided municipalities and county councils with greater autonomy regarding their organisation and also, partly, allowed them to develop their own policies in a few areas. However, the bulk of local tasks is regulated and monitored at the national level. Historically, two mechanisms have provided for unitary implementation. The first is the central role played by professionals. Many professionals are alumni from specialised degree programmes and are part of cultures characterised by strong professional norms and ethos. Second, large national 'reform bureaucracies' (Lindvall & Rothstein, 2006, p. 50) established in the 1930s and 1940s assured national standardisation. However, with NPM reforms the focus of many national bureaucracies shifted to performance management and monitoring: as a result the capacity of the central state to provide for standardised implementation was weakened, resulting in variation in implementation and service delivery (Hall, 2015). Internal delegation, corporatisation, contracting out and consumer choice models are among the organisational structures prevalent in Swedish welfare service delivery (Montin, 2015). Also, during the recent COVID-19 pandemic, the municipalities enjoyed great autonomy and many initiated their own measures; for example, restricting access to care homes before the Public Health Agency issued the respective recommendation to limit access (Kuhlmann et al., 2021, p. 7). In the early months of the pandemic, in particular, coordination problems between the national level and regional authorities were widespread and the government was criticised for not assuming a stronger role here (Ahlenius, 2020; see below).

In recent years, central-local relations have become more complex. On the one hand, there is still considerable autonomy for local governments regarding how they perform their tasks. On the other, central government increasingly focuses on centrally set standards through binding regulation to emphasise uniform implementation. According to Hall (2015), this central government turn to coercion results from decreasing public acceptance of differences in public service delivery, and from increasing pressure on ministers to be held accountable even if local governments are formally responsible. Overall, central-local relations are tense and this '"recentralization" trend reinforces already existing ambiguities regarding responsibility and accountability between the state and local governments' (Hall, 2015, p. 309).

Central Government Control and Politicisation

In a somewhat fragmented and decentralised public sector, coordination and steering have become more challenging over time. The central government has sought to regain control in various ways: through diminishing the role of commissions and controlling membership thereof, and through politicisation in the government offices and, partly, at the top of agencies.

With regard to policy-making, the role of the commissions as key actors has changed. For much of the twentieth century, commissions with representatives from major parliamentary parties occupied a central role in the Swedish policy-making system, serving as an important arena of negotiation between the government and interest groups. Their recommendations often shaped policy options and reforms and they had an important consensus-building function. And though the government continues to appoint commissions for key policies and their reforms, they are not as frequent as they used to be and their independence and representativeness have been weakened. Dahlström et al. (2021) analyse changes in the composition of commissions, and find a decrease in the share of politicians appointed alongside growth in the presence of civil servants. Overall, government control increases, and thus the authors conclude that the commissions have lost their key role as consensus-building arenas in Swedish governance (Dahlström et al., 2021).

Dahlström and Pierre (2011) document a steady and sharp rise in the number of political appointees in the Government Offices since the 1980s. These appointees, however, have not replaced civil servants, but rather have added a 'thickening layer' (Dahlström & Pierre, 2011, p. 199) to the organisation of the Offices. Increasing politicisation, Dahlström and Pierre argue, serves as an instrument for addressing long-standing coordination problems in the Government Offices (2011). This argument is supported by a comparative study exploring the roles of advisers in coordination in Denmark and Sweden: in the former, advisers have a rather indirect role in coordination as they serve to link the minister's positions to the party's position, whereas in Sweden, from a certain stage onwards they control coordination (Hustedt & Salomonsen, 2017). Political control has also become more relevant regarding the agencies: though agency heads are appointed on fixed-term contracts and are often recruited from leadership positions in other organisations, Dahlström and Holmgren (2019) show that Swedish agency heads leave their positions at greater rates after a change of government coalition. Moreover, they provide a number of prominent recent cases illustrating the political nature of recruitment decisions (Dahlström & Holmgren, 2019, pp. 832–833).

Crisis Management

Sweden is considered an outlier or special case with regard to how the country responded to the coronavirus from early 2020 onwards. In contrast to most other European countries, Swedish pandemic policy relied on voluntary recommendations rather than legally binding regulation. Only in the later stages of the pandemic did the government decide on a few legally binding measures. Next to their voluntary character, the policy measures were much less restrictive than in most other countries. At no point did Sweden institute a lockdown, school and child care facilities remained open (only higher education institutions moved to online teaching) and mask-wearing was not made mandatory.

While in many other countries the heads of government became central in formulating and communicating crisis response measures, in Sweden, Anders Tegnell, the head of the Public Health Agency (or the 'state epidemiologist') was the key actor. In contrast, early on the prime minister removed the Crisis Management Coordination Secretariat away from the Prime Minister's Office and was criticised for his passive stance (Andersson & Aylott, 2020). The Public Health Agency regularly issued recommendations that citizens were expected to follow and while they are not legally binding, recommendations are the strongest instrument the Public Health Agency has at its disposal (Kuhlmann et al., 2021). The government was in the 'backseat' (Pierre, 2020, p. 483) and left the key role to the experts at the Public Health Agency. And while this leaning back can, on the one hand, be understood as a normal implication of Swedish dualism with its strong role for independent agencies, it can—on the other—be interpreted as a politically convenient blame-shift on the part of the government. While trust in the agencies' recommendations was high overall—and the Swedish pandemic policy generally also enjoyed high levels of public support—criticism rose as the number of deaths vastly exceeded those of Sweden's Nordic neighbours, in particular among the elderly (Kuhlmann et al., 2021). However, criticism never became strong enough to change the policy response to the pandemic and, broadly speaking, the Public Health Agency remained shielded from criticism (Andersson & Aylott, 2020).

Mediatisation

Relationships between journalists and political sources have, in the Nordic countries, been defined as being based on 'professional distance' (Moring & Pfetsch, 2014; see also Hallin & Mancini, 2004). This professionalisation on the part of both journalists and political sources is confirmed by Johansson et al. (2019) in the context of Sweden, in particular, where exchanges between journalists and their sources are close but at the same time characterised by a recognition of each other's professional roles.

On the side of the media the relationship is affected by the downsizing of newsrooms, multi-platform production 24/7 and increased competition for unique news. These developments have made journalists more dependent on available sources. For their part, on the side of political sources, the professionalisation of government communication—including the appointment of more press advisers, greater coordination, and increased attempts to influence news reporting—makes news management more efficient and fosters centralising effects on executive systems. Together, these trends shift the balance between journalists and their political sources, favouring the latter in the context of a more mediatised political communication environment.

Within the Swedish context, Johansson and Raunio (2020, p. 1153) portray a similar image of a government which is increasingly able to control parts of its media coverage. They quote senior journalists who experience being 'in the hands of the government' and of press secretaries who act 'as a filter' between journalists and governmental actors (Johansson & Raunio, 2020, p. 1153). That perception is shared and confirmed by press secretaries within government, with Johansson and Raunio noting that:

> Both journalists and press secretaries described increasing resources on the political side—more coordination, more press secretaries, and more active work from sources to influence news reporting. Over time, the system has changed fundamentally in terms of accessibility and management. There is more control of information by press secretaries, according to the experienced journalists. (2020, p. 1153)

How has this professionalisation and centralisation been performed within the Swedish government and the PMO? How has Regeringskansliet (the Government Offices), in its professionalisation and more active media management (especially from the PMO), been organised and coordinated (Dahlström & Pierre, 2011, p. 205; Erlandsson, 2008) to the point that, to some extent, it 'holds the upper hand' vis-à-vis the media and journalists?

As noted by Hustedt and Salomonsen, '[t]he fact that policy is "tightly" coordinated facilitates "tight" coordination of also communication (SWEPRESS4) by creating a "mentality" (SWEPRESS3) that horizontal coordination is vital for both policy and communication' (2017, p. 401). This 'mentality' is fostered, or reinforced, by formal hierarchical modes of coordination, performed and led by press secretaries positioned at the centre of the government.

To understand how the Swedish government and the PMO performs the coordination and control of government communication, it is important to differentiate between the roles played respectively by permanent civil servants employed in government communications and the politically appointed press secretaries and political advisers who are also involved in managing the media. At the bureaucratic level the Government Offices' communication department was established to strengthen the coordination of government communication. This unit is part of the internal administrative unit staffed with permanent bureaucrats who coordinate non-political aspects of communication horizontally and control the government's website (SWEPRESS2; SWEHC1). To facilitate coordination in the line ministries, the heads of communication meet with the head of the Government Offices' communication department once a month (SWEHC1, SWEHC3). Amongst the bureaucracies it is emphasised that the communication performed from ministries is 'the government's policy and politics', rather than communication intended to promote individual ministries or ministers (SWEHC1).

For the politically appointed advisers and press secretaries the coordination of government communication—not least that which is performed to and via the news media—is strategically linked to the policy coordination by the central coordination unit. Coordination starts in the press unit in the PMO (although not as part of the prime minister's staff) (SWEPA4). Led by a head of press and a vice head of press, both recruited from each of the coalition parties, the unit approves all communication from ministers and the prime minister (SWEPRESS5). Those actors hold the authority to decide on the political aspects of communication, including the power to determine whether ministers are allowed to publish any given piece of communication (SWEPRESS5). Hence, coordination is related to communication of strategies and policy, and to attempts to control the government agenda.

This formal authority is reflected in a perception of a de facto authority, and is described as a 'strong center' (SWEPA3, SWEPA5, SWEPRESS4) which, from time to time, prohibits communication from line ministries (SWEPA2). While some latitude is experienced by press secretaries in ministries (SWEPRESS1; SWEPRESS2), Hustedt and Salomonsen explain that 'to ensure that policy issues are in line with the entire coalition government before they are communicated, press secretaries must seek approval from both the central coordination unit and the PM's press office (SWEPRESS4)' (2017, p. 401).

Over the years there has been a substantial increase in the number of press secretaries and other employees involved in government communication (Johansson & Raunio, 2020, p. 1151). The first press secretary entered the PMO in 1963 and by the beginning of the 1970s almost all ministers had at least one press secretary; these days there are normally one or two in each ministry (Dahlström & Pierre, 2011, pp. 204–205). More specifically, nowadays:

> There are four press secretaries to the PM. Two of them do regular press secretary work. One works mainly with social media. One works with communication matters relating to the EU and foreign policy, including the incoming international visits. There is also a press assistant, alongside the chief press officer and the deputy chief press officer. Moreover, there is the deputy chief press officer for the Green Party and a press secretary for the (Social Democratic) minister for EU affairs, both of whom are also based at the PMO. Furthermore, epitomizing the strengthening of the center, a new position was established in 2017 for the PM: media strategist, which is at the level of political advisor with responsibility for the government's long-term and strategic communication. (Johansson & Raunio, 2020, p. 1152)

All press secretaries are formally employed in the PMO press unit under the formal responsibility of the head of press, which points to the importance given to thinking as a government collegium rather than as individual ministries or parties—that disposition also applies within the corps of press secretaries. As one press secretary explains, this means that 'you should be able to be a bit "free standing" from your minister … we are not satellites; rather, we coordinate our policy' (SWEPRESS1).

This may cause conflicts: '[i]t is a balancing act how to defend your own portfolio externally while at the same time keeping a unified government. It is not good in the eye of the public if you see a government which is divided' (SWEPRESS3). However, demands for strong coordination are substantial, as a coherent and unified government is considered a crucial norm in Swedish government: as described by one adviser, the minister's interest and the government's interest are 'in principle the same' (SWEPA3).

Next to the fact that all formal employment of press secretaries takes place at the centre—a decision that was taken by the Social Democratic-Green Government when entering the Government Offices in 2014 (Johansson & Raunio, 2020, p. 1152)—there are other centralising coordination mechanisms in play which help to coordinate government communication. A short daily morning meeting among all press secretaries, led by the head of the press unit at the PMO, is the core coordination mechanism for reactive communication to the media (SWEPA3; SWEPA4; SWEPRESS1). (This initiative, too, was introduced by the Social Democratic-Green in 2014 (Johansson & Raunio, 2020, p. 1152).) Another central steering mechanism is the preparation of common talking points for communication on any given issue or policy. These guide ministers' communications, especially with the media, and are prepared by the centre (SWEPRESS5). The press secretaries exclusively handle media communication if in any way political (SWEPRESS2). Moreover, the head of press plans communication via a weekly document—which is based on the wishes of the press secretaries (SWEPRESS1) and resembles the former UK government's 'news grid'—that includes all planned communication activities.

Moreover, the press unit is strategically linked to powerful central actors through weekly meetings with the state secretaries in the PMO and with the central coordination unit. Hence, the news grid is difficult to 'go up against' or to disagree with (SWEPRESS5). Further, there is a monthly meeting of the same actors for long-term planning and coordination of events, government agenda and strategy (SWEPRESS5). In addition, the strategic links between the press unit and the coordination unit are underlined by ongoing informal contacts (SWEPRESS5).

In terms of horizontal coordination the press secretaries are primarily involved in communication issues, whereas their role within the ministries becomes intertwined with policy coordination with the political advisers (SWEPRESS2). However, the part they play in horizontal policy coordination varies and is, in general, rather limited (SWEPRESS5). To ensure that policy issues are in line with the entire coalition government before they are communicated, press secretaries must seek approval from both the central coordination unit and the prime minister's press office (SWEPRESS4).

Three additional mechanisms have been introduced by the current government to ensure the coordination of communication, indicating the ongoing trend towards increased centralisation. The first was the introduction of political advisers at the PMO who are responsible for coordinating the 'talking points'. Second, the role of the press secretaries is now regulated through a communication policy emphasising that '[c]ommunication by the Government Offices is based on its mandate to assist the Government and its ministers in their role as Government representatives and therefore not as party representatives' (Prime Minister's Office, 2012, p. 22). That policy also states that the PMO has 'ultimate responsibility for the coordination of both internal and external communication' (Prime Minister's Office, 2012, p. 5; for a similar interpretation see Johansson & Raunio, 2020, pp. 1152–1153). And third has been the introduction of a policy document regulating ministers' behaviour and communication in social media, and what has been described as 'a kind of social media communication policy' (Johansson & Raunio, 2020, p. 1153).

The description above indicates a clear trend towards the centralisation of control over government communication in Sweden, with the core executive playing the key role in ensuring the tight coordination of government communication in both the bureaucratic and political spheres of the Regeringskansliet. Centralisation has been performed by giving a larger role to political advisers and press secretaries, particularly in the PMO, in an attempt to make government speak with 'one voice' (Johansson & Raunio, 2020). This centralisation is to be seen in the context of attempts to address the challenges stemming not only from the management of coalition governments, but also from the need to strengthen the vertical coordination of media management between the very centre of the core executive and line ministries (Johansson & Raunio, 2020).

Concluding Remarks

Had Montesquieu been alive and well today, he would probably have looked at Sweden with some admiration. On the face of it, and despite various reforms, the general architecture of a dualist separation of power between the executive and administration appears, on the whole, to have stood the test of time. Dig a bit deeper, however, and it becomes apparent that quite a lot has happened inside the Government Offices over the last few decades—amounting to what we have argued are significant changes in the dynamics of Swedish state governance.

Swedish politics has experienced a considerable change of pace following EU membership and the general internationalisation of politics, not to mention the mounting complexities of public-sector management and policy-making. Such developments have arguably placed a greater burden on the political executive in its efforts to weave an increasingly intricate web of connections together in a coherent fashion, while enabling executive control and, not least, coordination.

The response has, in part, been the addition of a growing number of political appointees to the ranks of the Government Offices, notably media-related staff and so-called policy professionals. Moreover, the institution of the commission of inquiry—previously so important—has lost much of its neutrality and compromising function as a tool for policy analysis, as governments have sought to restrict both stakeholder diversity and the scope of investigation in their favour.

Likewise, NPM reforms (particularly in budgetary processes) have developed into means for centralised control, through the setting of various degrees of performance objectives but also—and perhaps this is more noteworthy—via biased budget allocations along partisan politics. Agencies have, accordingly, increasingly become hubs for performance monitoring. A commonly held view of NPM practices inside the agencies seems to be that they have not been fully integrated into everyday operations, but rather act as an ambiguity sitting on top of already existing routines. As a result, to a significant degree they have become a secondary burden lacking sufficient clarity and purpose: a source of tension between decentralisation and national standardisation.

On the whole, the interpretative openness of the Swedish Constitution presents a particularly interesting puzzle, which we might perhaps argue causes a slight disconnect between perception and pragmatism. On paper the separation of power appears almost set in stone, yet the reality is that the government has more means of control at its disposal than first meets the eye—and it has considerably strengthened central control in recent years through the various means described in this chapter. While EU membership and other developments we have highlighted have placed greater demands on government—and thus necessitated a strengthening of resources in the Government Offices—there is also the stark contrast provided by the pandemic policy, where the government shied away from centralising control, perhaps so as to divert uncomfortable responsibility. However, it would probably also be fair to say that the government has capitalised on these developments to further consolidate its steering power in the name of consensus—and that this has possibly been facilitated by these constitutional ambiguities. To a considerable extent such leeway seems also to be complemented by the informal mechanisms of Swedish consensus-making.

Likewise, we have noted the normative importance of political loyalty across the Swedish state—and, importantly, as something that is now more or less a prerequisite in the recruitment of agency heads, in spite of formal meritocracy. From such a perspective, Swedish consensus-making does not always come across as entirely voluntary, but as a phenomenon that is to some extent an enforced means of control.

While often perceived as something close to an exemplar model of state governance—an image Sweden certainly has not hesitated to boast about publicly over the years—we conclude with the sense that such a stellar reputation seems to precede from the actual reality of affairs. Stripped away, a tactically flexible realpolitik instead emerges, allowing the Swedish executive to pull the strings of centralisation from afar.

Note

1. Part of the description of the executive landscape within the Swedish government, as well as parts of the analysis of the mediatisation of the Swedish government, is based upon primary sources, including five interviews with politically appointed press secretaries (SWEPRESS); five interviews with politically appointed political advisers (SWEPA) and five interviews with heads of communications (SWEHC), who are employed as permanent civil servants. All interviews were performed in 2015, and all of the respondents were in office serving the minority coalition government at the time, led by the Social Democrats (Socialdemokraterna), headed by Prime Minister Stefan Löfven and including the Green Party (Miljöpartiet de gröna). The interviews were performed by some of the authors and some have been used in Hustedt and Salomonsen (2017).

References

Ahlenius, I. B. (2020, June 9). Regeringen har abdikerat. *Kvartal*. Retrieved October 2, 2021, from https://kvartal.se/artiklar/regeringen-har-abdikerat/

Andersson, C. (2004). *Tudelad trots allt: dualismens överlevnad i den svenska staten 1718-1987*. PhD Thesis, Stockholms Universitet, Statsvetenskapliga institutionen.

Andersson, S., & Aylott, N. (2020). Sweden and Coronavirus: Unexceptional Exceptionalism. *Social Sciences* (Basel), 9(12), 232.

Dahlström, C., & Holmgren, M. (2019). The Political Dynamics of Bureaucratic Turnover. *British Journal of Political Science, 49*(3), 823–836.

Dahlström, C., Lundberg, E., & Pronin, K. (2021). No More Political Compromise? Swedish Commissions of Inquiry 1990–2016. *Scandinavian Political Studies*. https://doi.org/10.1111/1467-9477.12205

Dahlström, C., & Pierre, J. (2011). Steering the Swedish State: Politicization as a Coordination Strategy. In C. Dahlström, B. G. Peters, & J. Pierre (Eds.), *Steering from the Centre: Strengthening Political Control in Western Democracies* (pp. 193–211). University of Toronto Press.

Ehn, P. (2015). The Public Servant. In J. Pierre (Ed.), *The Oxford Handbook of Swedish Politics*. Oxford University Press. https://doi.org/10.1093/oxfordhb/9780199665679.013.19

Ehn, P., Isberg, M., Linde, C., & Wallin, G. (2003). Swedish Bureaucracy in an Era of Change. *Governance, 16*(3), 429–458.

Elder, N. C. M., & Page, E. (1998). Culture and Agency: Fragmentation and Agency Structures in Germany and Sweden. *Public Policy and Administration, 13*(4), 28–45.

Erlandsson, M. (2008). Regeringskansliet och medierna: Den politiska exekutivens resurser och strategier för att hantera och styra massmedier. *Statsvetenskaplig tidskrift, 110*(4), 335–349.

Freivalds, L., & Heckscher, S. (2018) Politiker tjänstemän i Regeringskansliet. *Svensk Juristtidning*. Retrieved October 3, 2021, from https://svjt.se/svjt/2018/4

Government Offices of Sweden. (2021). *Public Agencies and How They are Governed*. Retrieved September 28, 2021, from https://www.government.se/how-sweden-is-governed/public-agencies-and-how-they-are-governed/

Grossi, G., Mauro, S. G., & Vakkuri, J. (2018). Converging and Diverging Pressures in PBB Development: The Experiences of Finland and Sweden. *Public Management Review, 20*(12), 1836–1857.

Hall, P. (2015). The Swedish Administrative Model. In J. Pierre (Ed.), *The Oxford Handbook of Swedish Politics*. Oxford University Press. https://doi.org/10.1093/oxfordhb/9780199665679.013.17

Hallin, D., & Mancini, P. (2004). *Comparing Media Systems. Three Models of Media and Politics*. Cambridge University Press.

Hustedt, T., & Salomonsen, H. H. (2017). Political Control of Government Coordination? The Roles of Ministerial Advisers in Government Coordination in Denmark and Sweden. *Public Administration, 95*(2), 393–406.

Hysing, E. & Olsson, J. (2012). *Tjänstemän i politiken* [Officials in Politics]. Lund: Studentlitteratur AB.

Jacobsson, B. (1984). *Hur styrs förvaltningen: myt och verklighet kring departementets styrning av ämbetsverken* [How the Administration is Governed: Myth and Reality about the Ministry's Governance of the Agencies]. PhD Thesis, Ekonomiska Forskningsinstitutet vid Handelshögskolan i Stockholm. Lund: Studentlitteratur. Retrieved September 29, 2021, from https://ex.hhs.se/dissertations/221882-FULLTEXT01.pdf

Jacobsson, B. (2001). *Hur styrs regeringskansliet?—om procedurer, prat och politik* [How is the Government Offices Managed?—On Procedures, Talk and Politics. *Score Rapportserie*, 8. Retrieved September 30, 2021, from https://www.score.su.se/polopoly_fs/1.26672.1320939808!/20018.pdf

Jacobsson, B. (2019) Den svåra samordningen—Regeringen och agenda 2030. *Förvaltningsakademin*, http://sh.diva-portal.org/smash/get/diva2:1294091/FULLTEXT02.pdf

Jacobsson, B., & Sundström, G. (2015). Governing the State. In J. Pierre (Ed.), *The Oxford Handbook of Swedish Politics*. Oxford University Press. https://doi.org/10.1093/oxfordhb/9780199665679.013.20

Johansson, K. M. (2008). Chief Executive Organization and Advisory Arrangements for Foreign Affairs: The Case of Sweden. *Cooperation and Conflict*, 43(3), 267–287.

Johansson, K. M., Malling, M., & Nygren, G. (2019). A Professionally Symbiotic Relationship. In K. M. Johansson & G. Nygren (Eds.), *Close and Distant Political Executive–Media Relations in Four Countries* (pp. 97–126). Nordicom.

Johansson, K. M., & Raunio, T. (2020). Centralizing Government Communication? Evidence from Finland and Sweden. *Politics & Policy*, 48(6), 1138–1160.

Klijn, E. H., & Koppenjan, J. (2015). *Governance Networks in the Public Sector*. Routledge.

Kuhlmann, S., Hellström, M., Ramberg, U., & Reiter, R. (2021). Tracing Divergence in Crisis Governance: Responses to the COVID-19 Pandemic in France, Germany and Sweden Compared. *International Review of Administrative Sciences*, 87(3), 556–575.

Larsson, T. (2002). Sweden. In R. Laking (Ed.), *Distributed Public Governance: Agencies, Authorities and other Government Bodies* (pp. 181–208). OECD Publishing.

Lindvall, J., Bäck, H., Dahlström, C., Naurin, E., & Teorell, J. (2020). Sweden's Parliamentary democracy at 100. *Parliamentary Affairs*, 73(3), 477–502.

Lindvall, J., & Rothstein, B. (2006). Sweden: The Fall of the Strong State. *Scandinavian Political Studies*, 29(1), 47–63.

Ministry of Finance. (2004). *Embedsmænds rådgivning og bistand*. Betænkning Nr. 1443. Copenhagen: Schultz.

Molander, P., Nilsson, J.-E., & Schick, A. (2002). *Does Anyone Govern? The Relationship between the Government Office and the Agencies in Sweden*. SNS.

Montin, S. (2015). Municipalities, Regions, and County Councils: Actors and Institutions. In J. Pierre (Ed.), *The Oxford Handbook of Swedish Politics* (pp. 367–382). https://doi.org/10.1093/oxfordhb/9780199665679.001.0001

Moring, T., & Pfetsch, B. (2014). European Political Communication Cultures and Democracy. In B. Pfetsch (Ed.), *Political Communication Cultures in Europe: Attitudes of Political Actors and Journalists in Nine Countries* (pp. 287–301). Palgrave Macmillan.

Niemann, C. (2013). *Villkorat förtroende: Normer och rollförväntningar i relationen mellan politiker och tjänstemän i Regeringskansliet*. PhD Thesis. Stockholm University: Department of Political Science.

Noreland, L. (2019). *Laga efter läge: Statsråds föreställningar om styrning i Regeringskansliet*. PhD Thesis. Uppsala Universitet. Retrieved October 24, 2021, from www.diva-portal.org/smash/record.jsf?pid=diva2%3A1287326&dswid=5343

Öberg, S. A. (2015). Introduction: Constitutional Design. In J. Pierre (Ed.), *The Oxford Handbook of Swedish Politics*. Oxford University Press. https://doi.org/10.1093/oxfordhb/9780199665679.013.42

Öberg, S. A., & Wockelberg, H. (2015). The Public Sector and the Courts. In J. Pierre (Ed.), *The Oxford Handbook of Swedish Politics*. Oxford University Press. https://doi.org/10.1093/oxfordhb/9780199665679.013.8

Petersson, O. (2015). Constitutional History. In J. Pierre (Ed.), *The Oxford Handbook of Swedish Politics*. Oxford University Press. https://doi.org/10.1093/oxfordhb/9780199665679.013.5

Pierre, J. (2020). Nudges Against Pandemics: Sweden's COVID-19 Containment Strategy In Perspective. *Policy and Society, 39*(3), 478–493.

Pollitt, C. (2005). Performance Management in Practice: A Comparative Study of Executive Agencies. *Journal of Public Administration Research and Theory, 16*(1), 25–44. https://doi.org/10.1093/jopart/mui045

Premfors, R., & Sundström, G. (2007). *Regeringskansliet*. Liber förlag.

Prime Minister's Office (2012). *Communication Policy for the Government Offices*. Retrieved October 3, 2021, from https://www.government.se/49baf5/contentassets/733006124df143acbc8ae762aa61a42f/communication-policy-for-the-government-offices.pdf

Regeringskansliet. (1974). *Regeringskansliets rättsdatabaser* [The Government Offices' Legal Databases]. SFS-nummer 1974:152. Retrieved September 30, 2021, from https://rkrattsbaser.gov.se/sfst?bet=1974:152

Regeringskansliet. (2008). *Regeringskansliet genom tiderna* [The Government Offices through the Ages]. Retrieved September 30, 2021, from https://www.regeringen.se/49bb57/contentassets/7f9d827dd80c4008a59b031f45620ab0/regeringskansliet-genom-tiderna

Regeringskansliet. (2021a). *Sveriges regering* [The Government of Sweden]. Retrieved September 26, 2021, from https://www.regeringen.se/sveriges-regering/

Regeringskansliet. (2021b). *Så arbetar regeringen och Regeringskansliet* [How the Government and the Government Offices work]. Retrieved September 29, 2021, from https://www.regeringen.se/sa-styrs-sverige/sa-arbetar-regeringen-och-regeringskansliet/

Regeringskansliet. (2021c). *Regeringskansliets anställda* [The Employees of the Government Offices]. Retrieved September 26, 2021, from https://www.regeringen.se/regeringskansliet/regeringskansliets-anstallda/

Statskontoret. (2021). *Statsförvaltningen i korthet* [State Administration in Short]. Retrieved September 26, 2021, from https://www.statskontoret.se/globalassets/publikationer/2021/statsforvaltningen-i-korthet%2D%2D-webb.pdf

Sundström, G. (2009). 'He Who Decides': Swedish Social Democratic Governments from a Presidentialisation Perspective. *Scandinavian Political Studies, 32*(2), 143–170.

Sundström, G. (2015). Administrative Reform. In J. Pierre (Ed.), *The Oxford Handbook of Swedish Politics*. Oxford University Press. https://doi.org/10.1093/oxfordhb/9780199665679.013.45

Sundström, G., & Lemne, M. (2016). Bo Smith-utredningen betraktad från andra sidan bron. *Politica, 48*(4), 455–480.

Sveriges Riksdag. (1996). *Regeringens proposition 1996/97:1: Förslag till statsbudget för budgetåret 1997, m.m.* [Government Bill 1996/97: 1: Proposed State Budget for the Financial Year 1997, etc.]. Retrieved September 29, 2021, from https://data.riksdagen.se/dokument/GK031

Sveriges Riksdag. (2017). *Svenska ambassadörer Svar på skriftlig fråga 2017/18:172 besvarad av Utrikesminister Margot Wallström (S)* [Swedish Ambassadors Answer to Written Question 2017/18: 172 Answered by Foreign Minister Margot Wallström (S)]. Retrieved September 16, 2021, from https://www.riksdagen.se/sv/dokument-lagar/dokument/svar-pa-skriftlig-fraga/svenska-ambassadorer_H512172

Sveriges Riksdag. (2021). *Riksdagens uppgifter* [The Tasks of the Riksdag]. Retrieved September 26, 2021, from https://www.riksdagen.se/sv/sa-funkar-riksdagen/riksdagens-uppgifter/

Ullström, A. (2011). *Styring bakom kulisserna: Regeringskansliet politiska staber och regeringens styringskapacitet*. PhD thesis, Department of Political Science, Stockholm University.

CHAPTER 10

The Danish Core Executive: From 'Duopoly' to 'Monopoly'?

Heidi Houlberg Salomonsen and Amalie Trangbæk

Introduction

For the last 30 years Danish prime ministers have, to a large extent, run their governments as a duopoly between the Prime Minister's Office (PMO) and the Ministry of Finance (MoF). They have navigated this nexus in the context of primarily minority, coalition governments. However, since the election in June 2019, the Danish core executive has changed, both when it comes to the participants and, to some degree, to the functioning of this inner court. First, the Mette Frederiksen government of 2019 was a minority, *single party* government, which is rather unusual in a Danish context.[1] Second, PM Frederiksen introduced a

H. H. Salomonsen (✉)
Department of Management, Aarhus University, Aarhus, Denmark
e-mail: hhs@mgmt.au.dk

A. Trangbæk
Department of Political Science, Aarhus University, Aarhus, Denmark
e-mail: amt@ps.au.dk

© The Author(s), under exclusive license to Springer Nature Switzerland AG 2022
K. Kolltveit, R. Shaw (eds.), *Core Executives in a Comparative Perspective*, Understanding Governance,
https://doi.org/10.1007/978-3-030-94503-9_10

number of structural changes which all point towards increased centralisation around the prime minister and her office.

The ambition of this chapter is to describe and discuss these recent changes within the Danish core executive. In addition, we reflect upon both how these changes fit into the established core executive framework and how the Danish case can potentially add to theoretical understandings of how inner courts of governments are set up and function (Rhodes, 2017, Chap. 7).

The chapter will empirically illustrate how the centralisation around the PM and the shift in power between the PMO and the Ministry of Finance materialises, both in formal institutional changes at the PMO and in the practices of policy coordination performed within government. In addition, the chapter also illustrates how centralisation is manifest in the central government's media management in Denmark.

The recent changes have occurred within a government which has lived most of its life in the context of the COVID-19 crisis. In crisis management, centralising is often part of governments' repertoire, at least in the early phases, and recent research has found that the COVID-19 crisis was no exception in such respects (Boin et al., 2021, p. 55). However, as we will illustrate, the changes leading to centralisation in the Danish case were announced and partly introduced before the COVID-19 crisis hit the country in February/March 2020.

Methods and Data

It can be challenging to get insights into not only the formal aspects but, more importantly, also the interpretation and descriptions of governing practices from actors inside the central government apparatus. Therefore, the chapter is based on both secondary and unique primary data, the latter including qualitative interviews spanning more than the three most recent Danish governments (spanning from 2011 to 2021) as well as field observations from 2019 to 2020.

The anonymised interviews are with politicians, permanent secretaries, heads of press and communication and politically appointed special advisers, and the majority of interviews were performed while the respondents were still in office. The primary data were collected for the following three research projects, all of which included participation from one of the authors: 31 interviews from the project 'Communicating Governments',[2] mainly covering the minority coalition governments headed by PM Helle

Thorning-Schmidt (2011–2015)[3]; 22 interviews from the project 'Comparative Cabinets',[4] mostly covering governments headed by Lars Løkke Rasmussen (2015–2019)[5] but also including interviews from previous governments; and insights from the 2021 PhD project 'Life at the top', which in the main covered the single party government led by Mette Frederiksen (2019–). The empirical material in the latter project consists of observations from 8 ministries and more than 30 interviews. Overall, the interview data cover accounts of the core executives spanning three different PMs governing for the last ten years. Some of the quotes used in this chapter have previously been used in other publications; when that is the case, reference to those publications is made.

The secondary data include official documents describing institutional changes at the PMO; news articles about these changes; a TV documentary portraying the now-former special adviser of the current PM, Martin Rossen (DR December 2020); an interview with Rossen performed in relation to a bachelors project from the University of Copenhagen (Engholm & Petersen, 2021); and different official reports and white papers (Bo Smith-Udvalget, 2015; Ministry of Finance, 1998a, 2004, 2013).

ACTORS AND INSTITUTIONS AT THE CORE OF DANISH GOVERNMENT

Danish governments operate in the context of parliamentary democracy and are organised according to the principle of ministerial governance. First, that principle entails that ministers heading ministries also hold ultimate formal authority. Ministers as political executives 'are placed on top of a hierarchy and endowed with formal authority to issue general instructions on any business within their portfolio and also to intervene personally into any decision falling within it' (Christensen, 2006, p. 999). Second, it also entails that ministers are formally accountable to parliament for all decisions and actions taken in the ministry (Grøn & Salomonsen, 2020, p. 126). However, the relatively high degree of autonomy thus granted to individual ministers is in practice restricted. As noted by Rhodes and Salomonsen (2018):

> The principle of ministerial governance *de jure* grants substantial autonomy to the individual ministers of the Danish cabinet. However, the close alignment of the Ministry of Finance (MoF) and the Prime Minister (PM) and

his office *de facto* reduces the policy autonomy formally granted to ministers individually and as cabinet members. (Rhodes & Salomonsen, 2018, p. 6; original emphasis)

According to the Danish Constitutional Act, it is the prime minister's prerogative to appoint ministers as well as decide the number and portfolios of ministries (Mortensen, 2014). However, this decision is often rather constrained by the preferences of other coalition party leaders.

Danish ministers are served by a permanent civil service, recruited and promoted on merit, as well as by a small number of Special Advisers (SpAds). Ministers have appointed SpAds since the late 1990s (Christiansen & Salomonsen, 2018). The importance of keeping the number of SpAds relatively low has been emphasised in government white papers regulating their use (Ministry of Finance, 2004, p. 185); however, if the minister is a member of one of the central cabinet committees (see below), they were allowed to recruit two or three SpAds (Ministry of Finance, 2013, p. 122).

Since their introduction, it has been stressed that SpAds should be positioned in staff functions and not hold formal authority vis-à-vis the permanent civil service (Ministry of Finance, 1998a, p. 222). The importance and roles of Danish SpAds have evolved over time, from being primarily media advisers to some also becoming central in terms of providing policy advice to their ministers (Christiansen & Salomonsen, 2018). However, their role in government coordination has, until recently, been very limited (Hustedt & Salomonsen, 2017).

The Danish PMO was established in 1914 (Knudsen, 2000, p. 87), but it was not until 1965 that it formally and *de facto* started to function as a political secretariat for the prime minister, as well as began to assume a coordinating role vis-à-vis preparing cabinet meetings (Knudsen, 2000, p. 91). Compared to PMOs in other European countries, the Danish Prime Minister's Office has traditionally been (and still is) relatively small. From 1980 until 1992 there were between 13 and 18 academically trained employees; from 1993 to 1999 that number increased to between 21 and 27 (Knudsen, 2000, p. 94). Since then there has been a more radical expansion. In August 2020, the PMO included 84 person-years (both academically trained and other types of employees) (Holst, 2020).

Since the MoF was established in 1848, it has been responsible for the state budget, where the core task is the yearly formulation of the Finance Bill (Ministry of Finance, 1998b, p. 3). Other responsibilities have changed through time: taxation, for instance, is now handled by the Ministry of

Taxation, and with increased digitisation the MoF became responsible for implementing digitisation policy, which is handled by the Agency for Governmental IT Services (Agency for Digitisation, 2021). In contrast with the PMO, the number of employees in the MoF has remained relatively stable in the past 20 years: in 1999 there were about 250 employees, while today that number stands at around 275 (Ministry of Finance, 1998b, p. 4; Ministry of Finance, 2021).

Compared to other European countries, the core executive in Denmark is characterised by 'the absence of a dedicated cabinet office' (Hansen, 2020, p. 119). This is partly the explanation for the historically close collaboration between the PMO and the MoF. As a former permanent secretary noted: 'Most of [the] Cabinet Office functions are actually taken care of by the Ministry of Finance in Denmark' (#6 FPS). Another called it 'an extended secretariat for the prime minister' (#5 PS; #13 PS) (see also Rhodes & Salomonsen, 2021, p. 79). As will be elaborated below, the MoF has a central role in the coordination of government policies. In addition, it functions as a 'scapegoat for the PM', meaning that those employed by the MoF, rather than the prime minister and the PMO, will 'get their hands dirty' and be the ones held politically accountable (Rhodes & Salomonsen, 2021, p. 79).

Frederiksen's Structural Changes at the PMO

As mentioned above, Prime Minister Mette Frederiksen has introduced a number of structural changes which point towards increased centralisation in the Danish core executive. The shift towards a strengthened prime minister, and hence an executive which is more 'monopoly' than 'duopoly', was already 'announced' by Frederiksen before winning the 2019 election. At a public conference even before the election was announced, she said: 'We have an incredibly small Prime Minister's Office, which does not drive anything in the political work. That does not suit my temper, if I am to be the prime minister of this country. Because it is my responsibility' (Korsgaard, 2019). In addition, in a book portraying her which was published three years before she was elected, she pointed to the hindering role played by the MoF in terms of developing new policy (Korsgaard, 2019).

One measure for strengthening the PMO has been the appointing of more SpAds. Mette Frederiksen was the first prime minister to appoint three special advisers, one being formally employed as chief of staff (*stabschef*). Other ministers (the Minister of Finance, the Minister of Taxation and the Minister of Justice) have also been allowed to have more than one special adviser probably because they are members of at least one of the two central cabinet committees (see below). This development can be seen as an attempt to get more assistance and to strengthen their position as politicians. In another bid to strengthen the PMO, it was announced that the number of person-years would increase by 15 to 20 person-years from 2021 (PMO, 2020b).

When Frederiksen became prime minister, she announced that the PMO would establish a political secretariat. The secretariat should have a particular focus on government-prioritised projects, policy developments and communication. In general, the secretariat would strengthen the strategic management of the government, as well as increase internal coordination between ministers and SpAds. The PMO announced that the political secretariat would be led by Martin Rossen, the SpAd who was employed as chief of staff, and would include both permanent civil servants and special advisers (PMO, 2019a). This gave rise to questions as to whether a political appointee would be able to supervise and give instructions to permanent civil servants (Christensen & Mortensen, 2019). The subsequent public debate led to a new decision in the PMO, reflected in a press release, clearly stating that Rossen would not be able to instruct and delegate tasks to permanent civil servants, and announcing that the political secretariat would consist of the three special advisers and a secretary to assist their work (PMO, 2019b).

COORDINATION OF GOVERNMENT POLICIES AND MEDIA COMMUNICATION

Intra-executive Coordination: Managing Danish Governments

Coordination across governments is a central task for any core executive. Until the recent shifts in the Frederiksen government, this task in the Danish core has mainly been performed by the prime minister, the PMO, the minister of finance, the MoF and the permanent secretaries serving the two ministers. These actors and institutions are what Rhodes and Salomonsen (2021) describe as 'a duopoly'.

The very centre of coordination comprises two cabinet committees. The first of these, the Coordination Committee (Koordinationsudvalget), is chaired by the PM. As described by the permanent secretaries interviewed in the projects this chapter reports on, the Coordination Committee discusses and coordinates 'all the matters of high political impact for the government', enabling the PM to be 'informed and in control of some of the bigger initiatives' (#6 PS) (see also Rhodes & Salomonsen, 2021, p. 76). The second committee, the Economic Committee (Økonomiudvalget), is chaired by the minister of finance and is 'taking decisions and discussing matters of economic importance' (#1 PS) (see also Rhodes & Salomonsen, 2021, p. 76). The minister of finance is also a member of the Coordinating Committee, cementing the position of the minister and his or her ministry at the very core of Danish government.

A handful of ministers (including the party leaders from the coalition partners when a coalition government is in office) have traditionally been permanent members of these two central committees, membership of which assures a certain place in the informal cabinet hierarchy. Party political considerations between coalition partners, as well as potential fragmentation within the PM's own party, are therefore taken into account when deciding who become permanent members of the Coordination and Economic committees (Nielsen, 2020). Note that there are no formal memos from meetings, and that the public is generally restricted from gaining insight into discussions therein (Nielsen, 2020).

Prior to meetings of both committees, policy issues are coordinated across government at the administrative level. That is, parallel preparatory government committee meetings consisting of permanent civil servants have been established. Mirroring the 'parent' committees, the permanent secretary of the PMO chairs the Coordinating Committee and the permanent secretary of the MoF chairs the Economic Committee. These preparatory government committees have been described by a former minister as 'a mirror image of the [Economic and Coordination] committee meeting itself. So, you're basically playing the whole thing, but without ministers' (#3 FM) (see Rhodes & Salomonsen, 2021, p. 76). In cases where the prime minister decides to change the composition of ministers in the committees (e.g., when reshuffling the government) this will also be reflected in the composition of the preparatory government committees—providing an instrument for the prime minister to also influence membership of the inner court in terms of administrative executives.

The Danish setup of two core committees is described by a former permanent secretary as 'a machine that has hand-on management of the whole government' (4 FPS), and to a large extent has run without conflicts between the different actors in the duopoly (see Rhodes & Salomonsen, 2021, p. 78). This smooth functioning between the committees has been possible partly due to the individuals holding key positions (as the two ministers are most often from the same party within the government coalition), but also, as a former minister noted, because 'all the institutions are designed to avoid that. It's simply—it's simply completely in the opposite direction of that' (#3 FM) (see Rhodes & Salomonsen, 2021, p. 78).

While both committees are central, the Economic Committee had come to play a more important role in the years leading up to the 2019 change in government. The Coordination Committee has previously been described as 'an inner cabinet' (Christensen & Jensen, 2011, p. 12): however, the Economic Committee is now 'where you hammer out deals between the (…) coalition parties' (#3 FM) (Rhodes & Salomonsen, 2021, p. 78).

A key to understanding the effectiveness of the duopoly lies in the discretion granted to the minister of finance, as well as in the central role played by the permanent secretaries of the PMO and the MoF. The former means that 'there can be no appeal to the Prime Minister of the decisions taken by the Minister of Finance' (#3 FM). If appeals were allowed 'the whole thing will collapse' (#3 FM)—so, 'the full backing of the Prime Minister underpins the authority of the MoF' (#3 FM). Similarly, 'the Coordination Committee isn't a court of appeal' (#5 PS)' (see Rhodes & Salomonsen, 2021, pp. 78–79).

The pivotal role played by the permanent secretaries of the PMO and the MoF is reflected in their presence in the committee meetings and the close collaboration between the two civil servants. To help the minister of finance and to ensure coordination across the PMO and the Coordination Committee, the PMO's permanent secretary has close contact within the MoF: that is, he or she is 'part of the Ministry of Finance's workflow, spends a lot of time in the Ministry, dines with the minister and his or her PS. He or she will always report to the PM on the decisions made and the obstacles facing the MoF' (#3 FM). Moreover, the permanent secretary of the PMO is 'physically in the Ministry of Finance for a lot of his time' (#3 FM) (see also Rhodes & Salomonsen, 2021, p. 79).

While coordination within the core of Danish government primarily occurs via the cabinet committees described above, there are also supplementary coordination mechanisms, including weekly formal cabinet meetings. However, these meetings have no *de facto* substantial importance in terms of ensuring coordination.

In addition to the formal coordination performed in the cabinet committees and the mirroring civil service preparatory government committees, informal coordination is important in the Danish core executive. This activity includes, but is not limited to, texts, phone calls and short discussions before and after meetings (Trangbæk, 2021b, pp. 259–261). The norm is to coordinate with others 'on your own level'; for instance, permanent secretaries coordinate with permanent secretaries, special advisers talk to other special advisers and so on.

Another important coordination mechanism is the often biannual government seminar (*regeringsseminar*) hosted by the PM and attended by both ministers and permanent secretaries. In these gatherings the PM briefs on the current state of affairs, on the government's work so far and on the most important policy initiatives going forward (#IP5, Trangbæk, 2021b). In continuation of that seminar, there might be an opportunity for each ministry to send a number of top civil servants to a one-day seminar where the PM will further explain the government's agenda, motives and reasoning.

Finally, also personal relations are important as a coordination mechanism within the Danish core executive, both when it comes to the relation between ministers and permanent secretaries but also among the permanent secretaries (Trangbæk, 2021b, pp. 87–101, 239–256). Knowing your colleagues is a crucial element of strategic interaction: one can better predict the reaction of colleagues (Trangbæk, 2021b, p. 249), it makes informal coordination easier and it enhances one's ability to decode colleagues' responses. Hence, it may be easier to coordinate and reach agreement when you can be more forward in your communication.

Changes in Coordination in Frederiksen's Cabinet

The 2019 Frederiksen government signalled stronger political control of the two most central cabinet committees. It is suggested that the political level is now more involved when preparing the agenda for meetings of the Coordination and Economic committees (Holstein, 2020a). PM Mette Frederiksen's ambition and active role in making the agendas for the Coordination Committee have also been acknowledged by special adviser Rossen (Engholm & Petersen, 2021). While committee agendas were previously constructed primarily on the basis of input from the other ministries, the ambition from the new PM and her PMO was to steer these in a way that was based more clearly on the cabinet's political priorities.

Frederiksen also established the practice of having special advisers participate in government committee meetings. Initially, Martin Rossen had a formal seat in the Coordination Committee (like the ministers), even though it was assured that he 'only' had the same scope for voicing his opinions as had any other civil servant (Prime Minister's Office, 2020b). While there were no legal constraints hindering this decision, it became a subject for rather intense parliamentary and public debate—and even a subject for discussion in the parliamentary presidium (Ritzau, 2019).

Rossen describes his role in the committee meetings as follows: 'I represented the general political ambitions. I represented the fact that we maintained our focus on certain strategic issues we had chosen' (Rossen, quoted in Engholm & Petersen, 2021, p. 27). Since he left his position as special adviser in 2020, no one has taken Rossen's formal seat on the committee. However, it has been announced that special advisers can participate in government committee meetings on the same terms as permanent civil servants (Prime Minister's Office, 2020b). According to Rossen, other SpAds from the PMO could listen in when the permanent secretaries held the preparatory cabinet committee meetings so as to ensure the political perspective was heard among permanent secretaries (Engholm & Petersen, 2021, p. 28). While it does not seem to have become the norm that special advisers participate in these meetings (Trangbæk, 2021b), it is difficult to assess how often this happens in practice.

Nonetheless, this (potential) participation of SpAds from the PMO not only ensures a more prominent role for the PM and the PMO vis-à-vis the MoF, but it further enables a stronger political grip and perspective vis-à-vis the administrative actors involved in government coordination. As explained by Rossen, ministers present at the cabinet committee meetings could 'use me to remind their respective systems [...] "it was good to hear your perspective, but we just have to remember that we are here to make some changes"' (Engholm & Petersen, 2021, p. 35). As such, the presence of the PMO's SpAds points to yet another means by which the prime minister can use her prerogative to strengthen her position vis-à-vis other parts of the political and administrative executives.

Previously, there appears to have been an almost symbiotic relation between the MoF and the PMO in Denmark. Now, it seems as if power is flowing back into the PMO (Holstein, 2020b). An indicator of this increasingly prominent role of the PMO in relation to the MoF is that line ministries focus on coordinating with both the MoF and PMO at various levels within the ministerial hierarchy, because the two core ministries do not necessarily agree (fieldnotes, Trangbæk, 2021b).

However, according to the now-former chief of staff in the PMO, the strengthening of the PMO and the prime minister has not been at the expense of the MoF. Rather:

> [t]he position of the chief of staff is an attempt to strengthen the overall steering of the government. The civil service is a very, very, very big body with very strong legs and very strong arms. The head consists of two parts, the PMO and the Ministry of Finance, and it has not been at the expense of the Ministry of Finance ... the reality is just that the PMO ... is very contingent upon the Ministry of Finance, and that we wanted to change—not at the expense of the Ministry of Finance, but on behalf of the whole government. (Engholm & Petersen, 2021, Appendix 2)

When asked which of the two cabinet committees he found most influential and important for the government, Rossen further noted: 'everything that is very, very important for the government, Mette will demand is being dealt within K [the Coordination Committee]'.

While the quotes from Rossen suggest that the MoF is still important, they also indicate that the PMO and the prime minister wish to regain control or power vis-à-vis the MoF. Concurrently, there are indications that the role of the Ministry of Justice is growing in importance in the core executive, though it is still too early to say whether that is contingent on the COVID-19 crisis or whether it will endure. In January 2020, it was announced that the permanent secretary in the Prime Minister's Office had been given a new position in the European Investment Bank and a new permanent secretary was therefore appointed: Barbara Bertelsen. Mette Frederiksen had previously appointed Bertelsen to the Ministry of Justice, where she served as a permanent secretary before starting in the PMO on 1 January 2020 (Prime Minister's Office, 2020a). At the MoJ Bertelsen spent five years working on re-shaping and adjusting the ministry's reputation, culture and goals after a stakeholder analysis clearly showed what the media referred to as a problematic and indeed dangerous culture in the ministry (Lund, 2016). Because of her background, therefore, Bertelsen is very familiar with the MoJ.

Another indication of the Ministry of Justice's increased importance relates to the ministry serving as a stepping stone for other positions in the core executive. Since Barbara Bertelsen was appointed to the PMO, two of six permanent secretaries appointed to ministries other than the MoJ had spent the majority of their careers in the MoJ before moving on. This appears to be part of a trend that an increasing number of permanent secretaries are appointed following a career in the Ministry of Justice (Trangbæk, 2021a).

Overall, there are several factors pointing to a centralisation and strengthening of the PMO during the time that Mette Frederiksen has served as prime minister. However, it is important to remember that the PMO has had a special status in the hierarchy for a long period (Knudsen, 2007). While the ministries *de jure* are equal, there is a *de facto* hierarchy between the actors, partly determined by their formal position: 'We actually have a government of ministers, meaning that no one is superior—but of course there still is. It goes without saying that this applies to both the prime minister in relation to the other ministers, and it also applies *de facto* to the Prime Minister's permanent secretary' (PS 3) (Trangbæk, 2021b, p. 253).

Extra-executive Coordination: Portraying the Executive in the Media

Over the years, Danish governments have responded to the increased media pressure experienced by most governments across modern democracies. As already mentioned, the introduction of special advisers from the late 1990s is one such response. The SpAds were introduced because ministers did not receive sufficient media advice from the permanent civil service due to limited competencies in terms of managing the media within the civil service, and also because of ministers' wishes that civil servants do not become too involved in this task in order to preserve their anonymity as well as neutrality.

Over recent decades this ability has changed through the establishment of communication units within ministries, aiming to help the minister and ensure 'good press' (Bo Smith-Udvalget, 2015; Ministry of Finance, 2013; Trangbæk, 2021b). At the same time, more SpAds have entered into the sphere of not only the political-tactical but also the policy advisory domain around ministers (Christiansen & Salomonsen, 2018). This is not least the case for the Frederiksen Cabinet. As noted by the former chief of staff in the PMO, Martin Rossen: 'We basically employed all the former political advisers from the Social Democratic party, they are now in the "central" ministries, the vast majority of them being policy-people' (Rossen, quoted in Engholm & Petersen, 2021, p. 27). Being recruited from former positions in the party as well as being described as 'policy-people' indicates that the SpAds in the current government reflect the shift towards less media and more policy and partisan people among the cadre of political advisers.

In the previous coalition government led by the Social Democratic party (2011–2015), there were a few strong efforts to coordinate government communication and media management across the different entities in the core executive. For instance, the prime minister established a communication unit in the PMO led by a permanent civil servant. According to the job description of the unit head (as described in the advertisement for the position), the purpose of the new communication unit was to coordinate the strategic communication of major political initiatives across the government and individual ministries (Ritzau, 2015). At the same time, the government launched a website for the government (Ritzau, 2015).

Under the current Frederiksen government, efforts to coordinate communication have increased. One initiative is the central coordination of communication across all ministries. This entails that the ministries have to coordinate with the PMO whenever they want to communicate new initiatives. More specifically, the PMO has an overview of the important government initiatives that need to be communicated. Based on that, there are 'green' time periods when ministries can actively communicate initiatives and 'red' time periods, when only the government's core initiatives should be communicated to the public. In these latter phases, other ministries should not communicate minor stories. This means that before they initiate press stories ministries need to check with the PMO whether they are in a red or a green zone (Trangbæk, 2021b, pp. 156–157).

Another (potential) centralising effort is the alleged 'politicising' of the civil service by employing heads of press (who are permanent civil servants) who have either personal or party-related ties to ministers (Lund, 2021; Vikkelsø, 2021). However, it is not the minister who decides who should be hired, even though technically they could interfere in this process: rather, it is top civil servants in the ministry who are usually in charge of hiring the head of press (fieldnotes, Trangbæk, 2021b).

Finally, it is worth noting the intense use of social media by Mette Frederiksen, which has also led to rather intense debate, particularly as this engagement is occurring simultaneously with recurring allegations that the PM is not willing to 'stand up to' interviews with journalists (Cordes,

2020). Communicating via social rather than traditional news media may be seen as a potential personal resource of prime ministers which, if used wisely, provides the opportunity to 'speak to' constituents in an unfiltered way, including by posting scenes from their professional or political and 'personal' live. Thus, Mette Frederiksen both posts pictures when acting as a prime minister and showcases more private sides of her life, including when she is polishing her windows or eating a traditional Danish lunch consisting of rye bread with mackerel. Posting the lunch not only hit the traditional news media and caused a public debate but also reached more than 18,000 likes on Instagram (Nyhus, 2021).

This type of communication may not only enhance the political capital of the government, but just as importantly enhance that of the prime minister vis-à-vis other politicians—including other ministers in her government. The number of followers does not give an indication of whether the communication performed via social media is effective in terms of building such positive political capital. However, it does point to whether or not there 'is an audience' to begin with. In the early spring of 2021, Mette Frederiksen had 388,000 followers on her Instagram profile, which is more than three times the number of people following all of the other leaders of parties in the Danish parliament taken together (Jensen, 2021). In 2020, which of course was during the COVID-19 pandemic, she received 5,500,000 reactions to her Instagram posts: the party leader with the second largest number received just 100,000 reactions on a similar social media platform (Jensen, 2021).

Conclusion: How Does the Danish Core Executive Fit into the Core Executive Framework?

The present chapter has shown recent changes within the Danish core executive. In this final and concluding section, we discuss how these changes in the inner core fit into the established theoretical frameworks of core executives and show how they can potentially add to both our empirical and theoretical understanding of the inner courts of governments (Rhodes, 2017, Chap. 7).

Despite recent changes, there is no doubt that the concepts of the core executive and the inner court still make sense in the Danish context. The preceding analysis indicates that Danish prime ministers now not only hold the *potential*, but also the *ability* to exercise their power (Heffernan,

2003), not least when they are able to 'marry' personal resources (e.g., personal relations across the political and administrative executives) with the institutional resources the PMO holds the potential to provide (Heffernan, 2003, p. 350). The relevance of this marriage has already been demonstrated in Chap. 2, in which the editors—citing Rhodes and Salomonsen (2021, p. 74)—note that in the Danish core executive the:

> PM is the focal point of these networks: the innermost network linking the set of networks that comprise the core executive. ... [T]he PM has more central resources to support the work. These resources increase the power potential of the PM.' In other words, while the power of the political centre may fluctuate depending on personalities and proclivities, location is significant as far as possession of key resources is concerned.

This was perhaps most evident when Mette Frederiksen formed her single party government in 2019. Even before she won the election, she was determined to run the government from a larger PMO, strengthened vis-à-vis the MoF, and with a firmer political grip vis-à-vis the administration. She used her political power to enhance the role of her advisers and her chief of staff, shifting the balance in the inner core of the executive. In addition, she used her personal relations to recruit a new permanent secretary, who, apparently as much as the PM herself, was able to demonstrate 'situated agency'.

As such, the analysis of Denmark demonstrates how there is 'fluidity' also in the inner court of the core executive. This fluidity—reflected in the recent changes described in this chapter—represents a shift in the inner core executive in Denmark, from being a duopoly towards what seems more like a monopoly. In addition, this shift is being seen as something not merely as caused by (and part and parcel of) the government's crisis management, but rather as a consequence of the prime minister's genuine wish to centralise and increase policy development, coordination and media management capacity. The COVID-19 crisis may have been the catalyst for change, but it was not the fundamental reason for it.

By using the notion of inner courts and court politics, the present chapter also points to the relevance of the interpretive approach to core executive studies suggested by Rhodes (and outlined in Chap. 3). An important contribution of this approach is not merely pointing to the need for moving beyond the structural and fixed accounts of core executives (in terms of deducing who core executives are and the power that those executives hold). It also includes emphasising the importance of understanding and gaining insight into actors' interpretations of practices, rituals and beliefs within the core executive—including those within the innermost court (Rhodes, 2017, Chap. 7). As Rhodes and Tiernan (2016) note, agency and not structure determines the 'ebb and flow' of interactions between ministerial colleagues. That argument departs from the assertion that structures are too 'vague' as heuristics for understanding the core executives (Bevir & Rhodes, 2008, p. 730)—among other things, because the concept of 'structure' detracts our attention from identifying practices and traditions (Bevir & Rhodes, 2006).

The analysis of the Danish core executive shows how committees and other coordination structures, when looked at more closely, 'dissolve' into these very traditions and practices. They become traditions started by the practices of former governments, which are inherited by their successors and continue to be reflected in their practices, not least on the basis of advice from relatively powerful permanent secretaries (Rhodes & Salomonsen, 2021). These practices turn into traditions, which in turn become what may be looked upon as rather stable and even fixed structures: but which, in the end, are malleable, fluid and subject to change if they do not 'do the job' for and 'suit the temper' of the prime minister of the day. Such an analysis also demonstrates how changes in core executive arrangements can be brought about through the agency of powerful prime ministers such as Mette Frederiksen, whose decisions let prime ministerial power flow back to the PMO and the Coordination Committee (a process helped by allowing SpAds to enter the domain of the Coordination Committee), as perceived by the advisers at the core. As noted by her former chief of staff, it was Frederiksen's decision to give him a place in the committees—she could even have chosen her father if she wanted to (DR, 2020), because it was within her formal discretion to do so.

However, the present picture painted of the Danish core executive also points to the fact that the ebb and flow of the prime minister's powers are not unchecked, but become subject to parliamentary and public debate—at least when the interpretation of traditions goes against the normative expectations of the Danish prime minister and the power exercised from the PMO. It also demonstrates the need for comprehending the workings of inner courts in the wider context of the government and the parliamentary situation, the better to fully understand the 'situated agency' of actors within the inner circle of the core executive (at least in the context of a parliamentary democracy). Finally, our analysis suggests that further investigation is needed on the question of whether the formation of a single party government is a precondition for centralising power within the PMO. As the recent such administration headed by Lars Løkke Rasmussen demonstrated, being a single party government is not a sufficient condition per se for the replacement of a duopoly with the form of monopoly we have described—but the question remains whether it is a necessary one in the context of Danish core executives.

Notes

1. Recent times have also seen a single party government headed by Lars Løkke Rasmussen of the Liberals (*Venstre*) from 28 June 2015 to 28 November 2016 (https://www.stm.dk/regeringen/regeringer-siden-1848/ visited 21 October 2021).
2. Funded by The Danish Council for Independent Research, Social Sciences, grant no. 0602-01612B.
3. Including the following governments: (1) Helle Thorning-Schmidt I Cabinet; a coalition government including The Social Democratic Party (*Socialdemokraterne*), the Social Liberal Party (*Det Radikale Venstre*) and the Socialist People's Party (*Socialistisk Folkeparti*) from 3 October 2011 to 3 February 2014; (2) Helle Thorning-Schmidt II Cabinet; a coalition government including The Social Democratic Party (*Socialdemokraterne*) and the Social Liberal Party (*Det Radikale Venstre*) from 3 February 2014 to 28 June 2015 (https://www.stm.dk/regeringen/regeringer-siden-1848/ visited 21 October 2021).
4. Funded by the Australian Research Council (DP 160100896). Patrick Weller (Griffith University), R. A. W. Rhodes (University of Southampton) and Heidi Houlberg Salomonsen conducted the interviews. We thank Patrick Weller and R. A. W. Rhodes for allowing us to refer to the project and its empirical findings in this chapter.
5. Including the following governments: (1) Lars Løkke Rasmussen II Cabinet; a single minority government including The Liberal Party (*Venstre*) from 28 June 2015 to 28 November 2016; (2) Lars Løkke Rasmussen III Cabinet; a coalition government including The Liberal Party (*Venstre*), the Liberal Alliance (*Liberal Alliance*) and the Conservative Party (*Det Konservative Folkeparti*) from 28 November 2016 to 27 June 2019. (https://www.stm.dk/regeringen/regeringer-siden-1848/ visited 21 October 2021).

References

Agency for Digitisation. (2021). About the Agency for Digitisation. Retrieved October 19, 2021, from https://en.digst.dk/about-us/

Bevir, M., & Rhodes, R. A. W. (2006). Disaggregating Structures as an Agenda for Critical Realism: A Reply to McAnulla. *British Politics, 1*, 397–403.

Bevir, M., & Rhodes, R. A. W. (2008). The Differentiated Polity as Narrative. *British Journal of Politics and International Relations, 10*(4), 729–734.

Boin, A., McConnell, A., & t'Hart, P. (2021). *Governing the Pandemic. The Politics of Navigating a Mega-Crisis*. Palgrave Macmillan.

Christensen, J. G. (2006). Ministers and Mandarins under Danish Parliamentarism. *International Journal of Public Administration, 29*(12), 997–1019.

Christensen, J.G., & Jensen, L. (2011). The Executive Core and Government Strategy in the Nordic Countries, : Department of Political Science, University of Aarhus, *Unpublished Paper*.

Christensen, J. G., & Mortensen, P. B. (2019). Mette Frederiksen fører Statsministeriet på afveje. *Politiken, 10*(07), 2019.

Christiansen, P. M., & Salomonsen, H. H. (2018). Denmark—Loyalty and the Public Advisor Bargain. In R. Shaw & C. Eichbaum (Eds.), *Ministers, Minders and Mandarins. An international Study of Relationships at the Executive Summit of Parliamentary Democracies* (pp. 53–71). Edward Elgar.

Cordes, T. (2020). Medier har i månedsvis forgæves forsøgt at få statsministeren til at deltage i et kritisk interview: "Det er et demokratisk problem". *Berlingske Tidende, 11*(12), 2020.

DR. (December 2020). Hvad var planen Martin Rossen, *DR documentary* Identified October 13 at https://www.dr.dk/drtv/program/hvad-var-planen-martin-rossen_224555

Engholm, C.H., & Petersen, G.T. (2021, May 28). Koordination eller konkurrence? Betydningen af de centrale regeringsudvalg for politisering af det danske embedsværk undersøgt gennem eliteinterviews. Bachelor Thesis, University of Copenhagen.

Grøn, C. H., & Salomonsen, H. H. (2020). Organizing Central Government: A Pragmatic Meritocracy? In P. M. Christiansen, J. Elklit, & P. Nedergaard (Eds.), *The Oxford Handbook of Danish Politics* (pp. 124–140). Oxford University Press.

Hansen, M. E. (2020). The Government and the Prime Minister: More than *Primus Inter Pares*? In P. M. Christiansen, J. Elklit, & P. Nedergaard (Eds.), *The Oxford Handbook of Danish Politics* (pp. 107–123). Oxford University Press.

Heffernan, R. (2003). Prime Ministerial Predominance? Core Executive Politics in the UK. *British Journal of Politics and International Relation, 5*, 347–372.

Holst, E.Q. (2020, August 28). Mette Frederiksen laver historisk udvidelse af Statsministeriet. *Altinget*.

Holstein, E. (2020a, August 28). Rossen efterlader sig dybe spor.

Holstein, E. (2020b, June 29). Året hvor embedsmændene mistede magten.
Hustedt, T., & Salomonsen, H. H. (2017). Political Control of Government Coordination? The Roles of Ministerial Advisers in Government Coordination in Denmark and Sweden. *Public Administration*, *95*(2), 393–406.
Jensen, M.S. (2021, April 4). Mette Frederiksens Instagram: Det er som Ude og Hjemme på Speed. *Altinget*.
Knudsen, T. (2000). Statsministeren og Statsministeriet. In T. Knudsen (Ed.), *Regering og embedsmænd. Om magt og demokrati i staten* (pp. 81–98). Systime.
Knudsen, T. (2007). Den stærke statsminister. In T. Knudsen (Ed.), *Fra folkestyre til markedsdemokrati. Dansk demokratihistorie efter 1973* (pp. 280–326). Akademisk Forlag.
Korsgaard, K. (2019, March 28). Mette Frederiksen vil have et mere magtfuldt statsministerium.
Lund, S.R. (2016, March 24). Justitsministeriet på historisk forandringsrejse.
Lund, S.R. (2021, June 7). Ministerier har ansat 27 nye presse- og kommunikationschefer under Mette Frederiksen. *Altinget*.
Ministry of Finance. (1998a). White Paper 1354/1998. *Betænkning fra Udvalget om forholdet mellem minister og embedsmænd*.
Ministry of Finance. (1998b). Resumé: At tjene og forme den nye tid– Finansministeriet 1848-1998. Published as part of celebrating the 150 year jubilee of the Ministry of Finance. Retrieved October 21, 2021, from https://fm.dk/media/10187/finansministeriet-1848-1998.pdf
Ministry of Finance. (2004). White Paper 1443/2004. *Betænkning nr. 1443— embedsmænds rådgivning og bistand*.
Ministry of Finance. (2013). White Paper 1537/2013. *Ministrenes særlige rådgivere. Serviceeftersyn. Government white paper on special advisors*.
Ministry of Finance (2021). The organization of the department. Retrieved October 19, 2021, from https://fm.dk/ministeriet/organisation/finansministeriets-departement/
Mortensen, P. B. (2014). Statens forvaltning. In J. Blom-Hansen, P. M. Christiansen, T. Pallesen, & S. Serritzlew (Eds.), *Offentlig Forvaltning—et politologisk perspektiv* (pp. 78–106). Hans Reitzels Forlag.
Nielsen, P. H. (2020). Ledelse og Koordination i danske regeringer 1958 til i dag. *Historisk Tidsskrift*, *120*(2), 407–446.
Nyhus, M. (2021, February 5). : Mette Frederiksens makrelmadder er effektive. *Journalisten*.
Prime Minister's Office. (2019a). Press Release 04.07.2019. Retrieved October 20, 2021, from https://www.stm.dk/presse/pressemeddelelser/statsministeriet-styrkes-med-nyt-politisk-sekretariat/
Prime Minister's Office. (2019b). Press Release 02.09.2019. Retrieved October 20, 2021, from https://www.stm.dk/presse/pressemeddelelser/organisationsudvidelse-i-statsministeriet/

Prime Minister's Office. (2020a). Press Release 09.01.2020. Retrieved October 20, 2021, from https://www.stm.dk/presse/pressemeddelelser/ny-departementschef-i-statsministeriet/

Prime Minister's Office. (2020b). Press Release 28.08.2020. Retrieved October 20, 2021, from https://www.stm.dk/presse/pressemeddelelser/styrkelse-af-statsministeriet-og-aendring-af-regeringsudvalgene/

Rhodes, R. A. W. (2017). *Interpretive Political Science: Selected Essays* (Vol. 2). Oxford University Press.

Rhodes, R.A.W., & Salomonsen, H.H. (2018, September 17–18). Duopoly, Court Politics and the Danish Core Executive. Presented at Seminar on *Cabinet Government for the Twenty First Century*, University of Cambridge.

Rhodes, R. A. W., & Salomonsen, H. H. (2021). Duopoly, Court Politics and the Danish Core Executive. *Public Administration, 99*(1), 72–86.

Rhodes, R. A. W., & Tiernan, A. (2016). Court Politics in a Federal Polity. *Australian Journal of Political Science, 51*(2), 1–17.

Ritzau. (2015, September 30). *Ny spin-enhed i Statsministeriet koster millioner.* Retrieved October 10, 2021, from https://www.denoffentlige.dk/ny-spin-enhed-i-statsministeriet-koster-millioner

Ritzau. (2019, September 11). Folketingets ledelse har drøftet omdiskuteret særlig rådgiver.

Bo Smith-Udvalget. (2015). *Embedsmanden i det moderne folkestyre.* Jurist- & Økonomforbundets Forlag.

Trangbæk, A. (2021a). *Does the Cradle of Power Exist? Sequence Analysis of Top Bureaucrats' Career Trajectories.* Working paper, Aarhus University.

Trangbæk, A. (2021b). *Life at the Top. Understanding Top Bureaucrats' Roles as the Link between Politics and Administration.* PhD Dissertation, Aarhus University.

Vikkelsø, M. (2021, May 7). Overblik: Disse pressechefer har forbindelse til S og ministrene. *Altinget.*

CHAPTER 11

The Norwegian Core Executive: Baronial Courts and Inner Circles?

Kristoffer Kolltveit and Jostein Askim

INTRODUCTION

To characterise the Norwegian core executive as consisting of baronial courts and inner circles, as the chapter title suggests, may sound strange to those who know Norway well. Most Norwegian nobility died out in the Middle Ages, with the local nobility mainly continuing as large landowners and farmers, and only a few foreign (Danish) nobles were later given titles and ownership over Norwegian territories. The Norwegian Constitution of 1814 forbade the establishment of new counties and baronies, and in line with the national romantic ideal of equality, the nobility have had little place in Norwegian society ever since.

Similarly, the existence of inner circles also sounds like an oddity in a country traditionally characterised by collegiality and consensus in government decision-making. In Norway, the cabinet has been seen as a decision machine wherein the ministers work on an equal footing. The cabinet

---

K. Kolltveit (✉) • J. Askim
Department of Political Science, University of Oslo, Oslo, Norway
e-mail: kristoffer.kolltveit@stv.uio.no; jostein.askim@stv.uio.no

© The Author(s), under exclusive license to Springer Nature
Switzerland AG 2022
K. Kolltveit, R. Shaw (eds.), *Core Executives in a Comparative Perspective*, Understanding Governance,
https://doi.org/10.1007/978-3-030-94503-9_11

collegium's strong position has been explained by the prime minister's lack of formal authority over other ministers and by a normative preference for a collegial working form (Christensen & Lægreid, 2002).

As we will show in this chapter, however, inner circles consisting of party leaders have been important in cabinet decision-making, even though the cabinet remains an important decision-making organ. We show the cementation of baronial courts, where cabinet ministers surrounded by a growing entourage of ministerial advisers and communication professionals preside as 'barons' over their own policy territories. Although the seeds of Norwegian baronial courts can be found in the principle of ministerial rule, we relate their strengthening to developments in the media and to the mediatisation of politics and the public sector.

Note the following limitation: rather than covering all actors in the core executive in equal depth, the chapter pays particular attention to the cabinet, cabinet ministers, politically appointed ministerial advisors and the top layer of the permanent civil service—the prime minister's office (PMO) and permanent secretaries and communication units in ministerial departments. Despite their being important institutions in the core executive, we pay less attention to directorates and other central agencies, even though they do perform some of the same functions in Norway's executive as do the institutions and actors we do focus on in the chapter (e.g. the provision of policy advice and cross-sectoral coordination).

The rise of populism represents another relevant societal development, and Norway offers an opportunity for studying how a populist party is included in governing. After the parliamentary elections in 2013, the Progress Party entered the Solberg government. After six years, the party chose to leave the coalition in January 2020, after what can be characterised as a successful endeavour. In the chapter, we relate this to the Progress Party behaving similarly to the other parties in the coalition, as well as to the strategy of Prime Minister Solberg in allowing the Populist Party to maintain some of its outsider identity.

Data

In addition to providing a general overview, based on laws, regulations, government documents and existing research, the chapter covers three governments in more depth: the 2001–2005 Bondevik II government, the 2005–2013 Stoltenberg II government and the 2013–2021 Solberg government (Table 11.1). In terms of primary empirical material, the

Table 11.1 Cabinets, parties and parliamentary support in Norway 2001–2021

Cabinet	Parties	Parl. Support (% of mandates)
Bondevik II (2001–2005)	Conservatives, Liberals, Christian Democrats	37.6
Stoltenberg II (2005–2013)	Socialist Left, Centre Party, Labour	51.5 (2005–2009) 50.9 (2009–2013)
Solberg (2013–2021)	Conservatives, Progressives Conservatives, Progressives, Liberals Conservatives, Progressives, Liberals, Christian Democrats Conservatives, Liberals, Christian Democrats	45.6ª (2013–2018) 47.3 (2018–2019) 52.1 (2019–2020) 36.2 (2020–2021)

ªWritten agreement with the Liberal Party and the Christian Democratic Party, ensuring a majority in parliament

chapter utilises élite interview and survey material. Thirty-four interviews were conducted between 2010 and 2012 with ministers, the chief of staff at the prime minister's office (PMO) and ministerial permanent secretaries (see Kolltveit, 2013). Sixteen additional interviews were conducted between 2018 and 2019 with current and recent ministerial permanent secretaries and heads of communication (marked N1–N16; see also Difi, 2019). Surveys to ministerial advisers were sent out in 2015, 2018 and 2020, returning 283 responses in total. The response rate was higher in the Stoltenberg II cabinet (76%, $n = 146$) than in the Bondevik II cabinet (65%, $n = 60$) and the Solberg cabinet (54%, $n = 77$) (Table 11.1).

Configuration of Actors and Institutions in Norway

Before drawing up the configuration of the relevant actors and institutions in the Norwegian core executive, we briefly visit the formal regulations. There are a few formal amendments related to the executive in the Norwegian 1814 Constitution (Holmøyvik, 2021). The constitutional rules on the executive—for example, government formation and organisation, procedural rules and decision-making—predate parliamentarism and are essentially limited to the relationship between the monarch and their cabinet. Internal regulations, guidelines and informal norms play prominent roles in the workings of the Norwegian core executive, supplementing the constitutional framework. For example, in contrast to the letter of the constitution, the monarch's role is symbolic and ceremonial; in reality, executive power lies with the cabinet as a collegiate body (Holmøyvik, 2021). The principle of ministerial rule applies, meaning that the whole ministerial organisation—that is, not only the ministerial department but also regulatory bodies, directorates and other subordinate agencies—submits to the formal authority of the minister as head of the ministry. However, the constitution states that the overall executive power rests with the king in council and that its political component (the government) carries general responsibility for the entire executive power. The individual minister acts on behalf of the collegium. Although the constitution states that cabinet decisions formally are taken in the ritual Council of State, which is led by the king, or in the ministries, weekly cabinet meetings attended by all cabinet ministers are the most important arena for political coordination and for deciding cabinet policy.

The sectorised departmental system with its weak formal coordination requirements pushes decisions upwards to the cabinet level. Per guidelines formulated by the PMO, cases with significant economic and administrative consequences, politically difficult cases and cases where two or more ministers disagree should be discussed at cabinet meetings (Prime Minister's Office, 1969, 2010). These are relatively loose regulations; in the 1990s, one in three Norwegian ministers experienced uncertainty about whether seeking cabinet approval for a project was necessary (Eriksen, 2003). The rules have been refined over time, and now, cabinet notes need to follow strict formal requirements (see below).

The Prime Minister and Prime Minister's Office

Norwegian prime ministers have traditionally been weak compared with the prime ministers in other parliamentary democracies (O'Malley, 2007). As 'primus inter pares', the prime minister has been called a political organiser but no superstar (Olsen, 1983, p. 81). The prime minister formally has no authority over cabinet members. However, the Government Instructions from 1909 declare that the prime minister is the chairperson of the Council of State (*statsråd*) and may demand all of the information on a given case (Prime Minister's Office, 1969). In reality, however, prime ministers lead the cabinet and are the decisive actor if disagreements or conflicts arise. According to the constitution, the king appoints members to the cabinet, and the prime minister has no formal right to dismiss ministers. In reality, however, prime ministers have selected and dismissed cabinet members (Narud & Strøm, 2011). Strong prime ministers in single-party cabinets have picked and reshuffled their ministers, while prime ministers in coalitions have had less opportunity to select or dismiss members representing other parties. The Council of State decides who will be the deputy prime minister. In a coalition government, the norm is for the leader of the second-largest party to be the deputy prime minister, irrespective of the political prominence of the portfolio he/she holds as a minister.

The PMO is comparatively small, with about 70–80 employees, and functions as both a secretariat for the prime minister and a support for the cabinet as a whole (Christensen & Lægreid, 2002, p. 75; Eriksen, 1988, p. 192; Olsen, 1983). The PMO works as a broker in clarifying conflicts and disagreements and preparing the cabinet agenda. Although the PMO is not formally superior to other ministries, it is in reality primus inter pares. The PMO's superiority in the core executive is thus a political fact more than a formal institution.

An important maxim has been keeping the PMO free of specific areas of responsibility. The Norwegian PMO has had an important role in facilitating cabinet decision-making and acting as a service organisation for the cabinet. Over the past few decades, there has been growth in both administrative personnel and political appointees. This has enabled the PMO to take a more active role in line departments and in coordinating cabinet policy. In the Stoltenberg II cabinet, a separate coordination minister was appointed in 2009 to ensure horizontal coordination in the cabinet, but this measure was not continued in the subsequent Solberg cabinet. In neighbouring countries Sweden and Denmark, European Union (EU) accession has driven new appointments at the PMO. Norway is not an EU member but the country is economically and politically affiliated to the union as part of the European Economic Area (EEA). The appointment in 2013 of a minister of EEA and EU affairs at the PMO is a Norwegian watered-down institutional innovation, one echoing the larger expansions of the PMO observed in EU countries.

Cabinet Ministers and Cabinet Committees

According to the constitution, the king chooses a council consisting of a prime minister and at least seven other members: the cabinet ministers. The ministers have constitutional responsibility for illegal behaviour while acting in their position. Impeachment processes are very uncommon in

Norway but would be relevant, for instance, if false information is given to parliament. In addition, cabinet ministers have a parliamentary responsibility, which means that they can be held accountable for all actions of their department and subordinate agencies (see the ministerial rule mentioned above). Formal proposals for votes of no confidence against either individual ministers or whole cabinets have occurred on average just shy of once per year since 1945, albeit with only five proposals resulting in ministers or cabinets resigning. For example, in the current Solberg government, a minister resigned in 2018 when it was clear there would be a parliamentary majority for a vote of no confidence against the minister. The cabinet, however, stayed in power (Wahl & Hem, 2018).

Norwegian ministers are cabinet members, ministry heads and party actors, hence giving them tripartite roles:

> They are the legal heads of their respective ministries and thus administrators and specialists. They are generalists by virtue of their membership in the cabinet and their participation in the collective decisions reached in that forum. Finally, they are partisans in the sense that they represent their particular political parties in the cabinet and in their own ministries. (Strøm, 1994, p. 45)

Norwegian cabinet ministers have much discretion over matters within their own areas. Ministerial decisions are formally made in the minister's name or by authority from the minister. Research has found that Norwegian ministers in the 1970s and 1980s spent most of their time on departmental matters (Eriksen, 1988), thereby functioning mainly as ministry heads and specialists (Strøm, 1994). However, the growth of state secretaries in the apparatus has enabled cabinet ministers to engage in more outreach activities outside the ministry because authority can be delegated to the state secretaries (see below).

Norway has had a tradition of cabinet committees within selected policy areas. For instance, the cabinet's security committee was established after World War II, along with the cabinet's research committee and economic committee (Bloch, 1963, p. 119). Various governments have also had employment committees, oil committees and even a foreign policy committee (Eriksen, 2003, pp. 132–133). Cabinet committees became less important in the 1970s and 1980s. Discussions and any decisions in the committees were not considered politically binding for the cabinet, and the most difficult political matters often ended up on the government's table anyway. Over time, the various committees have therefore primarily had the task of preparing matters for cabinet meetings. Today, cabinet committees are still in use, and they provide cabinets with the opportunity to discuss certain matters with a smaller group that can meet more frequently. How cabinet work is organised and the ability to reach agreements—thus the need for inner cabinets—varies across cabinets. Cabinet subcommittees have been present in Norwegian coalitions since 1983 (Narud & Strøm, 2003). The subcommittee usually consists of the prime minister, the finance minister and the party leaders, depending on the composition of the cabinets. This inner cabinet has sometimes been used to solve conflicts, and especially in Jens Stoltenberg's second cabinet (2005–2013), the cabinet subcommittee grew into a supplementary decision-making arena, as will be elaborated on below.

State Secretaries and Political Advisers

Norway has a long tradition of political appointees in ministerial departments. The state secretary position was established in 1947 to reduce ministers' workloads. The political adviser position has existed since the early 1990s and is a continuation and relabelling of the personal secretary position, which was introduced in 1946 as a provisional arrangement to unburden the busiest ministers. State secretaries are appointed by the formal Council of State, whereas political advisers are hired by the PMO. However, both types of political appointees serve a certain minister and leave when the minister resigns. It is now common to have one political adviser and two to three state secretaries in each ministry. State secretaries are mentioned in the constitution; they are not part of the cabinet but can act on behalf of the minister at the minister's discretion. State secretaries are supposed to assist the minister in leading the ministry, and they often are responsible for certain sections of the departments, where they go deep into specific issues (N7, N15). Over the past two decades, it has also become common to appoint state secretaries to work under a cabinet minister from a party other than their own. First established in the early 1980s, these cross-partisan advisers have become a natural ingredient in Norwegian coalition cabinets (see below).

The constitution does not mention the political adviser position. According to government regulations, the political adviser should be at the personal disposal of the minister and should perform the tasks the minister delegates. However, it is emphasised that political advisers cannot have independent decision-making authority: in reality, however, some function as state secretaries (N16) while others are designated communication tasks, almost taking the role as head of communication (N16). In Norway, there are no government-appointed spokespersons or central press offices. Official statements from ministries are channelled through the cabinet minister and their political appointees.

Permanent Secretaries and Communication Professionals

The permanent secretaries are important actors in the Norwegian core executive. They are the administrative heads of the ministerial departments and are responsible for internal management and coordination. At the same time, the permanent secretary functions as a key adviser to the minister. Permanent secretaries are not hired on fixed-term contracts and cannot be subjected to at-will replacement by ministers. This job security and their often long tenures enable permanent secretaries to provide professional advice of a different sort than do state secretaries and political advisers. Since their advisory functions to some extent overlap, there has been a lasting tension—or power struggle—between the permanent secretaries and the state secretaries (Grønlie & Flo, 2009).

The number of bureaucratic communication professionals across ministerial departments has grown considerably in the recent decades, from about 30 in the early 1990s to about 130 in 2020. As in other contexts, this development is explained by growing expectations and perceived needs for ministers to respond to media queries and to be visible in the press, including on online platforms. Over the same period, the number of ordinary civil servants in the ministerial departments grew from about 3500 to about 4500.

The communication units are organised directly under the ministry's top administrative and political level. However, the communication professionals are civil servants, not politically appointed, and are obliged to act in a way that enables them to maintain political neutrality (Christensen, 2005). Ethical guidelines ban all civil servants, communication professionals included, from participating in party political campaigning. The communication professionals are still 'special' in the sense that their offices are located physically close to those of the ministry's political leaders and that they are in frequent contact, travel together and have lunch with the politicians.

Decision-Making and Coordination in the Norwegian Core Executive

The principle of ministerial responsibility is the main reason for the strong departments and sectorised system in Norway, where few ministries have cross-sectoral policy responsibilities. In addition, structural developments have strengthened the system's 'silo' characteristics. Through so-called agencification (in new public management parlance), responsibility for policy delivery and implementation has been transferred from ministerial departments to directorates and other executive state agencies and to state-owned companies, making the public sector more differentiated and fragmented (Christensen & Lægreid, 2002). This agencification has streamlined the functional role of ministerial departments, allowing them to focus on policy-making, including preparing reforms and revising acts, and on serving as secretariats for the political leadership (Grønlie & Flo, 2009). Observers have argued that their strengthened political secretariat function and organisational detachment from policy delivery have weakened ministerial departments' role in policy coordination across ministries—tying them instead to the political project of the minister and his/her political party. It is therefore possible that horizontal coordination has been pushed upwards to the cabinet level, thus strengthening 'the core of the core' in executive government.

The so-called cabinet meeting notes system structures the decision-making process of the Norwegian core executive. Cases discussed in cabinet meetings are presented in 2-to-3-page notes. Draft notes are circulated among the ministers prior to cabinet meetings, and any disagreements between ministers are meant to be coordinated away or incorporated in the notes to make visible disagreements between ministers and ministries, thus giving focus to the cabinet's discussion.

To have as few comments and disagreements as possible, there are extensive formal and informal contacts across ministries, by both (top) civil servants and ministerial advisers. As one official notes, 'Often, people talk of coordination as something that is achieved further down in the system, but … ultimately, coordination should take place at cabinet level [even though] some coordination is needed [further down in the system] too' (N1).

To achieve coordination at the bureaucratic level, permanent secretaries play important roles. The permanent secretaries have close relations, and their weekly informal meetings are important arenas to notify other colleagues of issues in the pipeline, to sound out viewpoints from other departments and so forth (N8). According to our interviewees, the permanent secretaries are better suited for resolving disagreements than are civil servants at lower levels, who tend to focus on their own ministry and their own cases (N14). One interviewee said:

> Ordinary civil servants and even the directors general often miss the whole picture. The permanent secretaries see the totality and know their colleagues well. People further down the system will think: 'I have no responsibility for this'. They each sit in their own little spot. Eventually you have to bypass that level, and go higher up to get someone to understand the importance of coordination. (N1)

State secretaries are essential actors in interdepartmental coordination; they find solutions in cases that are too small for the ministers and too difficult for civil servants (N7). When disagreements arise, the state secretaries might resolve disputes with their colleagues in other departments, leaving the gravest disagreements for the ministers to handle. If the permanent secretaries believe that the state secretaries are unable to solve certain issues, they sometimes go straight to the minister (N6). As one research participant observed:

> We try to solve as much as possible at the bureaucratic level. If we succeed in reaching a consensus and solutions at that level, issues can be lifted into the cabinet for a formal decision. But if it stops [at the bureaucratic level], I ask a state secretary to take this with a colleague in the other ministry, or I might go straight to the minister. We try to minimise what is being raised to the political level, that is always what we work for. (N9)

Some of our respondents believed that state secretaries are used (and should be used) more to solve disagreements and ease tensions between parties and ministries—political coordination functions that in other contexts tend to fall on more junior officials such as political advisers. According to respondents, this political coordination should not typically occur in arenas such as formal committees. Rather, it is considered to be more useful for state secretaries to meet to coordinate on specific and more limited issues: for example, in connection with the submission of cabinet notes, writing government white papers and so forth. At the same time, several respondents claimed that state secretaries primarily promote their own minister. When asked about the importance of the state secretaries for coordination, the main impression from our informants was that they consider the state secretaries mainly oriented towards promoting their own minister: 'They do what they can to build on the minister's political project' (Difi, 2019). According to another informant, the state secretaries are silo defenders: 'I have a very hard time imagining a state secretary who can help break down silos' (Difi, 2019). Although state secretaries are important actors in cabinet coordination, at the same time, they seem to strengthen the baronial courts around their minister.

As mentioned above, Norwegian ministries have strange allies in the form of cross-partisan advisers (CPAs). The number of ministries housing CPAs grew considerably when the centre-left Stoltenberg II government took office in 2005. Stoltenberg appointed CPAs to four different line ministries as well as the PMO and the Ministry of Finance. The Solberg cabinet, which took office in 2013, extended the practice, with CPAs appointed to 9 out of 16 ministries (Askim et al., 2018). In the literature on coalitions, these actors are called watchdog junior ministers and mainly seen as measures to 'keep tabs' on the coalition partners and to monitor and control each other's behaviour' (Thies, 2001; Strøm et al., 2010). In Norway, however, this is not their only designated task. Norwegian CPAs monitor on behalf of their party, but—as one interviewee noted—they also provide cross-partisan advice to their minister and perform many of the same tasks as regular state secretaries, including exercising independent decision-making power: 'They are a 'listening post', but they can also help resolve issues. They have such double roles. They are often allocated to the ministries that are a bit demanding. If something [in the cabinet] is very difficult, if there are no good processes' (N4).

The inherent tensions in the sectorised system, the short deadlines on the cabinet notes, and the absence of formal regulations that force coordination at the early stages of the decision-making process means that the actors at the administrative and lower political levels are often unable to resolve disagreements. Therefore, many cases are pushed upwards and end up at the cabinet level.:

> Usually, disagreements between ministries are supposed to be cleared before issues are raised to cabinet meetings. However, all disagreements should not necessarily be coordinated away; important disagreements should be raised to the cabinet level, so every aspect is illuminated. If there is disagreement between two different parties, then it should be lifted, so the prime minister should know where the disagreement is. (N1)

Issues where disagreements are still present are discussed and decided on at the weekly cabinet meetings, which bring together the full cabinet. Thus, the cabinet has been called the most important coordination organ in Norway, and cabinet meetings have been called the pillars of the cabinet's collegial working form (Skjeie, 2001). In cabinet meetings, formal voting almost never takes place (Narud & Strøm, 2011). Instead, controversies between parties or ministers are either resolved after discussions in the meetings or discussed further and solved by smaller groups of ministers, often the prime minister, finance minister and relevant line ministers (Skjeie, 2001; Olsen, 1983).

It can be challenging to rate the importance of different decision-making arenas solely on the basis of élite interviews. In the electronic surveys, we asked the respondents to rate the importance of different arenas for reaching agreements in the cabinet. Table 11.2 shows the distribution.

The results support the notion that the weekly cabinet meetings were seen as very important venues for reaching agreements in the Norwegian cabinet. Table 11.2 also shows that important decisions can be reached at informal lunches, while formal cabinet committees have limited importance in the Norwegian core executive.

However, by looking at the respondents from Bondevik II and Stoltenberg II cabinets, the cabinet subcommittee is rated as more important than the full cabinet. Because of the parliamentary majority, proposals from the Stoltenberg II cabinet could become official policies without the involvement of opposition parties. Because decisions made in the cabinet were presumably final, the decision-making process became tenser, and it was difficult to reach agreements in the full cabinet (N3), increasing the need for the cabinet subcommittee to reach agreements. In Stoltenberg II, the cabinet subcommittee consisting of the three party leaders grew into a supplementary and decisive decision-making arena (Kolltveit, 2013).

In Solberg's cabinet (2013–), there was also a subcommittee that included party leaders and deputy party leaders. However, with only two parties in the coalition, Conservative party leader Erna Solberg and Progress party leader Siv Jensen met as PM and minister of finance discussing issues before every cabinet meeting, reducing the need for the inner cabinet (Stavenes & Strøm, 2021). Emphasis has also been placed on using the full cabinet more to solve disagreements (N1, N3). The return to cabinet meetings as the most important arena has been explained by Prime Minister Solberg's personal preference for deciding issues there:

Table 11.2 The importance of decision arenas to reaching an agreement in the cabinet; percentages and means per cabinet

	Not Important				Very Important	Mean (Std. Dev.)	N
	1	2	3	4	5		
Weekly cabinet meetings							
Bondevik II 2001–2005	0	3	3	31	64	4.6 (0.70)	36
Stoltenberg II 2005–2013	0	4	7	46	43	4.3 (0.77)	100
Solberg 2013–2020	0	0	7	23	71	4.6 (0.61)	75
Cabinet committees							
Bondevik II 2001–2005	3	6	11	67	14	3.8 (0.85)	36
Stoltenberg II 2005–2013	3	6	17	55	19	3.8 (0.92)	99
Solberg 2013–2020	11	17	35	33	4	3.0 (1.06)	72
Weekly informal cabinet lunch							
Bondevik II 2001–2005	0	3	11	31	56	4.4 (0.80)	36
Stoltenberg II 2005–2013	2	9	24	46	19	3.7 (0.95)	97
Solberg 2013–2020	1	1	15	51	32	4.1 (0.80)	73
Cabinet subcommittee							
Bondevik II 2001–2005	0	6	3	14	78	4.6 (0.80)	36
Stoltenberg II 2005–2013	0	0	3	10	87	4.8 (0.45)	98
Solberg 2013–2020	21	13	24	32	11	3.0 (1.32)	72

Question: Thinking of issues that were solved at the cabinet level, how important were the following areas to reaching an agreement? Five-point scale (not important at all, less important, neither/nor, quite important or very important)

Some issues [in the Stoltenberg cabinet] lived and lived and lived in the government apparatus before they were decided. This [Solberg] cabinet seems much better at making decisions. Both because the one at the top makes these decisions, and also because the processes in advance are better, and clarifications are made before issues come to cabinet level. (N9)

It's about what form of work the government itself chooses to operate with. It's simply how the prime minister wants to lead the work. Some prime ministers like to conclude quickly, while others want to spend some time on issues if there are strong objections. If so, there are new rounds to find a form of consensus, and it's very easy to transfer issues to a group of state secretaries. But, if you're a bit determined, you make a decision then and there, based on the information you have. It's about the personal leadership style of the prime minister. It is about how they chair the cabinet meetings and the PM's way of acting. (N10)

DEVELOPMENTS IN THE NORWEGIAN CORE EXECUTIVE

In the following section, we elaborate on how long-term developments in the media have cemented the baronial courts, where cabinet ministers are surrounded by ministerial advisers and communication professionals. Further on, we show how the inclusion of populists in the government had little impact on the Norwegian core executive because of the Progress Party's behaviour and strategy of Prime Minister Solberg.

Mediatisation and the Cementation of Baronial Courts

The Norwegian media system has traditionally been described as a democratic corporatist model (Hallin & Mancini, 2004), with a strong public service broadcaster and generous press subsidies. Over time, however, the system has moved towards the commercial, liberal model, with an increasing prominence of commercial media (Nord, 2008; Ohlsson, 2015). The emergence of commercial media's generic news formats, higher tempo and rolling news deadlines have affected some parts of the core executive.

As has been the case in Sweden (see Chap. 9), the growth of ministerial advisers can partly be attributed to developments in the media. Political advisers started as little more than personal assistants, and the state secretary position was introduced to ease the burden of ministers. Over the past few years, however, the media has affected the actual work and roles of these actors. It is now common to give one of the political appointees designated media tasks, making this person the 'media adviser', responsible for coordinating with the ministerial communication staff, preparing the minister's speeches and media appearances and advising the minister on the handling of urgent media issues (Askim et al., 2017). That development is captured in the following observation:

If you look at how political advisers have been recruited in many ministries in recent years, they now often come from the communications community. Often, they have been communication advisers in party groups in parliament or in the party organisation. There has been a transition from the traditional political adviser—the old bag carrier—to the new political advisers who see it as their main area of activity to work with communication, to make the minister look good. (N13)

Developments in the media can also clearly be related to the emergence of nonpartisan communication experts (as mentioned above). The interviewees saw the growth of communication units as a response to a more communication-oriented society with several PR agencies (N14), as well as developments in the media sector itself:

The most important reason why the communication unit [in the department] has grown is what has happened out there. Before, you had party newspapers that had a deadline once a day. Now you have the internet and media acting at a completely different pace. The politicians need help to deal with the pressure; they need help to systematise it. (N11)

As commercialisation and increased production pressures have increasingly centred attention on ministers (Figenschou et al., 2017), Norwegian communication departments have been streamlined to serve the needs of their minister. Communication professionals do not mainly produce information material directed towards citizens—rather, their major task is to convey in the best possible way the decisions that the ministry makes and communicate the policy being pursued (N12, N13). Thus:

Communication, politics and professional expertise form a sacred triangle. If all three do not work together, they will not succeed. Our job is to make the minister succeed rather than shine. As head of communications, you work very closely with the minister; we are travelling with them all the time. You need to get inside their heads, to be able to understand them, and to avert, explain and formulate [messages] in a language that is theirs. (N16)

First and foremost, communication professionals work to promote the policy and present *their* minister in the best possible light (N15):

It is clear that they should communicate the government's policy, not [that of] individuals. But we are most concerned with our own minister. No doubt about that. It's what we do in this ministry that we want to promote. (N12)

We work for our own minister; we really do. Maybe a little competition can sometimes be healthy too. I have never heard anyone complain about it. But we try to think a little holistically, we work for the government, so not everyone's fight is against everyone. (N15)

Together with the ministerial advisers and permanent secretaries, the communication professionals make up the baronial courts, which are increasingly focused on helping their ministers succeed. These developments have arguably underlined the sectorisation of the Norwegian system. At the same time, there have been few clear and permanent efforts from the centre to counter these tendencies. Norway has not witnessed the same process of the centralisation of government communication (Bjerkaas, 2021)—where the importance of entities like the PMO has increased and cabinet ministers have been marginalised—as has occurred in countries such as Canada (Marland et al., 2017; Thomas, 2013), Sweden (see Chap. 9) and Finland (Johansson & Raunio, 2020). The PMO chairs the biweekly meetings of the heads of communication. Here, media issues concerning several ministers can be coordinated (e.g. those concerning communication of the cabinet's budget proposals), but in the main these meetings are used for exchanging information and sharing experiences (N11, N16). Overall, the Norwegian PMO is more 'kept in the loop' than 'in control of events'; the PMO is notified immediately if difficult cases arise for the ministers but—contra the situation in Sweden—is not actively involved in approving media initiatives (N10).

The Inclusion of Populists in Government: Behaving Normally and the Strategy of PM Solberg

As mentioned in the introduction to this chapter, Norway also offers an excellent case for studying how the inclusion of a populist party in a cabinet can affect the core executive.

The Progress Party (Fremskrittspartiet) was first represented in parliament in 1973, building its electoral success on tax cuts and anti-immigration policies. Most scholars consider it a right-wing populist party (Bjerkem, 2016; Jungar & Jupskås, 2014), distinguishing it from far-right populist parties (Mudde, 2007; Rooduijn et al., 2019). Over time, the party has developed a broad political profile and built a professional party organisation. Following the 2013 elections in Norway, week-long negotiations between the party leaders of the Conservatives, the Progress Party, the Liberals and the Christian People's Party failed to reach an agreement because of major political differences, and only the Conservatives and Progress Party chose to form a cabinet (Aardal & Bergh, 2018; Allern & Karlsen, 2014). After six years, in January 2020, the party chose to leave the Solberg cabinet.

Comparisons of ministerial advisers from the Progress Party and those from other parties reveal that the opinions, behaviours and experiences of politicians from populist parties generally resemble those of the politicians from non-populist parties (Askim et al., 2021). While populist ministerial advisers are somewhat more concerned than other ministerial advisers about how their political party is portrayed in the media, Askim et al. (2021, p. 22) conclude that 'normality is a more accurate description than exceptionalism to describe what occurred when a populist party entered government for the first time'. Although new to governing at the national level, the Progress Party has almost 50 years of continuous parliamentary representation, substantial experience from governing at the subnational level and a party organisation moulded on the mass-party model, something that has eased their inclusion into government and limited the changes in the Norwegian core executive.

Populist parties in government are said to prefer a 'one foot in, one foot out' strategy; they influence policy on their core issues while maintaining their 'outsider identity' with 'attention-grabbing statements' and 'spectacular actions' (Albertazzi & McDonnell, 2010, pp. 1319–1329). This is a version of a broader phenomenon, with junior coalition partners of different ideological stripes handling the challenge of incumbency. In Norway, Prime Minister Solberg accepted that the Progress Party needed to keep their outsider identity. Although painful compromises were made in the coalition cabinet, the Progress Party was allowed to voice their different opinions in parliament. Although there have also been open disagreements in former coalitions, the extent of this in the Solberg cabinet was noticeable. In the newspapers, the strategy was called Solberg parliamentarism, a 'quiet acceptance' or 'conscious resignation' over the double communication of the Populist Party, where cabinet compromises were left undefended and the primary points of view were voiced in public (Stanghelle, 2017).

Conclusion

This chapter has reviewed how the Norwegian core executive is set up and has changed over time, with particular emphasis on developments since 2000. The picture we have painted is one wherein Norway's core executive consists of a strong cabinet, an inner court of party leaders and several baronial courts of cabinet ministers surrounded by ministerial advisers and communication specialists. Institutional features such as a hands-on PMO and strict routines for the use of cabinet notes do structure decision-making processes and cross-departmental coordination. Still, a low level of formal regulation allows room for informal processes where numerous actors are involved in a sequential and hierarchical political and policy coordination process. In Norway, central coordination should not just be seen as a 'philosopher's stone', 'ever sought, but always just beyond reach because it assumes both agreement on goals and a central co-ordinator' (Rhodes, 2007, p. 1258). Rather, the system forces some degree of coordination, and when it is not possible at the administrative and lower political levels, issues are elevated to the highest level, where the cabinet's working mode is such that it is possible to have real discussions in cabinet meetings and eventually to reach agreements. The cabinet collegium is a real and not just a ritual decision-making organ, and cabinet meetings remain important. However, an inner cabinet—an inner court—has emerged in some Norwegian coalitions. In Westminster countries, the power of the court has been said to ebb and flow with that of the prime minister (Rhodes & Tiernan, 2016, p. 340). In coalitions, by way of contrast, the inner court consists not only of the prime minister and their staffers, but also of the party leaders and political strategists of coalition partners.

The ministerial rule means that each minister in Norway is politically responsible for the department and subordinate agencies, and this principle has been identified as the reason for strong sectors, line ministries and ministers in the Norwegian system. In core executive parlance, this type of ministerial government has been labelled one of baronial courts, where ministers and their political advisers preside over their policy territories (Bevir & Rhodes, 2006; Shaw & Eichbaum, 2020). In the Norwegian case, the permanent secretaries and nonpartisan heads of communication should also probably be included in the baronial courts. The Norwegian baronial court is not isolated from the civil service. There is no active bureaucratic self-censorship (Shaw & Eichbaum, 2020, p. 14), and departmental advice is not rendered only in 'accord with the ministerial adviser's own views/perspectives' (Shaw & Eichbaum, 2020, p. 9). Rather, civil servants' maxim and informal mandate is to be the devil's advocate internally and defenders externally (N16). Over time, the growth of commercial media has spurred the professionalisation of communication departments in Norwegian departments. Together with state secretaries and political advisers, the communication experts help defend the minister and maintain their visibility in the media, something that can underline the sectorised departmental system and increase the need for actors and arenas to 'pull together'.

Over time, the Norwegian PMO has been strengthened and has become a key player in executive politics. Compared with developments seen in countries like Finland, Sweden, Canada and the UK, however, centralisation is limited and there is no linear development in Norway towards a stronger centre. In the UK, '[t]he increase in size [of the core executive] illustrates the centre's sense of its own weakness. It is a power grab, a reaction to felt weakness and shortcomings, a response to baronial power, and a frustration with the inability to pull effective levers' (Rhodes, 2007, p. 1254). In the Norwegian case, it is not a permanent power grab but rather a continuous fight to drag inwards and fight the centrifugal forces of baronial ministers.

According to our interviews, the leadership style of prime ministers can help explain the balance between cabinet collegium and the use of inner cabinets consisting of party leaders. The prime minister's craft can also be key in keeping the coalition together and remaining in power by allowing populist parties to voice their scepticism over coalition compromises. Overall, this suggests that both long-term and short-term changes can affect how the core executive is set up and functions.

References

Aardal, B., & Bergh, J. (2018). The 2017 Norwegian Election. *West European Politics, 41*(5), 1208–1216.

Albertazzi D. & McDonnell D (2010). The Lega Nord Back in Government. West European Politics 33(6), 1318–1340.

Allern, E. H., & Karlsen, R. (2014). A Turn to the Right: The Norwegian Parliamentary Election of September 2013. *West European Politics, 37*(3), 653–663.

Askim, J., Karlsen, R., & Kolltveit, K. (2017). Political Appointees in Executive Government: Exploring and Explaining Roles Using a Large-N Survey in Norway. *Public Administration, 95*(2), 342–358.

Askim, J., Karlsen, R., & Kolltveit, K. (2018). The spy who loved me? Cross-partisans in the core executive. *Public Administration, 96*(2), 243–258.
Askim, J., Karlsen, R., & Kolltveit, K. (2021). Populists in Government: Normal or Exceptional? *Government and Opposition.* https://doi.org/10.1017/gov.2021.30
Bevir, M., & Rhodes, R. A. W. (2006). Prime Ministers, Presidentialism and Westminster Smokescreens. *Political Studies, 54*(4), 671–690.
Bjerkaas, S. (2021). Statsministerens kontor: Begrenset, sterk eller suveren? En studie av SMKs rolle i regjeringens strategiske kommunikasjonsarbeid [Prime Minister's Office: Limited, Strong or Sovereign? A Study of the PMO's Role in the Government's Strategic Communication]. Unpublished Master's thesis, University of Oslo, Oslo.
Bloch, K. (1963). *Kongens råd. Regjeringsarbeidet i Norge.* Universitetsforlaget.
Bjerkem J. (2016). The Norwegian Progress Party: An Established Populist Party. *European View* 15(2), 233–243.
Christensen, T. (2005). The Norwegian State Transformed? *Western European Politics, 28*(4), 721–739.
Christensen, T., & Lægreid, P. (2002). *Reformer og lederskap. Omstilling i den utøvende makt.* Universitetsforlaget.
Difi. (2019). *På toppen av styringssystemet. Om samordning i de skandinaviske regjeringsapparatene* [Coordination in Scandinavian Governments]. Difi report 2019: 6. Norwegian Agency for Public Management and e-Government.
Eriksen, S. (1988). Norway: Ministerial Autonomy and Collective Responsibility. In J. Blondel & F. Müller-Rommel (Eds.), *Cabinets in Western Europe* (pp. 183–196). Macmillan.
Eriksen, S. (2003). *I kongens navn [In the Name of the King].* Statskonsult.
Figenschou, T. U., Karlsen, R., Kolltveit, K., & Thorbjørnsrud, K. (2017). Serving the Media Ministers: A Mixed Methods Study on the Personalization of Ministerial Communication. *The International Journal of Press/Politics, 22*(4), 411–430.
Grønlie, T., & Flo, Y. (2009). *Sentraladministrasjonens historie etter 1945. Den nye staten? Tiden etter 1980* [The History of the State Administration Since 1945. The New State? The Period After 1980]. : Fagbokforlaget.
Hallin, D. C., & Mancini, P. (2004). *Comparing Media Systems: Three Models of Media and Politics.* Cambridge University Press.
Holmøyvik, E. (2021). § 12. In O. Mestad & D. Michalsen (Eds.), *Grunnloven. Historisk grunnlovskommentar* [The Constitution. Historical Commentary]. Oslo: Universitetsforlaget.
Johansson, K. M., & Raunio, T. (2020). Centralizing Government Communication? Evidence from Finland and Sweden. *Politics and Policy.* https://doi.org/10.1111/polp.12370

Jungar A. & Jupskås A. (2014). Populist Radical Right Parties in the Nordic Region: A New and Distinct Party Family? Scandinavian Political Studies 37(3), 215–238.

Kolltveit, K. (2013). *Cabinet Decision-Making and Concentration of Power. A Study of the Norwegian Executive Centre* [Doctoral dissertation, Institutt for statsvitenskap].

Marland, A., Lewis, J. P., & Flanagan, T. (2017). Governance in the Age of Digital Media and Branding. *Governance, 30*(1), 125–141.

Mudde, C. (2007). *Populist Radical Right Parties in Europe*. Cambridge University Press.

Narud, H. M., & Strøm, K. (2003). Norway: A Fragile Coalitional Order. In W. C. Müller & K. Strøm (Eds.), *Coalition Governments in Western Europe* (2nd ed., pp. 158–191). Oxford University Press.

Narud, H. M., & Strøm, K. (2011). From Hønsvaldian Parliamentarism Back to Madisonian Roots. In T. Bergman & K. Strøm (Eds.), *The Madisonian Turn. Political Parties and Parliamentary Democracy in Nordic Europe* (pp. 200–250). The University of Michigan Press.

Nord, L. (2008). Comparing Nordic Media Systems: North between West and East. *Central European Journal of Communication, 1*, 95–110.

O'Malley, E. (2007). The Power of Prime Ministers: Results of an Expert Survey. *International Political Science Review, 28*(1), 7–27.

Ohlsson, J. (2015). *The Nordic Media Market*. Nordic Information Centre for Media and Communication Research (NORDICOM).

Olsen, J. P. (1983). *Organized Democracy: Political Institutions in a Welfare State—The Case of Norway*. Universitetsforlaget.

Prime Minister's Office. (1969). *Instruks for regjeringen* [Cabinet Instruction]. : Prime Minister's Office.

Prime Minister's Office. (2010). *Om r-konferanser. Forberedelse av saker til Regjeringskonferanse* [On Cabinet Meetings]. : Prime Minister's Office.

Rhodes, R. A. (2007). Understanding governance: Ten years on. Organization studies, 28(8), 1243–1264.

Rhodes, R. A. W., & Tiernan, A. (2016). Court Politics in a Federal Polity. *Australian Journal of Political Science, 51*(2), 338–354.

Rooduijn, M., Van Kessel, S., Froio, C., Pirro, A., De Lange, S., Halikiopoulou, D., Lewis, P., Mudde, C., & Taggart, P. (2019). *The PopuList: An Overview of Populist, Far Right, Far Left and Eurosceptic Parties in Europe*. www.popu-list.org

Shaw, R., & Eichbaum, C. (2020). Bubbling Up or Cascading Down? Public Servants, Political Advisers and Politicization. *Public Administration, 98*(4), 840–855.

Skjeie, H. (2001). Inne i 'beslutningsmaskinen'. [Inside the 'decision-making machine']. In: B.S. Tranøy & Ø. Østerud (eds.) Den fragmenterte staten. [The Fragmented State]. Oslo, Norway: Gyldendal.

Stanghelle, H. (2017). Den solbergske parlamentarisme [The Solberg Parlimentarism]. *Aftenposten*, 26, mai.
Stavenes, T., & Strøm, K. (2021). Norway: Towards a More Permissive Coalitional Order. In T. Bergman, H. Bäck, & J. Hellström (Eds.), *Coalition Governance in Western Europe* (pp. 482–516). Oxford University Press.
Strøm, K. (1994). The Political Role of Norwegian Cabinet Ministers. In M. Laver & K. Shepsle (Eds.), *Cabinet Ministers and Parliamentary Government* (pp. 35–55). Cambridge University Press.
Strøm, K., Müller, W. C., & Smith, D. M. (2010). Parliamentary Control of Coalition Governments. *Annual Review of Political Science*, 13, 517–535.
Thies, M. F. (2001). Keeping Tabs on Partners: The Logic of Delegation in Coalition Governments. *American Journal of Political Science*, 45(3), 580–598.
Thomas, P. (2013). Communications and Prime Ministerial Power. In J. Bickerton & B. G. Peters (Eds.), *Governing: Essays in Honour of Donald J. Savoie*. McGill-Queen's University Press.
Wahl, T., & Hem, P. E. (2018). *Mistillitsforslag, kabinettspørsmål og kritikkforslag—en oversikt*. Perspektiv 01/18. : The Norwegian Parliament.

PART V

Conclusion

CHAPTER 12

Continuity and Change: Explaining Developments and Looking to the Future

Kristoffer Kolltveit and Richard Shaw

INTRODUCTION

Thirty years ago Rhodes and Dunleavy sought to change the terms of a debate regarding the nature of executive government in the UK that had become a little arid. In shifting the focus of analysis away from the formal institutions of the prime minister and cabinet they placed functional rather than locational considerations at the heart of the study of executive power. Since then the concept has travelled beyond the UK to other Westminster countries and to places where multi-party governments are the norm. To our knowledge, however, the extent to which these empirical excursions have affected the concept as an analytical tool has not been systematically

K. Kolltveit (✉)
Department of Political Science, University of Oslo, Oslo, Norway
e-mail: kristoffer.kolltveit@stv.uio.no

R. Shaw (✉)
School of People, Environment and Planning, Massey University, Palmerston North, New Zealand
e-mail: R.H.Shaw@massey.ac.nz

© The Author(s), under exclusive license to Springer Nature Switzerland AG 2022
K. Kolltveit, R. Shaw (eds.), *Core Executives in a Comparative Perspective*, Understanding Governance,
https://doi.org/10.1007/978-3-030-94503-9_12

assessed. It is this lacuna we have sought to fill in the preceding chapters, and to which we now turn.

Specifically, in this concluding chapter we will draw on the various country cases and the wider literature to reflect on the matters captured in the explanatory template that has guided our contributing authors. We begin by reviewing similarities and differences in the over-arching institutional architecture of and the modes of coordination used within the various core executives canvassed in the preceding pages. Then we discuss the different ways in which societal changes have shaped the configuration and operation of these executives. Finally, we look at the way ahead, assessing the ongoing utility of the core concept and considering possible trajectories for core executive studies over the next 30 years.

Comparing Cores

In this section, we compare and contrast the configuration of the various core executives sketched in the country cases, and review the various modes of coordination deployed therein.

Institutionalising the Core: Convergence and Divergence

Myriad actors inhabit the institutional arrangements in the core of the government machineries studied here: prime ministers, ministers, the cabinet collegium, various cabinet committees, ministerial advisers and top civil servants. In short, the main institutional setup is found across all of the case studies, such that it seems reasonable to speak of an over-arching institutional core executive architecture, perhaps reflective of a sort of institutional isomorphism (DiMaggio & Powell, 1983) according to which core executive arrangements across jurisdictions seem to converge.

However, it would be unwise to assume that any such convergence is indicative of a linear development. Neither are things always as they appear—rather, we stress the importance of attending to the empirical evidence of movement within and amongst the structures and interactions that lie just beneath the formal arrangements.

For one thing, institutional features that may be common across contexts are often deployed differently. In Denmark, for instance, two cabinet committees are crucial to the business of government while ministerial advisers are rather less important than they are elsewhere. On the other hand, in Norway formal cabinet committees have limited importance (and at times this has also been so in Ireland), while informal inner cabinets, and especially the prime minister-finance minister nexus, ensure that decisions are reached. In the Netherlands, by dint of craft, guile and the astute leverage of both personal and formal resources, the prime minister has emerged as the dominant player on the park; elsewhere (Germany, say), the agency of the political chief executive is more routinely constrained. Swedish ministerial advisers focus in the main on communicating the government's narrative, but their counterparts in New Zealand spend much of their time clarifying and coordinating the policy contributions of governing (and parliamentary support) parties.

Divergence extends beyond these sorts of functional differences. There has been one especially significant development in the structural organisation of (most) core executives in recent decades which any contemporary account must accommodate. In each of the countries we have canvassed (and, we imagine, a good many more besides), ministerial advisers are much more prominent now than they were 30 years ago. The means of institutionalising the roles and contributions of this new actor vary across cases (see Shaw & Eichbaum, 2018): the point, however, is that more or less everyone *is* institutionalising the function. The emerging Danish practice of having advisers sitting in cabinet committees is a striking example; so, too, is the example of Sweden, in which advisers have become integral to the central government's investment in coordination. Indeed, this 'third element' (Wicks, 2003) is now so ubiquitous across mature democracies that the term 'executive triangle' has more or less become a synonym for the 'core executive'. As Craft (2015, p. 64) has noted, in this respect, at least, it is time to update the core executive 'gospel' and to broaden the initial cast of core executive characters.

Coordination and Conflict Resolution: Modes, Mechanisms and Instruments

Rhodes' 1995 definition of the core executive identified the coordination of central government policies as the primary function of government. As we elaborated in Chap. 1, coordination—understood as the achievement of coherent policies and the resolution of conflicts—can be achieved through various modes, mechanisms and instruments. On this count, the country chapters in this volume have shown a substantial degree of variation.

Concerning degree, Scharpf's (1994) definition of negative coordination seems the best fit in some countries. In Germany, for instance, the policy output of ministerial departments is said to represent the lowest-common denominator. In Norway, too, cabinet policy is the sum of individual ministries' policies, adapted to different views and domains through information exchange and consultation. It is more than just negative, but not fully positive coordination.

As to type, both formal and informal coordination takes place. While rules and stipulations provide an indication of how policies should be developed, there is substantial room in most countries for informal discussions and de facto decision-making outside of formal arenas. In Germany, the formal requirements according to which the federal government secures coordination have remained constant over recent decades, allowing some actors to take an informal lead in proceedings. Similarly, in Norway the cabinet regulations provide few concrete provisions specifying how ministries should consult each other, opening up room for informal contacts both at administrative and at political level. Even where there are more explicit institutional prescriptions—as, perhaps, in the Westminster cases—informality oils the machinery of decision-making.

Furthermore, and per Rhodes' standard functional conception, both administrative and political actors are involved in coordinating government policies in the core. In Germany, political disagreements and policy incompatibilities should be resolved at the lowest level of hierarchy possible; in Norway, too, the process is sequential such that first administrative and then political actors are involved. In most cases only the most difficult issues tend to end up at the highest level, where the cabinet can act as a tiebreaker in the case of deadlock. While meetings of the Dutch, Danish and Swedish cabinets may largely have evolved into settings in which ritual approval is given to decisions taken (informally) elsewhere, in Norway the cabinet remains a de facto decision-making organ. Broadly speaking—and individual leaders' proclivities aside—this also remains the case in Ireland, New Zealand and (to a lesser extent) the UK. Quite apart from anything else, what these competing empirical observations demonstrate is the folly of assuming that the institution which, according to the political organisational chart, *should* be the one in which definitive decision are taken (the cabinet) *is*, in practice, where those determinations are made (rather than ratified). Rhodes and Dunleavy are likely to say that this is entirely the point they were trying to make.

As to the matter of who acts as the final arbiter of conflict between different parts of the government machine, the prime minister seems to play the determinative role in all of the countries under study. However—and this also reflects the core executive admonition that formal appearances do not always provide the best answers—there are concentric circles of core actors revolving around different prime ministers. In both the Netherlands and Norway, for instance, smaller forums consisting of the prime minister and coalition party leaders have been especially important when the need to consolidate fragilities and keep the coalition together has arisen. This sort of relational and institutional plasticity is also a feature of most of the other accounts here: it is invoked most graphically, perhaps, in Rhodes' chapter on Cameron's court, in which the prime minister's role in 'the legion of inter-ministerial and inter-departmental disputes varied from initiator to referee to judge'. Each of these instances, one presumes, was played out across a slew of forums and demanded engagement with an ever-changing slate of participants. For prime ministers, it must sometimes feel interminable.

Resources in the Core Executive

Actors in the core executive exchange resources such as agenda-setting power, technical expertise, political know-how and decision-making authority. Some of these resources are formal and their trade is legitimised through official positions and arrangements; others are informal, secured and exchanged via actors' success at exploiting systemic openings and opportunities. No less than other institutional actors, then, those in the core executive need to keep an eye open for the main chance.

The balance of formal and informal resources varies across countries, of course, as does the mix as between personal endowments (such as the attributes Cole associates with a successful private secretary in Chap. 6) and institutional assets (as with Hundehege and Hustedt's discussion of the affordances of the German chancellor in Chap. 7, or the growing recourse to political advisers that is noted in several chapters). Certain chapters reveal an interplay between the two, or perhaps a compensation effect. For instance, what emerges from the Dutch case is, at first glance, a little counter-intuitive: a prime minister generally recognised as institutionally weak nonetheless dominates the executive landscape. The compensation for a lack of formal authority through the exercise of informal power seems to vindicate Rhodes' and others' scepticism of the heuristic merits of focusing on official arrangements. The importance of informality in particular, it seems to us, has implications for future research (more on which below), which amongst other things should pay greater attention to the intersection of resources (formal/informal) and the institutional attributes of leaders (strong/weak). This not only holds for the inner courts of prime ministers, but should probably also be kept in mind when studying the plethora of sub-courts (including ministerial offices and those formed in departments) that appear in the earlier chapters.

The Impact of a Changing World

As noted above, virtually all of the contributing authors detect signs of a realignment of core executive structures and interactions in recent times; a reconfiguration of intra-executive relationships in response to current contexts. In this section, therefore, we step back from the case-specific detail and reflect on the impact of a number of broad, macro-level changes on the composition, functioning and resourcing of the contemporary core executive.

The Many Faces of Government

The concept of the core executive first emerged in the UK, a constitutional setting with a long history of single-party administrations. Little surprise, then, that it has subsequently been most enthusiastically embraced by those seeking to explain governing conditions in broadly similar constitutional contexts. However, Russell and Serban's (2020) objections to the continued use of 'Westminster' as an explanatory shorthand notwithstanding (and see Flinders et al. (2021) for a rejoinder to these), it appears to us that the key independent variable for comparative purposes is not administrative tradition but the structural properties of governments.

Increasingly, including in several chapters in this book, Rhodes' and Dunleavy's concept is being put to work in jurisdictions with little or no (recent) history of single-party government. Across Europe, in particular, there is a long tradition of forming coalition administrations in which parties can constitute 'centrifugal forces' (Andeweg 1988), stretching the core executive and challenging its capacities to both coordinate policy and resolve conflict. But it is worth noting, too, that there is now also a good deal of experience of coalitions amongst our three Westminster cases; in Ireland and New Zealand multi-party governments have been the norm for the better part of three or four decades (and as Rhodes illustrates in Chap. 4, the UK also has its own recent, colourful experience).

The test, then—especially if it is to serve comparative purposes—is to see how the core concept measures up in these more complex governing circumstances. On the evidence marshalled in previous chapters, it retains its heuristic value—subject to one or two modifications. The first thing to be said is that applying the core executive framework in a coalition setting implies a broadening of the initial membership of the core. Most obviously, coalition party leaders are included in inner circles, as seen in Ireland, the Netherlands and Norway. Moreover, under conditions of minority government there is a case to be made that the leaders of parliamentary support parties should also be considered part of the core executive: sometimes, as on occasion has been the case in New Zealand, those actors do not routinely sit in the cabinet, but their support is nonetheless central to a government's capacity to organise and legislate its policy agenda. Beyond the political executive, coalitions also have consequences for the wider membership of the core. In Sweden, notably (as in Ireland), the advent of multi-party governments has increased the number of ministerial advisers (Dahlström et al., 2011; Shaw & Eichbaum, 2014), while in Norway it has necessitated the creation of a particular cross-partisan role for state secretaries.

Although this is not something we asked our contributing authors to address, it is also possible that in multi-party governments—which are routinely formed in each of the case studies with the exception of the UK—there exists the potential for intra-coalition conflict along party lines to be reproduced in contests between line departments and agencies (Trangbæk, 2021). The institutional architecture erected in most civil service contexts over the last 40 years or so is expressly designed to enhance appointed officials' responsiveness to elected officials' policy preferences. This reassertion of the 'primacy of democracy over bureaucracy' (Aucoin, 1990) means that contests within cabinets can be transmitted out into the administrative executive—the institutionalisation of responsiveness serving as the structural vector. To the extent that this occurs, it is not difficult to envisage the challenges it might pose for cross-government coordination, and the tensions it could create within and between departments.

There is a sense, then, that in countries where single-party government is not the norm the essential nature of the core executive is both more structurally elaborate and distributed than it tends otherwise to be. The recent innovation of the 'rotating Taoiseach' in Ireland is a specific instance of the former, while the institutional thickening of the core (via the creation of new roles, offices and appointments) to accommodate multiple governing parties—a feature of several of our cases—speaks to the second. A little conceptual elaboration of the original concept is required to capture this endogenous empirical variegation. In particular (and we return to this point in greater detail below), the successful application of the core executive concept beyond single-party administrations rests on its capacity to account for the interlocking courts, or circles of influence, which are a structural property of coalition governments (and which, of course, can also emerge in single-party governments).

Summitry and Political Leadership

As underlined by Johansson and Tallberg (2010, p. 213), the domestic delegation of political authority comes in two forms: internal authority inheres in the right of the chief executive to coordinate domestic interests, while external authority consists in the right of state leaders to represent the state in international negotiations. Apropos, part of the explanation for the growing transfer of resources to political chief executives and their offices has been the wish to avoid situations in which 'international summitry, overseas visits and visitors' consume too much of a prime minister's time, restricting his or her capacity to attend to other cabinet issues' (Dunleavy & Rhodes, 1990, p. 8).

As described in some of the country chapters in this volume—including in the Dutch, German and Irish cases—contemporary practices of summitry have ramifications for the asymmetric distribution of power and resources within the core, particularly in the context of those set-piece international events such as the European Council in which a prime minister is the sole national actor in attendance (per Chaps. 5 and 8). In such cases, the political chief executive has to carry the burden of mastering knowledge across a wide range of issues (albeit with the assistance of bureaucratic sherpas): by virtue of this, however, the prime minister also possesses considerable advantages (knowledge, connections, leverage, profile and exposure) over other ministers in the national political court. Put another way, the evidence from the chapters on Denmark, Netherlands, Ireland and Sweden add considerable grist to the prime ministerial predominance thesis.

The reports from those country cases complement Johansson and Tallberg's (2010, p. 213) finding that declaratory summits addressing a narrow set of issues only give rise to weak domestic change, whereas summits involving authoritative decision-making across a broad range of policy issues are more likely to generate power shifts in favour of chief executives (including in the form of beefed-up departmental resources, per the Irish experience). Several contributors to Poguntke and Webb's (2005) comparative analysis of presidentialisation also find that internationalisation has a discernible impact on the structure and resourcing of executive decision-making, particularly in EU contexts (although there is also support for this argument from some non-EU cases).

That said, the absence of a uniform trend in the country chapters in this volume is worth noting. In Germany, for instance, the strong departmental principle means that Europeanisation has not privileged the chancellery over other departments, suggesting there are institutional barriers to prime ministerial empowerment in some contexts. Put that point alongside the analyses in Chaps. 7 and 8 of the significance of individual leaders' skill and craft and it is clear both that (a) the context-specific intersection of personal and institutional variables needs to be accounted for, and (b) the exogenous and endogenous are always speaking to each other.

Mediatisation and the Core

Changes in media technology and in the media industry over the last two decades or so have transformed modern societies—and the nature of politics therein. The emergence of online news outlets and social media, in particular, have created 24/7, instantaneous news cycles which place both politicians and the wider government apparatus under relentless pressure.

That said, prime ministers, in particular, can benefit from the preference of media outlets to talk directly with or to hear from the political chief executive. It has long been a trend to focus attention on presidents, prime ministers and state leaders, and there are both push and pull forces at play in this mediatisation and personalisation (or intimisation) of political leadership (Bennett, 2012; Bracciale & Martella, 2017). Yet while intensified competition and commercialisation create production pressures and forms of reporting that focus on the personal and emotional aspects of 'news', contemporary politicians themselves have learned to master the arts of communication and exploit the opportunities thereby given. Mastery of social media, especially (more on which shortly), has become a prerequisite for leadership in a way it certainly was not 30 years ago.

In part this speaks to defensive, tactical imperatives: these days, political leaders and their entourages simply cannot afford not to engage with social media in the context of managing political narratives and guarding against (or responding to) the eruption of crises. But seen through a core executive lens, the new media modalities also afford political executives considerable scope for consolidating informal power and (prime ministerial) predominance. A Mark Rutte (Chap. 8) or Mette Frederiksen (Chap. 10), for instance, can exploit the 'dialogic nature' (McGuire et al. 2020, p. 371) of social media—reaching over the top of the institutions that have traditionally mediated contact between leaders and led, creating a sense of a shared experience with citizens and capturing the political, reputational and affective benefits of doing so. In short, an adept can use this new form of bully pulpit to boost their stocks of personal political capital and underpin their predominance relative to other core executive actors. What is a ubiquitous exogenous development is having endogenous institutional consequences.

In this regard it is worth noting that in several of the case studies the harnessing of informal political resources has been mirrored by a process of formal institutional 'thickening'. Put differently, the contemporary media environment has justified (or at least goes a long way to explaining) claims for additional resourcing within the core executive, the consolidation of resources within ministerial offices and departments in part reflecting the need to manage a more demanding mediascape and the various risks—particularly the playing out of blame-games (Hinterleitner, 2020; Hood, 2011)—attendant upon that. In Norway, for instance, an investment in and centralisation of government communication resources has taken place—including via the appointment of ministerial advisers and media staff—such that the tactical and strategic importance of entities like the PMO has increased (Johansson & Raunio, 2020). A similar accretion of resources at the centre has played out else, including in Denmark and Ireland.

Whatever the fundamental drivers (which extend well beyond the mastery of new media technologies), institutional thickening has taken other forms, too. Most chapters tell a story of political leaders seeking constant recourse to institutional levers (cabinet committees, the power of appointment, the creation of new agencies and so forth) to bolster their power and position relative to other core executive actors. Rhodes' vivid description of the 'rubber levers' (Rhodes, 2007, p. 1255) that political executives try in vain to tweak probably retains currency—but that does not appear to have stopped those leaders trying to find new levers that are made of sterner stuff.

On the face of it, this sort of institutional consolidation within (prime) ministerial offices and departments is consistent with Dahlström et al.'s (2011) thesis regarding the strengthening of the political centre. More particularly, where the new media platforms comprise an important part of a prime minister's personal resources, their effects may be magnified by virtue of the institutional endowments a prime minister possesses (and which are likely to mean that a post, tweet or like from a prime minister will attract more attention than activity amongst other core executive actors).

A cautionary note applies, however, because while the new technologies enable political chief executives to centralise influence, it is in their nature that they also generate contests between core executive actors. After all, prime ministers are not the only ones on Twitter—others in the various baronial courts are similarly active, such that the new media have emerged as critical weapons in the contest for courtly dominance. Norway is unlikely to be the only country in which certain ministers, surrounded by retinues of political appointees and communication professionals, have demonstrated rather less concern for the government's policy projects and agenda than for their own visibility. The resolution of this endogenous tension appears to depend on the wider political-administrative culture. A skilled prime minister backed by a solid institutional resource may get to control the narrative; equally, as the German experience (Chap. 7) demonstrates, a rule regime privileging strong departments may contribute to media effects that are centrifugal rather than centripetal.

TAKING STOCK: 30 YEARS ON, WHAT HAVE WE LEARNT?

Three decades after its introduction, it is appropriate to ask how much utility the concept of the core executive retains, what the nature of that utility is and whether or not there might be aspects of contemporary contexts it does not adequately capture.

On the Matter of Relevance and Currency

Regarding the first of those, on the basis of the evidence marshalled here there are ample grounds for reaffirming the fundamental sense-making merits of the term: irrespective of constitutional or administrative context, the marriage of (a) a willingness to eschew simplistic explanations of executive power based on formal appearances with (b) the right sorts of questions regarding who does what and with which resources continues to produce (c) accounts of governing arrangements that are satisfyingly full-bodied.

This is especially so when the functional epistemology of the core executive is used in conjunction with the case study method. In some respects this volume constitutes a positive defence of the descriptive, single-country case study—which, the examples of comparative research designs noted in Chap. 2 notwithstanding, remains the method of choice in core executive studies. Elgie (2011, p. 75), of course, was sceptical of the merits of adding more explanatory cases to the core executive mix. We take the point, but also maintain that the grounds for doing so are compelling, if not necessary. For one thing—and this is especially apposite in the context of the changing times sketched above—the detail contained in Chaps. 4–11 constitutes precisely the kind of rich, granular content required for an understanding of the nature of executive politics in situ. Moreover, these things—actors, instruments and resources—change over time and space, and in the interests of currency the shifting executive sands need to be recorded and revealed.

A further reason why there will—and should—'always be new examples to discuss' (Elgie, 2011, p. 75) is because descriptive narration allows new things to be revealed. In this volume, those recent things are both contextually and temporally specific (the craft of Angela Merkel and Mark Rutte) and more generally applicable (the widespread institutionalisation of ministerial advisers and the consequential effects of social media); both informal (the shifting balance of power as between sundry baronial courts) and structural (the accretion of resources to the centre). Politics is always in the process of becoming, and we counsel against dismissing too quickly the value of articulating the sorts of stories of core executives contained in this book.

Down in the Leadership Weeds

Prime ministerial incumbents feature prominently in some of the country cases (Chaps. 4 and 8 are particular cases in point). While this focus risks feeling a little locationally orthodox (as if it is about to slip into the sort of account of the prime minister and cabinet which the notion of the core executive was supposed to put an end to), recourse to the core executive lens ensures that the intellectual and empirical enquiry heads off in non-orthodox directions.

Amongst other themes, what emerges from these attempts to address the questions Rhodes and Dunleavy first posed are accounts of informal meetings with close confidantes (Chap. 4); the ways which the office of the prime minister accrues political capital simply by virtue of the fact that (at least in Europe) it is the leader who attends European summits, and is thus personally associated with his/her country on a global stage (Chap. 8); and the coalescing together and operation of political courts of various kinds (Chap. 11). (Although we acknowledge that there are more weekdays than weekends, and there are more decisions on the internal than the external stage).

This level of workload necessarily demands a good deal of any prime ministerial incumbent and generates a series of contextually specific roles. Van Dorp and Rhodes are the most explicit about this, identifying the key roles in the Dutch context as diplomat-in-chief, communicator-in-chief, crisis manager-in-chief and boundary spanner-in-chief—other jurisdictions will have their own roles. The point is that it is unlikely that this role typology would have emerged from a standard analysis of the formal resources and responsibilities of the Dutch (or any other) prime minister. For this kind of subtlety, an interrogation informed by a core executive disposition is required—much might otherwise have remained invisible.

Not One Core But Many?

But the country cases also make clear that, their institutional and other advantages notwithstanding, a prime minister is not a president—they need the engagement, support and resources of those around them to succeed. (Conversely, of course, the withholding or withdrawal of such support can produce harder landings, any number of which are recounted in Rhodes' analysis of the Cameron court.) The complex and contingent choreography *between* inner courts (both political and administrative) is a central theme of the Danish, German, Irish and UK cases, while the New Zealand chapter explores the sorts of relationships that can play out *within* one such context. In the end, contra the normative inference inherent in more classical models of cabinet government, the evidence emerging from these case studies is that executive decision-making is a distributed, collective process, much of which takes place at some distance from the cabinet. To draw on the language of the interpretivists: courts, coteries and baronial politics—not all of them connected to much less synonymous with the cabinet—are always in play.

(As a partial aside, the same observation regarding the unpredictable intersection of multiple, overlapping courts probably also applies in the administrative arena. None of our authors explicitly does so (at least, not in this book), but it seems probable that the distribution of bureaucratic power is also patterned, with some departments—including those, as in Germany's ministries of finance, justice and defence, which enjoy fundamental constitutional status—possessing greater resource capacities, and exercising more influence and playing more central coordinating roles, than others.)

There is a conceptual point to be made here, which is that there is much empirical nuance to be gained when one conceptual innovation—the notion of executive courts—is grafted onto a prior one (the concept of the core executive). Rhodes and Dunleavy decoupled function and location, and those possessed of a political ethnographic disposition stepped into the space thus prised open. Amongst other, Rhodes (2017), Rhodes and Salomonsen (2020), Rhodes and Tiernan (2016), Trangbæk (2021) and Van Dorp and 't Hart (2019) promptly saw an intricate, complex world of courtly interplay. Consequently, while reference to a (singular) core executive offers conceptual and empirical advantages over more traditional approaches, the intersection of interpretivism, political ethnography and core executive studies now demands acknowledgement of the existence of a flourishing ecosystem of differently constituted courts. Essentially, these days, core executive scholars are being asked to think on the executive equivalent of biodiversity.

Structure Matters

One of the things that happens when the concept of the core executive is applied under conditions of multi-party government, as it has been throughout this book, is that it quickly becomes impossible to avoid the perennial debate about the salience of structure.

Within core executive studies, this is a matter of some contest (which we accept may seem arcane to some) between proponents of the asymmetric power and differentiated polity approaches. Having reflected at length on the cases in this book, we are inclined to wonder if the degree of distance between the two positions has been over-stated, and suspect that it might flow from a misreading of Rhodes' and Bevir's observation that they found the concept of structure 'unhelpfully vague' (Bevir & Rhodes, 2008, p. 730).

Note that those authors did *not* say that structure does not matter (although that is how their position is often represented), they simply indicated that in the context of core executive studies the concept is under-specified (which is quite different). The problem is that under-specified concepts hinder the pursuit of theoretical clarity and empirical understanding: it is one thing to assert that structure matters but another to observe and precisely communicate how and why this is the case. For Rhodes and other interpretivists, a more compelling means of apprehending the particularities of the core executive lies in attending to interpretations of the practices, rituals and beliefs of those within the various political or departmental courts (per Chaps. 3, 4 and 8). These things are observable in a way that a 'structure' is not.

Moreover, and perhaps this brings us full circle and back to the original bone of contention, executive actors' practices and rituals will, over time, clot together into patterns of interaction which assume the character of institutions—at least per the standard definition of institutions as the constellations of rules and procedures that structure actors' behaviours (Lowndes, 1996). (Bevir and Rhodes themselves define rituals as 'a set of actions … that exhibit a pattern, perhaps even a pattern that remains stable across time' (2010, pp. 75–76), which looks a lot like Lowndes' conception of an institution to us.) In the end, this may be something of a storm in a core executive tea cup: whether called 'practices' or 'institutions', the conduct of actors in different core executive contexts has (temporal) structuring effects on the options and choices available to others.

The country chapters provide various examples of this. In both New Zealand and Norway, for instance, there are indications that institutional variables (not just the internal configuration of cabinet and its committees but also the associated artefacts such as coalition agreements and the compacts establishing confidence and supply) have distributive effects—the things distributed, including status, power, authority, access to departments' advice, expectations of access to the prime minister, slots on the formal policy agenda and so forth.

Equally, there is evidence that the relationship between structure and agency is not unidirectional. For example, while there is a compelling a priori case (one we have already made in this chapter) that the structural properties of multi-party governments of necessity create specific types of coordination challenges, in the Netherlands, at least, it is possible to overstate the influence of this feature on the challenge of coordination. Rather, what really counts—and this also appears to be so in Denmark, at least presently—is the character, tenacity and political craft of the leader.

Structure matters in others way, too, and at different levels. Because it was articulated in the context of a unitary state, there is perhaps a risk that a core executive lens is innately predisposed to analytical outcomes that overstate the role of the centre. Hundehege and Hustedt make this argument in their chapter, pointing out that federal arrangements in Germany have material consequences for the exercise of power. It is possible that this partially explains the relatively low uptake of the concept in studies of non-unitary states (see Chap. 2). However, while Rhodes' 1995 definition refers to organisations and procedures at the level of central government, it does not proscribe analyses of the impact of competing layers of government on those central activities. It simply draws the gaze to that particular level, and there is no reason the invitation to understand the actions of 'organisations and procedures' functioning on other strata could not also (and simultaneously) be incorporated. In short, our reading of Rhodes— and the empirics set out by several of our colleagues in their chapters—is that the core concept comfortably entertains dual or multiple competing centres.

A Way Ahead: The Future of Core Executive Studies

Having reviewed and reaffirmed the utility of a 30-year-old construct, we end by offering some brief views on the ways in which the trajectory of the concept of the core executive might unfurl—theoretically, methodologically and empirically—over the next three decades.

Theoretical Futures

In Chap. 2 we noted Elgie's (2011) observation that the core concept offered an heuristic framework which stood outside of an accompanying theory. Without wishing to hold Rhodes or Dunleavy to a test they did not set for themselves, we see merit in reflecting a little further on that point.

Roberts (2013, p. 16) has written about the importance of public administration getting to grips with 'large forces'; that is, those exogenous factors—a number of which have featured throughout this book—that 'give public administration its peculiar stamp in each country'. That is a useful reminder of the importance of, from time to time, pulling back from a concern with the minutiae of the rituals and practices of the court or the sets of institutional arrangements through which core executive actors cycle, and of assessing instead the broader, systemic imperatives behind such activity. Core executives are innately fascinating venues for study, to be sure, but their examination could usefully sit within other contexts.

For this to occur we need additional theoretical guidance. In particular, there is something to be said for exploring points of congruence between meta theories and the core executive concern with both meso-level institutional settings and the contextually situated rituals and practices which (depending on one's views of the utility of the term 'structure') either constitute or take place within those settings. Core executive studies presently lacks a well-developed relationship with theories of the state, in particular, and its capacity to 'travel' is correspondingly hamstrung. It is not necessarily a matter of deductively grafting an extant theory onto the core concept—which is, after all, a heuristic device and would likely struggle to bear that weight—but it may be a case of identifying a sympathetic theoretical companion and exploring a potential relationship. The global COVID-19 pandemic has given this mission additional impetus. One fruitful theoretical marriage, therefore, could be to align the core executive framework more closely with the study of crisis management. Indeed, that is what occurs in the chapters on Germany and Sweden, both of which bring core executive tools to their nuanced analyses of executive responses to various crises. More such endeavour would be welcome.

There are other possibilities, of course, some connected less to the contingencies of global pandemics than to the enduring ontological nature of core executives. Macfarlane (2019, p. 110) makes the point that '[d]iscourse choice forcefully shapes research directions'. Put another way, the language researchers use and the imagery they invoke shape the ways in which the object of study is seen and understood. If core executive studies is indeed institutionally agnostic, it must also be theoretically (and methodologically) non-normative, which logically permits of a variety of theoretical and research languages rooted in different assumptions regarding the human condition and producing different frames.

We already have, in play, imagery drawn from the worlds of human relations (courtesy of de Visscher and Salomonsen's (2012) 'ménages a trois'), physics (Wicks' (2003) 'third element'), geometry (the executive triangle) and medieval royalty and nobility (Rhodes' and others' baronial courts).

To this panoply, scholars could usefully add framing devices and interpretive logics from the ecology of complex organisms, which would seem especially appropriate given the emphasis in the core executive literature on interdependencies, exchanges, nodes, networks and fluid modes of interaction in which actors' interactions are nested in and inseparable from those of others. There is much here that is both ecological and complex.

Methodological Futures

Elgie (2011, p. 65) identified three overlapping, connected facets to Rhodes' thinking and scholarship on the core executive: (1) the elucidation of the central concept and the subsequent articulation of the resource-dependency approach; (2) the working of the language of the core executive into a broader narrative of the 'hollow state'; and (3) the theoretical and empirical elaboration of the interpretivist approach with Mark Bevir. Although our primary concern has been with the first of these, connections have also been made with the two other strands of Rhodes' work. Most obviously, the interpretivist turn finds expression in chapters 3, 4 and 8, while the language of the executive court is increasingly pervasive, albeit often in isolation from its interpretivist foundations.

Apropos the latter, Elgie (2011) also suggested that as a research design, interpretivism is a little niche. That may well change should Rhodes' call in Chap. 3 to use it a basis for comparative research (sans institutions and positions) catch on. Eschewing formal institutions such as cabinets (whether in the Napoleonic or Westminster senses) and positions (including prime ministers, premiers and presidents) in favour of the drawing of comparisons between rituals and practices does offer a way of broaching the walls that exist between administrative traditions. (The wall-breaching would also sit very comfortably alongside the reflections on the merits of using state size as an independent variable which are offered below.)

All of which raises the stock criticism of political ethnography, which concerns the difficulty of securing access to sources. Rhodes' own views on this matter are set out in Chaps. 3 and 4. For us, the importance of his advocacy of the mining of all publicly available information, 'irrespective of discipline, profession or format', lies in the way in which this 'makes fieldwork on secretive governments possible'. Surely that is entirely to the good, particularly if the alternative is for research on the inner political sanctum not to take place. This is not to uncritically wave political ethnographers through without interrogating their assumptions and methods (for one thing, a ritual or practice taking place here may mean something quite different to the same one occurring over there), but it is to accept that interpretivism supplements the more common positivist research designs with textured accounts of context, meaning and interpretation, and in so doing gives form to that which might otherwise remain shapeless and invisible to the scholarly (and public) gaze.

Of course, access to élite interview sources, and even ethnographic fieldwork, is feasible in some countries while impossible in others; insider accounts obtained through leaks to the press or in memoirs might be widely available in some places but almost non-existent elsewhere. There is no single methodological solution that will encompass all contingencies, and if core executive studies is to expand in new directions, healthy doses of methodological pluralism will be required. On this point, we certainly endorse Elgie's (2011) call for greater methodological catholicity in the study of core executive politics.

Empirical Futures

As to matters empirical, changes in national and global political economies in recent times—notably those associated with the global pandemic—will continue to have consequences for the (a) integrative functions of central government (the obvious research question here concerns the emerging balance as between rowing and steering in a post-COVID world), (b) the identity and mix of political and administrative actors responsible for those functions; and (c) the nature of the interactions between those actors.

Those matters will detain researchers for years to come. But in the process of addressing them—and we appreciate that in this we are eliding methodological and empirical concerns—the orthodox position of using administrative traditions as the default unit of analysis in comparative politics might usefully be interrogated. The benefits of this method are well established, but they diminish—and at some point 'vaporize' (Aberbach & Rockman, 1987, p. 476)—in proportion to the evidence of widespread diversity across cases within a tradition (Bekker et al., 1996; Russell & Serban, 2020; Yesilkagit, 2010). There is evidence of this within our own case selection. For instance, Ireland, New Zealand and the UK are amongst the 10 most commonly cited Westminster nations (Russell & Serban, 2020, p. 13), but there is a good deal of institutional variation across them: of the six most commonly cited features of Westminster, Russell and

Serban find that the only one these three countries share fully is their status as parliamentary democracies.[1]

There are, clearly, other ways of framing comparative research, and one such is suggested by the recent application of the core executive lens in the context of small states (Corbett et al., 2020; see also Connaughton, 2016). This empirical expansion is not simply a matter of utilising a concept in new places (although in this regard it is certainly welcomed), it is also an opportunity to expand its explanatory power and thus strengthen it. The conclusions Corbett et al. (2020) draw regarding micro states, particularly those concerning the extent to which coordination is less of a challenge than in larger polities, could perhaps also be valid in small states like Denmark, Ireland, New Zealand, Norway and the Netherlands.

This is a matter for empirical resolution, clearly, but it seems reasonable to suppose there might be something particular about the political culture in these contexts—a level of informality and proximity between political actors—that has a bearing on the core executive. Connaughton makes this very case in Chap. 5, pointing to the salience of personalism, localism and other facets of a small state for accounts of the functioning of the Irish political-administrative system. To the extent that her analysis applies more broadly, future studies should systematically investigate whether or not 'state size' (appropriately operationalised per Connaughton) can serve as an independent variable that affects actors and their resources, and the possibilities for successful coordination in the core.

If so, this would add to the standard repertoire of comparative implements, helping respond to the growing chorus of voices (see Corbett et al., 2020) calling for what is effectively the decolonisation of public administration research. In Chap. 2 we referred to Dunleavy and Rhodes' (1990, p. 3) criticism of the ethnocentrism of traditional accounts of executive government; one specific thing which the articulation of a 'small states' typology for comparative research purposes could help achieve is the decoupling of empire (in the form of the term 'Westminster') from the scholarly endeavour. That would do no harm at all to efforts to take the core executive lens out to a wider audience.

Conclusion: Core Executives in Troubling Times

Elgie (2011, p. 75) cautioned against 'the reossification of core executive studies'. He did so in the context of a call for greater methodological experimentation and catholicity, which we endorse. However, there are other ways in which that project can be pursued, including through greater theorisation up (with the help of, for instance, theories of the state), down (including by drawing on the results of prosopographic methods) and sideways (via conceptual alliances with cognate meso-level literatures). A richer empirical palette—combining an expanded menu of single-country cases from parts of the world that have yet to feature in the scholarship with formal comparative research—would also help.

In this endeavour it will be important to maintain and build on the fundamental strengths of Rhodes' and Dunleavy's concept, one of most important of which is its capacity to adapt to the dynamic nature of modern societies. In the context of the challenging times in which we live, this plasticity will be as important as it has ever been to our ability to apprehend and make sense of the organisation, distribution and wielding of executive power.

NOTE

1. Russell and Serban's (2020, p. 14) list of attributes includes a plurality electoral system, parliamentary democracy, single-party majority government, parliamentary sovereignty, unitary state and bicameralism.

REFERENCES

Aberbach, J., & Rockman, B. (1987). Comparative Administration: Methods, Muddles and Models. *Administration and Society, 18*(4), 473–506.
Aucoin, P. (1990). Administrative Reform in Public Management: Paradigms, Principles, Paradoxes, and Pendulums. *Governance, 3*(2), 115–137.
Bekker, H., Perry, J., & Toonen, T. (Eds.). (1996). *Civil Service Systems in Comparative Perspective*. Indiana University Press.
Bennett, L. (2012). The Personalization of Politics: Political Identity, Social Media, and Changing Patterns of Participation. *The Annals of the American Academy of Political and Social Science, 644*, 20–39.
Bevir, M., & Rhodes, R. A. W. (2008). The Differentiated Polity as Narrative. *British Journal of Politics and International Relations, 10*(4), 729–734.
Bracciale, R., & Martella, A. (2017). Define the Populist Political Communication Style: The Case of Italian Political Leaders on Twitter. *Information, Communication & Society, 20*(9), 1310–1329.
Connaughton, B. (2016). Confronting Interrelated Crises in the EU's Western Periphery: Steering Ireland-EU Relations Back to the Centre. In J. M. Magone,

B. Laffan, & C. Schweiger (Eds.), *Core Periphery Relations in the European Union* (pp. 166–178). Routledge.

Corbett, J., Veenendaal, W., & Connell, J. (2020). The Core Executive and Small States: Is Coordination the Primary Challenge? *Public Administration.* https://doi.org/10.1111/padm.12682

Dahlström, C., Peters, B. G., & Pierre, J. (Eds.). (2011). *Steering from the Centre: Strengthening Political Control in Western Democracies.* University of Toronto Press.

De Visscher, C., & Salomonsen, H. (2012). Explaining Differences in Ministerial Ménages a Trois Multiple Bargains in Belgium and Denmark. *International Review of Administrative Sciences, 79*(1), 71–90.

DiMaggio, P., & Powell, W. W. (1983). The Iron Cage Revisited: Institutional Isomorphism and Collective Rationality in Organizational Fields. *American Sociological Review, 4*(2), 147–160.

Dunleavy, P., & Rhodes, R. A. W. (1990). Core Executive Studies in Britain. *Public Administration, 68*(1), 3–28.

Elgie, R. (2011). Core Executive Studies Two Decades On. *Public Administration, 89*(1), 64–77.

Flinders, M., Judge, D., Rhodes, R. A. W., & Vatter, A. (2021). Stretched But Not Snapped': A Response to Russell and Serban on Retiring the 'Westminster Model. *Government and Opposition.* https://doi.org/10.1017/gov.2021.19

Hinterleitner, M. (2020). *Policy Controversies and Political Blame Games.* Cambridge University Press.

Hood, C. (2011). Risk and Government: The Architectonics of Blame Avoidance. In L. Skinns, S. Scott, & T. Cox (Eds.), *Risk* (pp. 62–84). Cambridge University Press.

Johansson, K. M., & Raunio, T. (2020). Centralizing Government Communication? Evidence from Finland and Sweden. *Politics & Policy, 48*(6), 1138–1160.

Johansson, K. M., & Tallberg, J. (2010). Explaining Chief Executive Empowerment: EU Summitry and Domestic Institutional Change. *West European Politics, 33*(2), 208–236.

Lowndes, V. (1996). Varieties of New Institutionalism: A Critical Appraisal. *Public Administration, 74*(2), 181–197.

Macfarlane, R. (2019). *Underland: A Deep Time Journey.* W.H. Norton & Co.

Rhodes, R. A. W. (2007). Understanding Governance: Ten Years On. *Organization Studies, 28*(8), 1243–1264.

Rhodes, R. A. W. (2017). Court Politics. In R. A. W. Rhodes (Ed.), *Selected Essays, Volume 2.* Oxford University Press.

Rhodes, R. A. W., & Salomonsen, H. H. (2020). Duopoly, Court Politics and the Danish Core Executive. *Public Administration.* https://doi.org/10.1111/padm.12685

Rhodes, R. A. W., & Tiernan, A. (2016). Court Politics in a Federal Polity. *Australian Journal of Political Science, 51*(2), 338–354.

Roberts, A. (2013). *Large Forces: What's Missing in Public Administration.* CreateSpace Independent Publishing Platform.

Russell, M., & Serban, R. (2020). The Muddle of the 'Westminster Model': A Concept Stretched Beyond Repair. *Government and Opposition.* https://doi.org/10.1017/gov.2020.12

Scharpf, F. W. (1994). Games Real Actors Could Play: Positive and Negative Coordination in Embedded Negotiations. *Journal of Theoretical Politics, 6*(1), 27–53.

Shaw, R., & Eichbaum, C. (2014). Ministers, Minders and the Core Executive: Why Ministers Appoint Political Advisers in Westminster Contexts. *Parliamentary Affairs, 67*(3), 584–616.

Shaw, R., & Eichbaum, C. (2018). Conclusion: New Directions in Studying Ministerial Advisers. In R. Shaw & C. Eichbaum (Eds.), *Ministers, Minders and Mandarins: An International Study of Relations at the Executive Summit of Parliamentary Democracies* (pp. 198–218). Edward Elgar.

Trangbæk, A. (2021). *Life at the Top: Understanding Top Bureaucrats' Roles as the Link Between Politics and Administration.* PhD dissertation, School of Business and Social Science, Aarhus University.

Van Dorp, J.-E., & 't Hart, P. (2019). Navigating the Dichotomy: The Top Public Servant's Craft. *Public Administration, 97*(4), 877–891.

Wicks, N. (2003). *Defining the Boundaries within the Executive: Ministers, Special Advisers and the Permanent Civil Service.* Ninth Report of the Committee on Standards in Public Life http://www.public-standards.gov.uk.

Yesilkagit, K. (2010). The Future of Administrative Tradition: Tradition as Ideas and Structure. In M. Painter & B. G. Peters (Eds.), *Tradition and Public Administration* (pp. 145–157). Palgrave Macmillan.

INDEX[1]

A
Administrative traditions, 13, 18, 66, 284, 296, 297
Advisers
  media/press, 131, 223, 224, 268
  ministerial, 12, 13, 34, 35, 37, 97, 148, 150–155, 157, 196, 197, 201, 206, 256, 257, 263, 268, 270–272, 280, 281, 285, 288, 290
  personal, 172
  political, 13, 20n1, 34, 35, 37, 101, 125, 127, 130, 134, 193, 196, 197, 215, 217, 218, 224, 226, 227, 229n1, 236, 240, 246, 247, 249, 261–262, 264, 268, 269, 271–273
  special, 81, 85, 89, 93, 98, 99, 101, 102, 105, 109, 127–129, 133, 171, 236–240, 243, 244, 246, 247, 250

  See also 'Spin doctors'
Agency/agencies, 6, 7, 16, 20n1, 29–31, 35, 37, 45, 57, 65, 66, 100, 114, 145, 156, 167, 169, 183n1, 213–215, 218–222, 228, 249, 250, 281, 285, 288, 293
Ahern, Bertie, 128
Andeweg, Rudy, 10, 14, 28, 33, 190–192, 195–198, 200, 204, 284
Anonymity, 95, 102
Anticipated reactions, 10, 167

B
Baronial courts, 35, 63, 65, 91, 93–94, 255–273, 289, 290, 295
Beehive, 151
Blair, Tony, 53, 56, 58, 66, 86, 98, 99, 107, 109
Bondevik, Kjell Magne, 256, 257, 266

---

[1] Note: Page numbers followed by 'n' refer to notes.

Brexit, 81, 94, 95, 104, 113, 125, 132, 135–136, 177
Brown, Gordon, 65, 66, 86, 99, 109
Bureaucracy, 12, 13, 15, 144, 152, 156, 158, 171, 172, 214, 218, 219, 224, 272, 285
See also Civil service

C
Cabinet
  coalition, 10, 14, 15, 63, 84, 98, 102, 127, 132, 139, 148, 153, 168, 192, 217, 238, 241, 251n3, 251n5, 293
  collective responsibility, 129, 148, 213
  collegium, 225, 256, 272, 273
  committees, 6, 7, 10, 31, 34, 38, 54, 84, 93, 96, 97, 100, 102, 124, 127–129, 134, 136, 138, 145, 168, 191, 194, 196, 238, 240–245, 259–261, 266, 280, 281, 288, 293
  majority, 195, 202, 236, 246, 247, 266, 284–286, 299n1
  meetings, 6, 10, 54, 64, 97, 98, 125–128, 131, 133, 167–169, 215, 216, 238, 243, 258, 261, 263, 265, 266, 268, 272, 282
  minority, 137, 145, 203, 215, 229n1, 235, 236, 251n5, 285
  multi-party, 9, 14, 205, 279, 284, 285, 292, 293 (*see also* Coalition)
  principle (*Kabinettsprinzip*), 168
  single-party, 14, 235, 237, 249, 251, 259, 284–286 (*see also* Coalition)
  subcommittee, 136–138, 261, 266
  See also Coalition

Cameron, David, 18, 63, 71, 79–114, 283, 291
Centralisation, 13, 16, 65, 134, 155, 156, 176, 178, 181–183, 212–214, 223, 226, 227, 229, 236, 239, 246, 270, 273, 288
Chancellery (*Bundeskanzleramt*), 167
Chancellor principle (*Kanzlerprinzip*), 166
Civil servants, 12, 13, 81, 85, 98–100, 109, 112, 125, 126, 128, 131, 136, 137, 145, 149, 152, 156, 157, 167, 169, 171, 174, 183n4, 190, 193, 194, 196, 198, 206, 213, 216, 217, 221, 224, 229n1, 240–244, 246, 247, 262–264, 273, 280
Civil service, 5, 84, 100, 124, 126, 127, 133, 134, 153, 171, 172, 217, 238, 243, 245–247, 256, 272, 285
Clegg, Nick, 63, 84, 85, 87, 91–94, 97, 103, 104, 110, 112
Coalition
  agreements, 147, 153, 168, 192, 198, 293
  cabinets, 63, 98, 132, 137, 168, 169, 192, 217, 238, 241, 251n3, 251n5, 259 (*see also* Cabinet)
COBRA, 116n13
Comparative research, 8, 35–36, 290, 296, 298, 299
Confidence and supply, 147, 293
Conflict, 5–11, 14, 15, 17, 32, 38, 45, 63, 93, 104, 113, 130, 132, 133, 137, 138, 144, 148, 153, 155, 157, 168, 169, 172–174, 178, 179, 182, 191, 194–196, 204, 206, 225, 242, 258, 259, 261, 281–285

Conservative Party
  Denmark, 251n5
  Germany, 171
  Netherlands, 202
  Norway, 266, 271
  UK, 56, 63, 66, 71, 90
Coordination, 4–16, 20n1, 28, 29, 31–33, 45, 65
  arenas, 4, 196
  formal, 10, 17, 135, 215, 217, 223, 243, 282
  horizontal, 6, 9, 13, 125, 133, 217, 223, 226, 259, 263
  informal, 10, 17, 243, 282
  instruments, 9, 10, 17
  inter-ministerial/cross departmental, 134, 135, 167, 169, 172–174, 177, 179, 241, 272, 285
  literature on, 4, 9
  mechanisms, 6, 9, 10, 17, 133, 138, 215, 225, 226, 242, 243, 281–283
  modes, 17, 280–283
  negative, 9, 13, 172–174, 282
  of policy, 7–10, 12, 13, 33, 34, 46, 128, 155, 158, 167, 169, 172–179, 204, 236, 239–248
  political, 215, 217, 223
  positive, 9, 173, 174, 282
  rules of, 10, 215
  stages, 9
  vertical, 6, 9
Coordination Committee (Koordinationsudvalget), 240–245, 250
Core executive, 3–19, 20n1, 20n2, 27–46, 54–62, 66, 68, 69
  definition of, 4, 7, 32, 41, 42, 46, 54–55, 60, 281

  resource dependencies, 14, 28, 29, 34, 35, 44, 55
  resources, 3, 11, 15, 29, 30, 33–39, 43, 44, 55, 56, 60, 67, 124, 131, 132, 144, 149–156, 182, 205, 248, 249
  utility/fit of concept, 3, 15, 37, 38, 41, 43, 248–251, 280, 289
Core executive studies, 27–46, 280, 290, 292–298
  asymmetric power, 30, 32, 37, 286
  differentiated polity, 29, 30, 32, 36, 292
  resource dependency approach, 14, 55, 296
Council of State (*statsråd*), 258, 259, 261
Court politics, 18, 30, 36, 42, 43, 53–71, 190, 192, 194, 196–199, 203, 206
  baronial, 35, 63, 65, 93–94, 255–273
  beliefs, 29, 58–62, 66–70, 80, 206, 293
  courtiers within, 6, 62, 64, 67, 80, 149
  inner, 6, 19, 46, 82, 83, 101, 103, 106, 109, 112, 249, 261, 266, 272, 273, 281
  practices, 6, 18, 19, 29, 36, 40, 41, 45, 54, 57–62, 66, 67, 69, 70, 79, 80, 85–109, 192, 196, 206, 250, 293
  rituals, 6, 29, 45, 68, 106–109, 195, 250, 293
Coveney, Simon, 135, 136
COVID-19, 4, 11, 16, 19, 37, 46, 129–132, 137–139, 175, 176, 180, 181, 220, 295, 297
  See also Crises

Crises, 11, 15–16, 70, 83, 91, 125, 135, 139, 174, 175, 178–180, 201, 202, 204, 212, 221–222, 236, 245, 249, 288, 291, 295
  global financial, 16, 136
  management, 201, 204
  See also COVID-19
Cummings, Dominic, 89, 101, 102, 104–106, 109, 113

D
Denmark, 16, 236, 239, 244, 249
Departmental principle (*Ressortprinzip*), 166
Departments, 6, 13, 14, 93, 98–100, 107, 109, 125–129, 131, 133–136, 145, 146, 149–152, 154–157, 193–196, 198, 200, 212, 213, 217, 224, 256, 258, 260–264, 269, 272, 273, 282, 284, 285, 287–289, 292, 293
  line, 128, 224, 259
  See also Bureaucracy
Dunleavy, Patrick, 3, 4, 7, 8, 10, 11, 13, 17, 19, 20n1, 27, 28, 30, 31, 34–36, 38, 40, 41, 43, 45, 46, 54, 70
Duopoly, 43, 126, 235–251

E
Economic Committee (Økonomiudvalget), 241–243
Elgie, Robert, 7, 8, 18, 27–30, 32, 35, 37–39, 41, 42, 45, 54, 55, 57, 70, 290, 294, 296–298
Elite interviews, 17, 39, 67, 81, 129–131, 134–137, 139, 183n4, 193, 205, 229n1, 236, 297
  See also Interpretive approach
Ethnography, 17, 18, 66–68, 292, 296

See also Interpretive approach
European Council, 135, 200, 286
European Economic Area (EEA), 259
Europeanisation, 14, 135–136, 139, 166, 170, 176–179, 181, 182, 190, 200–201, 204, 287
European Union (EU), 14, 19, 85, 90, 94, 102, 114, 127, 176, 179, 180, 200, 201, 213, 218, 225, 227, 228

F
Fianna Fáil, 124, 127, 132, 134, 138
Fine Gael, 124, 127, 131, 132, 134, 137, 138
Five Star Movement, 15
Fragmentation, 13, 37, 45, 55, 195, 196, 220, 241
Frederiksen, Mette, 235, 237, 239–240, 243–250, 288
Freedom Party, 15

G
Germany, 18, 46, 165–183, 281, 282, 287, 292, 294, 295
Gove, Michael, 83, 84, 86, 90, 92, 93, 95, 101–106, 108–112, 114
Governance, 7, 147, 148, 150, 157, 158, 199, 211–215, 218–227, 229, 237
Government Offices (*Regeringskansliet*), 212–214, 218, 220, 221, 223–228
Green Party, 128, 132, 134, 138, 225, 229n1

H
Heywood, Jeremy, 84, 85, 87, 91, 97–99, 101, 106, 116n12

I

Implementation, 9, 13, 44, 65, 134, 178, 182, 212, 214, 219, 220, 239
Instagram, 131, 248
Internationalisation, 213, 218, 227, 287
  See also Summitry
Interpretive approach, 17, 28, 54, 66, 114, 205, 249, 292
  See also Elite interviews; Ethnography
Ireland, 18, 40, 281, 282, 284–286, 288, 297, 298

J

Journalists, 64, 67, 80, 81, 95, 106, 109, 134, 193, 197, 203, 222, 223, 247

K

Kenny, Enda, 128

L

Liberal Democrats, 84, 87, 91–94, 111, 115n8, 202
Line ministries, 152, 244–245, 265, 272
Löfven, Stefan, 229n1

M

Mail on Sunday, 53
May, Theresa, 84, 90, 93, 101, 102, 104, 106, 107, 111, 116n12
Media, 4, 11–14, 16, 19, 45, 53, 64, 65, 79, 85, 87, 90, 95, 96, 102, 106, 108, 109, 113, 131, 134, 138, 139, 149, 150, 152, 155, 158, 172, 179–181, 197, 201, 222–227, 236, 238, 240–249, 256, 262, 268–271, 273, 287–289
  social, 12, 13, 16, 106, 131, 179, 197, 225, 227, 247, 248, 287, 288, 290
Mediatisation, 179–181, 212, 219, 222–227, 229n1, 287–289
Merkel, Angela, 175, 177, 178, 180, 181, 183, 290
Minister, 6, 12, 13, 15, 125–139, 144–146, 148–157, 166, 168, 169, 171, 172, 175, 176, 180
  cabinet, 10, 30, 39, 41, 42, 54–57, 80, 91, 93, 98, 102, 166, 168, 180, 190, 192, 193, 215, 237, 238, 244, 255, 256, 258–263, 268, 270, 272
  junior, 125, 128, 133, 170, 171, 192, 260–262, 264, 265, 268, 273
  watchdog, 265
Ministerial office, 18, 144, 145, 149, 151, 153–155
Ministerial responsibility, 237, 245, 250
  collective, 129, 148, 213
  individual, 199, 237, 242, 247, 258
Ministry/minister of Finance
  Denmark, 239, 244
  Germany, 167–169, 292
  Ireland, 125, 129, 136
  New Zealand, 144, 145, 149, 151, 153, 155, 157
  Norway, 261, 265, 281
  Sweden, 215
Ministry/minister of Justice
  Germany, 168, 169, 292
Ministry of Defence
  Germany, 169, 292

N

Napoleonic, 13, 296
Netherlands, 19, 189–206, 281, 283, 285, 286, 293, 298
Neutrality, 153
New Public Management (NPM), 13, 212, 218, 219, 228
  post-NPM, 4, 13, 158
New Zealand, 18, 40, 143–159, 281, 282, 284, 285, 291, 293, 297, 298
Norway, 15, 19, 255–263, 265, 266, 270–273, 280, 282, 283, 285, 288, 289, 293, 298

O

Osborne, George, 83, 84, 86–93, 95, 97, 98, 101, 106, 108, 111

P

Pandemic, 220–222, 228, 248
  See also COVID-19
Participant observation, 67, 235
Permanent secretaries/Secretary General (SG), 85, 125, 126, 131, 135, 138, 236, 239–246, 249, 250, 256, 257, 262–264, 270, 272
Personalisation, 12, 131, 166, 179–181, 287
Policy advice, 149–151
  supply of, 158
Policy networks, 7, 198
Politicisation, 131, 170, 171
Populism, 4, 11, 14–15, 181, 202
Predominance, 19, 30, 43, 54–58, 65, 68, 149, 157, 204, 205, 286, 288
President, 36–37, 63, 70, 287, 291, 296
Presidentialisation, 34, 36, 39, 203
Press secretaries/press officer, 172, 218, 223–227, 229n1

Prime ministers, 3, 5–7, 10–12, 19, 20n1, 53–58, 63–66, 69, 70, 213, 215, 216, 222, 224–226, 256, 258–259, 261, 265–268, 272, 273
  craft, 19, 61, 86, 87, 190, 203–205, 281
  strong, 189, 191, 199, 244, 245, 284
  weak, 189–206, 258, 283, 284
Prime minister's office, 12, 13, 41, 65, 288, 289, 291
  Germany (*Bundeskanzleramt*), 167
  Ireland (Department of Taoiseach), 124
  Netherlands, 189–206
  New Zealand (Department of the Prime Minister and Cabinet, DPMC), 145, 150
  Norway (Statsministerens kontor), 258
  Sweden (*Statsrådsberedningen*), 212, 216
  UK (No. 10 Downing Street), 63, 87
Primus inter pares, 189, 191, 196, 258, 259
Private secretaries, 85, 144, 149–155
Progress Party, 15, 256, 266, 268, 270, 271
Public Health Agency (Sweden), 220, 222

Q

Quad, 84, 85, 88, 92, 101, 111, 113, 137

R

Rasmussen, Lars Løkke, 237, 251, 251n1, 251n5
Realpolitik, 54, 58–60, 62, 114

Resources, 3, 5–7, 11, 14, 15, 17, 19, 55, 56, 60, 67, 281, 283–284, 286–288, 290–292, 298
  institutional, 5, 55, 56, 289
  personal, 15, 56, 151, 155, 156, 191, 248, 249, 281, 283, 289
  resource dependency, 14, 55
Rhodes, Rod, 3–8, 10–13, 17–19, 20n1, 27–32, 35–41, 43–46, 54, 55, 57, 66, 69–71, 80, 81, 107, 144, 145, 149, 152, 153, 156, 158, 159n2, 190, 236–242, 248–250, 251n4, 272, 273, 279, 281–286, 288, 291–296, 298, 299
Roberts, Alisdair, 11, 13, 15, 294
Rossen, Martin, 237, 240, 243–247
Rutte, Mark, 193, 195, 196, 201–203, 288, 290

S
Scandinavia, 10, 13, 19
Scharpf, Fritz, 5, 9, 170, 172, 282
Social Democratic party
  Denmark, 246, 247, 251n3
  Germany, 171
  Ireland, 124, 133, 137
  Netherlands, 202
  Norway, 257
  Sweden, 229n1
Social media, 12, 13, 16, 106, 131, 179, 247, 248, 287, 288, 290
Solberg, Erna, 256, 257, 259, 260, 265–268, 270–271
'Spin doctors,' 131
  See also Advisers
Spring, Dick, 133
State
  centring, 212–214, 223, 226, 227, 229, 288
  decentring, 165, 183
  'hollowing out' of, 7, 145, 296

  small, 28, 33, 35, 124, 132, 139, 298
  theories of, 295, 299
State secretaries, 217, 226
  See also Minister, junior
Stoltenberg, Jens, 256, 257, 259, 261, 265–267
Summitry, 166, 176–179, 200, 201, 204, 286–287
  See also Internationalization
The Sun, 107
Surveys, 257, 266
Sweden, 211, 214–216, 218, 221, 222, 227, 229, 281, 285, 286, 295
Syriza, 15

T
Tánaiste (Deputy Prime Minister), 125, 128, 133, 134, 136
Taoiseach (Prime Minister), 125–129, 131–136, 138, 139
Thorning-Schmidt, Helle, 236–237, 251n3
TikTok, 131
Twitter, 289

U
United Kingdom (UK), 10, 16, 40, 56, 63, 66, 71, 79, 90, 94, 97, 279, 282, 284, 285, 291, 297

V
Varadkar, Leo, 131

W
Weber, Max, 15
Westminster, 13, 18, 37, 39, 40, 44, 47, 54, 279, 282, 284, 296–298
Wicked problems, 125